Resources for Teaching Mathematics: 14–16

Also available from Continuum

50 Mathematics Lessons, Colin Foster

100+ Ideas for Teaching Mathematics, Mike Ollerton

Getting the Buggers to Add Up, 2nd edition, Mike Ollerton

Resources for Teaching Mathematics: 14–16

Colin Foster

A companion website to accompany this book is available online at:
http://education.foster.continuumbooks.com
Please visit the link and register with us to receive your password and to access these downloadable resources.
If you experience any problems accessing the resources, please contact Continuum at:
info@continuumbooks.com

Continuum International Publishing Group
The Tower Building 80 Maiden Lane, Suite 704
11 York Road New York, NY 10038
London
SE1 7NX

www.continuumbooks.com

British Library Cataloguing-in-Publication Data
A catalogue record for this book is available from the British Library.

ISBN: 9780826436030 (paperback)

Library of Congress Cataloging-in-Publication Data
Foster, Colin.
Resources for teaching mathematics 14–16 / Colin Foster.
p. cm. — (Resources for teaching)
Includes index.
ISBN 978-0-8264-3603-0 (pbk.)
1. Mathematics—Study and teaching (Secondary) 2. Curriculum planning.
3. Lesson planning. I. Title. II. Series.
QA11.F69 2010 510.71'2—dc22

Typeset by Pindar NZ, Auckland, New Zealand
Printed and bound in Great Britain by Bell & Bain Ltd, Glasgow

Contents

Acknowledgements

I would like to thank Edexcel for permission to reproduce the examination question in Lesson 4 and the carpet company, who wished to remain anonymous, for permission to reproduce their advertisement in Lesson 37. The table of numbers quoted in Lesson 27 is 'Freeware copyright © 2009 Thomas R. Nicely; released into the public domain by the author, who disclaims any legal liability arising from its use'.

I would like to thank the teams at Continuum and Pindar for all their hard work and I would particularly like to thank John Cooper and Tim Honeywill, among many other wonderful colleagues, for numerous extremely helpful conversations – and some solutions! Most of all, I would also like to thank the many learners who have put their energy into these tasks and taught me more about how people learn mathematics. And thank you to Megan Gay (Year 10) for the drawing on page 158.

Introduction

Resources For Teaching Mathematics: 14–16 comprises 70 lesson plans covering many topics commonly encountered at this age. The lessons seek to draw learners into thinking about the various ideas by posing questions and tasks that are not straightforward or routine. Learners of any level of prior attainment can gain satisfaction from thinking carefully about worthwhile mathematics, and although some lessons mainly target a 'Higher Tier' GCSE (or IGCSE) topic, in the hands of a skilful teacher, many would work well for all learners, however they are grouped or setted. Much of the material is designed to be divergent, with learners self-differentiating according to their current skills, interest, speed or mood. It is to be expected that different learners, beginning with the same starting point, will finish in quite different places. 'Answers' are given for the teacher's convenience rather than to suggest that they should be the optimum endpoint for everyone. It helps if the teacher is not too rigid in his/her mind about what the 'proper' route should be or how far learners must get during a particular lesson. The notion of 'finishing off' is problematic for many mathematics teachers when working with rich tasks, since when a mathematician answers one question they are likely to find themselves asking others.

The lessons are described under headings that indicate a possible beginning of the lesson ('Lesson Starter'), a middle (referred to as 'Main Lesson') and a suggested whole-class discussion to end ('Plenary'), but clearly a successful mathematics lesson does not have to follow that pattern slavishly. Beginning with a plenary or having one or more plenaries in the middle, or omitting a starter, etc., are all viable options, so there is no need to be too regimented about such matters. The teacher should not feel dictated to by resources such as this book and must be free to adapt, responding professionally to learners' progress, comments, questions and interests, and using their skills to lead the lesson in the most beneficial way possible. Photocopiable task sheets are provided for each lesson to help learners engage with the tasks at their own pace. Likely outcomes and objectives are indicated to help the teacher to think in advance about what may arise and what opportunities are available. Possible homework tasks are suggested, as are ways of extending the ideas for early finishers or those very confident with the topic. There are also suggestions of ways that a learner who finds the work particularly difficult might begin.

On many occasions in these lessons, learners are asked to generate their own mathematical examples. This can be beneficial by encouraging them to see what possibilities are available within the particular mathematical structure. Additionally, they also give the teacher valuable information, enabling him/her to assess the quality of a learner's understanding at that moment. What learners choose to create tells us about what possibilities they are aware of and able to access. Techniques such as specializing and generalizing in a problem-solving context are central to mathematics and are encouraged on many occasions.

Human beings possess the capacity to solve demanding problems and work with complex situations. The mathematical tasks presented in this book seek to draw on learners' innate abilities to make sense out of situations – to bring order out of chaos. Some of the material will be highly challenging, but if learners can be encouraged to struggle without giving up, and are given the time and freedom necessary to dig into the ideas, they can get a lot out of working with rich problems. Sometimes teachers feel under pressure to over-simplify and to try to turn every area of mathematics into a stepwise list of rules, so that the 'methods' come from the teacher and the learners' responsibility is merely to memorize and reproduce them on demand. If this happens, lessons are likely to degenerate into 'demonstration by the teacher' followed by 'practice' by the learners. Such a structure does not harness the natural mathematical talents that young people possess and tends to be unrewarding for everyone involved.

Some of the questions and prompts on the task sheets are linguistically demanding and learners who find this a barrier are likely to need in-class support in order to access the materials fully. At times the wording may appear vague, but this is in an attempt to move away from rigid instructions so as to provide space for learners to interpret in their own way and structure their own work. These lessons will succeed if learners and teachers are not trying to finish them as quickly as possible but are instead attempting to look around for interesting avenues to explore and generate questions and ideas of their own as they go.

The questions and prompts intended directly for learners are displayed in *italics* throughout the teacher notes. All of the task sheets are available online and other online resources are indicated by the mouse symbol.

1 A Tale of Two Numbers

Introduction

Learners are very likely to have encountered 'I'm thinking of a number'-type problems before. This lesson exploits the idea of 'I'm thinking of *two* numbers' to help learners work with dividing a given quantity into portions that are in a certain ratio to one another. Ratios do not always have to be integers, but in this lesson imposing that particular constraint provides an opportunity to work with fractions and partitions.

Aims and Outcomes

- find systematically all the factors of an integer
- understand how to split a quantity into a given ratio
- use factors to find all possible solutions to a numerical problem

Lesson Starter (10 min)

You could use mini-whiteboards to allow each learner to work independently. You might or might not wish to allow calculators.

I'm thinking of two numbers each time. Work out what they are. If you think there's more than one possible answer then try to get them all. If you think it's impossible, put 'impossible' and try to say why.

The sum of the numbers is 18 and one number is twice the other number. (6, 12)

The sum of the numbers is 18 and one number is eight times the other number. (2, 16)

The sum of the numbers is 18 and one number is 17 times the other number. (1, 17) (A hint, if needed, could be: *This is not as hard as it sounds!*)

The sum of the numbers is 18 and one number is $3\frac{1}{2}$ *times the other number.* (4, 14)

You will wish to vary the difficulty according to your impression of the class and how they are responding to the problems as you go.

Then have a mini-plenary: *How did you do it? Did you think any were impossible? Why?*

Main Lesson (30 min)

We're going to abbreviate 'one number is twice the other number' by writing '1:2'. If there are more than two numbers, we could write, say, 4:5:2. What do you think that would mean? This would mean 4 parts to 5 parts to 2 parts.

Splitting 18 in the ratio 1:2 gives 6 and 12, because 6:12 = 1:2 and 6 + 12 = 18, etc.

Give out the Task Sheet and ask learners to work on splitting 24 into all possible partitions.

Plenary (15 min)

Learners will need to think about the factors of 24: 1, 2, 3, 4, 6, 8, 12, 24. The numbers in the ratio (when simplified) must add up to one of these numbers (but 1:0 doesn't really count!). (If learners use unsimplified ratios in their problems, the answers may still be integers [e.g., a 5:5 ratio will give the same result as a 1:1], but they will have an infinity of possible solutions.)

The only possibilities with two-part ratios are: 1:1 (12, 12), 1:2 (8, 16), 1:3 (6, 18), 1:5 (4, 20), 1:7 (3, 21), 1:11 (2, 22), 1:23 (1, 23), 3:5 (9, 15), 5:7 (10, 14), 5:19 (5, 19), 7:17 (7, 17) and 11:13 (11, 13). With three-part ratios such as 1:1:1 (8, 8, 8), 1:1:2 (6, 6, 12), etc., there are obviously many more!

It is helpful for learners to see that 1:2, for instance, is all about 'thirds', because $1:2 = \frac{1}{3}:\frac{2}{3}$, and $\frac{1}{3} + \frac{2}{3} = 1$. In general, an $a:b$ ratio can be thought of as $\frac{a}{a+b}$ of the total and $\frac{b}{a+b}$ of the total, and this is a powerful idea.

Homework (5 min)

Learners could each be given a different number (their number in the register or their textbook number?) and asked to construct six ratio problems based on dividing their number into two or more portions. Some will need to use decimals or fractions in order to produce their six problems and some won't. Ask them to explain why this is the case.

To make it harder

Learners who make quick progress with this task could be asked to make up three ratios that equal 3:2, one 'easy', one 'medium' and one 'hard', justifying their order of difficulty. They could make an 'odd one out' question where three ratios are equal to 3:2 and one isn't, but looks as though it could be! Be as sneaky and cunning as possible!

To make it easier

Learners who find this task difficult could work with 12 rather than 24, as a total, and use practical equipment such as cubes to visualize the two groups.

A Tale of Two Numbers

Make up problems about splitting the number 24 into two or more parts.

All the *numbers* in the question must be *integers*.

All the *answers* must be *integers*.

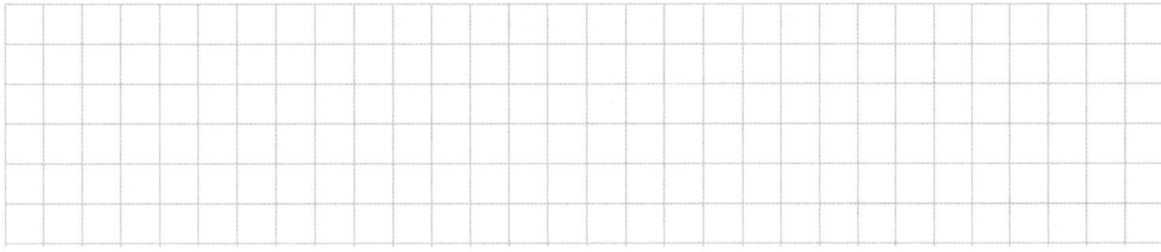

How many problems can you construct? Why?

How can you be sure that you have found all the possibilities?

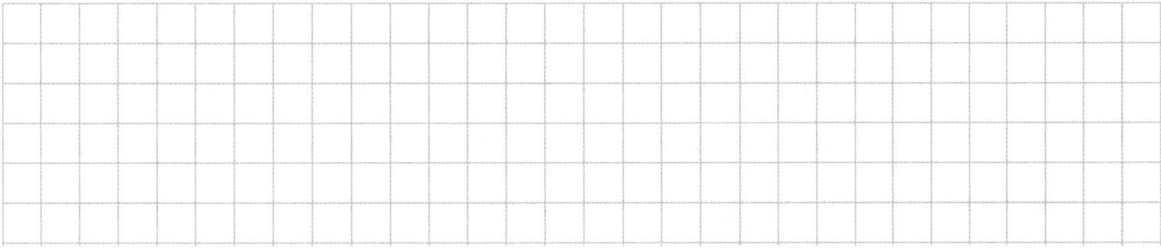

Try using a different number than 24.

Which numbers lead to plenty of questions? Why do you think this is?

2 Acting Your Age?

Introduction

This lesson uses a silly, humorous setting for some useful work on linear relations. Learners should enjoy criticizing the imaginary teachers' ridiculous points of view and looking at the rare instances when they may be talking sense! Comparing the teachers' judgements involves analysing different linear equations and looking for intersections of straight-line graphs. Formal methods of solving simultaneous linear equations may or may not be needed.

Aims and Outcomes

- relate the shapes and intersecting points of graphs to a context
- solve simultaneous linear equations to find where lines intersect
- understand how the features of a straight-line graph depend on its equation

Lesson Starter (10 min)

For young children, people sometimes say: attention span = 4 minutes per year of their age. What do you think of this formula?

Learners will probably try it out for certain ages and compare the answers with their experience. They may appreciate that a fixed formula, especially a linear one, has natural limitations. 'Attention span' will depend on what the person is doing, obviously, and on what is meant by 'attention span', what mood they are in, what they have been eating, how tired they are, their temperament, etc.

What does the formula make it for you? (Sorry, what were you saying?!) *Is that reasonable? What about for an adult or a grandparent?*

Learners may be amused that the formula breaks down completely outside a certain range. *Between what limits, if any, do you think that it is reasonable? Why?*

Do all real-life formulae break down at some values? Why/why not? *Can you think of examples?* There are helpful links here to the process of mathematical modelling.

Main Lesson (25 min)

Give out the Task Sheet and ask learners to compare the different teachers' views. It should be apparent that these are imaginary teachers and that the context is not to be taken seriously! The task could provide opportunities to work on solving simultaneous equations such as $n + 3 = \frac{n}{2} + 8$; alternatively, learners may draw or sketch the graphs on the same diagram and make comparisons in that way. If so, then they may need to consider whether it is appropriate to join the points, given that n must be an integer, or whether discrete points would be more sensible. It may also be necessary to think about whether the lines should be extended outside of a range like $7 \le n \le 13$ (depending on the structure of your school) or whether line *segments*, of finite length, would be better.

Plenary (20 min)

It is probably reasonable to say that the age of an average pupil in Year n is something like $n + 4.5$, though this will be an approximation, and some children in a Year group may be a year ahead or delayed. You might need to be careful to avoid embarrassing anyone in this position.

Taking a graphical approach, and using continuous lines for convenience, leads to a diagram such as the following:

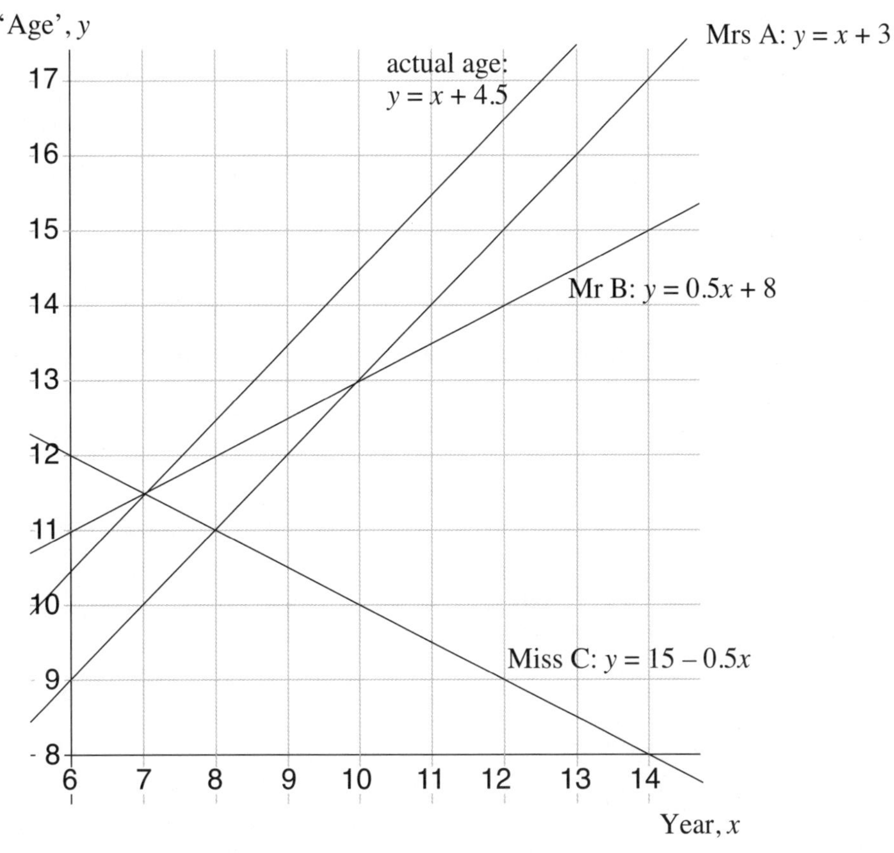

See what comments learners wish to make. You might want to have these graphs visible at the front, or not, depending on how the lesson has developed.

Mr B and Miss C view Year 7 pupils as acting their actual age, but underestimate all other Year groups, Miss C much more so, since she regards them as *regressing* as they get older, at the rate of half a year per year, so that by Year 13 they are acting as if they are 8.5 years old! Mr B has pupils *gaining* half a year per year, so that by Year 13 they are acting as if they are 14.5 years old – still rather rude! Mrs A believes that pupils gain a year per year but start from a base of only 10 years old in Year 7. She agrees with Miss C that Year 8s act as if they are aged 11 and with Mr B that Year 10s act as if they are aged 13. At the points of intersection, teachers swap in their relative order of judgements about the pupils.

Homework (5 min)

Make up four equations of four straight lines so that there are exactly six points of intersection. Is it possible to make the coordinates of all of the intersection points integers? Why / why not?

Can you get all six intersection points to lie on another *straight line? Why / why not? What possibilities are there?*

(Requiring *six* distinct intersection points prevents learners from having all their graphs parallel to the axes, so makes things a bit more interesting.) You can get *three* points in a line but no more than that if all the lines are distinct. Learners could investigate with more lines.

To make it harder

Learners confident with straight-line graphs might like to invent more complicated curves to represent teachers' views of learners' perceived ages. Learners might also like to consider the pros and cons of quadratics, hyperbolas, exponentials and sine graphs, depending on what they are familiar with or can find out about.

To make it easier

Learners who find these relationships hard to work with could start by focusing entirely on Mrs A, perhaps making a table of numbers of Mrs A's opinion against Year.

Acting Your Age?

Three secondary school mathematics teachers are complaining about their pupils.

Mrs A says: 'Pupils in Year n act as though they are only $n + 3$ years old!'

Mr B says: 'It's worse than that. I think that pupils in Year n act as though they are $\frac{n}{2} + 8$ years old!'

Miss C says: 'No, it's even worse. I think that pupils in Year n act as though they are $15 - \frac{n}{2}$ years old!'

Make a formula for the actual (average) age of a pupil in Year n.

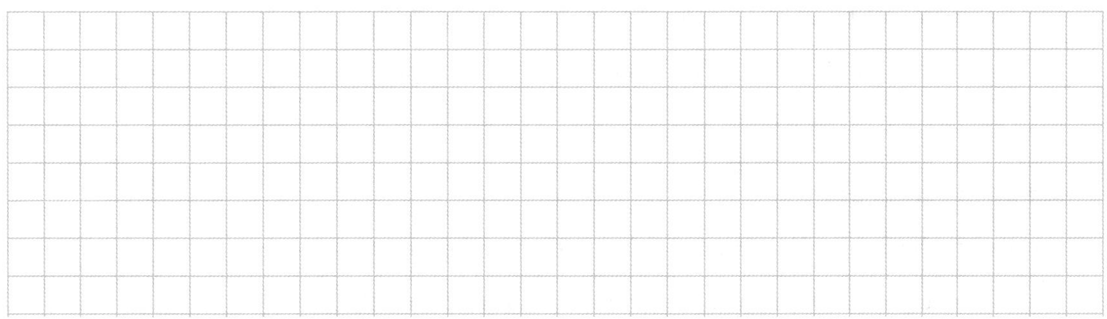

Compare the views of these three teachers.

Who has the lowest opinion about the pupils? Why?

Does it depend on which years you look at? Why?

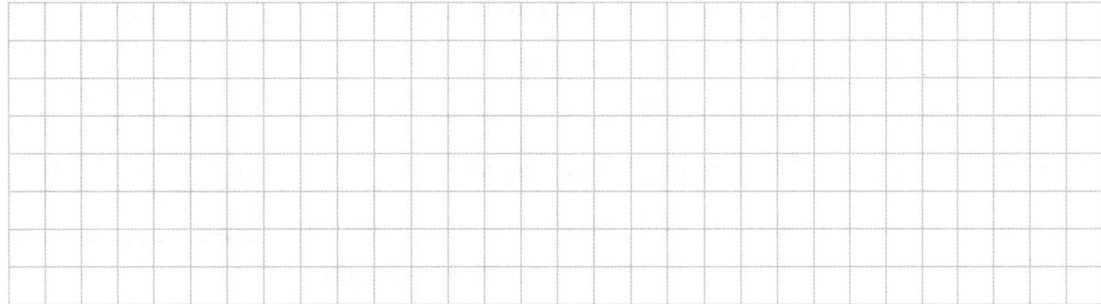

Are there any Year groups for which any of the teachers agree about the age learners act? Why / why not?

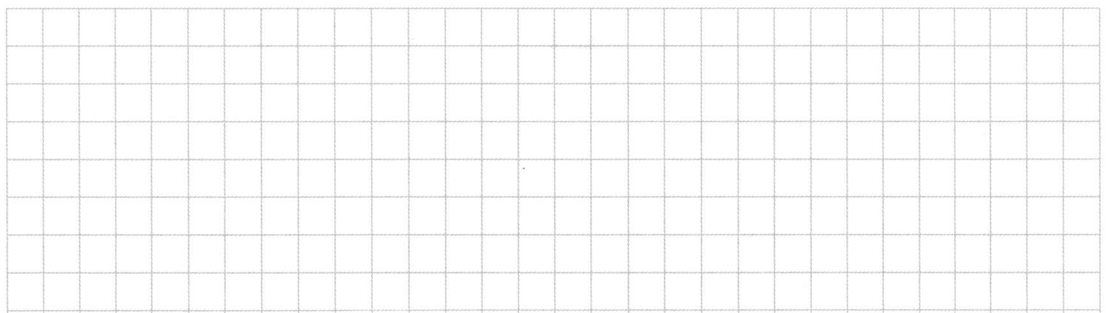

3 Arc Drawings

Introduction

When straight line segments and circular arcs are combined in shapes, considerable thought is often needed to calculate the area and perimeter of the entire shape. This lesson provides opportunities for different learners to follow different routes and then compare notes afterwards. It also offers some interesting and beautiful shape constructions, which can be made with ruler and compasses, and which might stimulate learners to invent their own. It is possible to have 'arcs' of all kinds of curves, but in the main part of this lesson they will all be portions of the circumference of circles, i.e., circular arcs.

Aims and Outcomes

- calculate the area and perimeter of shapes containing circular arcs
- carry out compass and straight-edge constructions accurately
- use the formula area $= \frac{1}{2}ab \sin C$ to find the area of a triangle

Lesson Starter (10 min)

What do you see? What else do you see?

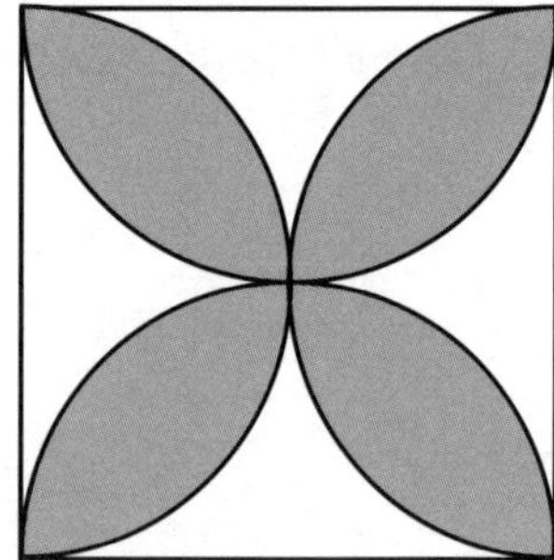

A flower? A butterfly? Encourage learners to use mathematical vocabulary to describe the different components.

How do you think it is constructed? Can you draw one accurately? Can you draw a similar but more complicated version?

This was constructed by making 180° circular arcs at the midpoints of the sides of a square, using a radius equal to half the side length.

Main Lesson (25 min)

How could we find the area and the perimeter of the flower/butterfly shape?

Let r be the radius of the circular arcs and perhaps label the four 'petals' A, and the four 'gaps' B, so considering the area of the whole square gives $4A + 4B = (2r)^2 = 4r^2$.

Looking at just one semicircular portion, $2A + B = \frac{\pi r^2}{2}$.

Simplifying and solving gives: shaded area $= 2r^2(\pi - 2)$

Perimeter is easier and comes to $4\pi r$. But there are other approaches that learners might take and it could be helpful to emphasize that there is not necessarily 'one right way'. It will be more interesting if different learners follow different paths and then you can compare in the plenary.

Give learners the Task Sheet. In the diagrams, anything that looks like a square *is* a square and all the curves are circular arcs. Unless learners wish to do otherwise, they could be advised to let the radius of the circular arcs be r in each case, but initially letting the radius be 1 or 10 might be easier. Learners may wish to construct the shapes for themselves first, as this can be a good way to get a feel for the different distances that are significant. Even if the constructions do not come out amazingly accurately, it can be a useful process to go through.

Plenary (20 min)

The answers are (this is also available online in case you would like to display it on the board, or print it out to give to your learners):

	Area	**Perimeter**
Lens A	$\left(\frac{\pi}{2}-1\right)r^2$	πr
Lens B	$\frac{r^2}{6}\left(4\pi-3\sqrt{3}\right)$	$\frac{4\pi r}{3}$
Axe-head	$2r^2$	$2\pi r$
Taijitu (half of the symbol), where *r* is the smaller radius	$2\pi r^2$	$4\pi r$
Egg, where *r* is the radius of the *complete* circle shown	$\left(3\pi-\sqrt{2}\pi-1\right)r^2$	$\frac{\pi r}{2}\left(6-\sqrt{2}\right)$
Arc square	$\left(1+\frac{\pi}{3}-\sqrt{3}\right)r^2$ (very hard – see http://nrich.maths.org/public/viewer.php?obj_id=1947&part=solution)	$\frac{2\pi r}{3}$ (from $4 \times \frac{2\pi r}{12}$)

Which ones were easier and which ones were harder? Why?

Which other shapes did you invent? Were you able to find their area and perimeter? How?

Homework (5 min)

Design an arc shape of some kind. It could have some straight-line segments in it, or not if you prefer. You could try to make the shape aesthetically pleasing in some way. Find the area and the perimeter and explain how you did it.

To make it harder

Learners confident with this work could find out about *ellipses*. Unlike a circle, whose size is completely specified by one number (the radius), *two* numbers are needed to describe an ellipse: a is called the *semi-major axis* and b is called the *semi-minor axis*.

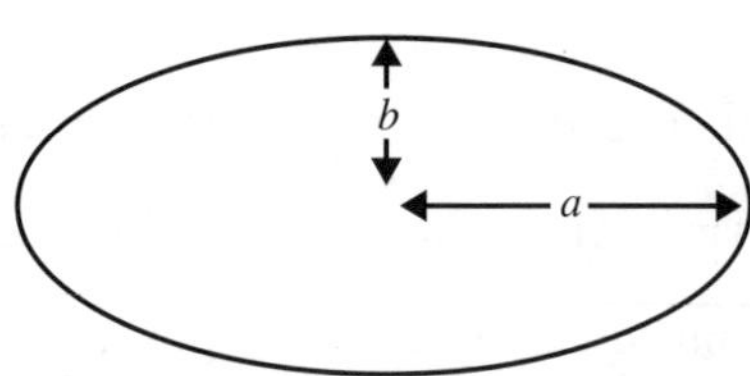

The area has a simple formula (area = πab), which you can see by imagining beginning with a unit circle (radius 1, area π) and stretching it by a factor of a in the horizontal direction (making an ellipse of area πa) and then by a factor of b in the vertical direction (making the area equal to πab). However, there is no simple formula for the exact perimeter of an ellipse, but one approximation is to imagine that it is approximately equal to the circumference of a circle with radius $\frac{a+b}{2}$, the mean of the semi-major and semi-minor axes, which would give a perimeter of $2\pi\left(\frac{a+b}{2}\right) = \pi(a+b)$.

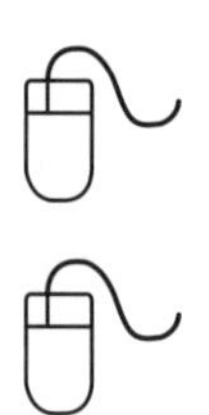

This is an *under*estimate for the true perimeter, unless the ellipse is an exact circle (where $a = b$). Learners could find out about other approximations (for example, see www.mathsisfun.com/geometry/ellipse-perimeter.html).

For more ideas of arc shapes, see www.mathematische-basteleien.de/arcfigures.htm.

To make it easier

Learners who find this hard could begin with shapes such as a *rounded rectangle* (a 'running track' shape).

Arc Drawings

Try to find the area and the perimeter of the shaded shapes.

Explain how you did it.

Which ones are easier and which ones are harder? Why?

Lens A

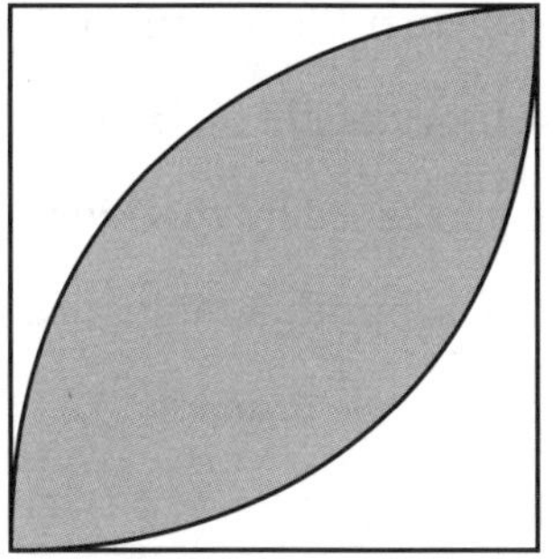

Lens B (*Vesica piscis*)

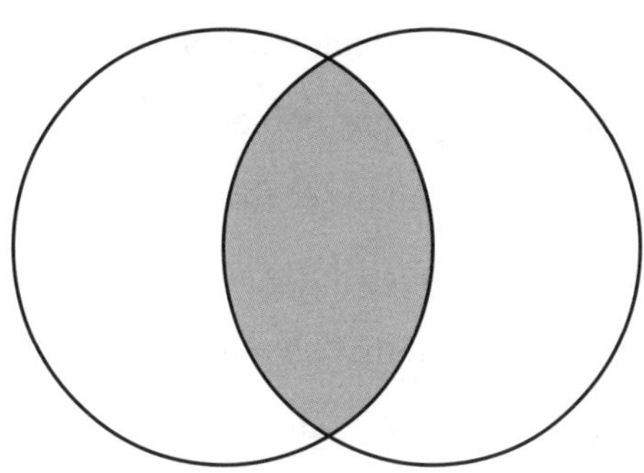

Axe-head

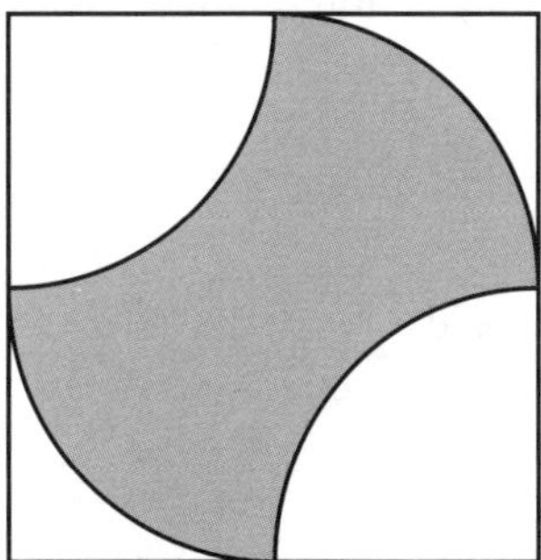

Taijitu (yin yang)

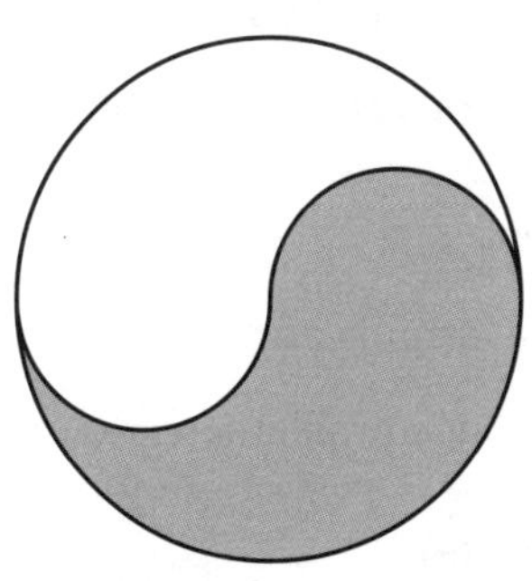

Egg

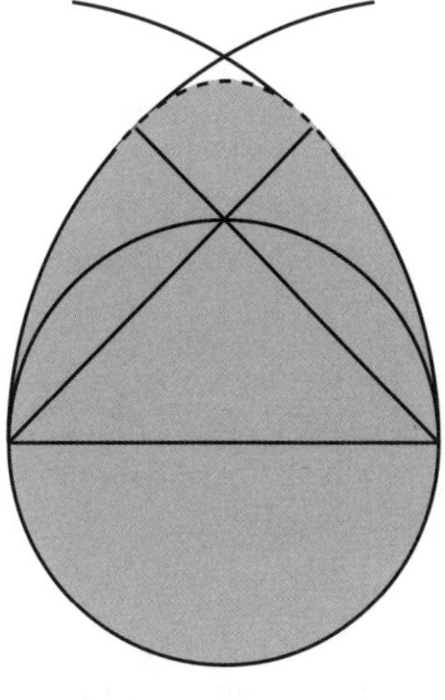

Arc Square

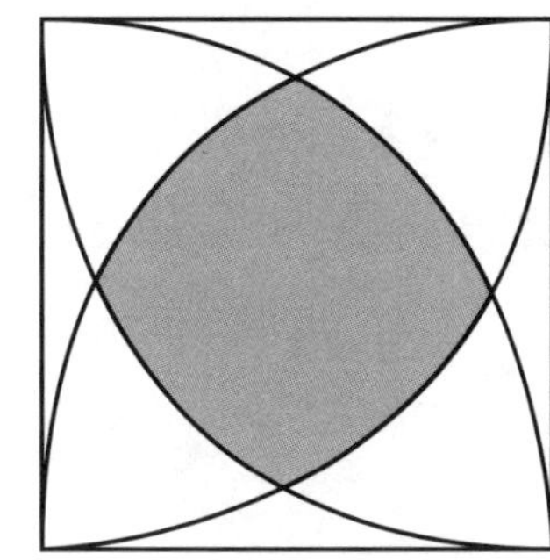

4 Area of a Triangle

Introduction

Learners will have been calculating the areas of triangles for many years by now, and 'half base times height' may be second nature. Learners are often puzzled, however, whether the formula is '*half-the-base* times the height' or 'half of *the-base-times-the-height*' or 'base times height divided by two' and may be surprised to see that $\frac{1}{2}bh=\left(\frac{1}{2}b\right)h=\left(\frac{1}{2}h\right)b=\frac{bh}{2}$. They may be persuaded by checking with some example numbers for b and h. For some reason, learners who are happy that multiplication is commutative (i.e., that $ab = ba$) are not always sure that it works with *triple* products (i.e., that $abc = acb = bac = bca = cab = cba$), especially if one of the three factors happens to be a fraction, as here. The fact that dividing by 2 is equivalent to multiplying by a half also complicates the story. Some diagrams of right-angled triangles (where the base and height may be interchanged without altering the triangle or its area) may help with seeing the equivalence.

Aims and Outcomes

- prove and use the formula area $= \frac{1}{2}ab \sin C$ to find the area of a triangle
- think critically about a problematic examination question

Lesson Starter (10 min)

What do you think the area of this triangle is? Why?

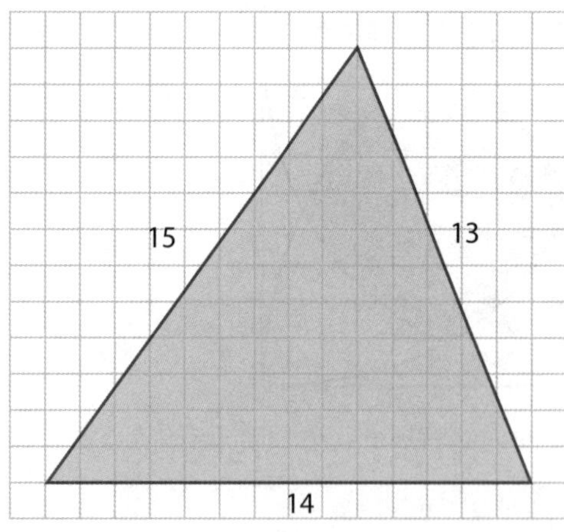

Learners may try all kinds of calculations, such as $13 \times 14 \times 15$, with or without dividing by 2. Alternatively they may try counting squares and part squares. Someone may get that the perimeter of the triangle is $13 + 14 + 15 = 3 \times 14 = 42$, and this could ring bells if anyone has come across Heron's formula, which says that the area of a triangle $= \sqrt{s(s-a)(s-b)(s-c)}$, where a, b and c are the lengths of the sides of the triangle and s is the semi-perimeter ($s = \frac{1}{2}(a + b + c)$). So substituting the numbers gives area $= \sqrt{21(21-13)(21-14)(21-15)} = \sqrt{21\times8\times7\times6} = 84$ square units.

However, a key length that is not marked on (though is countable if the triangle is drawn on a squared grid) is the height, which is 12 units. (This triangle can be thought of as the 12-13-14-15 triangle. It is an example of a *Heronian Triangle*, one with rational side lengths and area.) So $\frac{1}{2} \times$ base $\times$ height $= \frac{1}{2} \times 14 \times 12 = 84$ square units.

How could we change the triangle so that its area stays the same?

One option is to leave two of the vertices where they are and move the third parallel to the opposite side (i.e., perform a *shear*). This could lead to a right-angled triangle with base 14 and height 12, but the area is still 84.

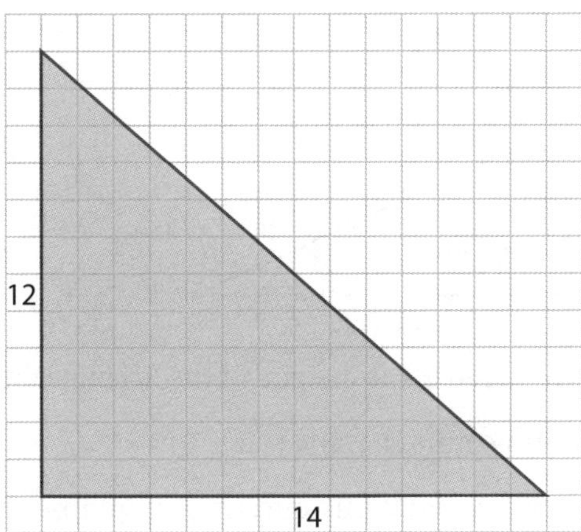

Main Lesson (25 min)

Give learners the Task Sheet and let them work through the first three questions. They should end up with three area expressions: area $= \frac{1}{2}ab\sin C = \frac{1}{2}bc\sin A = \frac{1}{2}ac\sin B$.

You could have a mini-plenary at this point: *Is it useful having three different formulae? When would you use each formula? Why?*

If a triangle is labelled *ABC*, learners may prefer to stick with the formula $\frac{1}{2}ab\sin C$ and re-label the triangle so that *C* is always the angle that is known (or to be found) rather than permuting the letters to obtain a formula that fits the problem. Alternatively, learners could dispense with the algebra and work with 'half the product of any two sides multiplied by the sine of the angle between them'.

Then ask learners to work on the problematic examination question.

Plenary (20 min)

(The question comes from Edexcel's IGCSE Mathematics paper [4H Nov. 08, Q14b].) If learners try calculating the area using the formulae just derived, they will get three different answers, depending on which angle they choose to use. The missing angle in the 'triangle' is 115°. So, using the formula just derived, area $= \frac{1}{2} \times 3 \times 7 \sin 115 = 9.52$ cm^2 (correct to 3 significant figures), which was the answer expected. However, if you use the sine rule to calculate the third side of the triangle, you get either $\frac{7\sin 115}{\sin 40} = 9.86975\ldots$ cm or $\frac{3\sin 115}{\sin 25} = 6.43352\ldots$ cm, which are different. Using each of these answers to find the area gives either $\frac{1}{2} \times 3 \times 6.43352 \ldots \times \sin 40 = 6.20\,\text{cm}^2$ or $\frac{1}{2} \times 7 \times 6.43352 \ldots \times \sin 25 = 9.52\ \text{cm}^2$ or $\frac{1}{2} \times 3 \times 9.86975 \ldots \times \sin 40 = 9.52\ \text{cm}^2$ or $\frac{1}{2} \times 7 \times 9.86975 \ldots \times \sin 25 = 14.6\ \text{cm}^2$, all correct (or incorrect!) to 3 significant figures. So there are three possible answers, by this way of thinking: 6.20 cm², 9.52 cm² and 14.6 cm². Maybe some learners will think that they should find their mean!

The problem arises because the triangle as described cannot exist. If learners try to construct it accurately they will end up with something like this:

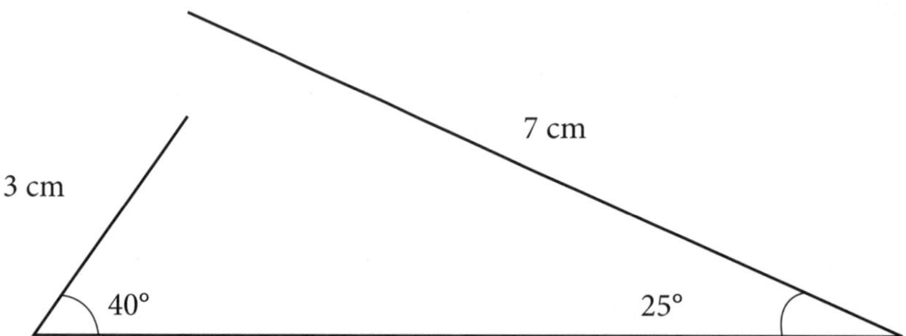

This can be seen numerically if learners try to calculate the 'height' of the 'triangle', because 3sin40 $\neq$ 7sin25, so $a\sin B \neq b\sin A$, or $\frac{a}{\sin A} \neq \frac{b}{\sin B}$, contravening the sine rule.

It will be interesting to hear learners' views on how this question should be fairly marked. Does excessive leniency penalize the strongest candidates, who would have been able to answer it correctly if it had been a possible question? What if some people spent an excessively long time worrying about this to the detriment of the other questions?

You may want to reassure learners that awarding bodies try hard to be fair in the rare situations in which problems like this arise, but, like the rest of us, they are only human!

Homework (5 min)

Find out what the Penrose Triangle *is and why it is impossible.* (This is a very different kind of 'impossible triangle'.)

To make it harder

Another (trickier) problem is realizing why any of the sides (not necessarily the longest one or the one drawn horizontally on the page) may be taken as the base and when multiplied by the perpendicular height will give the same value for the area:

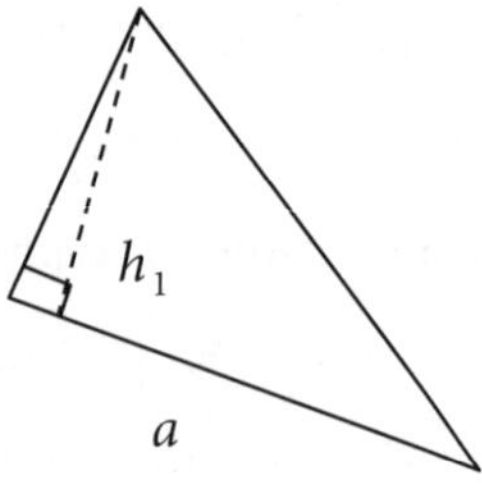

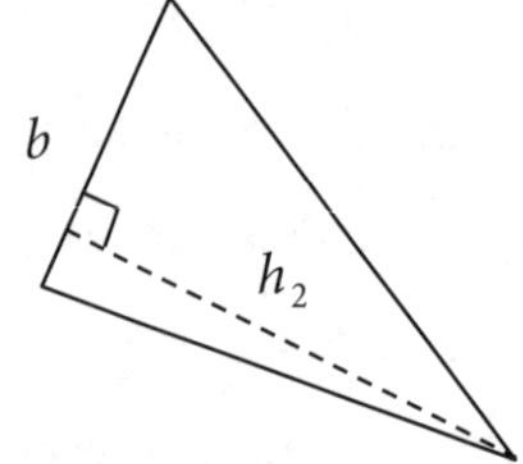

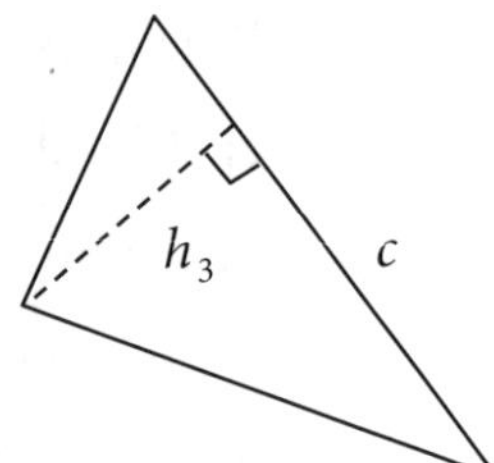

Why should $\frac{1}{2}ah_1 = \frac{1}{2}bh_2 = \frac{1}{2}ch_3$? This is quite hard to answer, but some drawing of triangles, perhaps on squared paper, can help. The above three triangles are online in case you would like to display them on the board.

To make it easier

Learners who find it hard to work with general lengths could draw specific triangles accurately on 1 cm × 1 cm squared paper and find their areas. This could scaffold generalizations later.

Area of a Triangle

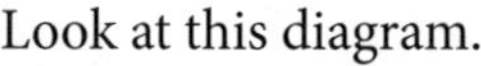

Look at this diagram.

Upper-case letters indicate angles.

Lower-case letters indicate side lengths.

Side a is opposite angle A, etc.

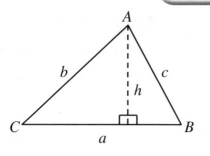

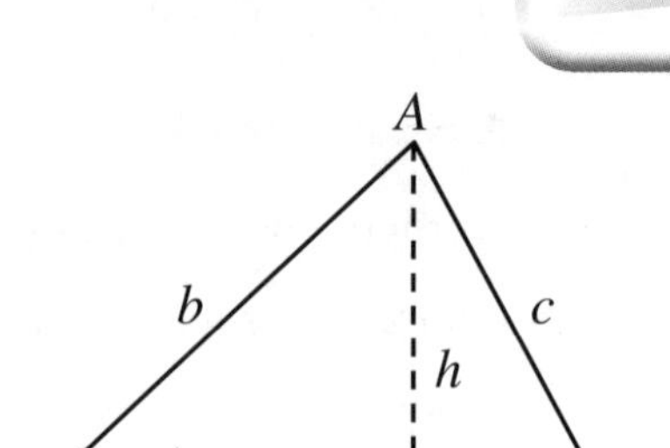

The *altitude* (marked h) divides the triangle ABC into two right-angled triangles, one on the left and one on the right.

1. Use trigonometry in the left triangle (drawn again here) to find an expression for h **in terms of angle C and side b**.

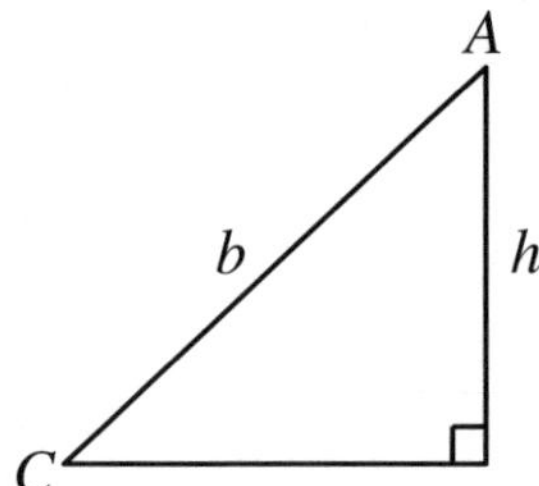

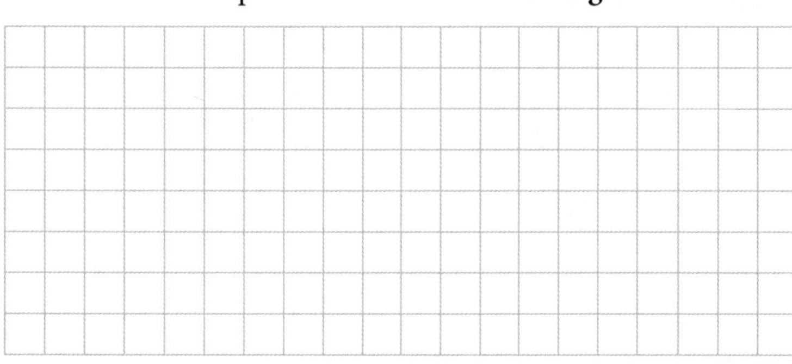

2. Use your answer to find an expression for the area of triangle ABC.

3. What if you began again, this time using the altitude going through B or C, rather than the one going through A. What expressions would you end up with for the area? Why?

Here is a question from an examination paper.

There is something wrong with the question.

Try to explain what is wrong.

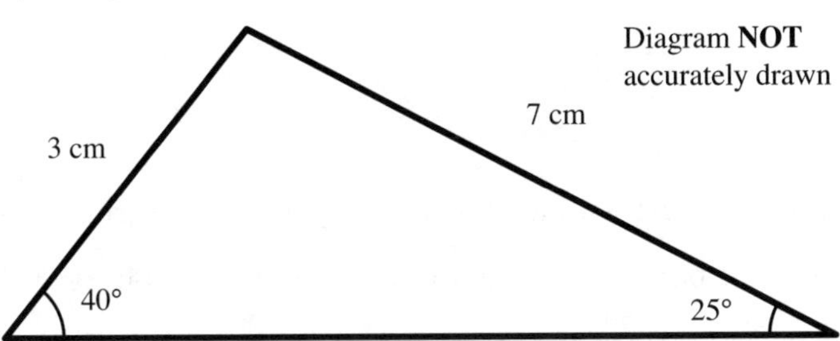

Calculate the area of the triangle.
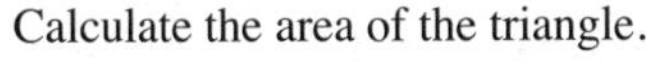
Give your answer correct to 3 significant figures.

Source: Reproduced with the kind permission of Edexcel Limited.

Try to construct an accurate drawing of this triangle.

You will have a problem.

Try to describe what the problem is and why it happens.

What is it about the numbers that makes this happen?

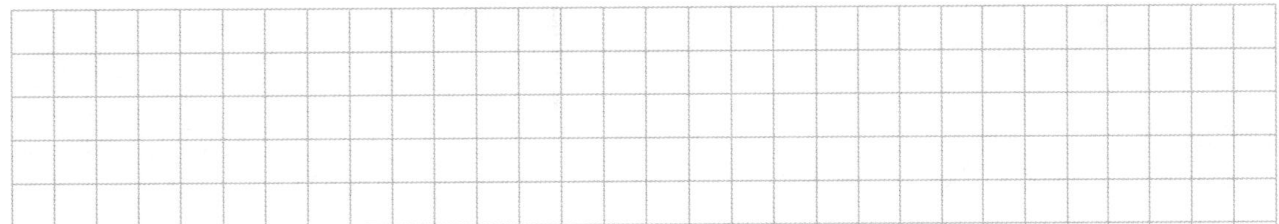

What is the smallest change you can make to the numbers to fix the problem?

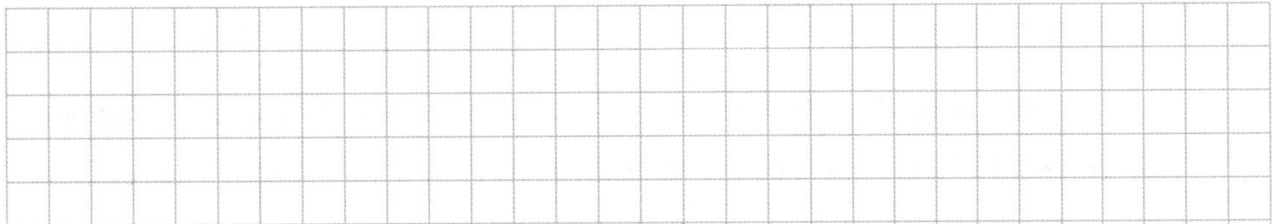

What possible methods/answers do you think the examiners should accept for this question? Why?

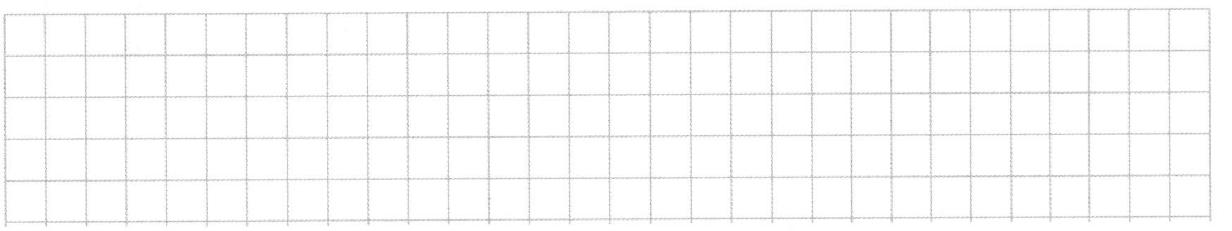

5 Bearings

Introduction

Bearings provide a helpful context for working with angles, and in this lesson learners have to work systematically to find all the possible bearings of positions from other positions on a clock-face. Unlike measuring work on maps, for instance, the bearings here can be calculated exactly *or* measured. It is common for learners to fail to go clockwise, or from the North direction, so these will be things you will probably need to remind learners of more than once!

Aims and Outcomes

- practise measuring and calculating bearings
- use facts, such as equal base angles in an isosceles triangle, to find angles
- work systematically through all possible cases in a mathematical problem

Lesson Starter (15 min)

Draw a square on the board and add the two diagonals. Label the vertices *A* to *D*.

Decree that North is upwards, with a suitable arrow:

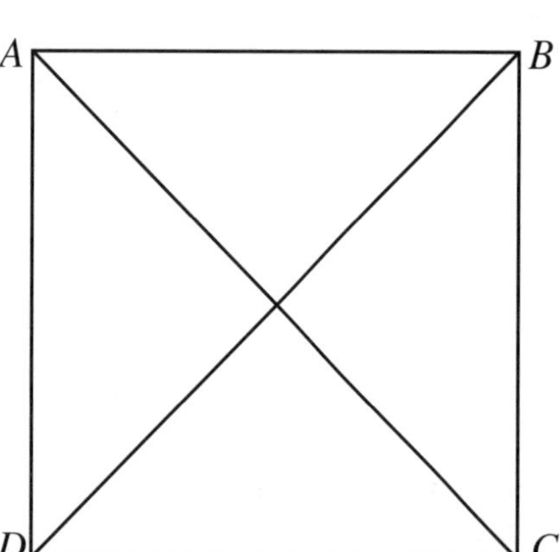

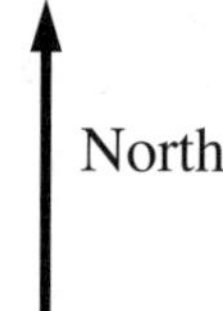

Ask questions like: *Given that ABCD is a square, what is the bearing of A from C, C from A, etc?*

Learners could answer individually or write their answers on mini-whiteboards, or they could complete a two-way table to show the bearing 'of everywhere from everywhere':

	The bearing *of* ...				
The bearing *from* ...		*A*	*B*	*C*	*D*
	A	–	090	135	180
	B	270	–	180	225
	C	315	000	–	270
	D	000	045	090	–

Main Lesson (20 min)

Give out the Task Sheet, which would be easier to use if enlarged onto A3. Some learners may choose to measure the bearings with a protractor, in which case they will need to draw in North lines at each of the positions around the circle. Others should be able to calculate the values by forming isosceles triangles (by joining the points to the centre of the clock-face) and then angle chasing. If learners are daunted by how many there are to do, they may be encouraged that symmetry will help, because whatever the bearing is, say, of 2 from 1, once you have worked that out you immediately have the bearing of 3 from 12, because the line 3-12 is parallel to the line 2-1. *Which other bearings must also be the same as these? Why?*

Plenary (20 min)

The answers (in degrees) are:

	The bearing *of* ...												
The bearing *from* ...		1	2	3	4	5	6	7	8	9	10	11	12
	1	–	135	150	165	180	195	210	225	240	255	270	285
	2	315	–	165	180	195	210	225	240	255	270	285	300
	3	330	345	–	195	210	225	240	255	270	285	300	315
	4	345	000	015	–	225	240	255	270	285	300	315	330
	5	000	015	030	045	–	255	270	285	300	315	330	345
	6	015	030	045	060	075	–	285	300	315	330	345	000
	7	030	045	060	075	090	105	–	315	330	345	000	015
	8	045	060	075	090	105	120	135	–	345	000	015	030
	9	060	075	090	105	120	135	150	165	–	015	030	045
	10	075	090	105	120	135	150	165	180	195	–	045	060
	11	090	105	120	135	150	165	180	195	210	225	–	075
	12	105	120	135	150	165	180	195	210	225	240	255	–

(All bearings are exact and given as three digits.)

There are many patterns here that learners may comment on. The relationship between a bearing and a 'back-bearing' (e.g., the connection between the bearing of *A* from *B* and the bearing of *B* from *A*) is an interesting one, and this may emerge during the lesson if learners are not already familiar with it. The table provides lots of data for a discussion (perhaps leading to a proof) of the connection: back-bearing = (bearing + 180) mod 360 (learners might prefer to express this less formally).

Did you work out every value in the table or did you use the patterns to help you?

How confident were you that the patterns would always continue? Why?

Which values did you have to calculate/check and which did you 'assume' or reason? Why?

Homework (5 min)

Design your own geometrical shape, and find the bearing of every vertex from every other vertex. Did you measure or calculate? Why?

Find out about the claim that cattle in a field mostly tend to face in a North–South direction (see http://news.bbc.co.uk/1/hi/sci/tech/7575459.stm.) *Try to investigate this claim on* Google Earth *by zooming in on fields of cows.*

To make it harder

Learners who complete this task early might be asked to consider what connections there are with circle theorems or investigate similar problems in other shapes such as a regular hexagon or regular heptagon.

To make it easier

Learners who struggle with bearings could be encouraged to visualize 'North' as being towards the front of the classroom (whether that is actually the case or not) and then position themselves at certain specified bearings from other learners. Helpful teacher feedback can address misconceptions quickly.

Clock Bearings

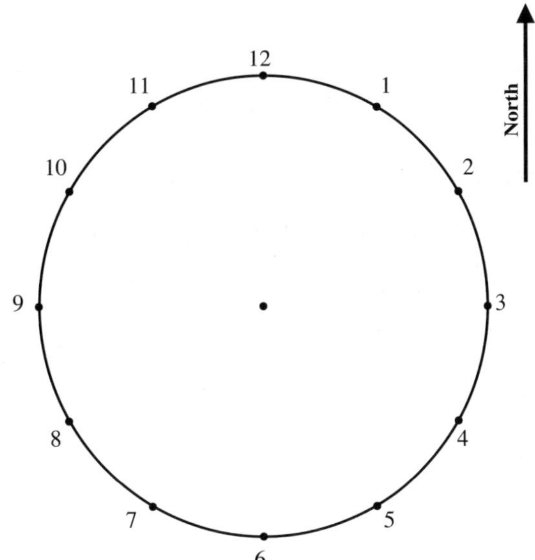

Work out or measure the bearing from each number to every other number.

	The bearing *of* ...											
The bearing *from* ...		**1**	**2**	**3**	**4**	**5**	**6**	**7**	**8**	**9**	**10**	**11**	**12**
	1	–											
	2		–										
	3			–									
	4				–								
	5					–							
	6						–						
	7							–					
	8								–				
	9									–			
	10										–		
	11											–	
	12												–

What patterns do you see in your results?

Can you explain them?

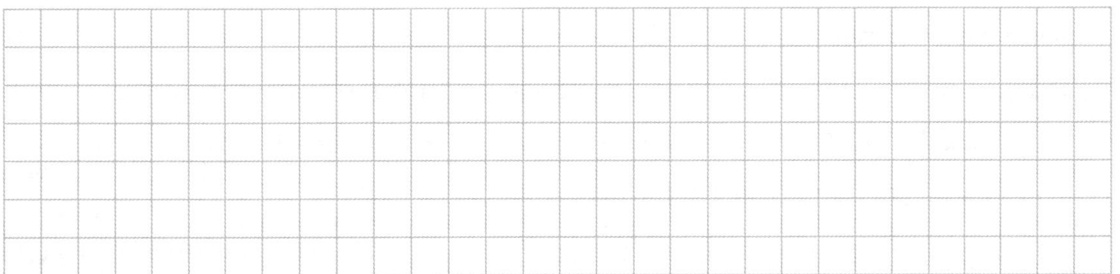

6 Beat the Calculator!

Introduction

At times, learners may be inclined to over-rely on their calculators and accept too indiscriminately the answers that they produce. The idea that the calculator can be wrong, and even that our reasoning can be superior, may be revolutionary! You can have fun with 'almost integers', such as $e^{\pi\sqrt{43}}$, which comes out as 884,736,744 'exactly' on a calculator, but is certainly not an exact integer. In a technological age, discernment over answers provided by calculators is a very important skill. We need to know when we can trust our machines and when we should be sceptical.

Aims and Outcomes

- appreciate the power of algebra to simplify numerical calculation
- develop a healthy scepticism about the answers provided by calculators
- interpret standard form to represent very large or very small numbers
- simplify algebraic expressions involving brackets

Lesson Starter (10 min)

Which do you think is cleverer, a calculator or a pupil? Why?

Depends on the pupil?! Depends on the calculator? Depends what we mean by 'cleverer'?

Suppose we are interested in accuracy and speed. Lots of calculations are quicker and more accurate on a calculator.

Can you think of anything that is quicker or more accurate if done by a person?

(E.g., 111 111 111 111 111 + 1 or 111 111 111 111 111 111 111 111 111 × 2.)

Why do these go wrong on a calculator? (*Try them.*) Answers will be given in standard form and to a limited degree of accuracy, due to memory and display limitations. The calculator can't appreciate structure – it just plods through digit by digit until it runs out of room. Also the calculator never says, 'I think so' – it always appears equally definite about its answers, so human beings need to use calculators intelligently and cautiously. So don't completely trust your calculator!

Main Lesson (25 min)

Today we are going to work on calculations that are better done *without* a calculator.

Give out the Task Sheet and ask learners to work on the various calculations.

Start with: $111\,111\,111\,111^2 - 111\,111\,111\,110^2$.

Learners could try to think of a 'clever' way of doing this, perhaps working in pairs. 'Long multiplication' of 111 111 111 111 × 111 111 111 111 is likely to be *very* 'long', though not impossible, if learners appreciate the structure as they go.

Misconceptions, such as that $111\,111\,111\,111^2 = 222\,222\,222\,222$ or $111\,111\,111\,111^2 = 111\,111\,111\,111$, etc., may dealt with by encouraging learners to check what happens with 11^2 or 111^2, say, where the calculator's answers *can* be trusted and pen-and-paper (or mental) methods are not too lengthy. Exploring patterns in $1\ldots1^2$ could prove interesting in itself.

Learners could explore what happens when two consecutive numbers are squared and subtracted by looking at, say, $5^2 - 4^2$, $6^2 - 5^2$, etc., and trying to see what is going on.

Learners may think for themselves of expressing the relationship between the numbers algebraically. You might wish to suggest something such as the following:

Let a = *111 111 111 110. In terms of* a, *what have we got?*

$(a + 1)^2 - a^2 = a^2 + 2a + 1 - a^2 = 2a + 1$

$= 222\,222\,222\,220 + 1 = 222\,222\,222\,221.$

What does the calculator say? Why?

What other calculations could we do using the same algebra? (E.g., $333\,333\,333\,333^2 - 333\,333\,333\,332^2 = 666\,666\,666\,665$, etc.) The business of finding other calculations of the same structure can be very helpful for showing the power and economy of algebraic statements.

Encourage learners to continue working on the calculations from the sheet.

At suitable opportunities, encourage learners to make up some of their own. Start with inventing some algebra that simplifies in a neat way. Then put some numbers in.

Plenary (20 min)

Ask learners to share their answers and reasoning. Try to avoid being the one who has to say 'Yes, that's the right answer'. An answer must be right if it follows from good logical reasoning, so the class should be able to decide which answers they will accept and which will need modifying. In this context, calculators can usually be trusted to give answers of *approximately* the right size.

With $111\,111\,111\,112^2 - 111\,111\,111\,110^2$, there is potential for doing this using similar algebra to that for the first one. We could have $a = 111\,111\,111\,111$ or $a = 111\,111\,111\,110$, for instance – perhaps some learners will have made one choice and others the other choice. It would be good to see that these (hopefully!) give the same result.

If $a = 111\,111\,111\,111$ then we have $(a + 1)^2 - (a - 1)^2 = 4a = 444\,444\,444\,444$.

$222\,222\,222\,222 \times 111\,111\,111\,112 - 222\,222\,222\,223 \times 111\,111\,111\,111 = 111\,111\,111\,111$, because if $a = 111\,111\,111\,111$ then we have $2a(a + 1) - a(2a + 1)$, which simplifies to a.

There may be many naïve answers to $\frac{222\,222\,222\,222^2}{444\,444\,444\,444}$ based on cancelling 2s and 4s, but checking with something like $\frac{22^2}{44} = 11$ may be helpful.

Let $a = 111\,111\,111\,111$, so we have $\frac{(2a)^2}{4a} = a = 111\,111\,111\,111$.

$$\frac{222\,222\,222\,222^2 - 111\,111\,111\,111^2}{111\,111\,111\,111} = 333\,333\,333\,333$$

Let $a = 111\,111\,111\,111$, so we have $\frac{(2a)^2 - a^2}{a} = 3a = 333\,333\,333\,333$.

In some situations, such as here, it may not be necessary to introduce a letter: factorizing the numbers may be sufficient, so

$$\frac{222\,222\,222\,222^2 - 111\,111\,111\,111^2}{111\,111\,111\,111} = \frac{(2 \times 111\,111\,111\,111)^2 - 111\,111\,111\,111^2}{111\,111\,111\,111}$$

$$= \frac{4 \times 111\,111\,111\,111^2 - 111\,111\,111\,111^2}{111\,111\,111\,111}$$

$$= \frac{3 \times 111\,111\,111\,111^2}{111\,111\,111\,111} = 3 \times 111\,111\,111\,111$$

$$= 333\,333\,333\,333.$$

Learners may find this harder, which could be a good reason for doing it. At any rate, no one should be in any doubt that algebra is infinitely more powerful than a calculating machine.

Homework (5 min)

Find out about Fermat's Last Theorem and work out why mathematicians should be worried when they see $1782^{12} + 1841^{12} = 1922^{12}$.

Fermat's Last Theorem was proved by Andrew Wiles in 1995 and states that no three positive integers can satisfy the equation $a^n + b^n = c^n$ for any integer value of n greater than 2. So if $1782^{12} + 1841^{12} = 1922^{12}$ were true it would be a counterexample, which would disprove the theorem. You can see that it cannot be true, since the left-hand side must be odd (because 1782^{12} is even and 1841^{12} is odd, since an odd number raised to any integer power is always odd), whereas the right-hand side, by similar logic, is even. It *appears* to be true on a calculator because the numbers are so large that rounding errors conceal the difference. This 'equation' appeared in an episode of *The Simpsons*, 'Treehouse of Horror VI' (season 7, episode 6); another, more plausible, one ($3987^{12} + 4365^{12} = 4472^{12}$) appeared in a later episode, 'The Wizard of Evergreen Terrace' (season 10, episode 2).

To make it harder

There are many opportunities for self-differentiation in this lesson. Keen learners could look up *Heegner numbers* and *Ramanujan's constant* on the internet and try to make some 'almost integers' of their own. Learners may also like to play with a website such as www.wolframalpha.com which *will* do calculations to many digits of accuracy.

To make it easier

Learners who are less familiar with algebraic identities such as 'the difference of two squares' could begin with additions and subtractions.

Beat the Calculator!

Here are some hard calculations.

Your calculator may not get them right. Can you?

Think about how to convince everyone that your answer is better than the calculator's.

$$111\,111\,111\,111^2 - 111\,111\,111\,110^2$$

$$111\,111\,111\,112^2 - 111\,111\,111\,110^2$$

$$222\,222\,222\,222 \times 111\,111\,111\,112 - 222\,222\,222\,223 \times 111\,111\,111\,111$$

$$\frac{222\,222\,222\,222^2}{444\,444\,444\,444}$$

$$\frac{222\,222\,222\,222^2 - 111\,111\,111\,111^2}{111\,111\,111\,111}$$

Find other calculations that match the structures of these ones.

Make up your own calculator-unfriendly calculations. Make sure that you have a way of doing them!

7 Being Human

Introduction

Very often in mathematics problems all the necessary information is carefully provided, with no extraneous details. In real life, necessary information usually has to be sought out and separated from a wealth of irrelevant background. The internet is a wonderful source of information, but mixed in with the facts are plenty of misconceptions, myths, deliberate misinformation and errors, and people in the modern world need to be able to access information discerningly and with sound judgement if they are not to be led astray. This lesson attempts to stimulate learners into asking challenging questions and then seeking out the necessary facts (or estimating appropriate values) to answer them. It also encourages learners to draw conclusions from 'suggestive' data.

Aims and Outcomes

- convert measures into different units
- estimate approximate sizes in everyday contexts, making appropriate assumptions
- select necessary information from a large quantity of data

Lesson Starter (5 min)

'The average human body contains enough sulfur to kill all of the fleas on an average-sized dog, enough carbon to make 900 pencils . . . enough fat to make seven bars of soap, enough phosphorus to make 2200 match heads, enough water to fill a . . . [40-litre tank] and enough iron to make a three-inch nail.' (Various versions of this appear on the internet, such as at www.triviafactoids.com/2009/06/what-average-human-body-contains.html and http://news.bbc.co.uk/1/hi/special_report/1998/05/98/the_human_body/93773.stm.)

How do you feel about that? Do you believe it? Do any of those statements surprise you? Do any seem impossible? Why? How would you check these claims?

Main Lesson (30 min)

Give out the Task Sheet and let learners have a look and discuss.

Do you believe the claims at the top? Do you believe the 'facts' underneath? Which ones surprise you? Do any seem impossible? Why? How could you check them, approximately? Would it be possible to decide that any of them were definitely incorrect?

What possible questions could you ask from these data?

Collect questions on the board.

For example:

- How much does all your DNA weigh? (About 600 g)
- How far would it stretch if it were all laid out in a long line? (About 2×10^{13} m)
- How much do all your electrons weigh? (About 20 g)
- If you had a life-size solid-gold statue of yourself, how much would it be worth?
- How much would your weight in salt, say, be worth? Or chocolate? Or potatoes?
- How many atoms/cells can you put on the head of a pin (say, 2 mm diameter)? (See www.cellsalive.com/howbig.htm) (About 100 000 cells)

Learners could guesstimate the answers first ('off the top of your head'). Then calculate an approximate answer, making appropriate assumptions as they go. If learners might be sensitive about their weight or height, it might be better, instead of thinking about themselves, to consider 'Mr or Miss Average Adult', who weighs, say, 70 kg and is about 1.7 m tall.

Plenary (20 min)

It is very likely that questions will be asked and answered that the teacher could not have anticipated prior to the lesson, so you will not always be in possession of 'answers' and different groups may have answered similar questions and obtained very different answers. Handling the debate mathematically, being ready to consider different people's arguments and comparing different ideas, will make for a very worthwhile discussion. Of course, the actual final values may not be particularly important – it is the thinking and reasoning that has gone in to them that is valuable. (Why should anyone really care, for example, how long their fingernails actually might grow in a lifetime? But the process of thinking about it could be very engaging.) If a real dispute arises over values that are too different to be reasonable, and it is looking difficult to resolve one way or the other, you might have to record both claims and do a bit of checking yourself, perhaps on the internet, before the next lesson, and report back – or encourage learners to do the same.

Homework (5 min)

Prepare a poster outlining 'fascinating facts' discovered or calculated during today's lesson, together with how you worked them out or why you believe them to be true.

To make it harder

Learners who are comfortable with handling very large (and very small) numbers can set themselves greater challenges, including ones related to volume; for example, how many people could fit into the Grand Canyon, or how many glasses of water could you fill from a swimming pool?

To make it easier

Learners who find this lesson difficult could be encouraged to focus initially on comparisons of length rather than those of area or volume.

Being Human

What are You Made of?

Here are some claims:

- An average person, in a lifetime, will walk the equivalent of five times around the equator of the earth.
- There are about 100 000 hairs on a typical human head. 'Even the hairs of your head are numbered' (Bible, Luke 12.7).
- In one day, your blood circulates a distance of about 12 000 miles around your body.
- In one human lifetime a person takes 300 million steps, spends $3\frac{1}{2}$ years eating, 12 years watching TV and the same amount of time talking, consumes 160 kilograms of chocolate, grows 28 metres of finger nails and 950 kilometres of hair on their head, blinks 415 million times and has about 3 billion heart beats.

(For these and other claims, go to http://news.bbc.co.uk/1/hi/special_report/1998/05/98/the_human_body/93773.stm.)

Human Data Sheet

These values may be helpful for your calculations. They may also suggest different questions you could ask.

The values are obviously all approximate.

If you need values that are not here, you could estimate them or use the internet or books to find them out.

- average human mass = 70 kg
- average human height = 1.7 m
- average human volume = 70 litres
- number of atoms = 10^{28}
- number of (human) cells = 10^{13}
- total number of cells (including bacteria, etc.) = 10^{14}
- mass of DNA per cell = 6×10^{-12} g
- length of DNA molecules in one cell (all 46 chromosomes unravelled and put together) = 2 m
- cell diameter = 10^{-6} m
- atom diameter = 10^{-11} m
- electrons contribute about 0.03% to the total mass of an atom

1 cm^3 = 1 ml	10 mm = 1 cm	1 000 mm = 1 m
1000 cm^3 = 1 litre	1000 g = 1 kg	100 cm = 1 m
1000 litre = 1 m^3	1000 kg = 1 tonne	1000 m = 1 km

Element	Amount/kg	Element	Amount/kg
oxygen	43	chlorine	0.084
carbon	16	magnesium	0.019
hydrogen	7	silicon	0.018
nitrogen	1.8	iron	0.0042
calcium	0.98	lead	0.000 12
phosphorus	0.77	copper	0.000 07
sulfur	0.14	gold	0.000 01
potassium	0.14	uranium	0.000 000 09
sodium	0.098		

Source: Emsley, J. (2003), *Nature's Building Blocks: An A–Z Guide to the Elements*. New York: Oxford University Press.

Human hair grows at about 0.4 mm per day; fingernails at 0.1 mm per day (toenails at a third of that speed).

- distance to the moon = 384 000 km
- distance to the sun = 149 600 000 km
- density of gold = 19.3 g/cm^3
- density of salt = 2.2 g/cm^3
- density of chocolate = 1.3 g/cm^3

What questions can you ask and answer relating to this data?

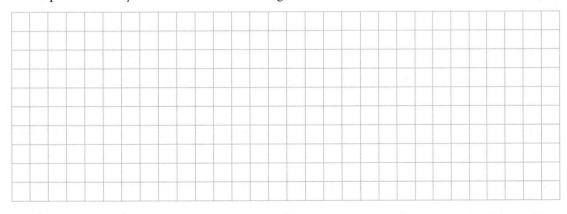

8 Being Irrational

Introduction

The divide between rational and irrational numbers is an important one mathematically. Typically learners encounter square roots of non-square numbers from quite an early age and become used to rounding these to a few decimal places in much the same way as they might with a fraction such as $\frac{3}{7}$, without realizing that anything different is going on. So much is happening when learners first encounter Pythagoras' Theorem that there may not be much time to think about irrational numbers – this is perhaps more likely to take place when meeting the relationship between the circumference and diameter of a circle, and the transcendental number π. This lesson provides an opportunity to focus on irrationality and to consider why some numbers are irrational, what irrationality means and what happens when you combine rational and irrational numbers in different ways.

Aims and Outcomes

- appreciate relationships between irrational and rational numbers
- understand that irrational numbers are numbers that cannot be expressed as an integer divided by an integer

Lesson Starter (15 min)

Try to think of a square number that is twice as big as another square number.

Learners often suggest 1 and 2 or 2 and 4, and this gives an opportunity to clarify what a square number is.

Learners can hunt for numbers in pairs or small groups.

Then add '*... is three times as big ...*', '*... is four times as big ...*', etc. on the board.

Learners will find that some are impossible and some are possible. *Why?*

From this it seems that a square number can only be a square number times bigger than another square number. Algebraically, if a and b are integers and $a^2 = kb^2$, then k must be a square number. *Why should this be?*

Learners may be encouraged to think about (prime) factors of a^2 and b^2. Since every prime power that is in a will appear *twice* in a^2, it follows that the indices of the prime factors of square numbers are always even. So $a^2 = kb^2$ can work only if k also contains only even indices of prime numbers; i.e., k must be a square number too. So $a^2 = 2b^2$, for instance, is impossible, so $\frac{a^2}{b^2} = 2$ is also impossible and so $\frac{a}{b} = \sqrt{2}$ is also impossible.

What does this mean? What is it saying about the square root of 2?

This leads to the definition of 'irrational' as a number that cannot be expressed as an integer divided by an integer.

Which other square roots will be irrational?

The argument above indicates that the square roots of any non-square numbers will be irrational (i.e., surds). In other words, square roots of positive integers are either integers or surds. Similarly, the same logic shows that cube roots of non-cube numbers will also be irrational, and so on.

Main Lesson (20 min)

Give out the Task Sheet and help learners to consider the various possible cases by both specializing (thinking of particular examples and seeing what happens) and generalizing (by writing rational numbers as an integer divided by an integer).

Plenary (20 min)

Many of the answers are 'sometimes', giving good opportunities for learners to consider different people's examples.

$a + 1$ is always irrational. Irrational ± rational will always be irrational. It is possible to argue this by thinking about the non-repeating, non-recurring decimal places of irrational numbers or by a 'proof by contradiction' method: if $a + 1$ were rational, it could be expressed as $\frac{m}{n}$, where m and n are integers with $n \neq 0$. Then subtracting 1 from both sides would give $\frac{m}{n} - 1 = \frac{m-n}{n}$, which would show that a is rational, since $m - n$ is an integer, so a is expressed as an integer over an integer. This is a contradiction, since we began by assuming that a was irrational. Therefore it must be wrong to think that $a + 1$ could be rational. So it is irrational.

A similar approach works with a general rational number in place of 1.

$a + b$ may be irrational (e.g., $\pi + 2\pi = 3\pi$) or rational (e.g., $(3 + \pi) + (3 - \pi) = 6$).

$a - b$ may be irrational (e.g., $3\pi - \pi = 2\pi$) or rational (e.g., $\pi - \pi = 0$).

ab may be irrational (e.g., $\sqrt{2}\sqrt{3} = \sqrt{6}$) or rational (e.g., $\sqrt{2}\sqrt{8} = \sqrt{16} = 4$).

$\frac{a}{b}$ may be irrational (e.g., $\frac{\sqrt{6}}{\sqrt{2}} = \sqrt{3}$) or rational (e.g., $\frac{\sqrt{12}}{\sqrt{3}} = \sqrt{4} = 2$).

$\frac{1}{a}$ is always irrational, provided $a \neq 0$ (which it cannot be, since a is irrational), because if it were rational then it could be expressed as $\frac{1}{a} = \frac{m}{n}$, where m and n are integers with $n \neq 0$, and inverting both sides of this would give $a = \frac{n}{m}$, so a would be rational, which is a contradiction. So $\frac{1}{a}$ cannot be rational if a is irrational. This is another 'proof by contradiction' argument, similar to the one above.

a^2 may be irrational (e.g., $\left(\sqrt[3]{2}\right)^2 = \sqrt[3]{4}$) or rational (e.g., $\left(\sqrt{3}\right)^2 = 3$).

Homework (5 min)

Find out why Greek mathematicians were so worried about irrational numbers. What was the Delian Problem*?*

Which do you think that there are more of – irrational numbers or rational ones? Find out.

Learners often assume that most ordinary numbers are rational, which may be true in the sense of most numbers commonly encountered in everyday life or school mathematics, but considering all *possible* numbers, 'almost all' of them are irrational, and almost all irrational numbers are *transcendental*. (*Find out about Georg Cantor* [*1845–1918*].)

To make it harder

Confident learners might like to repeat the sheet but with a irrational and b *rational*.

Very keen learners might like to grapple with this difficult proof: If a and b are *irrational*, is it possible for a^b to be *rational*? A clever argument proves that it *is* possible. (It is an example of a 'non-constructive proof'.) Suppose that $a = \sqrt{2}^{\sqrt{2}}$ and $b = \sqrt{2}$. Maybe $\sqrt{2}^{\sqrt{2}}$ is irrational (in fact, it is and it is also *transcendental*, but the clever thing is that you don't need to know whether it is or isn't). If $\sqrt{2}^{\sqrt{2}}$ is rational, then that would give us an example of $\textit{irrational}^{\textit{irrational}}$ = rational. But, on the other hand, if $\sqrt{2}^{\sqrt{2}}$ *is* irrational (as is in fact the case) then $a^b = \left(\sqrt{2}^{\sqrt{2}}\right)^{\sqrt{2}} = \sqrt{2}^2 = 2$, which is rational, so that proves it. So either way the statement is proved.

To make it easier

Learners who are finding this difficult could begin by folding a piece of paper down the middle and listing as many rational numbers on one side and irrational numbers on the other as they can think of. Obviously there are infinitely many of both, so rather than laboriously constructing endless examples, learners could be encouraged to find 'interesting' or 'different' examples and then to experiment with combining them in various ways.

Being Irrational

Suppose that *a* and *b* are *irrational* numbers.

Depending on which irrational numbers *a* and *b* are, are these expressions always, never or sometimes irrational?

If you think an expression is *always* irrational, try to say *why*.

If you think an expression is *never* irrational, try to say *why not*.

If you think an expression is *sometimes* irrational, try to say *when* and *why*.

$a + 1$

$a + b$

$a - b$

ab

$\frac{a}{b}$

$\frac{1}{a}$

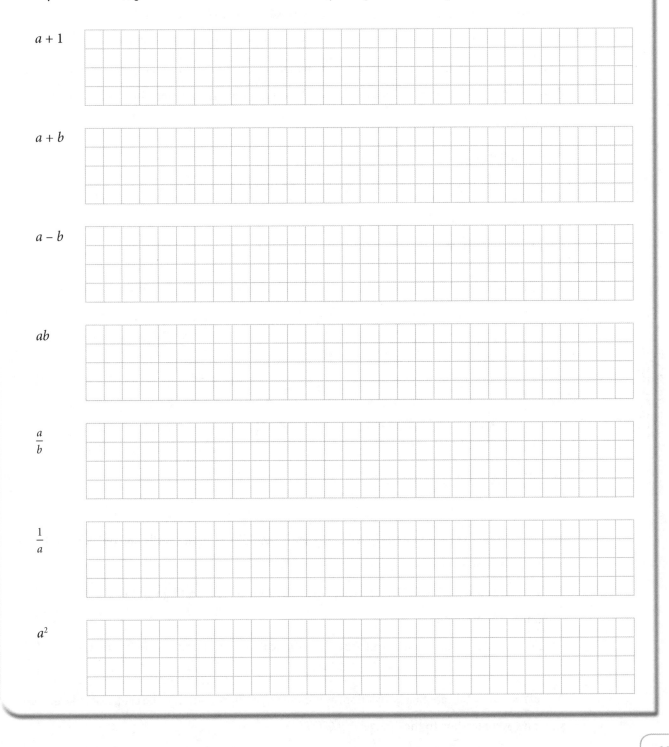

a^2

9

Building a Wall

Introduction

This lesson provides an opportunity for learners to investigate enlargements; in particular, the effect on the image of changing the position of the centre of enlargement while keeping the scale factor and the object position constant. The effect of changing the scale factor is comparatively straightforward to understand, with scale factors greater than 1 leading to an increase in the size of the shape, scale factors between 0 and 1 leading to a decrease in the size of the shape and negative scale factors giving an inversion as well as a change in size. But moving the centre of enlargement does not affect the size or the orientation of the image, only its position. In this lesson, learners investigate *how*.

Aims and Outcomes

- investigate enlargements of a rectangle with different centres of enlargement

Lesson Starter (10 min)

Draw a diagram such as:

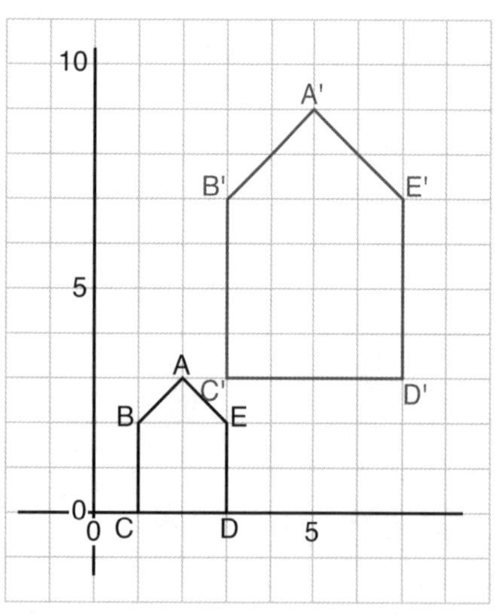

This could be with or without the letters, axes, etc. (Such diagrams are easily and quickly produced using graph-drawing software.)

What do you see? Maybe 3D, if learners mentally join corresponding vertices.

How was it produced?

A'B'C'D'E' is an enlargement of *ABCDE* with scale factor 2 and centre of enlargement (–1, –3).

Learners may talk about a 'projection', as if there were a light source at the centre of enlargement and 'rays' were leading to the 'image' *A'B'C'D'E'*.

What would happen if we moved the centre of enlargement but kept everything else the same? The shape, size and orientation of the image would stay the same, but it would translate to a different position.

How could we find the centre of enlargement if we just had the object and image shapes?

You could put in the 'rays', joining corresponding vertices and the point where they meet will be the centre of enlargement. *Will they always all meet at a single point no matter where you place the object and image? Why/why not?*

Yes, they will, provided that the object and image are similar and in the same orientation.

Main Lesson (25 min)

Give out the Task Sheet.

Starting with one 'brick', with vertices at (0, 0), (2, 0), (2, 1) and (0, 1), 'build a wall', just using enlargements of this first brick, scale factor 2, and varying only the centre of enlargement. All the bricks in the wall should be the same size as each other, and with twice the dimensions of the original given brick.

Learners should try to find the required centres of enlargements.

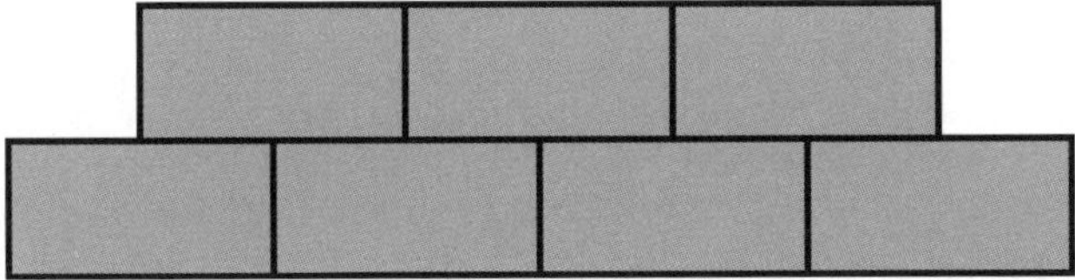

Plenary (20 min)

There is plenty of scope for generalizations. All learners should be able to find some correct centres of enlargements, but as patterns develop it is natural to try to express these algebraically.

Learners may be surprised that the centres of enlargement make a rectilinear arrangement of dots. Sometimes people expect the dots to be closer together nearer the starting brick and more widely spaced further out, perhaps curving upwards (or downwards) too. It might be worth asking learners at the beginning to say how they think it is going to turn out before they start.

The bottom row (row 1) can be made by using centres of enlargement $(4n, -1)$ and the second row by using $(4n + 2, -3)$, where n is an integer. In general, row r requires centres of enlargement $(4n + 1 + (-1)^r, 1 - 2r)$.

Homework

Make another design using a similar process but a different starting 'brick'. List the centres of enlargement that you are using for each image brick.

To make it harder

Learners who are confident with this task could vary the dimensions of the original brick. *How does this affect the centres of enlargement needed? Can you generalize to an original brick with vertices (0, 0), (2a, 0), (2a, a) and (0, a)?*

Here, centres of enlargement will need to go at $a(4n + 1 + (-1)^r, 1 - 2r)$.

What other generalizations are possible?

Learners could try making wallpaper patterns by repeating an image in a pattern across the paper. *Where do the centres of enlargement have to go to make the pattern work? Why?*

To make it easier

Learners who find themselves getting confused could begin with a blank piece of 1 cm × 1 cm squared paper, draw a rectangle anywhere they like and any size they like (although not too big) and try to explore where they can place the centre of enlargement, and what scale factor they can use, so that the image will lie completely on the piece of paper. Experimenting to get a feel for the 'dimensions of possible variation' will help when working on the main task.

Building a Wall

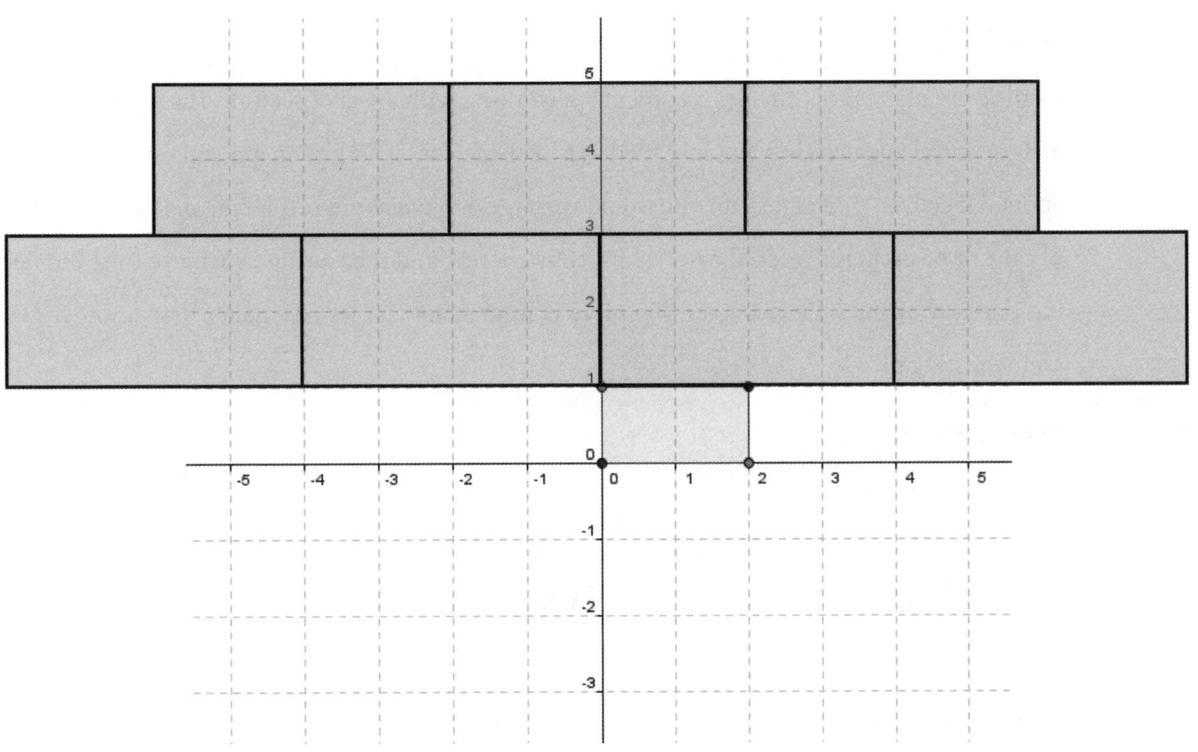

Start with one 'brick', with vertices at (0, 0), (2, 0), (2, 1) and (0, 1).

Build the wall shown, just using enlargements of this first brick, with scale factor 2, and varying the centre of enlargement.

All the bricks in the wall should be the same size as each other.

Where does the centre of enlargement have to be to generate each brick? Why?

Extend the wall downwards, and upwards.

What if you use a different shape or position for the first brick?

How does this change things?

10 Cake-Cutting Contest

Introduction

Cutting circular cakes provides a context for working with areas of sectors. The setting is deliberately artificial and certainly not intended as a 'real-life context'– just an amusing situation to think about. Of course, in practice, no one would worry too much about producing precisely equal slices of cake or be prepared to do the necessary constructing and measuring to achieve this! But deciding one way or the other whether one piece is in principle larger or smaller than another can be an interesting puzzle.

Aims and Outcomes

- find the areas of sectors of circles
- understand and use circle theorems
- use the formula area = $\frac{1}{2}ab\sin C$ to find the area of a triangle

Lesson Starter (15 min)

How many ways can you find of cutting a square cake into two pieces, with just one cut, so that both pieces have exactly the same area?

Learners could draw their ideas on the board. It is not necessary for the cut to go through a vertex or through the midpoint of a side.

Point at somewhere at the edge of the cake: *If I start cutting here, where should I stop?, Can I start cutting anywhere?* Any straight cut through the centre of the cake (the position where the two diagonals intersect) will give 'halves', and neither 'half' can be larger than the other!

What if there is some icing on a rectangular portion of the cake (not central). Is it possible then?

This time there is just one solution, found by joining the centres of the square and the rectangle (and extending the line obtained to the edges of the cake). Because the line goes through both centres, it must contain equal amounts of cake and equal amounts of icing. (If the centre of the icing coincides with the centre of the cake, then of course there will be infinitely many possible solutions, and the situation is identical to that where there is no icing.)

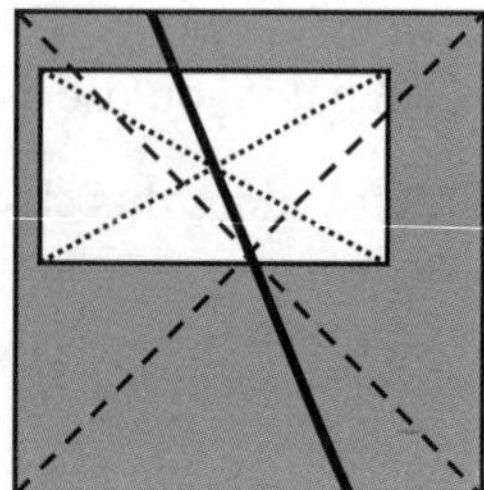

(Dotted and dashed lines here show the diagonals of the rectangle and the square respectively. The centres of the square and rectangle are joined by the thick solid line, which is where you would cut.)

Main Lesson (25 min)

Give out the Task Sheet. Learners may need to be advised to draw in additional radii in the diagram and to consider *segments* (the region between a chord and an arc) as the difference between a *sector* (formed by two radii and an arc) and a *triangle* (formed by two radii and a chord). Learners may like to estimate the order of size of the different pieces before doing any calculations.

Plenary (15 min)

Some of these may be estimated fairly easily by eye, but others are probably too close to call, which provides a motivation for some of the calculations. But even when it is fairly certain which slice is bigger it could be important to know *how much* bigger. Quantitative reasoning, without precise calculation, can also come into play: it is worth reasoning out why, for example, E must be equal to C.

$A = \frac{\pi r^2}{6} = 0.524r^2$ (correct to 3 decimal places)

$B = \frac{1}{2}r^2 \sin 120 = \frac{\sqrt{3}}{4}r^2 = 0.433r^2$ (correct to 3 decimal places)

$C = \frac{\pi r^2}{3} - B = 0.614r^2$ (correct to 3 decimal places)

$D = \frac{\pi r^2}{12} + \frac{1}{2}r^2 \sin 150 = \left(\frac{\pi}{12} + \frac{1}{4}\right)r^2 = 0.512r^2$ (correct to 3 decimal places)

$E = C$, since the segments are exactly identical

$F = \frac{\pi r^2}{2} - D - E = \frac{\pi r^2}{2} - \left(\frac{\pi}{12} + \frac{1}{4}\right)r^2 - \left(\frac{\pi}{3} - \frac{\sqrt{3}}{4}\right)r^2 = \left(\frac{\pi}{12} - \frac{1}{4} + \frac{\sqrt{3}}{4}\right)r^2 = 0.444r^2$ (correct to 3 decimal places)

So the ordering is $B < F < D < A < C = E$, so C and E win!

Homework (5 min)

Find out what a plat diviseur *is* (spell it out) *and design one of your own. Do you think it would be useful in practice? Why / why not?*

To make it harder

Learners who finish early might work out A to F as percentages of the whole cake (divide by πr^2 and multiply by 100) and draw a 'pie chart' ('cake chart'?!) to illustrate how the slices would look if they all went conventionally from the edge to the centre.

To make it easier

Learners who find this very hard could start with cuts that all go through the centre (i.e., are diameters) and explore how many twelfths each slice of cake is worth. *What happens with parallel chords that do not go through the diameter?*

Cake-Cutting Contest!

A cake is marked into 12 equal sections around its edge, with points positioned like the numbers on an analogue clock. The centre is also marked.

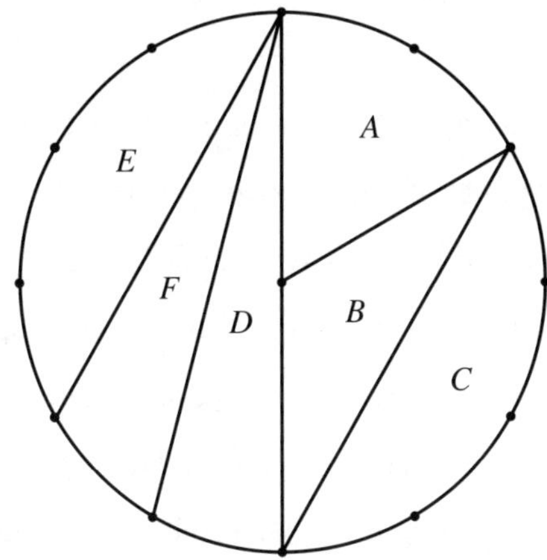

This diagram <u>is</u> drawn accurately

Six strange people, A to F, cut six strange slices of cake:

Who do you think gets the most? Why?

Who gets the next largest slice? And so on? Why?

Try to say how much bigger one slice is than another.

Try to judge first just by looking at the drawing.

Then calculate and see if you were right.

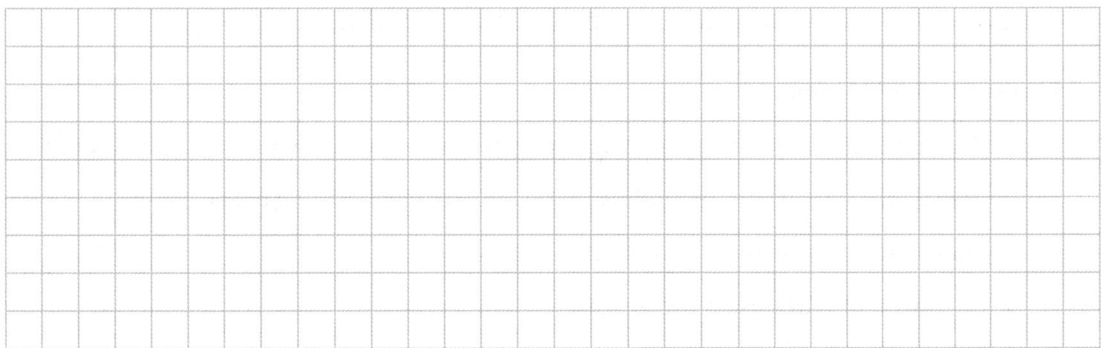

Invent another crazy cake-cutting contest like this in which some of the slices look about the same size. Work out which are actually bigger.

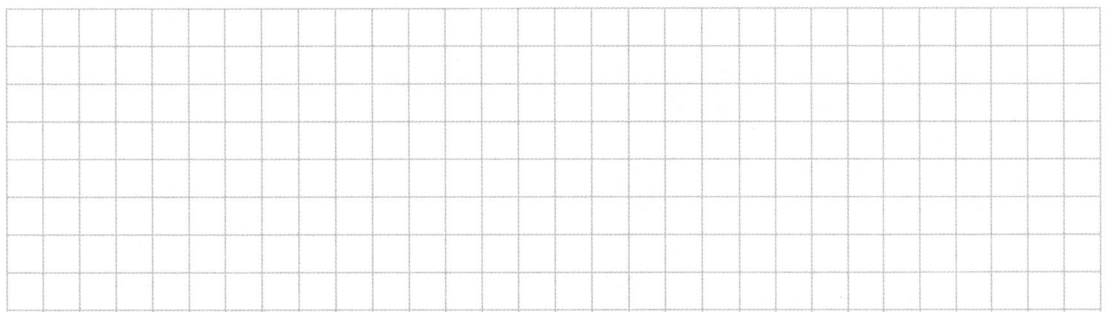

11

Circle Theorems

Introduction

The topic of circle theorems presents one of the best opportunities in the 14–16 curriculum to work on the conjecture and proof of a set of related theorems. If done in a lecture format, where the results and their proofs are presented by the teacher and the learners merely 'apply the rules', then the topic loses much of its challenge and purpose. If learners are simply referring to a diagram and a rule that says 'the angle at the centre is twice the angle at the circumference', then their work reduces to mentally rotating a diagram to match the picture and then doubling or halving a number! This lesson aims to give learners the opportunity to get a feel for the relationships between different angles associated with line segments in a circle and to formulate theorems and begin to think about their proof. It is common practice to use dynamic geometry software at some point during this topic, and that would certainly make for a valuable experience before or after this lesson. The aim here is to focus in depth on one or two specific cases, but the alternative of sweeping through lots of possible diagrams would complement this lesson very well.

Aims and Outcomes

- apply circle theorems to solve angle problems
- prove circle theorems using the properties of isosceles triangles

Lesson Starter (10 min)

Fluency with the *ABC* method of referring to angles will be important for the main task in this lesson, otherwise there is likely to be endless confusion over what is being talked about! So the Starter aims to introduce/practise this convention.

Draw a shape such as this on the board:

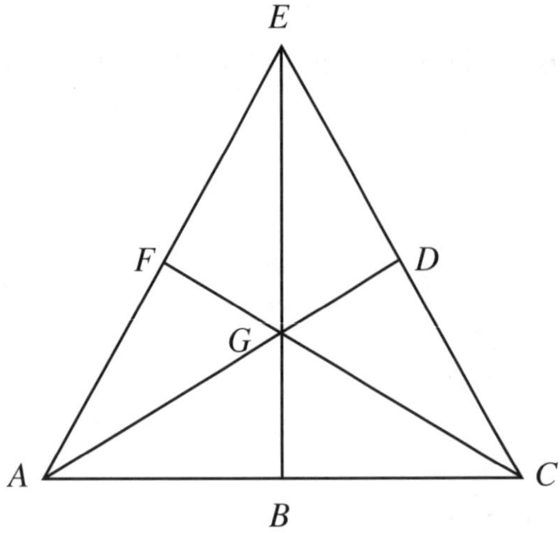

Say what you see – describe this drawing.

It looks like an equilateral triangle with three perpendicular – or angle – bisectors. Once you reach this conjecture, you could agree that that is *exactly* what the drawing is going to be taken as and ask for further comments and observations.

What do you notice about how it has been labelled?

There is a cyclic convention about where to put the letters. Explain or remind learners about the angle-naming conventions; for example, *AGF*.

Why can't we just call that angle 'angle G'? There are at least six different angle positions at *G*, possibly more if you count angles like *AGE*, so it would be ambiguous.

Say an angle that is 90°. And another, and another … How many are there? There are six.

Say an angle that is 30°. And another, and another … How many are there? There are six.

Say an angle that is 60°. And another, and another … How many are there? There are nine.

Say where angle AEC *goes to if the whole drawing is rotated 120° clockwise about G*, etc.

Main Lesson (25 min)

Give learners the Task Sheet (they will need protractors) and invite them to answer the questions. When it comes to the 'why' questions, you may need to draw learners' attention to the fact that each of the triangles in the drawing is *isosceles*. (This will also be true for their drawing in the final section.) 'What is the same about all the triangles?' may be a useful question. This observation is critical for proving the circle theorems.

Plenary (20 min)

This phase of the lesson would work well as a collecting and summarizing exercise, with some emphasis on proof, depending on how you gauge the lesson to have proceeded. Theorems likely to be encountered are 'the angle in a semicircle is 90°', 'the angle at the centre is twice the angle at the circumference', 'angles in the same segment are equal' and 'a radius and a tangent meet at 90°'.

Homework (5 min)

Summarize the conclusions and theorems from today's lesson and write about why you think they are true, perhaps with illustrative examples.

To make it harder

Learners who are comfortable with the circle theorems could make up problems in which 'minimal information' is given and angle-chasing and application of circle theorems (perhaps including the Alternate Segment Theorem) enable '*x*' to be found.

To make it easier

Those who find this topic hard could focus on accurate drawing and measuring and making and testing conjectures.

Circle Theorems

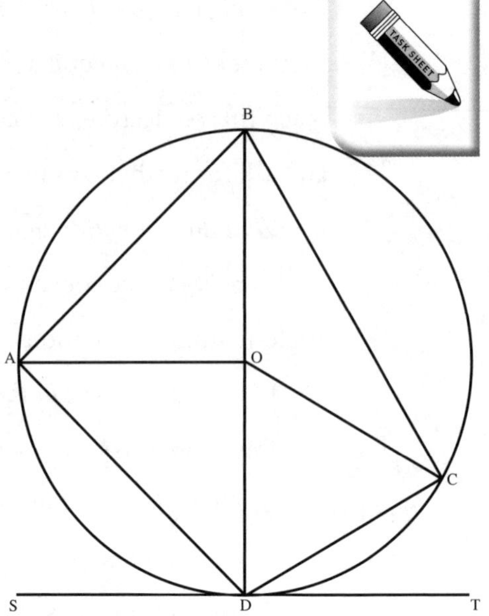

This diagram has been drawn accurately.

O is the centre of the circle.

A, *B*, *C* and *D* are points on its circumference.

SDT is a straight-line tangent to the circle.

On the diagram, carefully measure and label as many angles as you can find, such as *COB*, *COD* and *CDT*, etc.

Look for connections between the sizes of different angles.

If two angles are the same size, is there a reason for this?

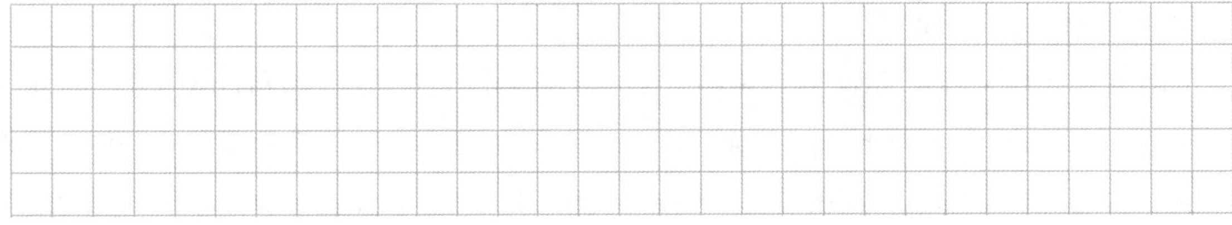

Find an angle that is twice the size of another angle.

Is there a reason for it?

Find an angle that is 90°. Why is it 90°?

Repeat for the other 90° angles.

Summarize your observations in words.

Make a similar drawing of your own, keeping B, O, D, S and T in the same places but moving A and C along the circumference of the circle to positions nearer to D.

Carefully measure the angles again.

Which ones are still the same size? Why?

Which ones have changed? How have they changed? Why?

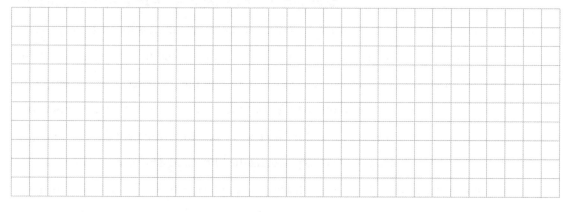

Which connections that you saw in the first diagram are still there in the second? Why do you think this is?

Summarize your conclusions and compare your ideas with those of other groups.

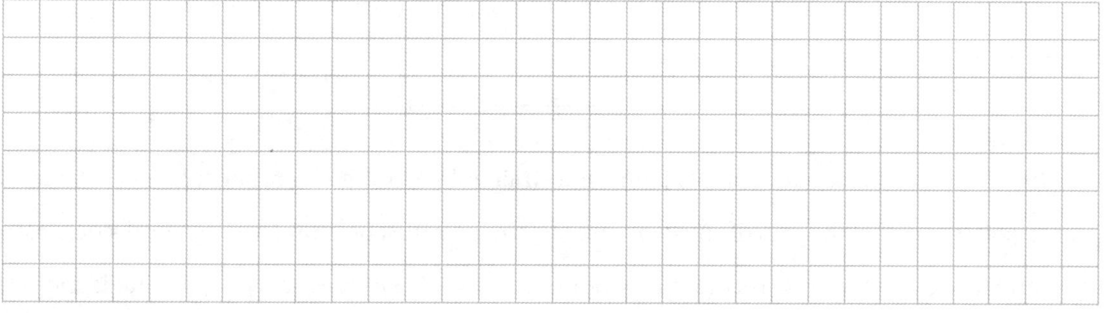

12 Circular Argument

Introduction

Many learners first encounter the number pi (π) as a consequence of measuring the circumference and diameter of a collection of cylindrical objects, being urged by a teacher to divide, and 'discovering' a recurring 'three and a bit', arising as an experimental result. It is then left to the teacher to say that 'actually' the number is π, that it is an irrational number, and thus not a ratio, even though it has been introduced as the 'ratio' of the circumference to the diameter. This can be confusing! Learners can be left with an impression that π 'goes on forever' or 'is such a huge number you can't write it all down' and lose the sense that it is 'three and a bit'. Unfortunately there is no easy proof that π is irrational, but this lesson seeks to persuade the 'three and a bit' through logic rather than experimental measurement. This can help learners to appreciate that all circles are similar and the fact that 'the same π' applies to all circles of any size whatsoever, which doesn't always emerge so well from measuring objects.

Aims and Outcomes

- appreciate the relationship between the circumference and diameter of a circle and understand that this is the same for *all* circles

Lesson Starter (10 min)

Draw the lines below on the board to a similar scale.

Trace the two journeys with your finger: *Which is further or are they the same?*

(In these diagrams we are assuming that line segments that *look* the same *are* the same and that angles that *look* like right angles *are* right angles, etc.)

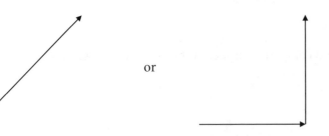

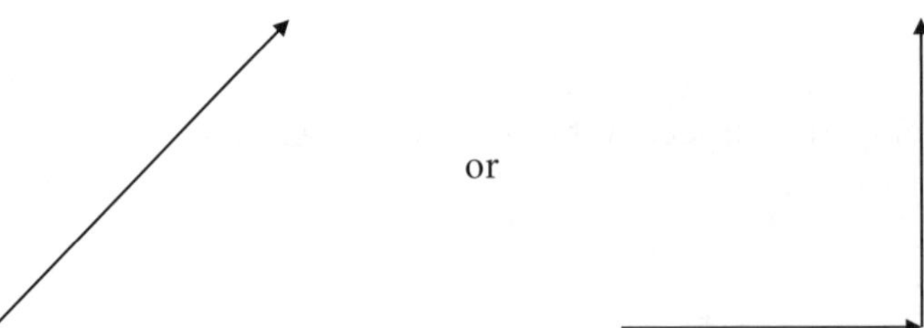

The shortest distance between two points is a straight line, not 'going round a corner'. The triangle inequality says that the sum of any two sides of a triangle must be more than the third side. Learners familiar with Pythagoras' Theorem may notice that $\sqrt{a^2+b^2} \leq a+b$, equality happening if and only if either a or b is equal to zero.

Do we need to measure to be sure? Learners may appreciate that measuring a specific example is a less powerful approach than thinking logically and abstractly about a general case. There are always inevitable inaccuracies associated with measuring and limitations with a finite number of particular examples.

Main Lesson (20 min)

Give out the Task Sheet and encourage learners to decide, perhaps in small groups, which they think is further in each case and why. There is nothing to stop them from using a ruler to measure, but the emphasis should be on explaining with words or pictures rather than resorting to measuring the diagrams given. If learners seem to be relying on measuring the diagrams, you could ask: *Do you think that will always be the case? Why/why not?* Learners may be less familiar with mathematical proofs such as this that do not involve algebra.

For the third case, you might need to suggest that learners draw in diameters, to help them to make the comparison more easily.

Plenary (25 min)

Words such as 'circumference' and 'diameter' will obviously be useful and if they are not brought in naturally you might choose to define and use them.

1. Straight there and back must be shorter than going around in a circle. This establishes that a circumference must be greater than twice the diameter; i.e., that $2d < c$. You could stress that this must be true for *every possible circle* – any circle ever imagined and all circles yet to be imagined by anyone!

2. Superimposing the two pictures may help learners to see that the circle 'cuts each corner' and is therefore shorter. The two radius lengths at each corner must be longer than the quarter arc. So comparing the circumference of the circle with the perimeter of the square we find that $c < 4d$. And again, we can be sure of this for all circles.

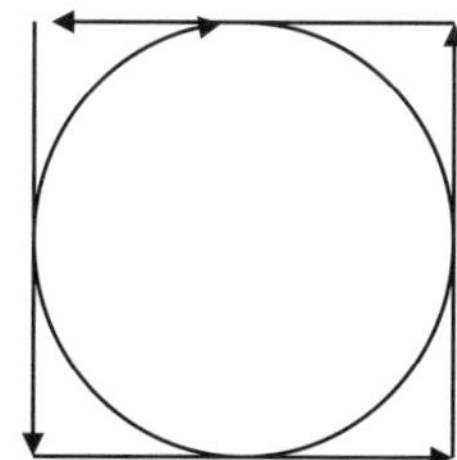

   So far we have that $2d < c < 4d$, so inviting comments at this stage is likely to lead to the conjecture that c is probably $3d$, which is almost right but not exactly. One more diagram is necessary to dispel the idea that $c = 3d$.

3. Again, superimposing the pictures is helpful, and it should be clear that this time the circle is longer than the hexagon, because all the vertices of the hexagon lie on the circumference of the circle, yet the circle does not join them in the shortest possible way, with straight line segments, as the hexagon does.

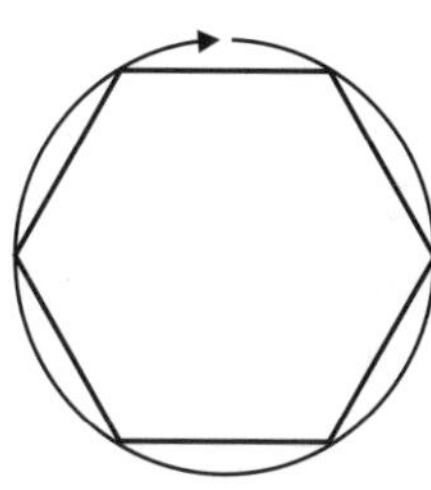

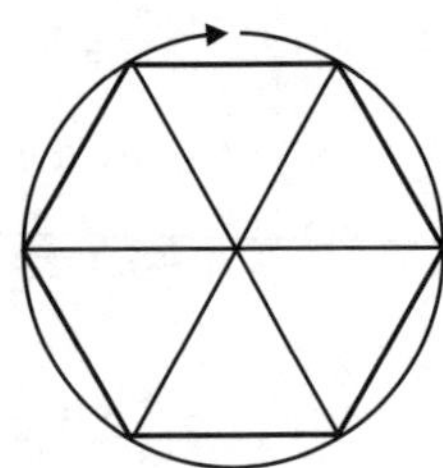

Including the diameters creates six equilateral triangles, all with sides of length r (the radius of the circle). So the perimeter of the hexagon is $6r$ or $3d$.

So $3d \neq c$ as we might have supposed. In fact, $3d < c$. Combining this with the previous results, we have that $3d < c < 4d$. From which it may be reasonable to believe that, exactly, $c = \pi d$.

Homework (5 min)

Find out six interesting facts about π and be ready to share them next lesson. (It will help their internet searches if learners are clear that there is no 'e' in the word 'pi'!)

To make it harder

Learners who are comfortable with trigonometry might like to find a more accurate approximation to π by fitting n-gons inside and outside a circle and comparing either the perimeter or the area of the n-gon with the circumference or the area of the circle. This leads to results such as $n\sin\left(\frac{180}{n}\right) < \pi < n\tan\left(\frac{180}{n}\right)$ and $n\sin\left(\frac{180}{n}\right)\cos\left(\frac{180}{n}\right) < \pi < n\tan\left(\frac{180}{n}\right)$. Substituting large values of n into these expressions gives good approximations for π.

To make it easier

Some learners may find it helpful to use string (or tape measures) to make approximate measurements of the circumferences of circles, to confirm their reasoning or to suggest conjectures to test.

Circular Argument

1. Which is further and why? Or are they the same?

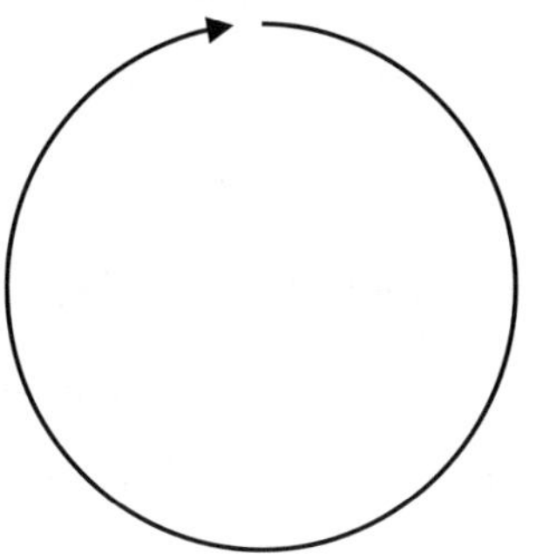

or

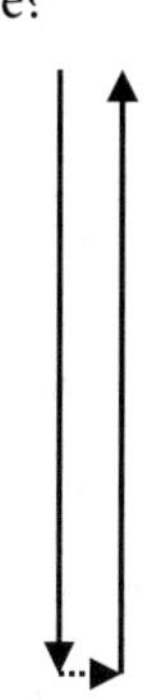

2. Which is further and why? Or are they the same?

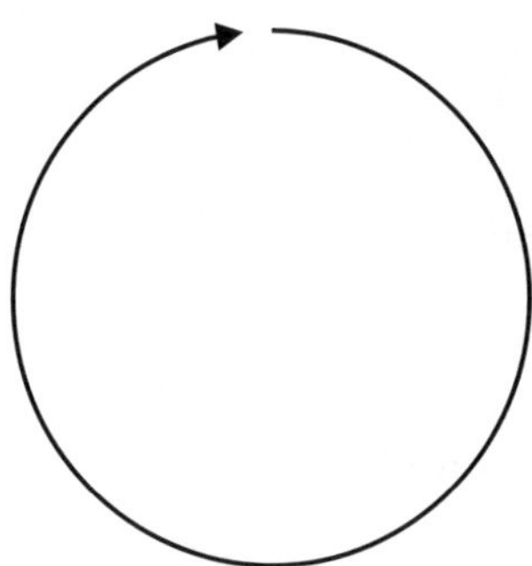

or

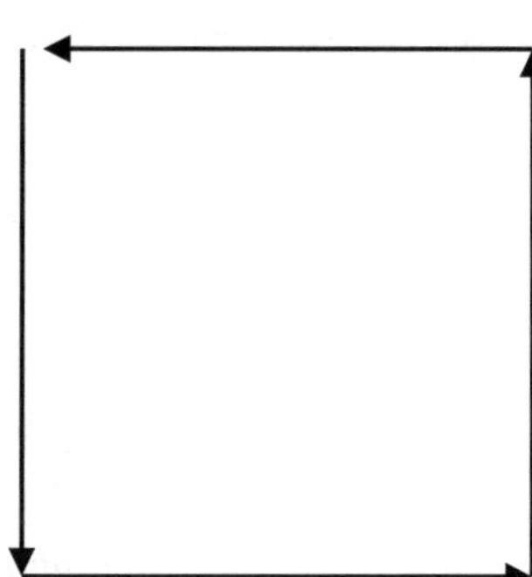

3. Which is further and why? Or are they the same?

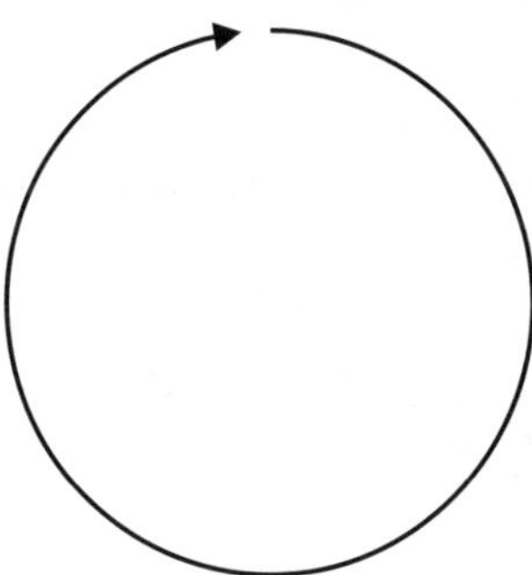

or

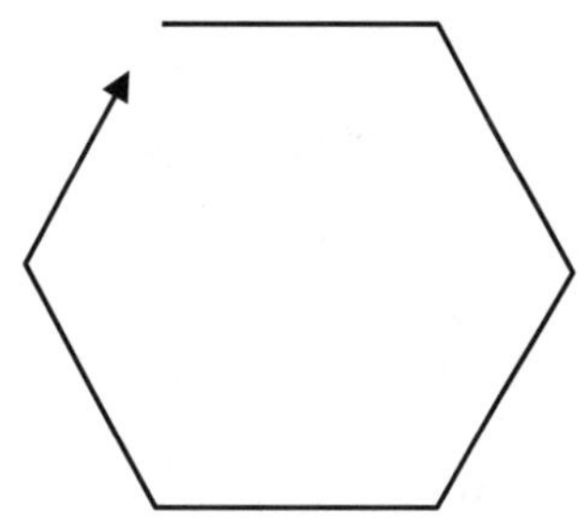

Explain your conclusions as clearly as you can.

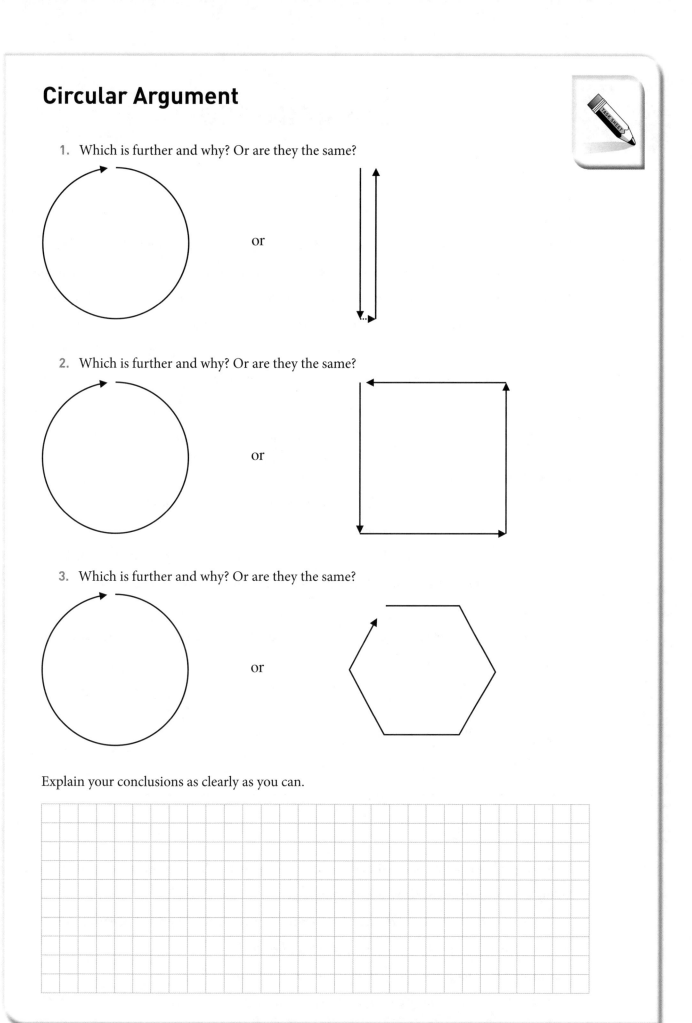

13

Congruence

Introduction

This is traditionally seen as a difficult topic. Learners struggle with the notation of sides and vertices of shapes and also with abbreviations such as AAS (angle-angle-side, meaning that two angles of a triangle are specified along with one side that is *not* the side in between them). Consequently, the topic can easily be reduced to a collection of rules which are used without being well understood. The starting point of this lesson is the idea of a 'uniquely specified' shape, meaning one where the given information is sufficient to describe one and only one triangle.

Aims and Outcomes

- understand the conditions under which two triangles are congruent

Lesson Starter (20 min)

Draw a triangle where two of the sides have length 6 cm and one of the angles is 30°.

Have we all drawn the same triangle? Why / why not?

Learners could be encouraged to use rulers and protractors (or compasses) and to make accurate constructions, or they could sketch the possible triangles without attempting an accurate diagram.

There are *two* possible triangles, both isosceles, but different depending on whether the 30° is in between the two 6 cm sides or not:

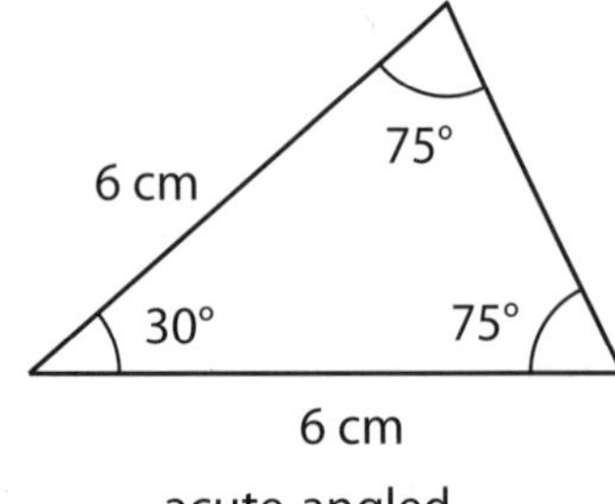

acute-angled

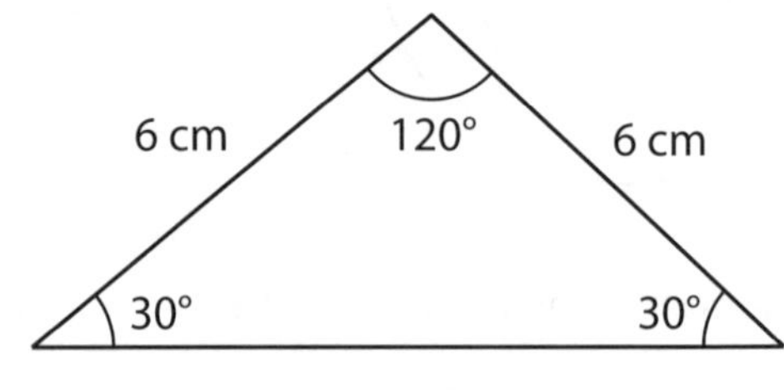

obtuse-angled

Learners might think that 'one of the angles is 30°' means that '*only* one of the angles is 30°', thereby ruling out the second possibility, and this might generate a useful discussion.

Let's change the instructions and see what happens. Learners could suggest different sets of information. *When is more than one triangle possible and when does it have to be just one triangle? Why? Can there ever be more than two possible triangles? Why / why not?*

When there are two possible triangles, is one always acute-angled and one obtuse-angled? Why / why not?

You could mention the phrase 'uniquely defined' to mean that there is just one possible triangle that can be made from the given information.

Main Lesson (20 min)

Give out the Task Sheet and ask learners to consider the various possibilities, making sketches or accurate drawings to help them. This works best if learners are in pairs or groups, so that they are trying to find exceptions and counterexamples to each other's ideas. A learner working individually can be too easily self-convinced!

Plenary (15 min)

There are $2^3 = 8$ possible three-letter triads of the letters A and S, and they have the following properties:

- AAA $\Rightarrow$ similarity
- AAS, ASA, SAA $\Rightarrow$ congruence
- SAS $\Rightarrow$ congruence
- SSA, ASS $\Rightarrow$ two possibilities
- SSS $\Rightarrow$ congruence

When you know any two angles of a triangle, you effectively know all three angles, since you can calculate the third angle by using the fact that the sum of the interior angles of a triangle is 180°. So any two A's and any corresponding S will always lead to congruence. But it is *not* true that if you start with any two S's you can find the third S, because the length of the third side depends on the angle between the two given S's. That is why SSA (or ASS) are problematic (the so-called 'ambiguous case') when SAS isn't.

Homework (5 min)

Give three sets of written instructions telling someone how to draw a triangle, without providing a diagram (e.g., by text message). In two cases, make them descriptions of a unique *triangle and in the third case make it so there are* two *possible triangles. Draw the four triangles accurately.*

To make it harder

Learners who finish early might like to consider what conditions are necessary to prove congruence between two *quadrilaterals*, or polygons with more than four sides. It can get complicated here! Learners could imagine constructing (or actually construct) SSSS out of cardboard and paper-fasteners and see that it may be 'wobbly', unlike SSS with a triangle. (*Are* all *quadrilaterals deformable? Even if a quadrilateral cannot be smoothly deformed into another one, if you disconnect the pieces perhaps they can be fitted together differently to make a different quadrilateral?*) It is fairly easy to see that SASAS will prove congruence and so will SSSSA in any order. A drawing may convince learners that ASASA also works. What about SASAA, etc? Learners might also want to try including 'D' for a diagonal.

To make it easier

Learners who are stuck might wish to spend longer drawing specific triangles for given information before thinking more generally.

Triangles

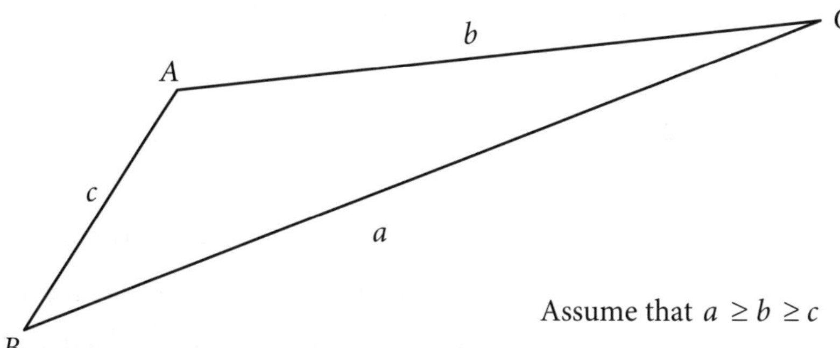

Assume that $a \geq b \geq c$

Is it possible to make a triangle with these measurements?

If not, why not?

If you can, how many different triangles is it possible to make? Why?

	a cm	**b** cm	**c** cm	**A**	**B**	**C**	**Conclusions**
1	10	8	7				
2	10	5	4				
3	10	(<10)	(<10)		100°		Impossible, because the biggest side must be opposite the biggest angle.
4							
5							
6							

What other possible situations are there?

What *impossible* situations can you invent?

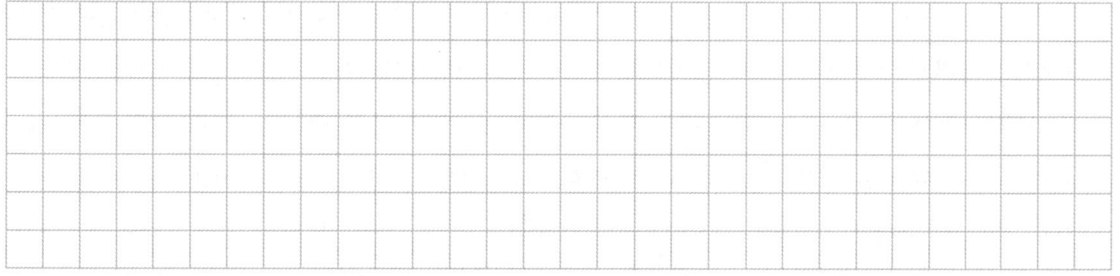

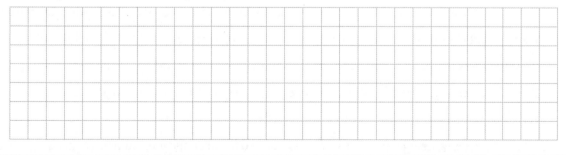

14 Connect Four

Introduction

Learners frequently write algebraic *expressions* in order to answer stated questions rather than because of a real desire to *express* something mathematical. This lesson aims to create a situation in which learners notice connections between different values, represented by letters, and then seek to express those connections in algebraic form. The economy of expression given by the language of algebra should become apparent, and there is plenty of opportunity to practise the arbitrary conventions of algebraic notation while at the same time appreciating the ways in which numerical quantities can be linked by operations. The task of rearranging an equation can be seen as finding alternative ways of expressing the same connection between the various quantities.

Aims and Outcomes

- rearrange equations to make a different letter the subject
- substitute numbers into algebraic formulae

Lesson Starter (10 min)

Can you make 24 from the following numbers? (You have to use all the numbers once each.)

1, 2, 4 and 5? (e.g., $4 \times (5 + 2 - 1) = 24$)

2, 4, 10 and 10? (e.g., $10 \times (2 + 4 \div 10) = 24$)

2, 2, 2 and 9? (e.g., $2 \times (2 + 9) + 2 = 24$)

Ask learners to make up a 24 puzzle like this, involving four integers. *Make it hard but not too hard! You certainly need to make sure that* you *can do it!* Encourage learners to choose their best creation and share it, perhaps explaining why they consider it to be their best one.

Main Lesson (20 min)

Give us four numbers, please. (You could specify integers between zero and ten if you wish or leave it completely open.) It may be helpful to choose four learners with different initial letters of their names and then to use these letters for the four values; for example, *A*jay, *P*arminder, *R*euben and *U*wati might choose 5, –2, 7 and 19, respectively, leading to $a = 5$, $p = -2$, $r = 7$ and $u = 19$.

Write these on the board and then pause as though you are thinking. Then say something like, $2r + a = u$. *Can you explain why?*, perhaps writing the equation on the board. (If someone chooses zero, that will be particularly easy to incorporate!)

See how many other connections learners can find between the four numbers. Encourage them to express them in correct algebraic notation; for example, no multiplication signs (5*ad* rather than

$5 \times a \times d$), number first ($5ad$ rather than $a5d$) and letters alphabetically where possible ($5ad$ rather than $5da$).

Can you say something that includes a power, a root, a division, etc?

Learners can decide whether they think that each equation has to include *all* four letters and whether repeats are allowed.

Give out the Task Sheet. Learners could choose their four numbers individually or in groups – or you might prefer for the whole class to agree on the numbers initially and work with the same ones. Learners may think that all the numbers need to be different, so that if $s = 6$ then k cannot be 6 as well, and you may wish to try to undermine this assumption deliberately.

Plenary (20 min)

Learners could present their equations in poster form rather than orally during discussion. This would allow members of different groups to circulate and look at and 'check' other groups' work. Queries could be resolved by discussion, with teacher arbitration where necessary!

Homework (10 min)

Begin with some formulae and try to construct numbers that will fit them. This is equivalent to finding solutions to four simultaneous equations in four unknowns. For example, a possible set of four equations could be:

$ab = d$

$2c = b$

$abc = d$

$b^2 + c = a$

with solution $a = 5$, $b = 2$, $c = 1$ and $d = 10$. Here, numbering the equations 1 to 4 in order, equations 1 and 3 together imply that c must be 1. So equation 2 gives that b must be 2. Substituting those values into equation 4 gives that $a = 5$, so that $d = 10$ from either equation 1 or equation 3.

Learners could try to solve these equations and to construct their own one. Do their sets of equations have exactly one solution or more than one solution? Why?

To make it harder

Confident learners could try to work with a really awkward set of four numbers, whatever the class might think that to be. The class could seek to construct four numbers among which they felt that there would be 'no or very few' connections. Then a suitable challenge might be to find some connections, or to find a better set of four 'disconnected' numbers.

To make it easier

Learners who are stuck could begin with adding and subtracting connections between the variables. Coding different letters with different colours (e.g., using cyan for a letter c and black for a letter b) may help some learners to articulate connections.

Connect Four

$a =$

$b =$

$c =$

$d =$

Choose four numbers for the letters *a*, *b*, *c* and *d* above.

How many connections can you find between *a*, *b*, *c* and *d*?

Write each one in algebra.

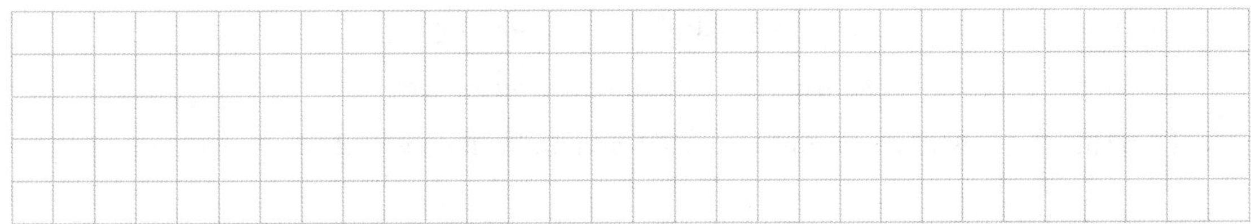

Choose one of your equations and try to write it in a different way, still expressing the *same* connection.

Try to make your ideas as interesting and creative as you can.

Are some sets of four numbers easier to use than others? Why / why not?

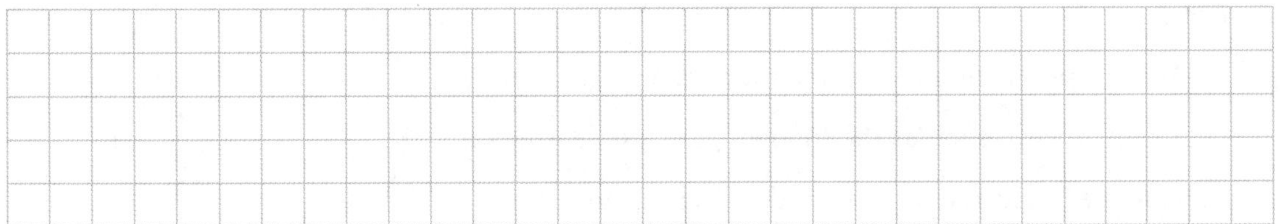

15 Constructions

Introduction

Constructions are often learned instrumentally, and learners can get trapped in a 'step 1 – step 2, . . .' kind of procedure. If they lose the thread somewhere along the way then everything can fall to pieces. This lesson aims to address the thinking behind *why* constructions work. Sometimes learners are confused about why they need to do constructions; if you are given the lengths of the three sides of a triangle (SSS), is it really easier or more accurate to construct it using compasses and ruler than it is using just ruler, pencil and rubber? Many learners can produce more accurate triangles using the 'guess – rub it out – guess better' strategy, with a couple of iterations, than they can with a wobbly pair of compasses! But constructions are important mathematically because of the geometrical principles behind their use, even if the finished drawings are not particularly accurate. Constructing with compasses is 'exact in principle', even if not in practice.

Aims and Outcomes

- appreciate that not just any three lengths will make a triangle
- investigate possible integer triangles with different perimeters
- know how to construct a triangle given SSS and understand why this construction works

Lesson Starter (10 min)

Close your eyes (if you wish). Imagine a circle of any radius. Imagine a second circle with any radius. Try moving the second circle around.

What different things can happen? Can you sum up the different possibilities?

When do the circles cross? How many times? Why?

When will one circle be inside *the other? Why?*

When will the circles just touch? *Why?*

Were you thinking on a flat surface or on a sphere? Or something else?

On a sphere can you say which circle is inside *which? When? How?*

At some point you may wish to move to a physical drawing on the board, such as the following, or ask learners to come to the board and draw what they were seeing.

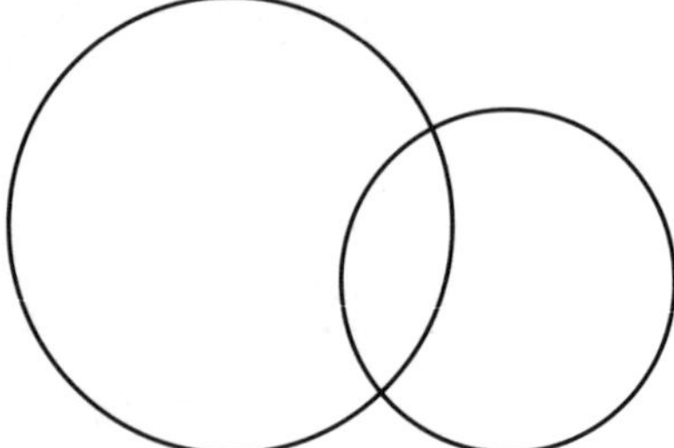

You could add in the centres A and B of the circles and join them to make a line segment AB.

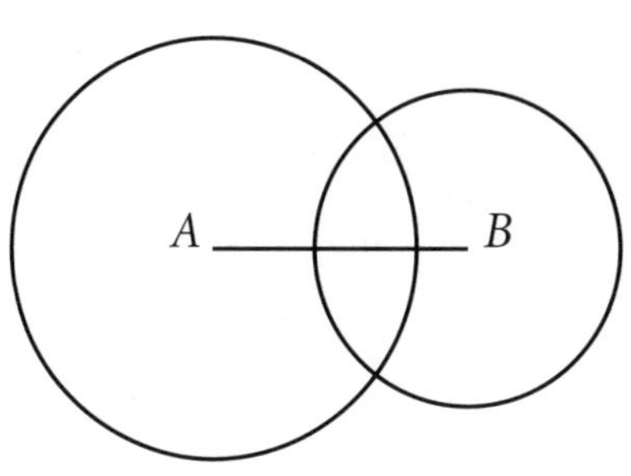

Place your finger somewhere on the circumference of the left circle (centred on A) and ask: *How far am I from* A*?* Repeat, moving your finger round to other positions on the circumference of the left circle.

Do the same thing on the other circle, asking: *How far am I from* B*?*

Ask learners what is special about the crossing points; this leads in naturally to the standard construction of a triangle, by joining either of the intersection points to both A and B.

Main Lesson (25 min)

Give out the Task Sheet and ask learners to work on the problem, either sketching or drawing accurately (using the procedure established) each triangle that they find. You may want to provide real sticks (e.g., headless matchsticks) or not, as you feel appropriate for your class. Encourage learners to write down their ideas as they go.

Plenary (20 min)

There are only two triangles that can be made from 10 sticks: (2, 4, 4) and (3, 3, 4). It may surprise learners that there are so few.

Why aren't there any more? How can you be sure? What would you say if I said that I have another one?

These are good questions for probing how systematic and logical learners have been in their search. Did they just happen to find only two triangles or do they know that there *can* be only two?

With only nine sticks you can actually make *more* triangles – three: (1, 4, 4), (2, 3, 4) and (3, 3, 3). Having to use the tenth stick constrains what triangles can be made.

No. of sticks (perimeter)	**No. of possible triangles**	***a***	***b***	***c***	***A* (°)**	***B* (°)**	***C* (°)**
1	0	–	–	–	–	–	–
2	0	–	–	–	–	–	–
3	1	1	1	1	60	60	60
4	0	–	–	–	–	–	–
5	1	1	2	2	29	76	76
6	1	2	2	2	60	60	60
7	2	1	3	3	19	80	80
		2	2	3	41	41	97
8	1	2	3	3	39	71	71
9	3	1	4	4	14	83	83
		2	3	4	29	47	104
		3	3	3	60	60	60
10	2	2	4	4	29	76	76
		3	3	4	48	48	84
Total	**11**						

The 11 possible triangles are shown on the previous page, where (a, b, c) are the lengths of the sides and (A, B, C) are the angles (in degrees) opposite the three sides respectively. Knowing the angles can be useful for learners to self-check the accuracy of their constructions, so you might want to provide these.

With n sticks, when n is even, the number of possible triangles is $\left[\frac{n^2}{48}\right]$; when n is odd the number of possible triangles is $\left[\frac{(n+3)^2}{48}\right]$ – where the square brackets indicate rounding to the nearest integer. For more details and proofs, go to www.maa.org/features/integertriangles.pdf.

Homework (5 min)

A stick is broken into three pieces at random. What is the probability that the three pieces will make a triangle? Why? (This time the broken pieces don't have to be of integer length – and neither does the starting stick, though it does have to be straight.)

The longest stick must be less than half the length of the original stick, because of the triangle inequality. The answer is $\frac{1}{4}$, and there are many different solutions that can be found on the internet (search for 'broken stick problem') – see also Haigh, G. (1981), 'The glass rod problem', *Mathematical Gazette*, **65**, 37–8.

Learners may have come across 'QED' written at the end of proofs. You could ask them to find out what 'QEF' stands for.

QED stands for *quod erat demonstrandum*, indicating that a proof has been completed because the last line was 'what was to be demonstrated' – the thing we set out to prove in the first place. QEF stands for *quod erat faciendum*, and is sometimes (less often) used at the end of a construction, meaning that what has been achieved is that 'which was to have been done' or 'which was what we were trying to do in the first place'.

To make it harder

Learners who are comfortable with this work may like to think about how the possible number of integer triangles is related to the perimeter, by combining the triangle inequalities with the number of partitions of the perimeter into three.

To make it easier

The task as given should be accessible to all learners, particularly if practical equipment such as headless matchsticks is available.

Sticks

You have 10 sticks, each of length 1.

Can you arrange them to make a triangle? Why / why not?

If you can, can you do it in more than one way? Why / why not?

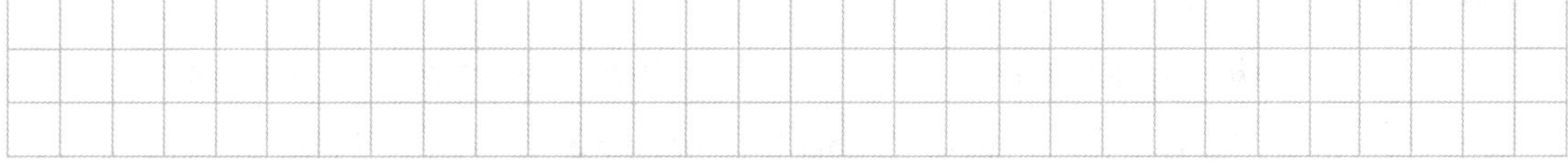

Try with a smaller number of sticks, still of length 1.

Can you make triangles this time? Why / why not?

Suppose you have *up to 10* sticks, still of length 1.

This time you *don't have to use all of the sticks.*

What is the total number of triangles you can make now? Why?

(Before you try, you could say roughly how many you might expect to find.)

Construct all the triangles, with ruler and straight edge, and explain why there can't be any more.

What happens if you use sticks of a different length? Why?

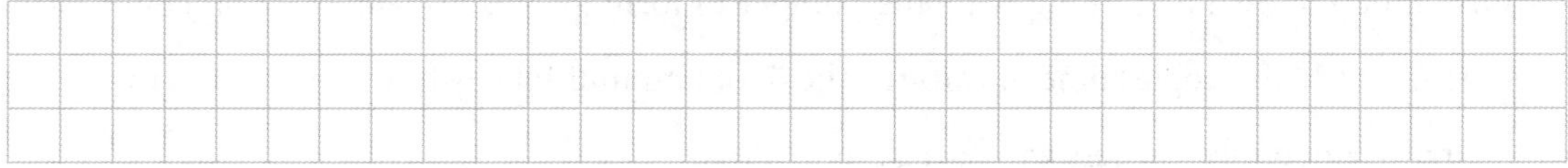

What happens if you try to make other shapes?

Investigate.

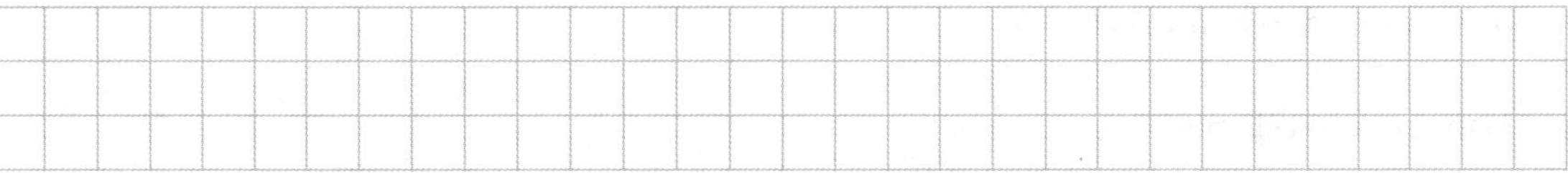

Find out about *integer triangles.*

16 Counting Squares

Introduction

Everyone knows how to count, but counting large numbers efficiently, even in an approximate way, can be challenging. This lesson assumes that learners have an 'exercise book' consisting of pages of squared paper. It can be a fruitful first lesson with a class, if you have just given out a new book to every learner, as it is a way of establishing some of the ways in which you may want to work in future lessons and can seem like a natural mathematical question to arise when receiving this new book!

Aims and Outcomes

- devise intelligent strategies for simplifying problems
- estimate large numbers
- work with large numbers on a calculator

Lesson Starter (10 min)

Suppose you wanted to know roughly how many people were present in assembly – how would you count them?

How do you think the police estimate crowds at demonstrations?

How would you estimate the number of people attending a football match?

There are lots of possible methods of estimating numbers such as these. You could count a small area or a row and multiply up. In a school you could estimate the average number of people in a form group or Year and multiply by the number of form groups or Years. Or you could estimate the rate at which people come in through the door and multiply by how long it takes for everyone to arrive. Hopefully learners will have several ideas.

What's the same about all these methods?

They all give a 'near enough' answer. They don't give you an exact number, but often you can't or don't need to know that.

Main Lesson (25 min)

Give out the Task Sheet. You might want to spend most of the time on just one of the problems, or ask different learners to work on different problems. Encourage them to use whatever methods they can think of but to write down what they are doing and be ready to explain later on what they did and why.

If learners seem insecure, repeatedly asking you for more information (e.g., 'But how many pages are there in an exercise book?' or 'But we don't know how thick a piece of paper is?' or 'But where does it say how big a football pitch is?') you could handle this by saying, honestly, that you don't know (if you don't!) and leaving them to decide what to do about that. Or you could more actively encourage them to guesstimate the value themselves. Learners who are not used to working in an approximate way may feel that the tasks are impossible unless you supply them with further information, so it may be a challenge to modify the dynamics so that they feel that it is their responsibility to come up with the best answer that they can – and be prepared to justify it to the class – rather than your responsibility to keep telling them what to do and rushing around digging out information for them.

Plenary (20 min)

It will be natural to share different learners'/groups' answers and compare and discuss their methods. *How much difference do you regard as acceptable and why?*

What other estimation questions can you ask and answer?

Do we believe the answers that we're being told? Why / why not?

As a last resort it might be necessary to go to the internet (either during the lesson or before the next lesson) to settle disputes, although learners should be aware that information displayed on the internet is hardly infallible!

Homework (5 min)

Invent three more estimation problems and work out suggested solutions. Be ready to share them next lesson with your reasons.

To make it harder

Learners who finish early might be invited to think about the problem of also counting squares that are bigger than 1×1. For example, there will be many 2×2 or 3×3 squares on a page of squared paper. How much difference will including these make? Counting all possible squares means, for instance, that there are a lot more than 64 squares on a chessboard. Learners might be advised to begin with a small notepad-sized page rather than a whole exercise book page!

Competent learners could also consider error bounds and try to decide between what limits they think the true answers lie and why.

The answer to the 'squares within squares' problem is the sum of squares. On an 8×8 chessboard there are 204 squares altogether, which is the sum of the first 8 square numbers. If you count all possible *rectangles* (i.e., including the square ones) you get 1296, which is the sum of the first 8 *cube* numbers.

To make it easier

Learners daunted by the problem could begin with a smaller piece of squared paper. If they wish to count each square individually, the experience of trying this might motivate a more efficient multiplicative approach.

Estimation Problems

How many squares do you think there are in your exercise book? Why?

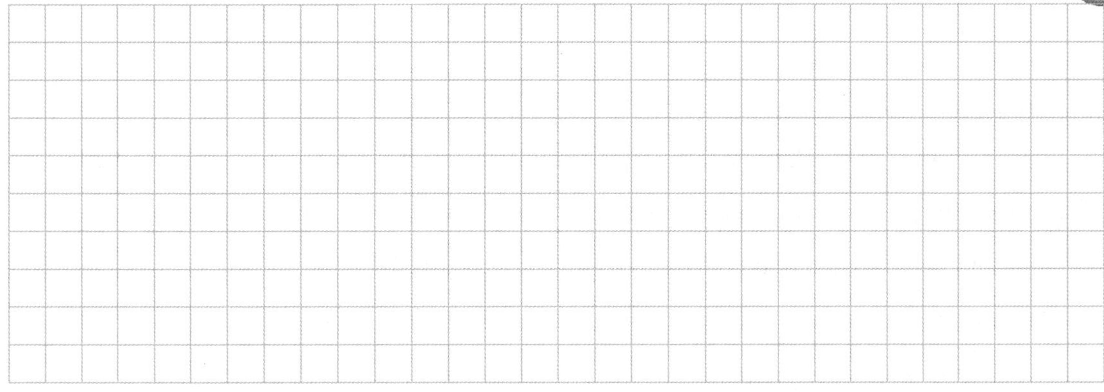

If you took out all the furniture, people and objects, how many sheets of A4 paper do you think you could stack in your classroom? Why?

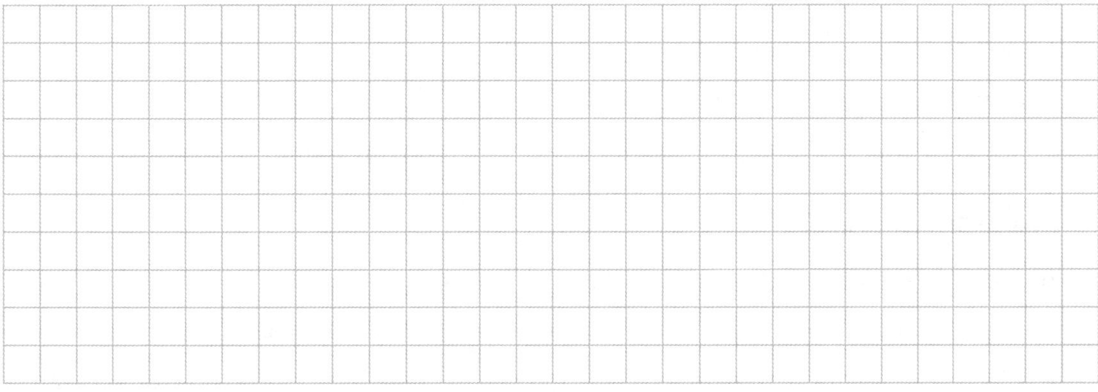

Imagine some 1 cm × 1 cm × 1 cm cubes.

How many do you think would fit in your pencil case? … in your classroom? … in a football stadium? Why?

17 Cutting a Square

Introduction

In mathematics textbooks cakes are almost always circular. So this lesson chooses to exploit *square* cakes for the purposes of establishing and using facts about angles and parallel lines. Learners are often told that corresponding angles are equal, that vertically opposite angles are equal and that alternate angles are equal, and then they tend to ask why and it is sometimes difficult for the teacher to explain or give a proper reason – 'They just are: look at them!' seeming rather unsatisfactory. In this lesson, it should be the *learners* who work on the problem, end up feeling that such angles *must* be equal and try to express in words why they feel this.

Aims and Outcomes

- know the relationships between angles on parallel lines
- use systematic thinking to find all possible cases in a geometrical context
- use the fact that the sum of the interior angles of a triangle is 180° to find angles

Lesson Starter (5 min)

You could begin with some mental visualization: *Imagine a circular (i.e., ordinary cylindrical) cake. If you make some plane (flat) slices with a knife, what is the largest number of pieces you can get with 1, 2, 3, 4, … slices?* (The slices can be horizontal as well as vertical.) Different learners could think about making different numbers of slices.

This is quite hard to imagine accurately and a good mental exercise. The answers are the so-called *cake numbers*: 2, 4, 8, 15 (not 16!), … which satisfy the expression $\frac{1}{6}(n^3 + 5n + 6)$ for positive integer n.

Main Lesson (25 min)

We are going to use square cakes and just think about line slices in two dimensions.

Give out the Task Sheet and encourage learners to be systematic and try to cover exhaustively all the possible situations. They should not be constrained by the number of squares drawn on the Task Sheet. They will need to think about special cases, such as where a cut goes through a vertex. It may be worth specifying that the knife remains in position after the cut, sticking out at both ends, so we get angles between the edge of the cake and the protruding parts of the knife as well as angles within the body of the cake.

Plenary (25 min)

How did you decide when to stop? How did you decide that you had found all the possible situations?

The various possibilities are shown below:

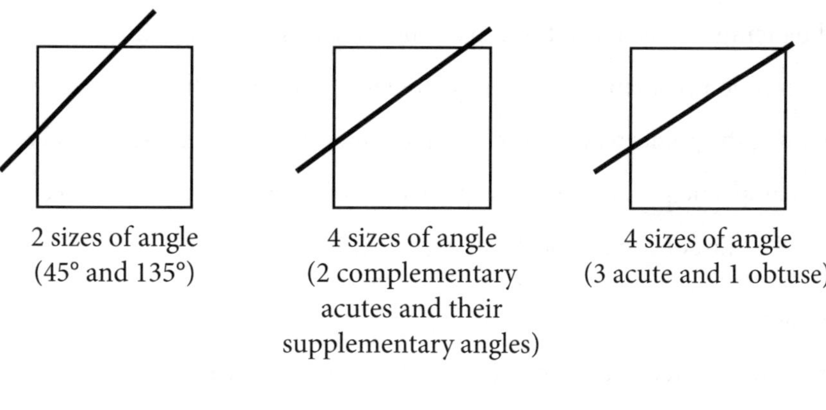

2 sizes of angle (45° and 135°)

4 sizes of angle (2 complementary acutes and their supplementary angles)

4 sizes of angle (3 acute and 1 obtuse)

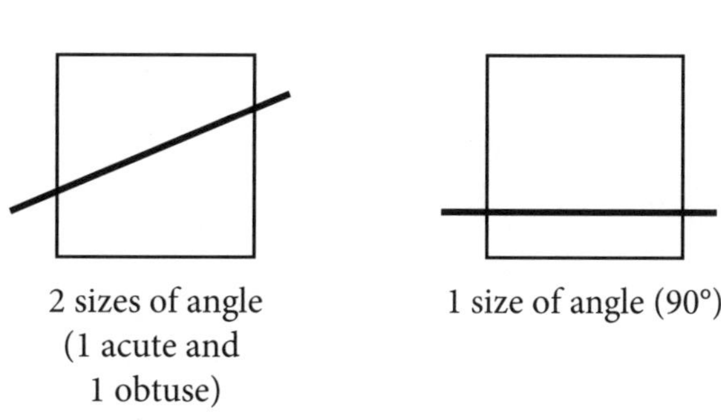

2 sizes of angle (1 acute and 1 obtuse)

1 size of angle (90°)

Learners might experiment with cutting, say, equilateral triangle cakes, leading to the following possibilities:

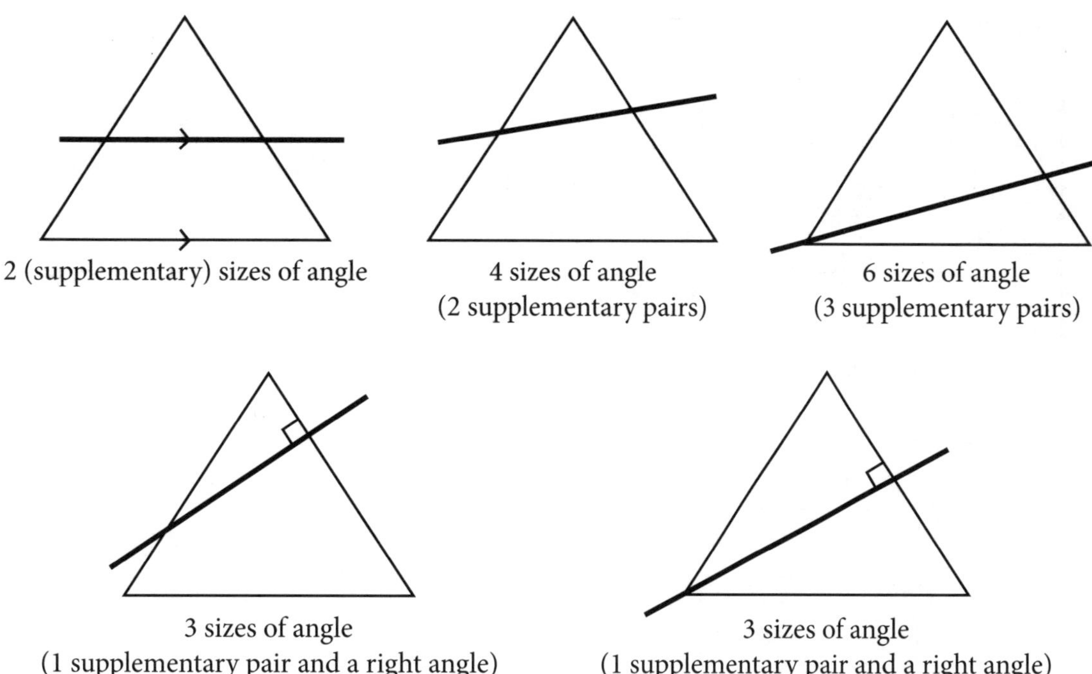

2 (supplementary) sizes of angle

4 sizes of angle (2 supplementary pairs)

6 sizes of angle (3 supplementary pairs)

3 sizes of angle (1 supplementary pair and a right angle)

3 sizes of angle (1 supplementary pair and a right angle)

Other possible shapes to work with would be right-angled triangles and rectangles.

Homework (5 min)

Learners could extend and continue the investigation, perhaps trying trapeziums (isosceles or right-angled, say).

To make it harder

Learners who rapidly succeed with this topic could consider working with a *circular* cake (the limiting case of an n-gon as n tends to infinity). To define the angles here, it is necessary to imagine *tangents* drawn at the points where the cutting line meets the circumference. There will always be two different (supplementary) angles, except when the line passes through the centre of the circle, when there will be just one angle (90°).

To make it easier

Scissors and square pieces of paper (or card) may aid some learners in developing their visualization.

Cutting a Square

Draw a straight line through one of the squares below.

How many different-sized angles are created between this line and the sides of the square?

Why?

Alter the position of the line. Try to think about all the different possibilities.

How does the number of different-sized angles created between the line and the sides of the shape change? Why?

What other shapes of cake could you try?

You could work on other regular polygons or other quadrilaterals or different kinds of triangles.

Write down what you think will happen before you try it.

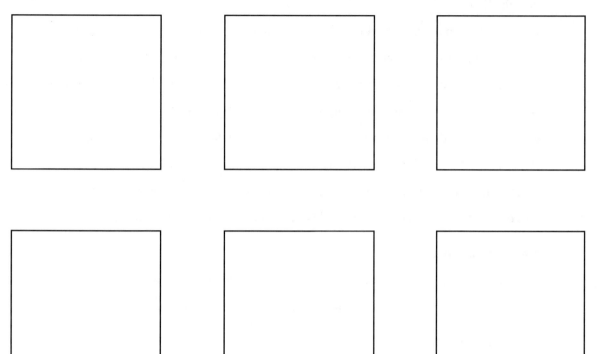

18 Equable Sectors

Introduction

Once learners know about formulae for the area and circumference of a circle, it may seem a short step from there to finding areas and perimeters of sectors. But the fact that the area of a sector or the length of an arc is proportional to the angle at the centre is not always obvious. Learners may accept it for a semicircle or a quadrant but not necessarily in general. For many years previous they are likely to have divided circular cakes into sectors and talked about fractions of a whole, so invoking these ideas may help. In this lesson, although there is numerical equivalence between area and perimeter, the dimensions (units) are necessarily different, so measuring in different units would give different answers. Learners might like to explore this too if they finish early.

Aims and Outcomes

- plot data points on a scatter-graph and discuss patterns and exceptions
- Use ratio (and formulae) to calculate the area and perimeter of sectors

Lesson Starter(10 min)

Ask learners to come and draw a rectangle on the board (use a squared board). Alternatively, learners can do this individually on mini-whiteboards.

Work out the area and the perimeter. Which is larger?

Put it where it belongs on this graph:

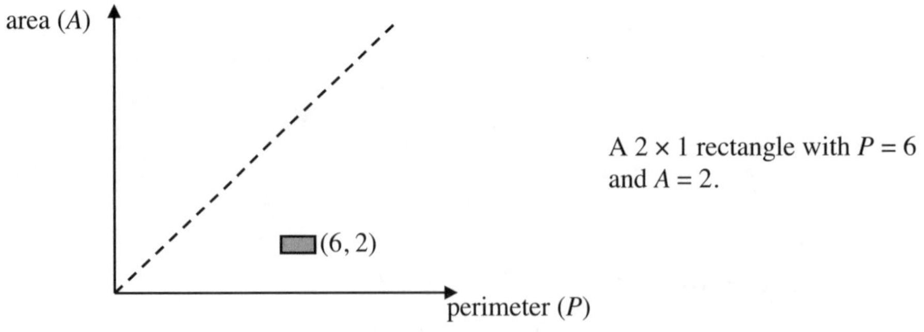

Repeat this with a couple more rectangles, drawn by other learners. The size of your board should limit the rectangles that can be drawn, and therefore the necessary extent of the axes on your graph.

What is special about the diagonal line? Along this line, $A = P$. (Such rectangles are known as *equable* rectangles, but this is probably not a very important term for learners to know beyond this particular lesson!)

Can we find some shapes that go on the diagonal line? For example, a 4 × 4 square has $A = P = 16$.

Can you find a circle that will go somewhere on the diagonal line? There is only one possibility, because $\pi r^2 = 2\pi r$ (for $r > 0$) only if $r = 2$.

Are any positions on the graph impossible? Why / why not?

Main Lesson (25 min)

Give out the Task Sheet, and perhaps some blank paper, protractors and scissors, and invite learners to consider possible sectors and general formulae.

Plenary (20 min)

In general, the perimeter of a sector is given by $P = 2r + s = 2r + \frac{2\pi r\theta}{360}$. (The 2 and the 360 could be cancelled down in the second fraction, but by leaving it in this way the origin of the formula is clearer.)

And the area: $A = \frac{\pi r^2\theta}{360}$.

So for $A = P$ we have $\frac{\pi r^2\theta}{360} = 2r + \frac{2\pi r\theta}{360}$, so $\pi r^2\theta = 720r + 2\pi r\theta$, and since $r \neq 0$, $\pi\theta(r - 2) = 720$, showing that $r \neq 2$ (unlike with a circle, where $r = 2$ is the *only* situation where $A = P$). In fact, since $\theta < 360$, r must be greater than $\frac{2}{\pi} + 2$. For example, if $r = 3$, then $\theta = \frac{720}{\pi} = 229.2°$ (correct to 1 decimal place).

It would be worth making accurate drawings of some of these solutions to see whether their areas and perimeters 'look' equal by eye (quite a difficult thing to establish!).

Homework (5 min)

Learners could be asked to look into *radians*, as an alternative measure of angle, and find out how it simplifies these formulae. They could make a poster summarizing their findings.

To make it harder

A task for learners who complete these tasks quickly would be to sketch the graph $\theta = \frac{720}{\pi(r-2)}$, perhaps using graph-drawing software, and examine its properties in the range $0 < \theta < 360$. They could also look at what happens if you measure equable sectors in a different unit (e.g., inches and square inches). They might like to think about why the equality disappears and which one they would expect to be larger and why. The fact that area and length have different scale factors (area scale factor = (linear scale factor)^2) may help. Alternatively, learners could begin with any sector they like and construct a suitable unit such that the sector would be equable.

To make it easier

Learners who are stuck could try drawing sectors accurately on 1 cm × 1 cm squared paper and estimating their area. How close are their estimates to the calculated values?

Sectors

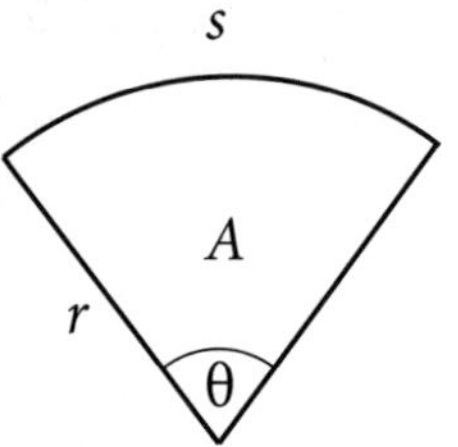

The angle of this sector is θ, the radius is r, the arc length is s and the area is A.

Express the perimeter P in terms of r and s only.

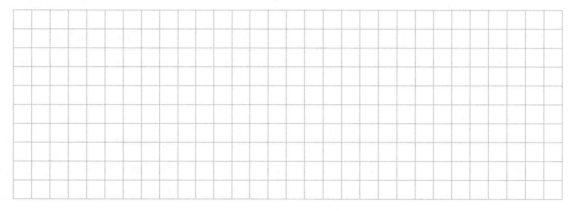

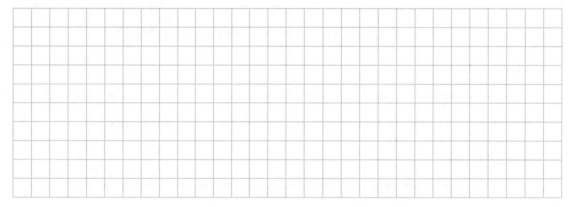

Express the perimeter P in terms of r and θ only.

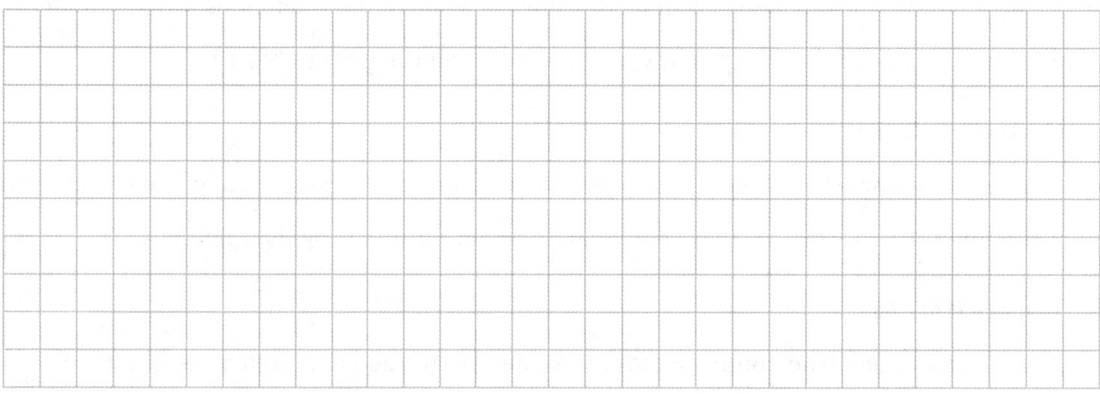

Express the area A in terms of r and θ only.

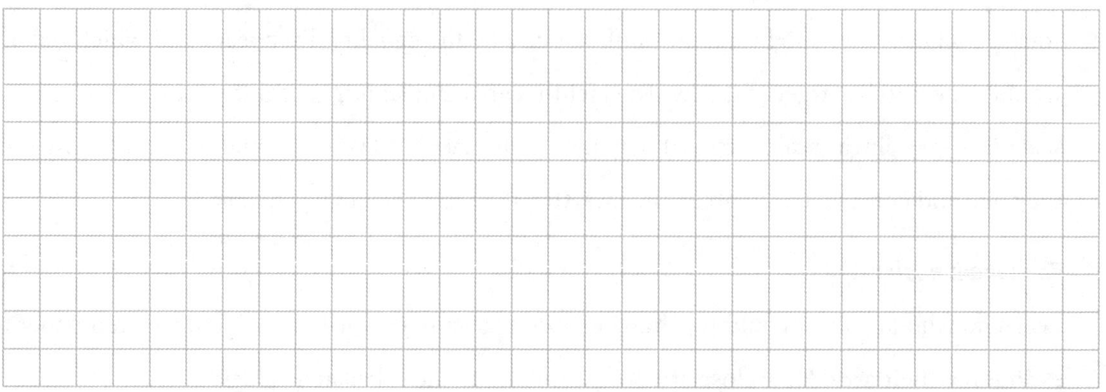

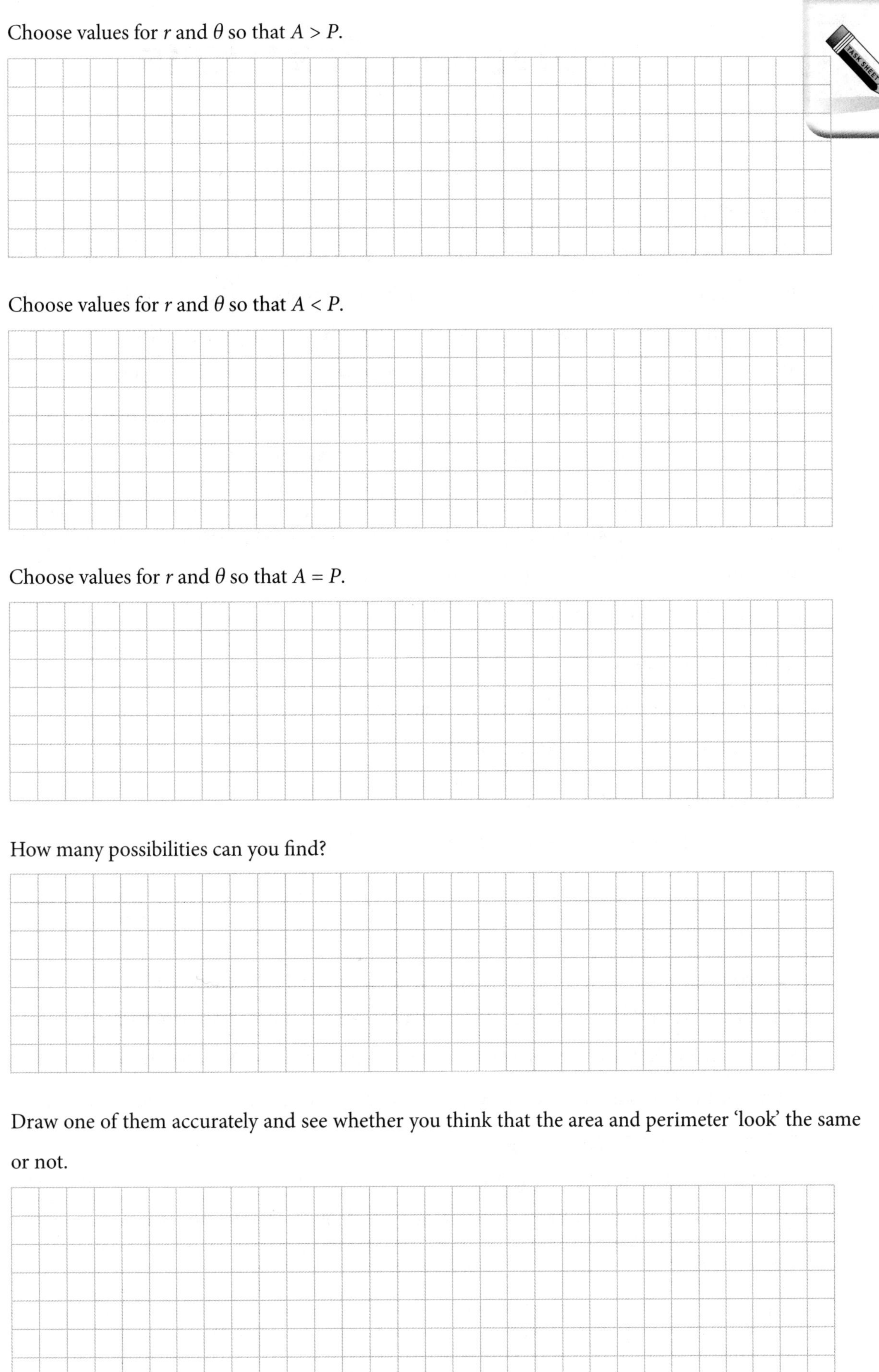

Choose values for r and θ so that $A > P$.

Choose values for r and θ so that $A < P$.

Choose values for r and θ so that $A = P$.

How many possibilities can you find?

Draw one of them accurately and see whether you think that the area and perimeter 'look' the same or not.

19 Equivalent Fractions

Introduction

The idea of equivalent fractions lies at the heart of all fraction work. It may seem odd to learners that the same number can be represented in multiple ways (e.g. $\frac{3}{4}=\frac{6}{8}$, etc.), but the same is true of decimals in cases such as $1.3\dot{9}=1.4$, as well as the more obvious kind such as 1.400 = 1.40 = 1.4, etc. When adding or subtracting fractions, finding fractions *equivalent* to the original ones, but with a common denominator, turns a difficult addition or subtraction into an easy one. So a sum like $\frac{3}{4}+\frac{5}{6}$, for instance, becomes a much easier $\frac{9}{12}+\frac{10}{12}$. In multiplication, equivalent fractions again mean that if $\frac{3}{4}\times\frac{5}{6}$ can be seen as the same as $\frac{3}{6}\times\frac{5}{4}$, then it can be replaced by $\frac{1}{2}\times\frac{5}{4}$, which lies behind the more usual cancelling procedure: $\frac{\not{3}^{1}}{4}\times\frac{5}{\not{6}^{2}}$. Even division can be approached by means of common denominators: $\frac{3}{4}\div\frac{5}{6}=\frac{9}{12}\div\frac{10}{12}=\frac{9}{10}$, although in many cases that might be less efficient than the more usual 'multiplying by the inverse': $\frac{3}{4}\times\frac{6}{5}$.

Aims and Outcomes

- understand when and why fractions are equivalent to one another
- use equivalent fractions to solve problems

Lesson Starter (15 min)

What fractions do you think go in the spaces below and why?

$\frac{1}{12}$ $\frac{1}{6}$ $\frac{1}{4}$ $\frac{1}{3}$ … $\frac{1}{2}$ … … etc.

Learners may take some time to realize that this is a linear sequence going up in $\frac{1}{12}$'s – the $\frac{1}{12}$-times table, in fact. Rewriting the fractions with common denominators makes it obvious. If no one sees this, you could ask learners to put the fractions in order (which they already are, but they may not realize this) or to think about what they would do if they wanted to add them up. The missing fractions, therefore, are $\frac{5}{12}, \frac{7}{12}, \frac{2}{3}$, etc.

You could ask learners, perhaps in pairs, to try to construct another puzzle like this, perhaps using a denominator like 18 or 24 – something with plenty of factors will work best.

For example,

$\frac{1}{18}$ $\frac{1}{9}$ $\frac{1}{6}$ $\frac{2}{9}$ …

The answer is $\frac{5}{18}$, since the sequence is $\frac{n}{18}$, for positive integer n.

$\frac{1}{24}$ $\frac{1}{12}$ $\frac{1}{8}$ $\frac{1}{6}$ ...

The answer is $\frac{5}{24}$, since the sequence is $\frac{n}{24}$, for positive integer n.

More complicated sequences are possible, such as:

$\frac{1}{3}$ $\frac{1}{2}$ $\frac{3}{5}$ $\frac{2}{3}$ ...

The answer is $\frac{5}{7}$, since the sequence is $\frac{n}{n+2}$, for positive integer n. What other fraction sequences can learners generate?

Main Lesson (20 min)

Give out the Task Sheet and ask learners, perhaps in pairs or groups, to think about the statement – which is wrong. It is worth spending plenty of time asking learners to think about what is wrong and why, and perhaps encouraging them to invent similar wrong statements.

Plenary (20 min)

There are many issues relevant here. One is the meaning of an equals sign to say that two expressions have the same value rather than to indicate 'this is what I did next', such as when learners write calculations such as '$3 \times 4 = 12 \div 2 = 6^2 = 36$'.

If learners convert the fractions to decimals they may then realize that 0.75×2 cannot be the same as 0.75. (Nothing can be doubled and remain the same – except zero, and perhaps 'infinity'!)

Learners may correct the statement by thinking of multiplying both the numerator *and the denominator* by 2 to obtain an equivalent fraction: $\frac{3}{4} \times \frac{2}{2} = \frac{6}{8}$.

Or they may prefer to correct the answer to multiplication by 2, perhaps by thinking of 2 as $\frac{2}{1}$, so $\frac{3}{4} \times \frac{2}{1} = \frac{6}{4}$ or $\frac{3}{\not{4}^{2}} \times \frac{\not{2}^{1}}{1} = \frac{3}{2}$.

Learners may relate this to such things as the ratio 6:8 not being 'twice as big' as the ratio 3:4 but expressing exactly the same relation between the two quantities.

Homework (5 min)

Learners could design a poster to illustrate correct ways of adding, subtracting or multiplying fractions, together with pitfalls to avoid and common misconceptions. Why do they think that the misconceptions arise? Are they inevitable or could they be avoided?

To make it harder

Learners confident about the details of this task could think about squaring or square rooting both numerator and denominator (e.g., $\frac{3}{4} \stackrel{?}{=} \frac{9}{16}$ and $\frac{9}{16} \stackrel{?}{=} \frac{3}{4}$). With equations you can 'do the same thing to both sides of the equation', such as squaring or adding 6 or multiplying by 2, but with a fraction you cannot add or subtract the same quantity to the top or bottom of a fraction without changing its size (unless it happens to equal 1) – nor can you square or square root both the top and bottom of a fraction (again, unless it happens to equal 1, or –1, in the case of squaring) – but you *can* multiply or divide by the same amount. Learners might like to ponder why this should be.

To make it easier

Learners who have trouble beginning could be given a fraction, such as $\frac{2}{3}$ and asked to make a list, as long as they can, of fractions equivalent to it. Why do they think that their fractions are equivalent? Diagrams could help.

Equivalent Fractions

Look at this statement.

It is wrong.

Can you say why?

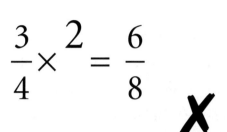

$$\frac{3}{4} \times {}^{2} = \frac{6}{8}$$

What do you think is wrong with it? Does this matter?

How would you convince someone that it is wrong?

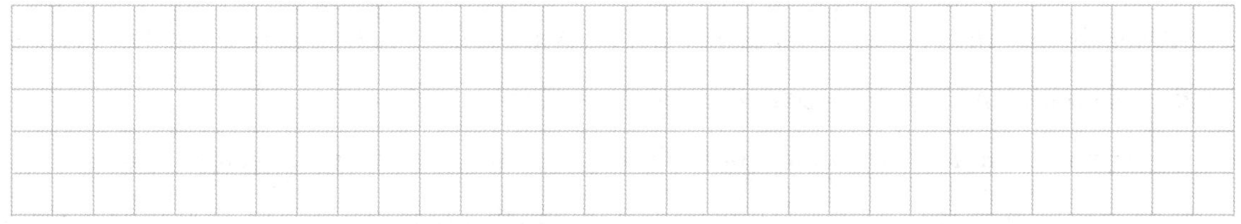

Why do you think that someone would write this?

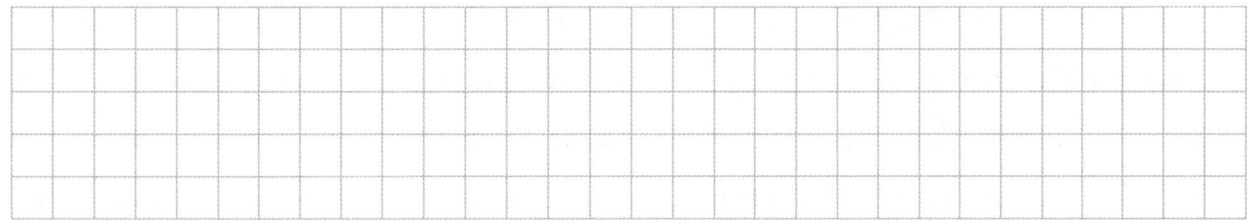

How would you correct it? Can you find more than one way?

How would you explain your correction to the person who wrote it?

20 Factorizing Quadratics

Introduction

This lesson focuses on *monic* quadratic expressions (quadratic expressions in which the coefficient of x^2 is 1, when the equation is rearranged into the usual form, and x is the variable). Learners sometimes follow a rule based on finding pairs of numbers which add up to the coefficient of x and multiply to make the constant term. To ensure that this is more than a mindless routine, it can help learners to appreciate what is going on by working backwards, either in general from $(x + a)(x - b)$ or with specific numbers. Alternatively they can write, for instance:

$$x^2 + 8x - 20 = x^2 + 10x - 2x - 20 = x(x + 10) - 2(x + 10) = (x - 2)(x + 10).$$

Although this might be tedious if carried out every time, it could help to indicate the reason why the rule works and be good preparation for factorizing *non*-monics.

Finding numerical factors turns out to be important in this lesson, and it may be useful for the teacher to be aware that a quick way of finding the number of factors of, say, 72, is to prime factorize it first: $72 = 2^3 \times 3^2$. If we split 72 into two factors, there are four possible powers of 2 (2^0, 2^1, 2^2 or 2^3) and three possible powers of 3 (3^0, 3^1 or 3^2) for the first factor, and the second factor will be whatever is left to make the product up to 72. So for each of the four possibilities for the power of 2, there will be three possibilities for the power of 3, so there must be $4 \times 3 = 12$ possibilities altogether, which means that 72 has 12 factors (which are: 1, 2, 3, 4, 6, 8, 9, 12, 18, 24, 36 and 72). In general, a number that factorizes to, say, $2^a \times 3^b \times 5^c$, will have $(a + 1)(b + 1)(c + 1)$ factors. There is no need to go through this with learners, but if they haven't encountered it before some may benefit from working on it for themselves alongside the main activity for this lesson.

Aims and Outcomes

- begin to gain a sense of when quadratics do and do not factorize
- practise factorizing monic quadratic expressions

Lesson Starter (15 min)

Everybody knows the 'I'm thinking of a number ...' game. Today 'I'm thinking of two *numbers'.* Learners could use mini-whiteboards for this.

One number is 3 more than the other one. And they multiply to make 70. (7, 10) or (–7, –10)

One number is 3 less than the other one. And they multiply to make 10. (2, 5) or (–2, –5)

One number is 8 more than the other one. And they multiply to make –15. (–3, 5) or (3, –5), etc.

End with:

One number is 4 more than the other one. And they multiply to make 10.

It is highly unlikely that learners will be able to do this one without forming and solving a quadratic equation. *What makes this one different?* There are two possible pairs of answers: $\sqrt{14}-2$ and $\sqrt{14}+2$ are one pair, and the other pair are $-\sqrt{14}-2$ and $-\sqrt{14}+2$. Can learners verify that those numbers work if you tell them?

Main Lesson (25 min)

What is a quadratic expression? Can you give a definition or an example?

What is the difference between an expression *and an* equation*?*

What does factorize *mean?*

You could convert the questions from the starter into algebra such as $x(x + 3) = 70$ and solve them algebraically, to give *two* solutions.

Can you give an example of a quadratic expression that factorizes and one that doesn't?

Try to make up one that looks *as though it* does *(or might) factorize but* doesn't.

Try to make up one that looks *as though it* doesn't *factorize but* does.

$x^2 - 6x + 7$ and $x^2 + 14x - 72$ would be a possible pair of answers. The former cannot factorize, since '$b^2 < 4ac$', but perhaps looks as though it might, since $7 = 1 \times 7$ and $-6 = -7 + 1$; the latter is $(x + 18)(x - 4)$ but because people are usually more familiar with tables up 12 they are more likely to think of 72 as 8×9 or 6×12 than as 4×18.

To make things trickier (and easier at the same time!), we are just going to allow integers (whole numbers) today. But an integer can be negative.

Give out the Task Sheet and encourage learners to try to find *all* the possibilities and to have a good reason why there can't be any more.

Plenary (15 min)

Will there always be as many possible box values as there are factors of the constant term? Why / why not?

If the constant term is a square number, what happens? Why?

Factor pairs of 40 are (1, 40), (2, 20), (4, 10), (5, 8) and the same but with both numbers negative in each case. So the possible coefficients of x are ±13, ±14, ±22 and ±41 (i.e., eight solutions). With −40 as the constant term, the possible box values are ±3, ±6, ±18 and ±39 (again, eight solutions). There are eight (positive) factors of 40 (1, 2, 4, 5, 8, 10, 20 and 40; since $40 = 2^3 \times 5$), so a conjecture might be that the number of possible box values is equal to the number of factors of the constant term. This will always work unless the constant term is a square number, where the number of possible box values will be one less than the number of factors of the constant term (since there is a repeated factor).

All the factors of an odd number will be odd, in which case all the possible box values will be odd ± odd = even. But not all the factors of an even number will be even (1 will always be a factor, at least, even if the constant term is a power of 2), so the possible box values can never all be odd. This sort of argument doesn't require algebra, just some careful logical thought.

Homework (5 min)

Learners could look at the related problem of finding the possible box numbers in situations such as $x^2 + 10x + \square$.

To make it harder

Encouraging learners to generalize and to investigate methods of finding the number of factors of a number without writing them all out (e.g., by prime factorization) gives a lot of scope for productive work. Learners displaying lots of confidence could consider non-monics, by putting a number such as 2 or 3 as the coefficient of x^2.

To make it easier

Reducing the size of the '40' (start with 1, perhaps) will make the problem more accessible for learners who find this very difficult.

Factorizing Quadratics

Look at this quadratic expression.

The coefficient of x is shown by a box.

$$x^2 + \square x + 40$$

What integers can go in the box, if the expression is going to factorize?

The coefficient of x can be positive or negative.

You should find eight possible answers.

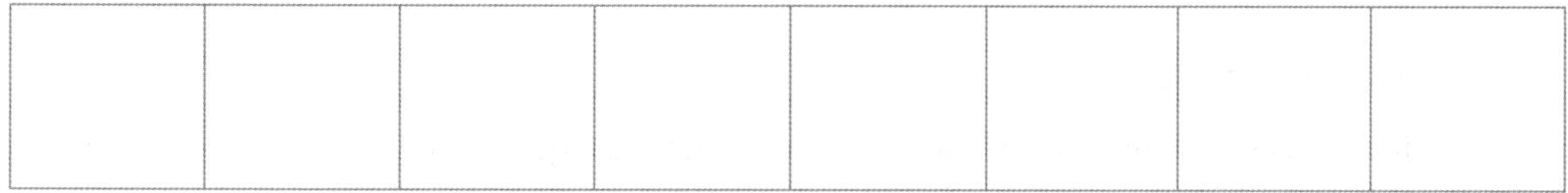

Why must there be *exactly eight* possible answers?

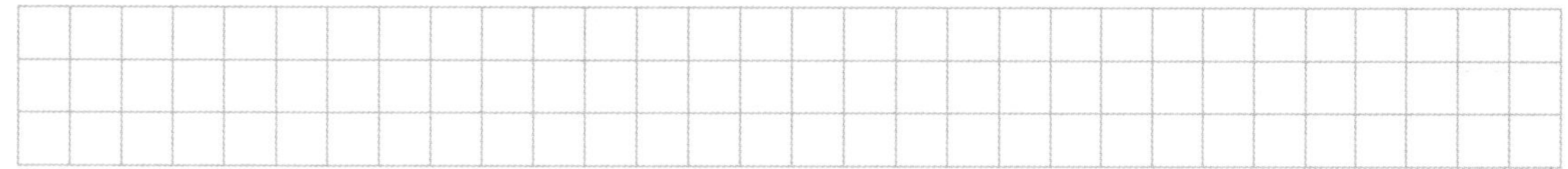

Suppose we change the 40 into –40, so the expression becomes:

$$x^2 + \square x - 40$$

How many possible box values are there this time, if the expression is going to factorize? Why?

Imagine that the 40 (or –40) can be any number.

Will the possible box values ever be all odd or all even? Why?

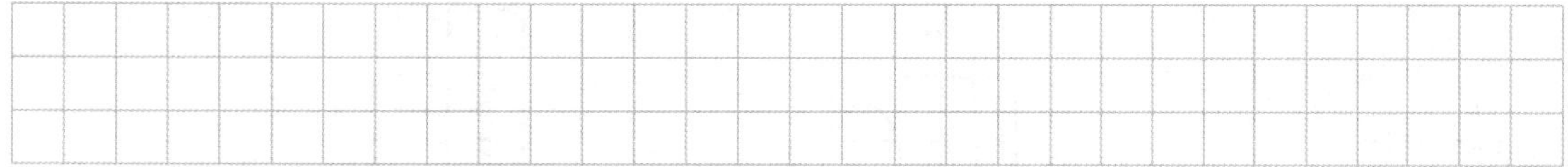

Investigate the patterns in the list of possible box numbers.

Fill it Up!

Introduction

Placing numbers sequentially into boxes laid out in different arrangements leads to many interesting patterns. This lesson gives learners the opportunity to choose their own layouts and explore the sequences generated. There is plenty of scope for extending the task to complex arrangements of boxes or for limiting to rectangular arrays so as to work with linear rather than quadratic formulae.

Aims and Outcomes

- investigate triangle numbers and other quadratic sequences arising from staircase grids of cells

Lesson Starter (15 min)

Look at this drawing:

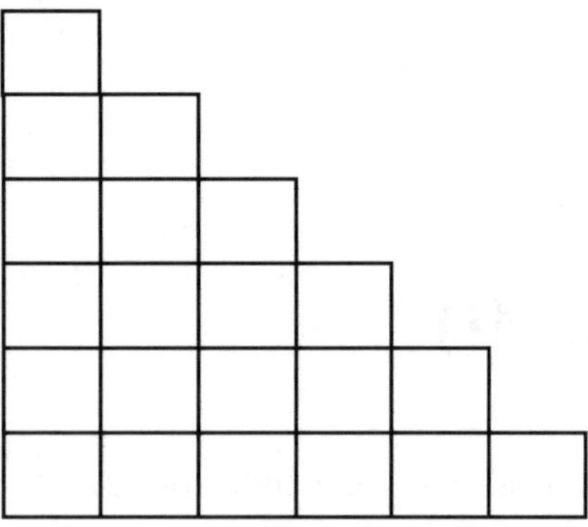

We're going to fill this grid with the positive integers, in order. Where shall we start?

What pattern shall we follow with where the numbers go? Let's start with a simple pattern.

Go with whatever learners suggest provided it is not overly complicated.

For example,

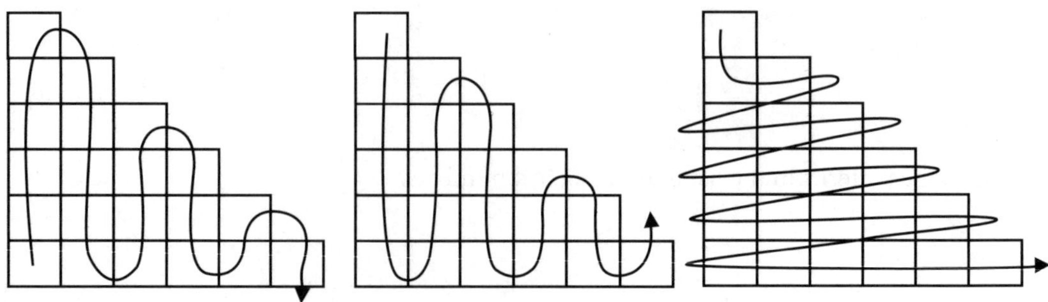

(You could imagine that you were laying out exam papers on desks, if that would be a topical reference!)

After a few numbers have been entered, stop writing in numbers and ask questions like these:

What number will appear at the top/bottom? Why?

What numbers will appear at the ends of the rows? Why?

What number will be at the beginning of the 100th row? Or 1000th row? Why?

What other questions can you ask?

Main Lesson (25 min)

Give out the Task Sheet and ask learners to work on different possible situations. Some 1 cm × 1 cm squared paper will be useful as well. The task could lend itself to some interesting display work, where learners could be encouraged to pose questions about their sequences, with answers underneath flaps, perhaps, to make an interactive display for the wall. Spreadsheet software might make it easier to keep the different cells lined up and connected, but if used thoughtlessly could lead to learners dwelling on creating massive grids of numbers rather than observing their structures more carefully.

Plenary (15 min)

Ask learners to share their different arrangements. This could be easier if learners have been using spreadsheets and can show their arrangements via a data projector. It might be too tedious and time consuming to have learners writing all their numbers up onto the board. Alternatively, learners could draw out their grids on poster-sized paper and hold them up or tack them to the board while explaining their work.

For example, the arrangement below gives triangle numbers $\frac{1}{2}n(n + 1)$ as the end number (nth number) of the nth row.

1					
2	3				
4	5	6			
7	8	9	10		
11	12	13	14	15	
16	17	18	19	20	21

The left-hand column is $\frac{1}{2}n^2 - \frac{1}{2}n + 1$, where n is the row number and, in general, the number in the nth row and the rth column is $\frac{1}{2}n^2 - \frac{1}{2}n + r$, provided that $r \leq n$.

Where will the number 1000 come? The answer is in the 45th row and the 10th column.

Other arrangements shown below also lead to interesting quadratic sequences:

1	2					
3	4	5				
6	7	8	9			
10	11	12	13	14		
15	16	17	18	19	20	
21	22	23	24	25	26	27

Here the left-hand column are the triangle numbers, so the formula is $\frac{1}{2}n^2 + \frac{1}{2}n + r - 1$, provided that $r \leq n + 1$.

1										
2	3	4								
5	6	7	8	9						
10	11	12	13	14	15	16				
17	18	19	20	21	22	23	24	25		
26	27	28	29	30	31	32	33	34	35	36

Here the left-hand column is $(n - 1)^2 + 1$, so the formula is $(n - 1)^2 + r$, provided that $r \leq 2n - 1$.

Where do the square numbers come? Why?

They come on the end of each line, because $r = 2n - 1$ in those positions and when you substitute $r = 2n - 1$ into $(n - 1)^2 + r$ you get n^2.

1	2								
3	4	5	6						
7	8	9	10	11	12				
13	14	15	16	17	18	19	20		
21	22	23	24	25	26	27	28	29	30

Here the left-hand column is $n^2 - n + 1$, so the formula is $n^2 - n + r$, provided that $r \leq 2n$.

1			
2			
3	4		
5	6		
7	8	9	
10	11	12	
13	14	15	16
17	18	19	20

Here it is easier to take odd and even rows separately.

For the *odd* rows, the left-hand column is $\left(\frac{n+1}{2}\right)^2 - \left(\frac{n+1}{2}\right) + 1$, the same structure as in the previous situation, so the formula for the odd rows is $\left(\frac{n+1}{2}\right)^2 - \left(\frac{n+1}{2}\right) + r$, provided that $r \leq \frac{1}{2}(n + 1)$.

For the *even* rows, the left-hand column is $\frac{1}{4}n^2 + 1$, so the formula for the even rows is $\frac{1}{4}n^2 + r$, provided that $r \leq \frac{1}{2}n$.

These results are given for your convenience rather than because it is envisaged that learners will necessarily deduce all of this. 'Getting the formula' need not always be seen as the ultimate aim of this sort of investigative work, and it would be good to respond positively to whatever observations and deductions learners make and see what follow-up questions emerge from discussion.

Homework (5 min)

Explore spiral *situations such as the following:*

10	11	12	13
9	2	3	14
8	1	4	15
7	6	5	16
20	19	18	17

What patterns can you find and explain here?

This arrangement is sometimes called an *Ulam Spiral*: all prime numbers (except 2) lie along diagonal lines, since they are all odd numbers, but interestingly some diagonal lines contain many more than others.

To make it harder

There should be plenty of scope to develop more or less complicated situations to explore. Shading multiples of different numbers in different colours may help learners to notice points of interest.

To make it easier

The task as given should be accessible to all learners, provided that a sufficiently simple rule is chosen for how the cells should be filled.

Fill it Up!

Try putting consecutive integers into these boxes according to different rules.

What patterns do you find? (Look for patterns in the columns, in the rows, in the diagonals, for example.) Can you predict/explain/prove?

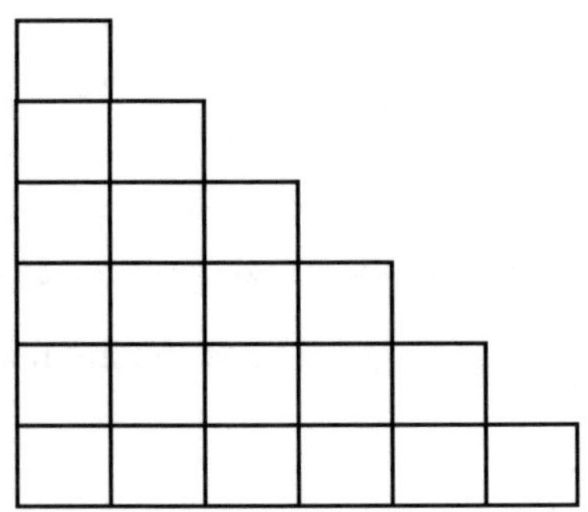

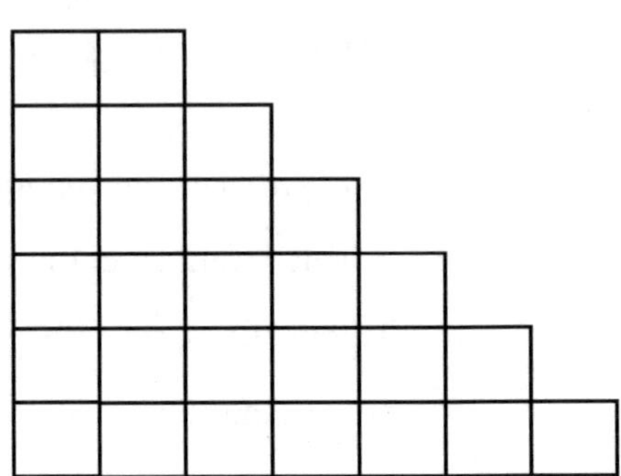

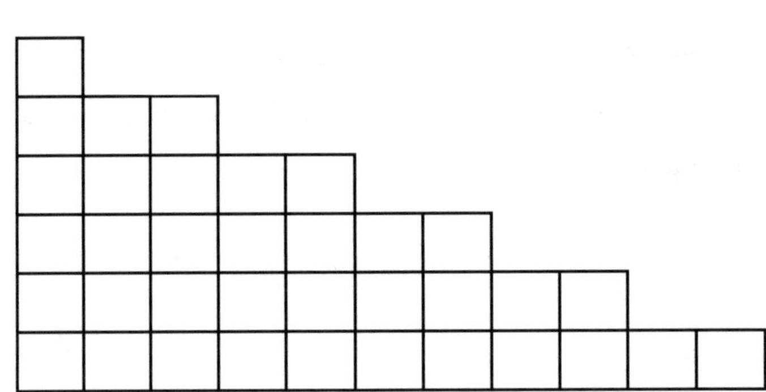

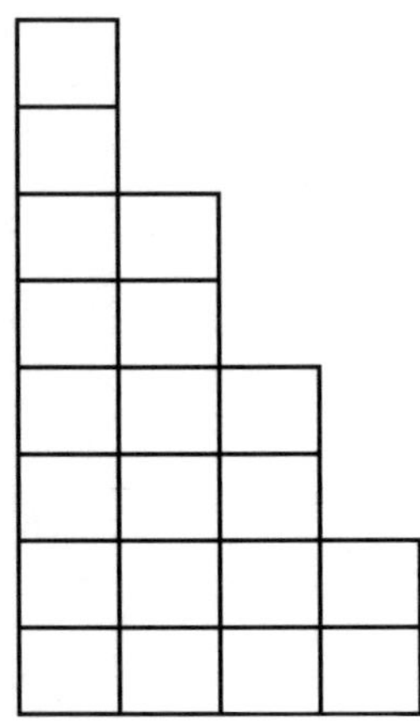

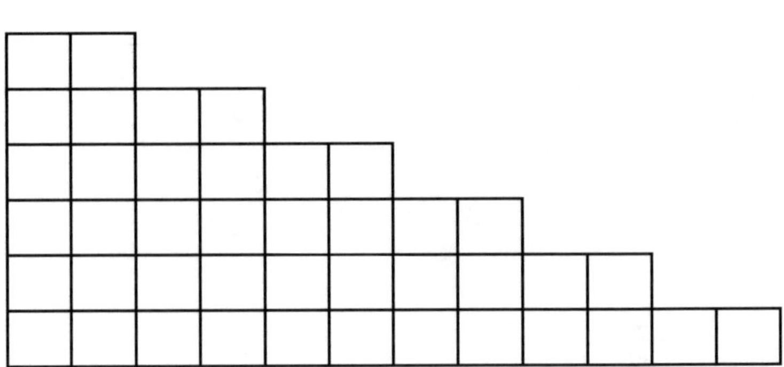

Questions to Ask for Different Arrangements

Imagine the boxes continuing forever.

Where would the number 100 be? Why?

What about 1 000 000? Why?

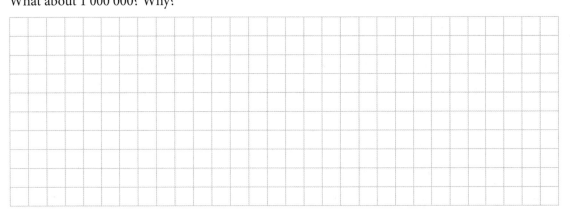

Invent some other box arrangements.

Try filling them up with consecutive integers.

Try filling them up with other sequences of numbers.

What patterns do you find?

Can you explain your results?

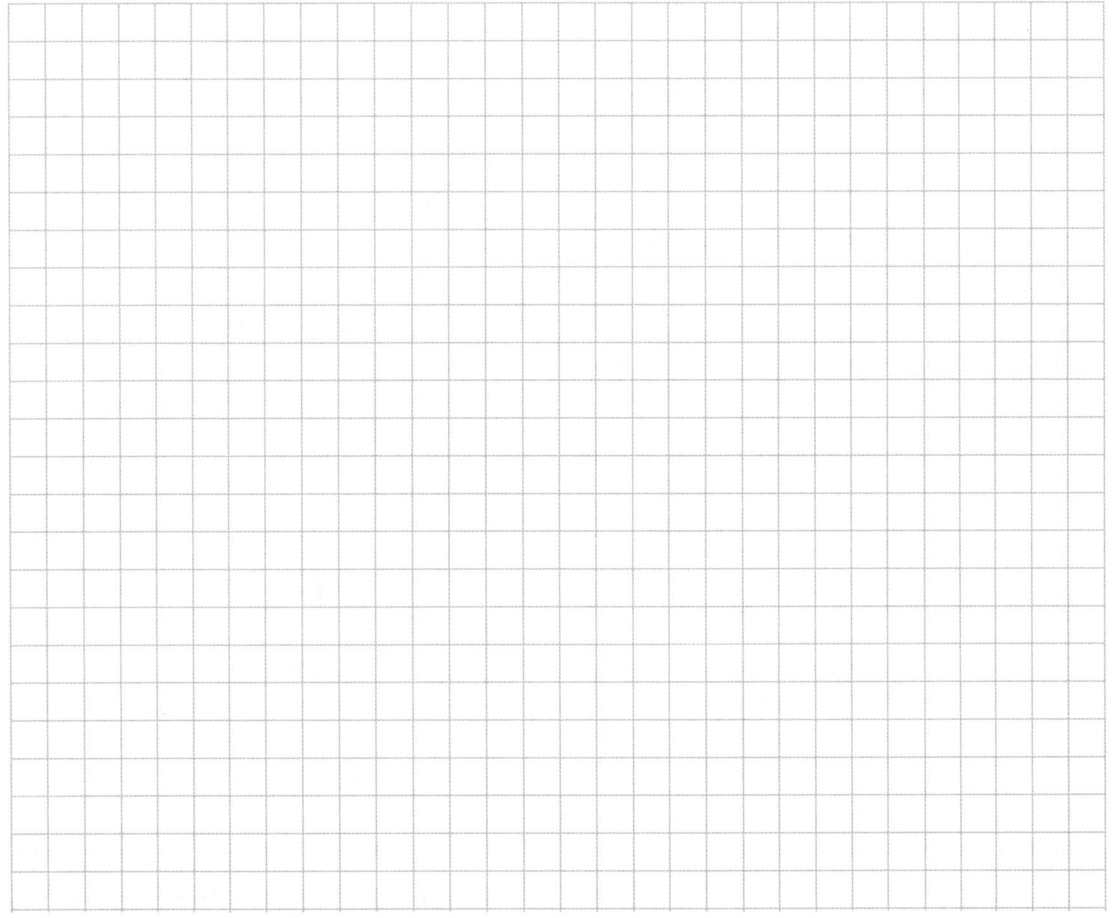

Fly on the Wall

Introduction

Many learners find it hard to make a connection between a 3D object and its 2D representation on paper, and having some models available in the classroom can obviously be extremely helpful. The mental transformation between the 3D world and its 2D version is important in life, a good mental discipline and worth working on, though some people may find this much more difficult than others. In this lesson, the 3D objects are represented as clearly as possible and learners might be advised when working on triangles (often right-angled) found within them to draw a simple (2D) sketch of the relevant triangle, with its vertices labelled and any information known about it marked clearly on the diagram, before trying to apply Pythagoras' Theorem or use trigonometry.

Aims and Outcomes

- find lengths and angles in 3D objects using Pythagoras' Theorem and trigonometry in right-angled triangles

Lesson Starter (15 min)

Show or draw these pictures in sequence, adding line segments to the previous drawing each time.

What do you see when you look at this?

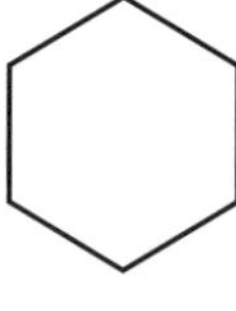

and now?

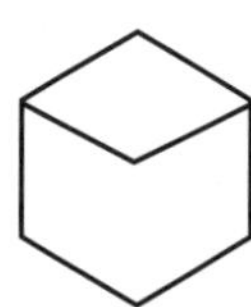

and now?

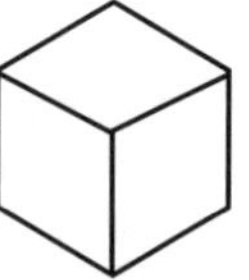

and now?

What about this?

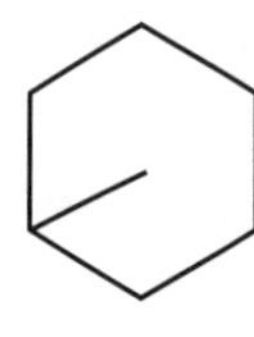

and now?

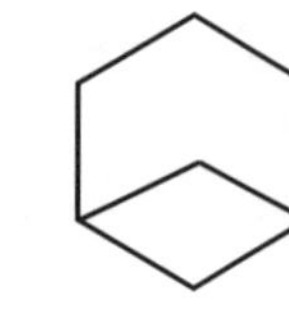

and now?

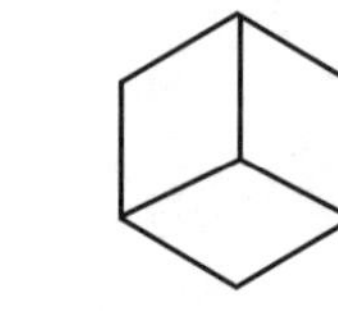

and now?

It may be interesting to compare what different people see at different stages, perhaps inviting discussion after the second drawing in each sequence. Some may think 'cube' from the very beginning whereas others may not see it even in the fourth drawing – especially in the second 'upside down' set.

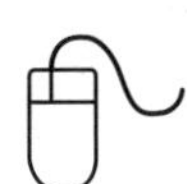

At what stage, if any, did it 'become 3D'? What do you think triggered that for you?

What do you see when you look at this?

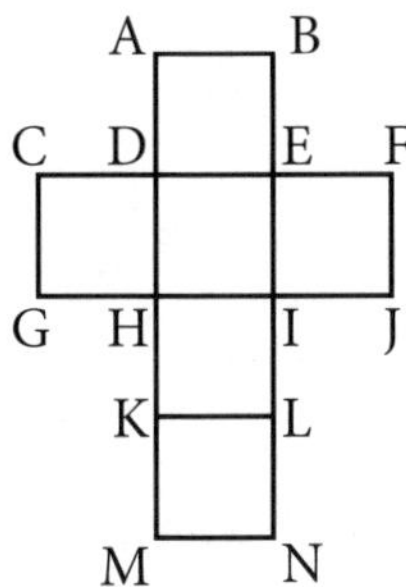

(The labelling here is deliberately contrary to normal 'cyclic' conventions.)

Then try questions like those below (learners could answer on mini-whiteboards if you wish). Push to get all possibilities before moving on. There may be more than learners think!

When folded up to make a cube, can you name a pair of vertices that will meet at the same point? And another? And another . . .? (E.g., *G* and *K*.)

When folded up to make a cube, can you name a pair of edges that will meet? (E.g., *AD* and *CD*.) *And another, and another . . .?*

When folded up to make a space *diagonal of the cube?* (E.g., *AI*.) *And another? And another . . .?*

When folded up to make a cube, can you name a face *diagonal* parallel *to* AE? (E.g., *KI*.) *And another? And another . . .?* Here there is only one other.

When folded up to make a cube, can you name a face *diagonal* perpendicular *to* AE? (E.g., *KI*.) *And another? And another . . .?* Here there are only *two* others.

Non-parallel non-intersecting lines (which cannot happen in 2D but can in 3D) are called *skew lines*.

Main Lesson (20 min)

Give learners the Task Sheet and ask them questions to encourage an accurate appreciation of the 3D nature of the drawings. For example: *In the cuboid, which vertex is vertically above* B? *Which plane is parallel to* OCDG? *Can you give another diagonal equal to* OE?, etc.

Then invite them to answer the questions and prompts, perhaps in pairs.

If you have time, and it seems appropriate, learners could consider the 'fly on the wall' problem:

A fly wants to move across the space diagonal of a cube (or cuboid). It could fly directly or it could rest its wings and walk the shortest distance across the surface of the cube. How much longer is it to walk than to fly? Twice as far? Why?

Learners might like to estimate before calculating.

Plenary (20 min)

For the cuboid, $OB^2 = OA^2 + AB^2$ (1) and

$OE^2 = OB^2 + BE^2$ (2).

Substituting equation (1) into equation (2) gives $OE^2 = OA^2 + AB^2 + BE^2$, which is the 3D version of Pythagoras' Theorem. (Learners who have met vectors may need to be careful not to confuse a sum of squares such as $OB^2 = OA^2 + AB^2$ with the vector sum $\overrightarrow{OB} = \overrightarrow{OA} + \overrightarrow{AB}$.)

For the square-based pyramid, learners are likely to begin numerically and look for relationships, but in general $CF^2 = \frac{AB^2}{2} + EF^2$. Because EF is the perpendicular height and CF is a slanting side, CF must be greater than EF, and the equation above shows that the amount by which CF^2 is greater than EF^2 is always $\frac{AB^2}{2}$.

For the second part, if the square $ABCD$ has sides of length x, then the height EF will be $\frac{\sqrt{2}x}{2}$ and all the triangles in the figure, such as AEF or AEB or ABC or AFC will be right-angled isosceles, with 45° acute angles. The triangular faces are all equilateral, so the square-based pyramid is half of a regular octahedron.

For the 'fly on the wall' problem, if we take the dimensions of the cube to be one unit, the diagonal length is $\sqrt{3}$. Drawing the net of the cube is the easiest way to track the shortest path along the surface. The fly will have to walk across two faces; i.e., along the hypotenuse of a 1×2 triangle, so the length is $\sqrt{5}$. If the fly were to walk along an edge, then a face diagonal, then another edge, the total would be $2 + \sqrt{2}$, and $\sqrt{3} < \sqrt{5} < 2 + \sqrt{2}$, as expected. In different cuboids there will be more different possible length routes and the trade-offs can be more complicated. There is plenty for learners to explore.

Homework (5 min)

Learners could construct problems at an appropriate level depending on how they are getting on with the topic. Some learners could be asked to write questions (with worked solutions!) about the lengths of different line segments in a cube or cuboid. Others might work with pyramids or octahedra.

To make it harder

Learners who seem competent with this work might like to consider these questions:

How many different length line segments are there in a cube from any vertex to any other vertex?

Three: side length, face diagonal, space diagonal. (This excludes zero-length 'lines' from a vertex to itself.)

How many of each are there?

There are 12 edges, 12 face diagonals (two on each face) and four space diagonals.

What are the possibilities in a cuboid?

A cube is an example of a cuboid with all its edge lengths the same, but a cuboid may have two different edge lengths (in which case it has a square end and is called a *square cuboid*), or three different edge lengths (a *non-square cuboid*).

For a square cuboid that is not a cube, there are eight edge lengths of one length and four edge lengths of a different length; eight face diagonals of one length and four face diagonals of another length; and four identical space diagonals – so five different lengths altogether.

For a non-square cuboid, there are four small edge lengths, four medium-sized edge lengths and four long edge lengths; four small face diagonals, four medium-sized face diagonals and four long face diagonals; and four identical space diagonals – so seven different lengths altogether.

What about other 3D solids?

Keen learners could find out about *hypercubes*.

To make it easier

Learners who get stuck may find that making a cuboid box from folding a cardboard net helps with their visualization and appreciation of the problem.

3D Geometry

Cuboid

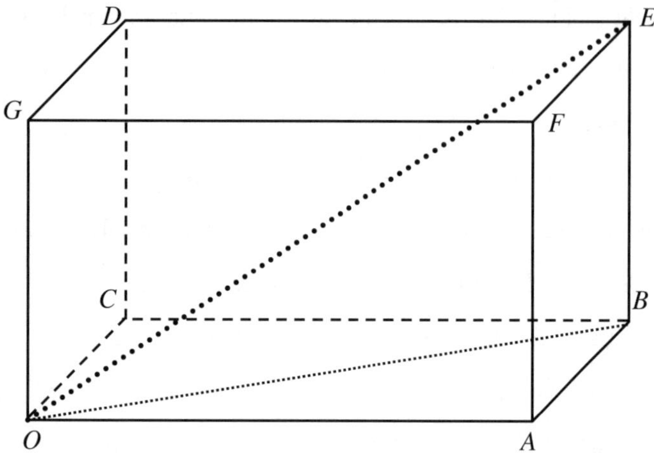

Explain why triangles *OAB* and *OBE* are right-angled triangles even though they might not look like it in the drawing.

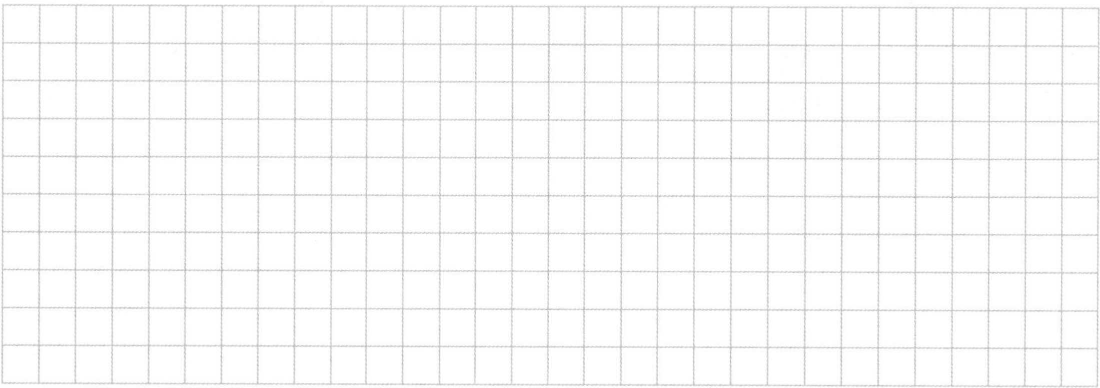

Use Pythagoras' Theorem in triangle *OAB* to find an expression for *OB*.

Use Pythagoras' Theorem in triangle *OBE* to find an expression for *OE*.

Combine your two results to find a connection between *OA*, *AB*, *BE* and *OE*.

Square-based pyramid

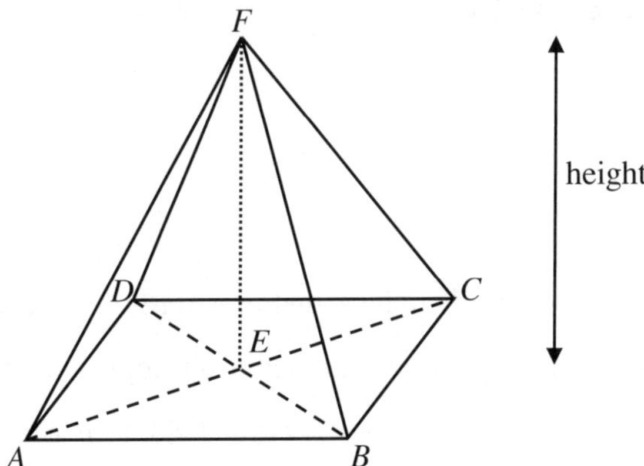

ABCD is a square. Choose some lengths for *AB* and *EF*, such as 6 cm or 10 cm.

Work out the length of *CF*.

Is it going to be more or less than the height *EF*? Why?

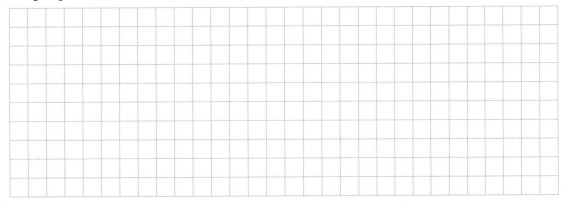

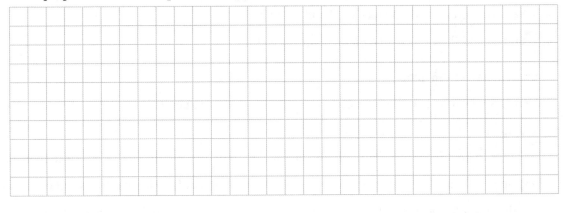

Suppose that the slanting lengths *AF*, *BF*, *CF* and *DF* are all equal to the length *AB* of the side of the square *ABCD*.

What properties does this square-based pyramid have? Why?

23 Functions

Introduction

The idea of a 'function machine' is one that learners are likely to have met previously. The Lesson Starter works with the idea of a 'mystery machine' giving output numbers from input numbers according to some known or unknown rule. Functions can be a notational minefield, with learners often thinking that a composite function such as $fg(x)$, for example, means multiplication: $f(x).g(x)$. There is real potential for notational confusion: the brackets on both sides of a statement such as $f(x) = 5(x + 2)$ mean completely different things, as do the superscripts in $f^2(x) = x^2$ or $f^{-1}(x) = x^{-1}$, although learners may have come across $\sin^{-1}$ (along with $\cos^{-1}$ and $\tan^{-1}$) to mean 'the inverse sine function'. Rather than focusing learners' attention on relatively arbitrary conventions, this lesson seeks to exploit their sense-making capacities by offering a sheet of combined diagrams and algebraic statements in need of organizing and completing. Learners may have met $p(x)$ notation for probability, perhaps, in cases such as p(heads) to mean 'the probability of getting heads when throwing a coin', or p(3) as 'the probability of getting a three on a die', so familiarity with probability functions may help learners to appreciate that f(3) is not a multiplication of some 'f' by '3' but a function f *acting on* a number 3. Learners are encouraged to work inductively to build a 'concept image' of a function – this can later be developed into a more formal 'concept definition'. (See Alcock, L. and Simpson, A. (2009), *Ideas from Mathematics Education*. Birmingham: The Higher Education Academy, chapter 1.)

Aims and Outcomes

- become familiar with the $f(x)$, $f^n(x)$ and $f^{-1}(x)$ notations
- understand the concept of a mathematical function

Lesson Starter (15 min)

Learners may have played the 'function game' when younger, but it is something that can be well adapted to a more sophisticated mathematical level. One person (perhaps the teacher, initially) pretends to be 'the machine', and others offer a variety of 'input numbers' to which the machine responds with an 'output number'. The object is to guess the 'rule' being used. Instead of blurting out the rule, anyone who thinks they know what it is could be invited to test their conjecture by asking: 'Would three come out as ten?', for example. As the game progresses, more and more learners become members of the 'in' group who know the 'secret rule'. Of course, *many* rules may be possible at times, so alternatives should be encouraged and accepted wherever consistent with the accumulated data so far. In the 'silent' version of the function game, communication is restricted to writing numbers on the board (perhaps with a smiley face to indicate when the correct output has been given).

Main Lesson (20 min)

If learners have not come across the

way of representing a function, then it would be good to relate this to some of the functions encountered in the Starter. A function may be one operation (e.g., '+ 3' or '× 10') or a sequence of operations (e.g., '+ 3 × 10'); i.e., a *composite* function, where the order is usually important.

Give out the Task Sheet and ask learners to try to make sense of the diagrams and the notation underneath each one. They should look very carefully for any missing details and fill them in – perhaps in pencil, so that they can make corrections later on if necessary. Learners could begin by grouping together those cases where they know that the function is 'f' and they are given (either in the diagram or underneath) both the input and the output. They will be able to conjecture from this that the f function is a '× 3 + 2' function, which will help them to complete the rest of the sheet.

Plenary (15 min)

The most puzzling ones are probably the f^2 and f^3 functions, which are repetitions of the f function two and three times respectively. The incomplete statements should be:

$f(2) = 8$, $f^2(5) = 53$, $f(x) = 3x + 2$, $f^3(1) = 53$, $f(3) = 11$, $f^{-1}(17) = 5$, $f(4) = 14$, $f(y) = 3y + 2$, $f(0) = 2$ and $f(-7) = -19$.

Which one of these do you think is the most helpful in telling you about the function f? Why?
Learners will probably choose either $f(x) = 3x + 2$ or $f(y) = 3y + 2$ as being equally informative about what the function is doing. Number inputs get 'jumbled up' (i.e., simplified) and emerge as just another number output, 'hiding the working', so to speak, whereas a *letter* input comes out as an *expression*, still showing what has been done to it, in the same way as a number like π or $\sqrt{5}$ would, if given as an exact answer: for example, $f(\pi) = 3\pi + 2$ or $f(\sqrt{5}) = 3\sqrt{5} + 2$.

Homework (10 min)

As a class, decide on a two- or three-step function g, say. Agree what it is going to be and write it as $g(x)$ = an expression involving x. Then ask learners to make up ten statements to do with g, such as $g^2(7)$ = something, or $g(x^2)$ = something, etc., to illustrate how confident they are about using function notation. Some might like to combine g with the f used in the lesson to make statements about $gf(x)$, etc.

To make it harder

Learners confident with this work could bring in other functions, g and h, of their choice, and investigate, perhaps initially by substituting numbers, whether statements such as these are always, sometimes or never true:

$\mathrm{fg}(x) = \mathrm{gf}(x)$

$(\mathrm{fg})^{-1}(x) = \mathrm{g}^{-1}\mathrm{f}^{-1}(x)$

$\mathrm{f}(\mathrm{gh})(x) = (\mathrm{fg})\mathrm{h}(x)$

If they are *always* true, say why; if they are *sometimes* true, say when and why; if they are *never* true, say why not.

If $\mathrm{fg}(x) = \mathrm{gf}(x)$ for all values of x, then the functions f and g are said to *commute* with each other. For example, if $\mathrm{f}(x) = x + 2$ and $\mathrm{g}(x) = x - 7$, then f and g will commute, because $(x + 2) - 7 = (x - 7) + 2$, but if $\mathrm{f}(x) = x + 2$ and $\mathrm{g}(x) = 2x - 7$ then they won't, because $2(x + 2) - 7 \neq (2x - 7) + 2$.

Composition of functions is always *associative*, so $\mathrm{f}(\mathrm{gh})(x) = (\mathrm{fg})\mathrm{h}(x)$ for all values of x, provided that at each stage the output values from the previous function are appropriate input values for the next (i.e., lie within the *domain*).

Some functions do not have inverses, but if all the functions written exist then $(\mathrm{fg})^{-1}(x) = \mathrm{g}^{-1}\mathrm{f}^{-1}(x)$, whatever functions f and g are, and this can be seen by drawing out function machines for both sides and seeing that they are the same. (See Lesson 30.)

To make it easier

Learners who find this difficult could avoid using letters until they have developed confidence with numbers as inputs and outputs.

Functions

Fill in the gaps below and try to explain what is going on.

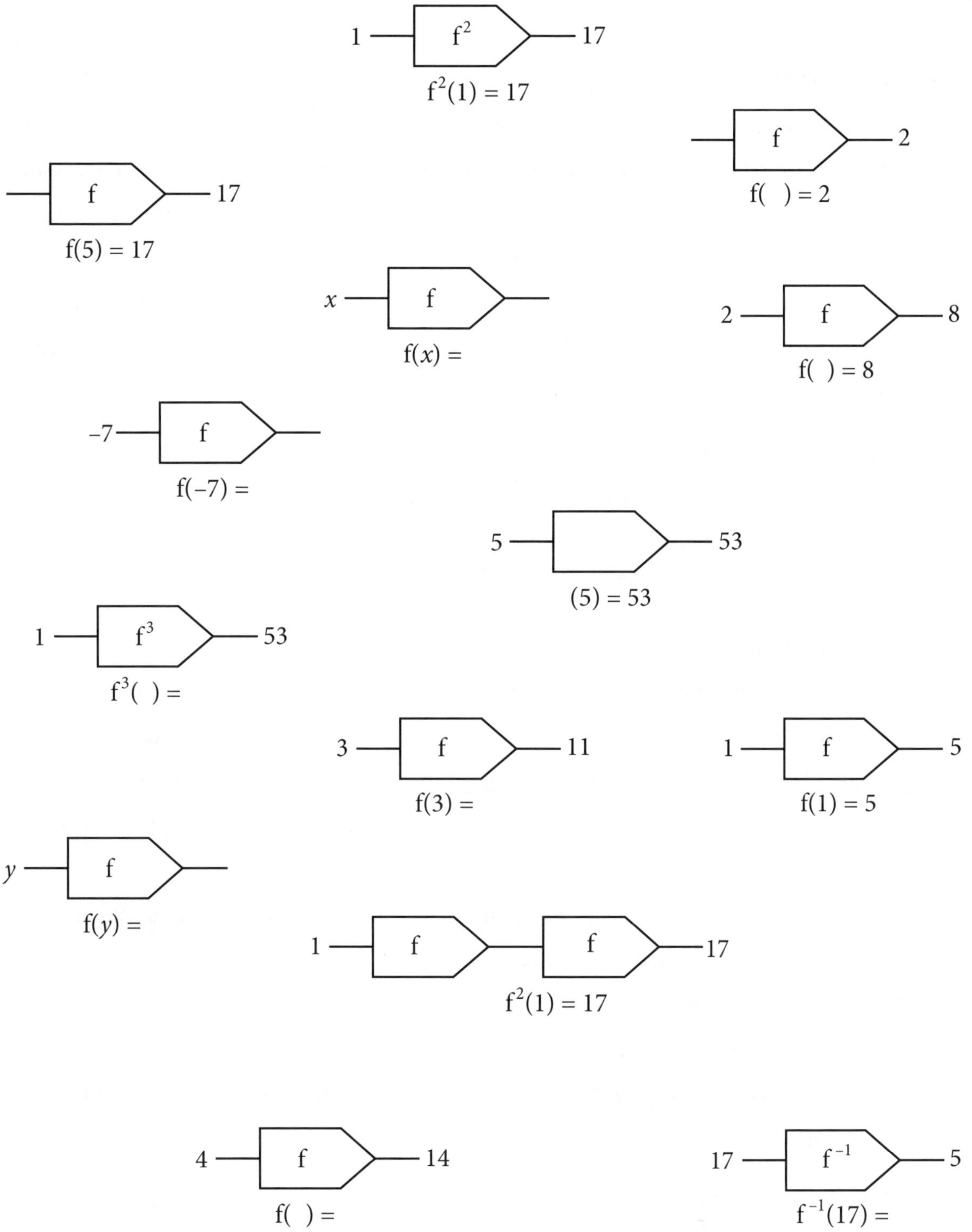

1 — f^2 — 17

$f^2(1) = 17$

— f — 2

f( ) = 2

— f — 17

f(5) = 17

x — f —

$f(x) =$

2 — f — 8

f( ) = 8

–7 — f —

f(–7) =

5 — — 53

(5) = 53

1 — f^3 — 53

$f^3(\ ) =$

3 — f — 11

f(3) =

1 — f — 5

f(1) = 5

y — f —

$f(y) =$

1 — f — f — 17

$f^2(1) = 17$

4 — f — 14

f( ) =

17 — f^{-1} — 5

$f^{-1}(17) =$

Golden Rectangles

Introduction

The golden section or golden ratio crops up all over the place, in human art and architecture as well as in the natural world. It also has mathematical links with topics such as the *Fibonacci sequence*. For more information, go to www.maths.surrey.ac.uk/hosted-sites/R.Knott/Fibonacci/fib.html or see Livio, M. (2002), *The Golden Ratio: The Story of Phi, the World's Most Astonishing Number*. London: Review. The golden rectangle provides a convenient context for learners to work with ratio and to devise a questionnaire to test out the hypothesis that people prefer the shape of golden rectangles to those of other rectangles.

Aims and Outcomes

- carry out a study and write a questionnaire to test a hypothesis
- understand that similar rectangles have the same 'aspect ratio'
- use ratio to explore the shapes of rectangles

Lesson Starter (10 min)

If you have a data projector (with or without an electronic whiteboard), open a word-processing package and ask a learner to come to the board and use the drawing tools to draw a rectangle. Ask another learner to draw a different rectangle. And another.

What is the same and what is different about these shapes? There are many points that learners can make.

Choose one of these rectangles, fix the 'aspect ratio' (by right-clicking and choosing 'properties') and make enlarged and reduced versions of it.

What stays the same? What changes?

Will it fit on top of one of the other rectangles? Why / why not?

Similar rectangles may have different areas and perimeters but the same ratio of sides – the same overall 'shape'.

Main Lesson (25 min)

Hold up a large golden rectangle (for example, a 26 cm × 42 cm rectangle cut out of gold-coloured A3 paper). Fold off a square from the shorter end and tear it off.

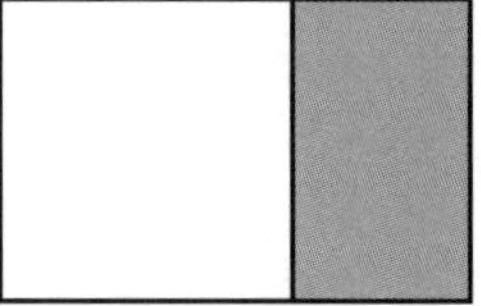

Look at the shape produced – it is the same shape as the original rectangle.

How can you tell? What does it mean that they are 'the same shape'?

You can rotate the new rectangle 90° to make it easier to compare their shapes.

Repeat the process of tearing off a square with this rectangle. *What do you think is happening? Why?*

(The rectangles produced can be lined up, with vertices at a common corner, or 'centred' to illustrate the process. This can make an interesting display, perhaps justifying the use of gold-coloured card for a brief activity!)

Give out scrap paper and ask learners, in groups, to try to cut out a rectangle that will do the same thing.

They will probably find it hard: even if you are only a little bit out, your new rectangle won't match the old one! Learners should be able to find by trial and error the approximate dimensions of the rectangle that will do it.

Then give out the Task Sheet and ask learners to think about how they will test the hypothesis: most people think that golden rectangles look more pleasing to the eye than other-shaped rectangles.

Plenary (20 min)

Some learners may be able to calculate the appropriate dimensions of a golden rectangle using algebra. If the starting golden rectangle has sides of length 1 and x (where $x > 1$), then $\frac{x}{1}=\frac{1}{x-1}$, because the rectangle remaining when the 1×1 square has been removed has dimensions 1 by $(x - 1)$, and it is also 'golden'.

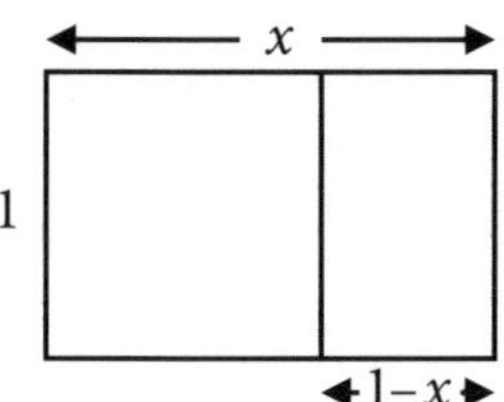

Rearranging, this gives $x^2 - x - 1 = 0$, so $x=\frac{1+\sqrt{5}}{2}$ (rejecting the other root, since $x > 1$), so $x =$ 1.618033989… This enables learners to draw rectangles with the appropriate proportions.

Alternatively, learners can use a compass construction, beginning with a unit square.

Centre the compasses on the midpoint of one side of the square and set the pencil on an opposite vertex. Use this radius to draw an arc, which then defines the 'long' dimension of the golden rectangle:

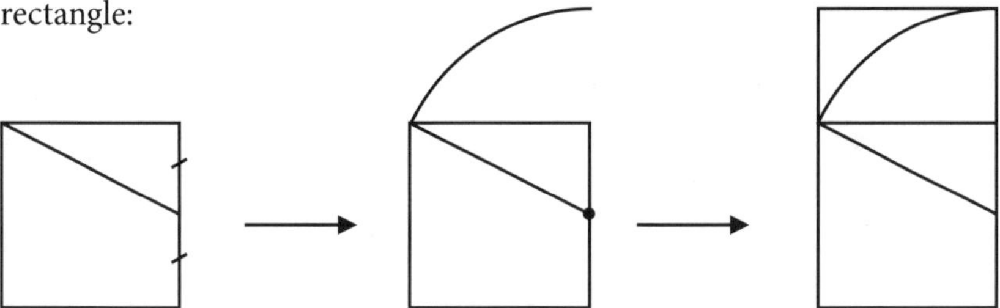

They can measure the sides of the finished rectangle to see how accurate their construction has been.

If the construction begins with a unit square, then the radius of the arc must have length $\sqrt{1^2+\left(\frac{1}{2}\right)^2}$, by Pythagoras' Theorem, so the vertical side of the rectangle has to be $\frac{1}{2}+\sqrt{1^2+\left(\frac{1}{2}\right)^2}$, which simplifies to $\frac{1+\sqrt{5}}{2}$, the golden ratio.

You might wish to ask learners to try out their questionnaire at home and discuss the results in the next lesson.

Homework (5 min)

Use the questionnaire on peers, teachers, family members or other suitable people. You might wish to warn learners not to approach strangers.

To make it harder

Keen learners could find out about where the golden rectangle appears in art and architecture and look into some of its other mathematical properties.

To make it easier

Learners with weaknesses in literacy will need support (small-group or one-to-one) in framing and writing the questions.

Golden Rectangles

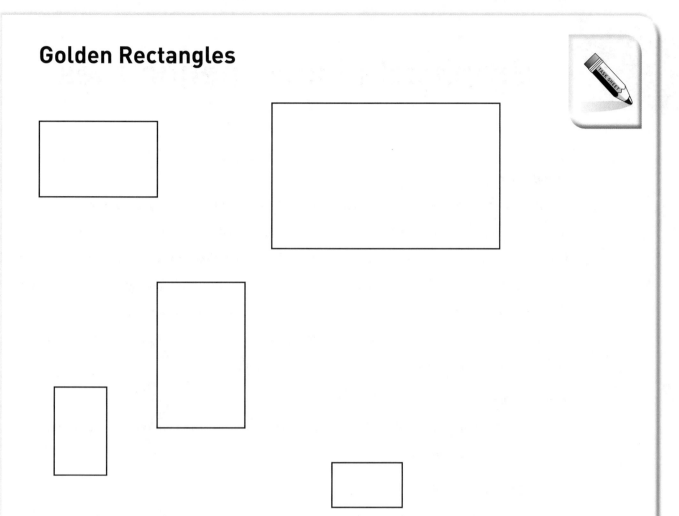

Design a questionnaire to see whether the golden rectangle is most people's 'favourite' shape of rectangle.

You could ask them to draw a beautifully shaped rectangle and then measure it afterwards.

Or you could offer a series of different shapes and ask people to choose the 'best looking' one.

Which approach do you think is better? Why?

How can you make it a 'fair test'?

Should all the shapes be rectangles? Should they all have the same area? Should they all have the same orientation? Why?

Would you try to put them in some kind of order? How would you arrange the rectangles on the page?

Where would you place the *golden* rectangle(s)? Why?

How will you choose who to ask?

25 Graphical Linear Inequalities

Introduction

Learners often approach a problem such as 'Shade the inequality $2x + y < 6$' as a mechanical list of instructions: draw the graph of the *equality* $2x + y = 6$ (with a *dashed* line here, since the inequality is $<$ and not $\leq$); pick a test point that is not on the line and evaluate to see whether those x and y values do or do not satisfy the inequality; and then shade out the unwanted region, etc. This lesson aims to help learners visualize the value of a two-variable function such as $f(x, y) = 2x + y$ across the entire coordinate plane by evaluating at many points, so that drawing lines, shading regions and testing points may be based on a sturdier understanding.

Aims and Outcomes

- draw graphs of linear inequalities in two variables and interpret the solution sets given by regions in the coordinate plane

Lesson Starter (15 min)

Learners could have mini-whiteboards with a square grid suitable for drawing axes and graphs. Alternatively, learners can draw axes, say, from –10 to 10 in both directions, on paper or in their books. Another option, depending on how many learners you have, and the layout of your room, is to seat learners in a rectangular array and label each person with coordinates. (Obviously do it upside down from your point of view so that that the learners see it the right way around!) The 'origin person' could either be near the centre of the room or be at the back-right corner (from the teacher's perspective).

Then say:

- *Put a cross somewhere where the* y-*coordinate is twice the* x-*coordinate* or *Stand up if your* y-*coordinate is twice your* x-*coordinate.*
- *Stand up if your y-coordinate is* more than *twice your* x-*coordinate.* (A lot more people should stand up this time.)
- *Stand up if your* y-*coordinate is* at least *twice your* x-*coordinate.*
- *Stand up if the sum of your x- and y-coordinates is less than 5.'*
- *Stand up if the difference between your x- and y-coordinates is less than 3.*
- *Stand up if your y-coordinate is less than 3 more than your x-coordinate.*
- (And so on . . .)

At each stage, you can invite comments on who is standing and why.

- *Who hasn't stood up yet? Invent a rule that will get* you *standing!*
- *Invent a rule that will cause* exactly four people *to stand up.*
- *Invent a rule that will cause* only girls/boys *to stand up.*
- *Invent a rule that will cause* everyone/no one *to stand up.*

Main Lesson (20 min)

Give learners the Task Sheet and encourage them to fill in the correct numbers in the circles. The patterns in the answers should encourage self-checking as they go.

When learners have completed the sheet, ask them to draw and shade another inequality, perhaps one containing a > or ≥ sign. *Do you need to work out all the values? Why / why not?* The idea of a 'test point' could emerge from this.

Plenary (20 min)

The sheet should eventually look something like this:

$$2x + y < 6$$

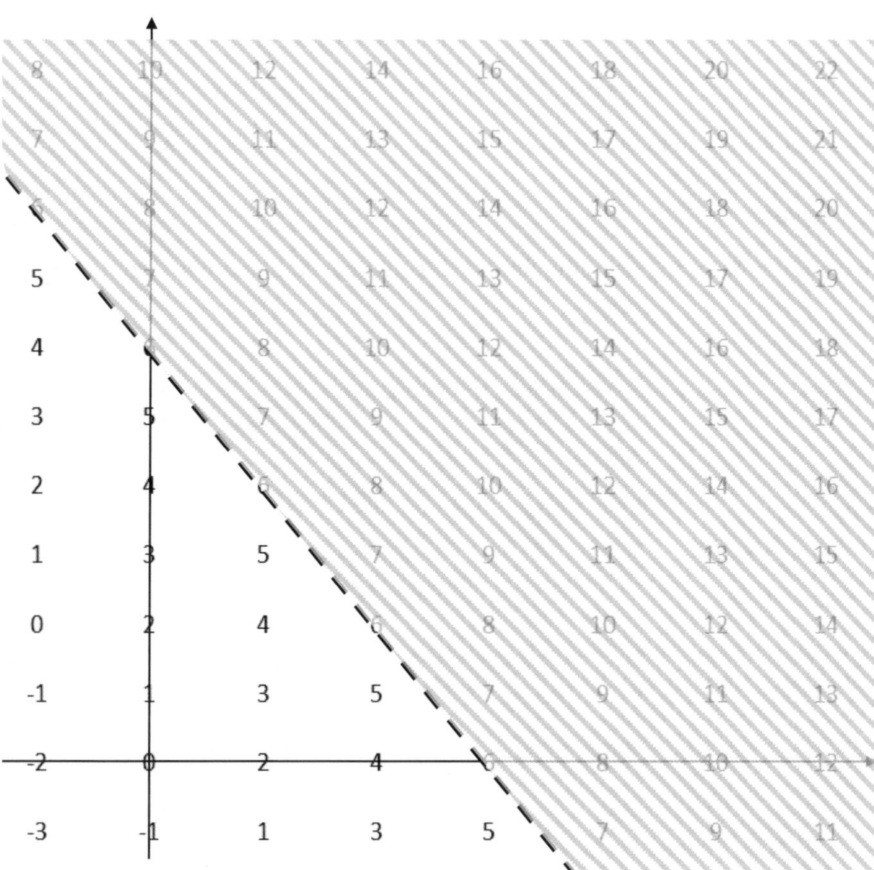

Why do the 6's lie along a straight line?

Why are the numbers bigger than 6 above the line?

Why are the numbers smaller than 6 below the line?

Will this always happen? Why / why not?

The idea that a line represents the boundary between two 'opposite' regions is a very useful one. Often in graph work we focus on lines and curves; for inequalities we focus on the *regions in between* lines and curves. For example, the line $x = 5$ represents all those points exactly five units to the right of the y-axis, but it can also be thought of as the boundary between points which are strictly *more* than five units to the right of the y-axis and those which are strictly *less* than five units to the right of the y-axis. Here, places where $2x + y$ is exactly 6 form the boundary between an area where $2x + y > 6$ (above the line) and one where $2x + y < 6$.

Homework (5 min)

Construct three inequalities which when taken together *define a region containing only* three *integer lattice points; for example, (1, 1), (2, 1) and (1, 2).* (A possible answer would be the three inequalities $x > 0$, $y > 0$ and $x + y < 4$.) *Make up other problems like this. Can* any *three 'adjacent' points be done in this way with just three straight lines? Why / why not?*

What if they are not *adjacent?*

To make it harder

Non-linear inequalities provide an extra challenge for learners who are comfortable with this topic. *What would* $2x^2 + y < 6$ *look like?* Again, it is helpful to begin with the equality $2x^2 + y = 6$ and then test points either side. (The required region is the 'underneath' portion of the graph $y = 6 - 2x^2$, although of course learners might choose to shade *out* the upper region.)

To make it easier

If $2x + y < 6$ is too daunting initially, simpler inequalities to begin with would be $y < x$ or $x < 3$, for example.

Inequalities

$$2x + y < 6$$

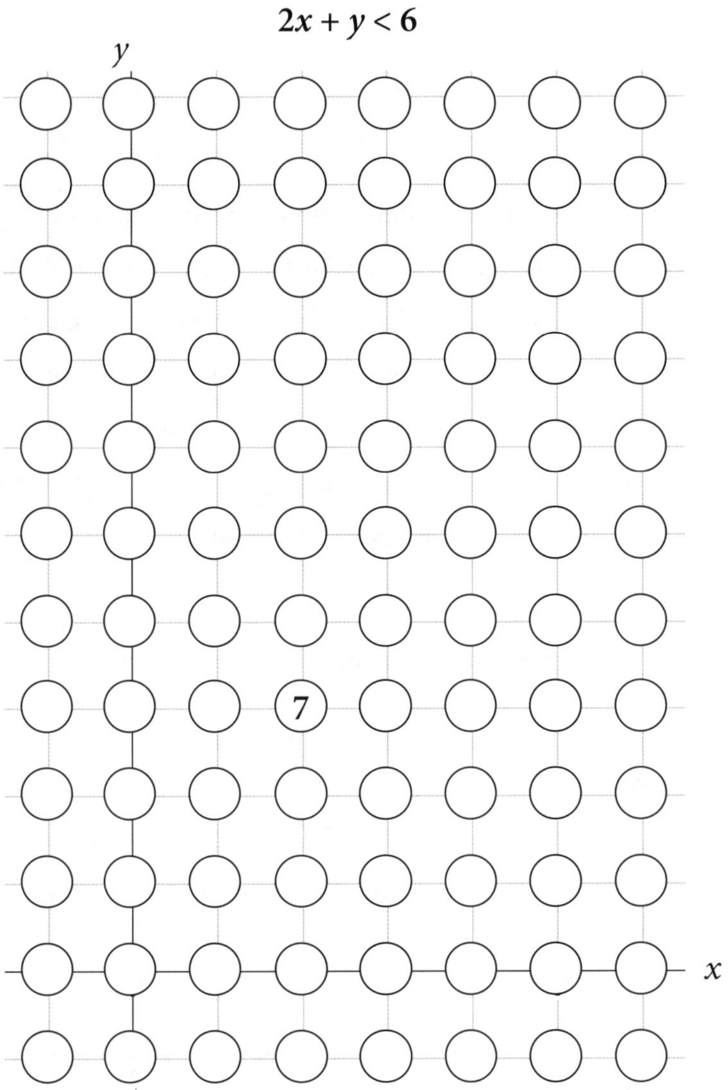

The thicker lines show the axes, with values going up in 1s. They cross at (0, 0).

The circle at position (2, 3) contains the number 7.

This is because if you take x as 2 and y as 3 (which is what (2, 3) means) then when you work out $2x + y$ you get $2 \times 2 + 3 = 7$.

Fill in all the other circles with the right numbers.

Describe any patterns you see in the numbers.

Can you explain why you get these patterns?

Colour *red* the circles which are *equal* to 6.

Colour *green* the circles which are *more than* 6.

Colour *blue* the circles which are *less than* 6.

(If you don't have these particular colours, use whatever you have, but make a key.)

What do you notice?

26 Graphical Solutions of Equations

Introduction

This is another strategy, like trial and improvement, for finding approximate solutions to equations. As with trial and improvement, in principle any desired degree of accuracy can be obtained by drawing graphs on increasingly finer scales (corresponding to 'trying' more – and 'improving' more – in 'trial and improvement'). In this lesson, the solutions obtained are readily found algebraically instead, and the emphasis is on seeing that the intersection points of two graphs have x-values equal to the solutions obtained by solving the equations simultaneously. This often turns out to be a difficult concept so you may need to be patient if learners get quite muddled!

Aims and Outcomes

- solve polynomial equations by finding the points of intersection of two graphs

Lesson Starter (10 min)

The solution is '$x = 3$', *what could the equation be?*

You could begin with writing '$x = 3$' at the *bottom* of the board and learners could successively add lines above it, increasing in complexity, burying the solution deeper and deeper underground, so to speak:

for example,

$$x = 3 \quad \rightarrow \quad \begin{aligned} x + 5 &= 8 \\ x &= 3 \end{aligned} \quad \rightarrow \quad \begin{aligned} 7x + 5 &= 8 + 6x \\ x + 5 &= 8 \\ x &= 3 \end{aligned} \quad \rightarrow \quad \begin{aligned} \frac{7x + 5}{2} &= 4 + 3x \\ 7x + 5 &= 8 + 6x \\ x + 5 &= 8 \\ x &= 3 \end{aligned}$$

You could do several of these, or learners could construct them in groups and share on the board for others to *de*construct.

Main Lesson (25 min)

How would you solve the equation $x^2 + x - 6 = 0$*?* If they know about quadratic equations, then learners are likely to suggest algebraic methods, such as factorizing to $(x + 3)(x - 2) = 0$, so that $x = -3$ or 2 or using 'the formula'. This lesson will be about *other* ways of finding the solution $x = -3$ or 2.

What would the graph of $y = x^2 + x - 6$ *look like?* Some learners may wish to draw up a table of numbers, say integers from $x = -5$ to $x = 5$, and work out the y-values. Learners will obtain $y = 0$ for $x = -3$ and $x = 2$, and you could then relate that back to the factorized form of the equation:

$(x + 3)(x - 2) = 0$. Alternatively, learners may see that the graph $y = x^2 + x - 6 = (x + 3)(x - 2)$ is going to be a 'happy' ('positive' coefficient of x^2, therefore U-shaped) parabola, passing through (–3, 0) and (2, 0).

Why are the x*-intercepts the solutions to the equation* $y = 0$*?*

They can be thought of as the intersections of the two graphs $y = x^2 + x - 6$ and $y = 0$.

What would be the significance of the points where $y = x^2 + x - 6$ *and* $y = 1$ *intersect?* These would be solutions to $x^2 + x - 6 = 1$ or $x^2 + x - 7 = 0$. You can't factorize this equation, so it might be easier to read off the approximate solutions than to use the quadratic formula on the equation.

Give learners the Task Sheet and see whether they can work out which equations are necessary, perhaps by working backwards from the solutions $x = -3$ and $x = 2$ if necessary.

Plenary (20 min)

The graph that needs to be added in each case is a straight line:

$y = 6 - x$, $y = 5 - x$, $y = 6$ and $y = -x$.

Learners should draw on these lines accurately and confirm that the intersection points are always at $x = -3$ and $x = 2$, the solutions to the original equation $x^2 + x - 6 = 0$.

Why are the y*-values not always the same?*

This can be a good question for probing learners' understanding of what is going on.

Homework (5 min)

Find four graphical methods of solving $x^2 + 2x - 8 = 0$*. Try to make each one the intersection between a* curve *and a* straight line*. Which one do you think is quickest/easiest/most convenient?*

Check that the solutions are the same each time. Do they match what you get algebraically?

The solution is $x = -4$ or 2.

To make it harder

Some equations *cannot* be solved algebraically, so numerical and graphical methods are the only options. This is *not* the same as saying that no one has worked out an algebraic method yet – maybe they will in the future – it can be proved, for instance, that you definitely can't find a general formula for all *quintics* (polynomials in which x^5 is the highest power of x) or higher, like you can for quadratics, say. Learners could look up the *Abel–Ruffini theorem* and *Galois theory* on the internet. For example, $x^5 - x + 1 = 0$ cannot be solved algebraically. *Try finding solutions to this by looking for points of intersection between* $y = x^5$ *and a straight-line graph. Which straight-line graph do you need?*

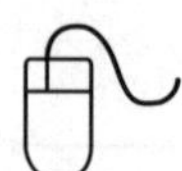

The graph needed is $y = x - 1$ and the solution is $x = -1.1673$ (correct to 4 decimal places). A website such as www.quickmath.com can be useful for finding approximate solutions to equations.

To make it easier

Learners finding the quadratic element problematic could begin by solving simultaneous *linear* equations graphically.

Solving Equations

$x^2 + x - 6 = 0$

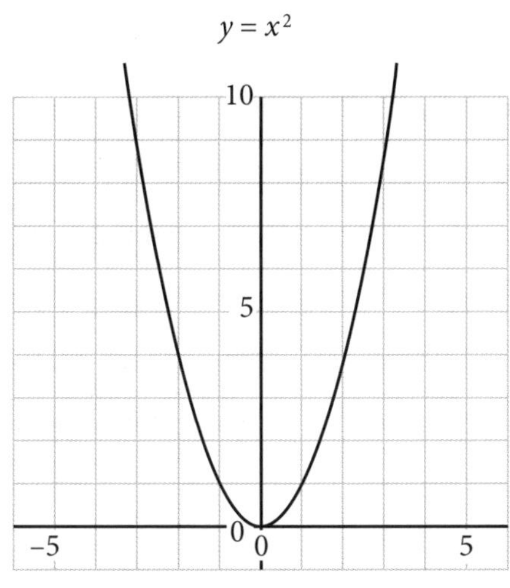

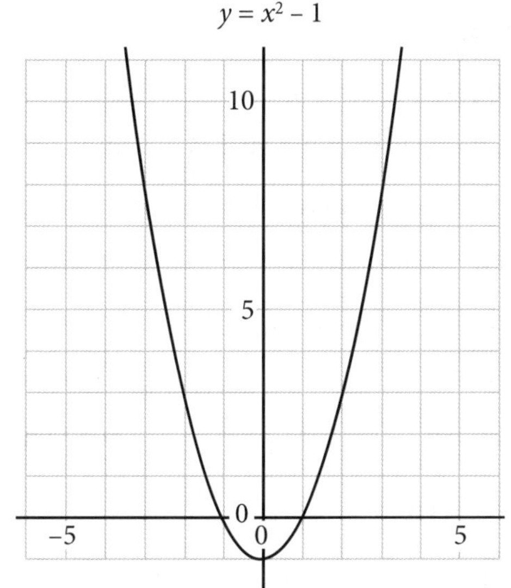

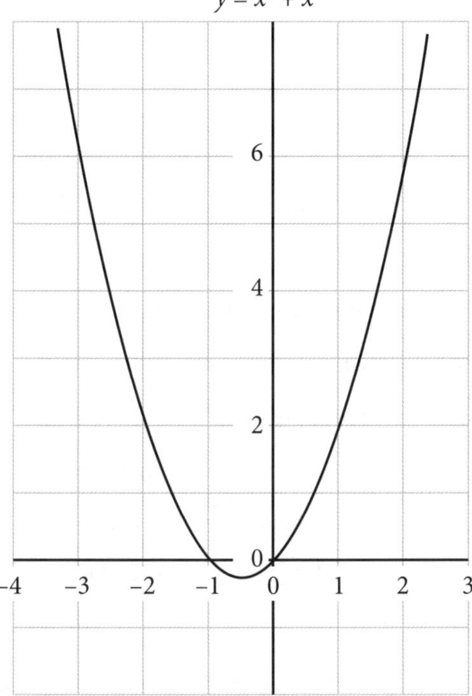

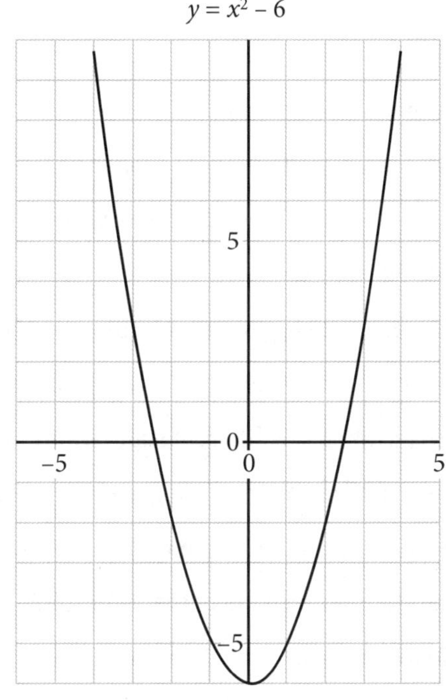

How can you use each of these graphs to solve the equation $x^2 + x - 6 = 0$?

Knowing that the solution is $x = -3$ or $x = 2$ may help.

27

Histograms

Introduction

To appreciate the purpose of histograms, learners need to see the distortion that is produced when data grouped with unequal class widths are represented naïvely in a 'bar chart'. One way to achieve this is to have different groups of learners draw 'grouped bar charts' from the same data but using different (and unequal) groups. The drastic differences in the appearances of the graphs may persuade learners that they need to take account of the width of the bars when drawing. This leads to the idea of 'histograms'. Bringing prime numbers into the picture allows a mathematical application of some mathematics, scoring two goals with one kick.

Aims and Outcomes

- appreciate that a 'bar chart' with unequal class widths is misleading
- explore the distribution of the prime numbers
- understand that a histogram gives a fair representation of data containing classes of unequal widths

Lesson Starter (20 min)

The manager of a swimming pool decides one morning to record the age of each person using the pool at a certain time. These are the results: 3, 4, 5, 8, 8, 14, 17, 17, 17, 18, 18, 20, 21, 25, 25, 27, 28, 29, 29, 29, 34, 41, 78.

He divides the ages into categories, makes a frequency table and draws a bar chart.

Look at the different ages listed, from youngest to oldest. What categories would you use?

Write down the different suggestions given. Learners will probably think that there needs to be a reasonable number of categories (not too few; not too many) and may have different opinions about what should be done with the 78-year-old outlier. They may suggest equal-width categories or not. (For convenience, the swimming pool data are given at the top of the Task Sheet, so you could give this out now if you wish.)

If you have, say, three suggested divisions of the data, assign learners to three groups and ask each group to make a frequency table and draw a bar chart for one of the suggested sets of categories.

For example, you might have:

Age (n)	Number of people
$0 \le n < 5$	2
$5 \le n < 15$	4
$15 \le n < 20$	5
$20 \le n < 30$	9
$30 \le n < 80$	3

Age (n)	Number of people
$0 \le n < 20$	11
$20 \le n < 40$	10
$40 \le n < 60$	1
$60 \le n < 80$	1

Age (n)	Number of people
$0 \le n < 10$	5
$10 \le n < 20$	6
$20 \le n < 40$	10
$40 \le n < 80$	2

(You might wish to warn learners as they do this that there is something 'wrong' about what you are asking them to do, but obviously spelling out exactly what is 'wrong' would defeat the point of the exercise!)

The bar charts will look very different.

Do you think they are fair to the data? Why / why not?

Do they give you an accurate impression of who was using the pool at that time? Why / why not?

Learners should see that where there are unequal bar widths, the larger-width bars overemphasize that category in proportion to their width while the small-width bars understate that category.

Main Lesson (20 min)

Give out the Task Sheet (if you haven't already) and ask learners to answer the questions about the awards data.

The frequencies are:

Number of awards (n)	Frequency (f)
$0 \le n < 10$	5
$10 \le n < 20$	6
$20 \le n < 30$	4
$30 \le n < 60$	15

So half the class (15 out of 30) obtained 30 or more awards. It looks like three-quarters of the class did, judging by area (what the eye naturally takes in), since the width of the 30–60 bar is three times the width of the others. So this is a *misleading* graph.

You could introduce the idea of *frequency density* here and then discuss how to represent the prime number data.

Then ask learners to draw histograms for the prime number data.

Plenary (15 min)

The prime number data, extended further, is as follows:

Number (n)	Frequency	Frequency density
$0 < n \leq 100$	25	0.25
$100 < n \leq 200$	21	0.21
$200 < n \leq 300$	16	0.16
$300 < n \leq 400$	16	0.16
$400 < n \leq 500$	17	0.17
$500 < n \leq 600$	14	0.14
$600 < n \leq 700$	16	0.16
$700 < n \leq 800$	14	0.14
$800 < n \leq 900$	15	0.15
$900 < n \leq 1000$	14	0.14
$1000 < n \leq 2000$	135	0.135
$2000 < n \leq 3000$	127	0.127
$3000 < n \leq 4000$	120	0.12
$4000 < n \leq 5000$	119	0.119
$5000 < n \leq 6000$	114	0.114
$6000 < n \leq 7000$	117	0.117
$7000 < n \leq 8000$	107	0.107
$8000 < n \leq 9000$	110	0.11
$9000 < n \leq 10\,000$	112	0.112

Source: Data adapted from information at www.trnicely.net – used with permission: copyright © 2009 Thomas R. Nicely. (Released into the public domain by the author, who disclaims any legal liability arising from its use.)

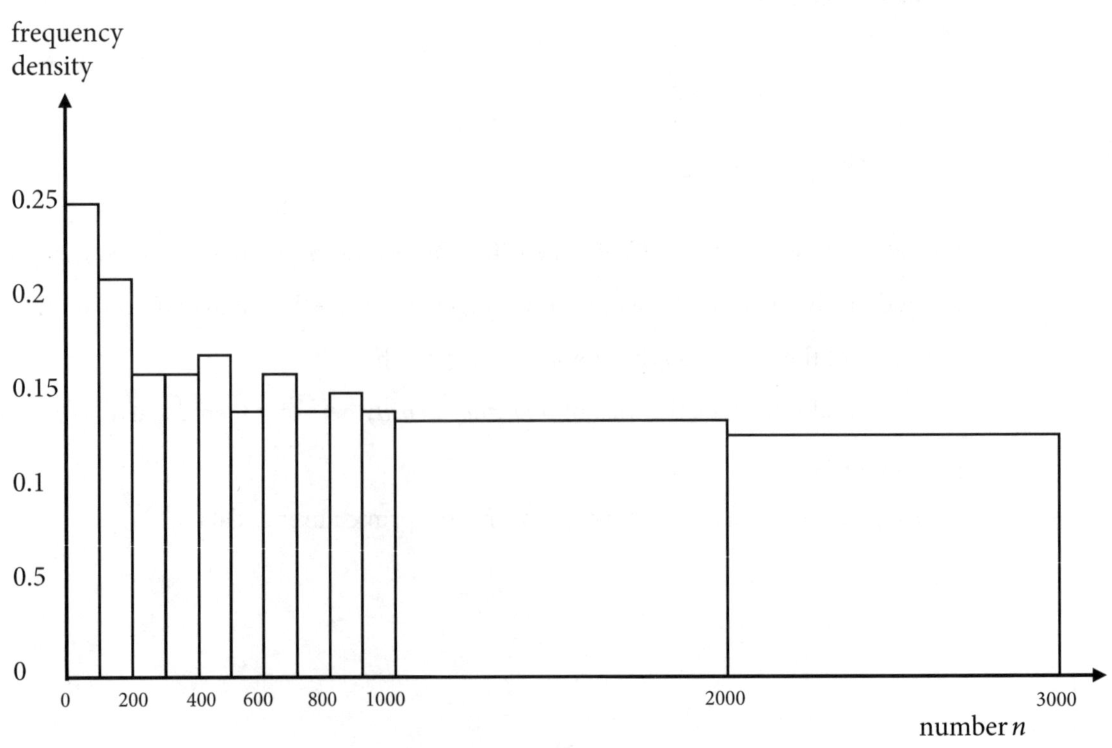

On the one hand, prime numbers seem to appear 'at random' at unpredictable spots on the number line, but on the other hand there are laws predicting how many will arise by what point. An internet search for 'prime number theorem' will lead to lots of interesting information.

If you have time, you could go back and discuss the original swimming pool data, and how, by calculating frequency density, the three graphs would have looked much more similar and would have accurately presented the data:

Age (n)	Frequency	Frequency density
$0 \le n < 5$	2	0.4
$5 \le n < 15$	4	0.4
$15 \le n < 20$	5	0.5
$20 \le n < 30$	9	0.9
$30 \le n < 80$	3	0.06

Age (n)	Frequency	Frequency density
$0 \le n < 20$	11	0.55
$20 \le n < 40$	10	0.5
$40 \le n < 60$	1	0.05
$60 \le n < 80$	1	0.05

Age (n)	Frequency	Frequency density
$0 \le n < 10$	5	0.5
$10 \le n < 20$	6	0.6
$20 \le n < 40$	10	0.5
$40 \le n < 80$	2	0.05

Homework (5 min)

Possible tasks would be to draw histograms of the swimming pool data or to find out about the prime-counting function $\pi(x)$. There is some interesting information at http://primes.utm.edu/.

To make it harder

Learners may be surprised to know that Paul Erdös (1913–1996) was only 18 years old when he showed that for all integers $n > 1$ there is always a prime number between n and $2n$. Interested learners could find out about his life and also about *Goldbach's conjecture*.

To make it easier

Learners who find this difficult might benefit from help choosing categories and devising appropriate scales for their graphs.

Graphs of Data

Swimming pool data

3, 4, 5, 8, 8, 14, 17, 17, 17, 18, 18, 20, 21, 25, 25, 27, 28, 29, 29, 29, 34, 41, 78

Awards data

Look at this graph, which is drawn to scale.

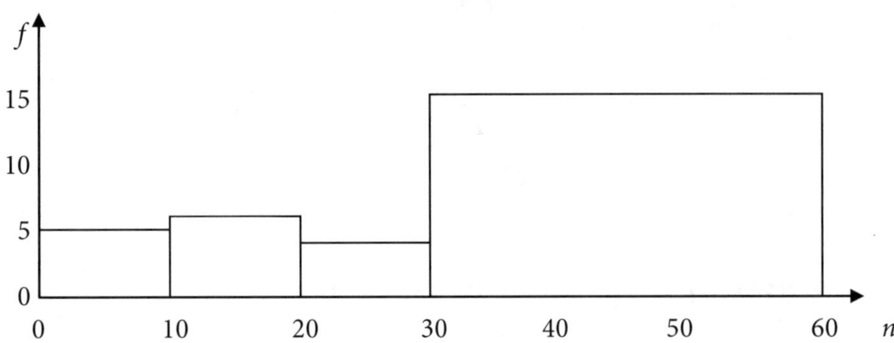

Describe in as much detail as you can the data it is showing.

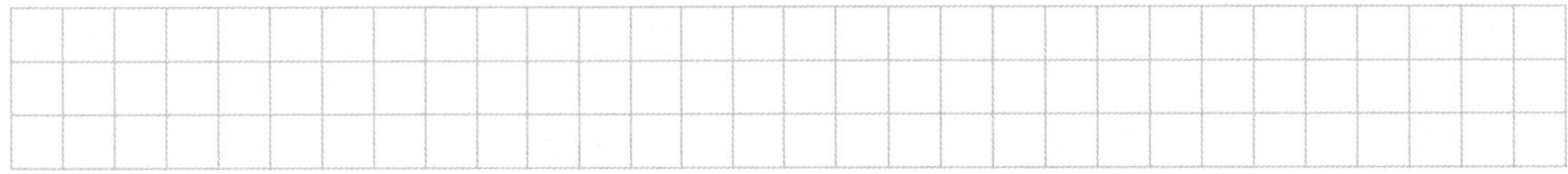

The graph is an attempt to show the number of awards (n) received by a class of 30 learners over a certain period of time. f is the frequency.

Complete the table below using the data in the graph.

Number of awards (n)	Frequency (f)
$0 \le n < 10$	
$10 \le n < 20$	
$20 \le n < 30$	
$30 \le n < 60$	

What *proportion* of the class obtained 30 or more awards?

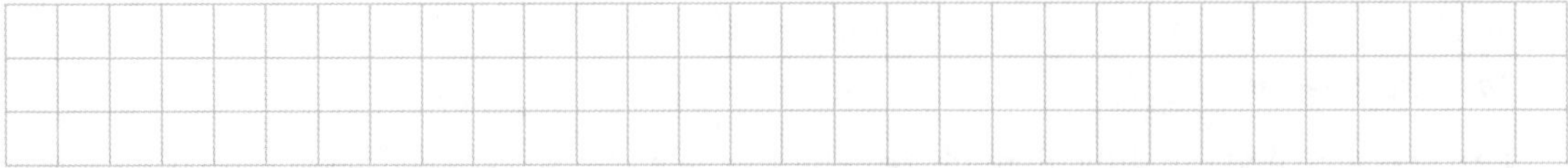

Shade in the part of the graph corresponding to these learners.

Why does the graph make it look like *more* than half the class did this?

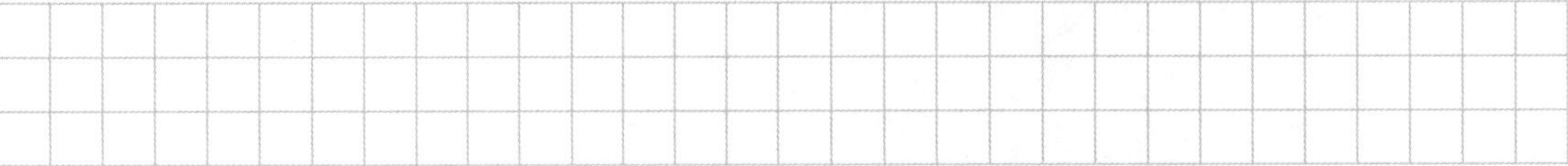

Here is the same data for the same class but with the highest group divided up into three smaller categories.

Number of awards (n)	**Frequency (f)**
$0 \le n < 10$	5
$10 \le n < 20$	6
$20 \le n < 30$	4
$30 \le n < 40$	5
$40 \le n < 50$	4
$50 \le n < 60$	6

Would a bar chart of this data look similar to the bar chart above? Why / why not?

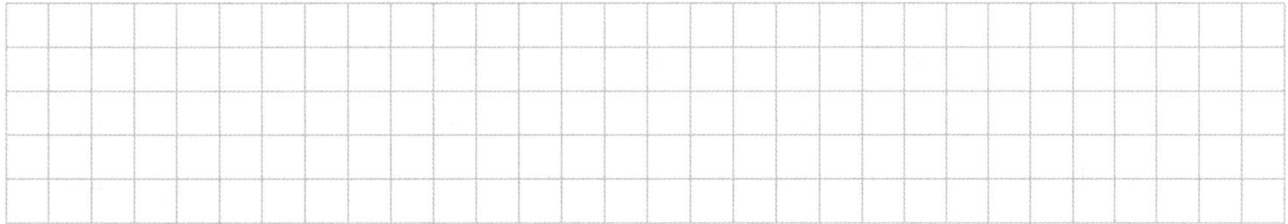

Prime numbers data

The first 170 prime numbers are:

2	3	5	7	11	13	17	19	23	29
31	37	41	43	47	53	59	61	67	71
73	79	83	89	97	101	103	107	109	113
127	131	137	139	149	151	157	163	167	173
179	181	191	193	197	199	211	223	227	229
233	239	241	251	257	263	269	271	277	281
283	293	307	311	313	317	331	337	347	349
353	359	367	373	379	383	389	397	401	409
419	421	431	433	439	443	449	457	461	463
467	479	487	491	499	503	509	521	523	541
547	557	563	569	571	577	587	593	599	601
607	613	617	619	631	641	643	647	653	659
661	673	677	683	691	701	709	719	727	733
739	743	751	757	761	769	773	787	797	809
811	821	823	827	829	839	853	857	859	863
877	881	883	887	907	911	919	929	937	941
947	953	967	971	977	983	991	997	1009	1013

Decide how to present this data graphically.

Identities

Introduction

This lesson gives learners the opportunity to explore various properties of numbers and to specialize and generalize. It also focuses on the idea of impossibility, which is an important idea in mathematics and one which learners can be resistant to. It can sound defeatist (arrogant, even) to claim that something *definitely cannot* be done – ever, by anyone. Learners frequently feel that such statements have a tendency to be proved wrong – science is littered with examples, such as Lord Kelvin, who said in 1895: 'Heavier-than-air flying machines are impossible', only eight years before Orville and Wilbur Wright built one! When learners are able to develop their own arguments against the possibility (rather than probability) of something happening, they are more likely to see the power of such thinking. If their only encounter with the word 'impossible' in mathematics has been as the end-point of a probability scale, they may see it as very close to possibility, rather than as its complete opposite.

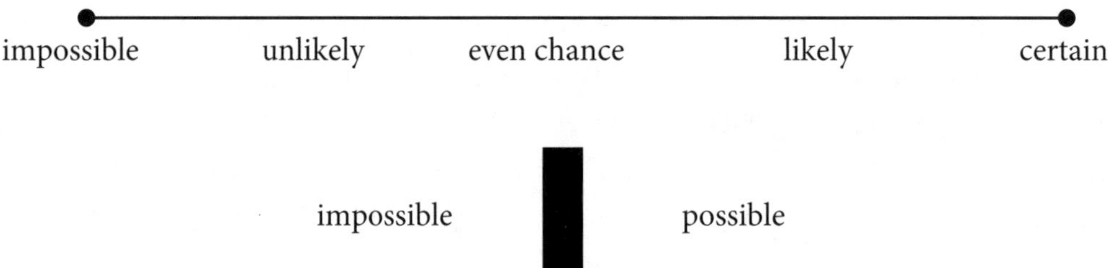

Different depictions of 'impossibility' in mathematics

Aims and Outcomes

- appreciate the significance of identities, which are true for *all* possible values
- experience how algebra can help to answer questions about possibility and impossibility
- solve quadratic equations to deal with problems concerning number patterns

Lesson Starter (10 min)

Look at this statement:

$$\square \times \square = \square \times \square$$

What possible numbers can you think of that will work? E.g., $6 \times 8 = 2 \times 24$.

Learners may wonder whether the blank boxes have to be the same as each other, which can be a fruitful discussion.

Invite lots of learner-generated examples: integers, decimals, fractions, negatives.

Make a simple example, a complicated example, a funny example, a surprising example, etc.

If you are restricted to positive integers, in which cases of a left-hand side is there only one possibility *for the right-hand side?* E.g., $1 \times 13 = 13 \times 1$. This happens only with prime numbers.

What if all the numbers have to be different? In which cases of a left-hand side is there only one possibility *for the right-hand side?* E.g., $2 \times 3 = 1 \times 6$ or $2 \times 4 = 1 \times 8$. This happens only with numbers that have exactly four factors; i.e., products of two primes or cubes of a prime.

What if you are not allowed to use 1? E.g., $2 \times 6 = 3 \times 4$. Then it is numbers with exactly six factors. *What kinds of numbers have exactly six factors?*

What other questions can you ask?

Main Lesson (20 min)

Give learners the Task Sheet. They may initially raise the issue of whether any of the boxes are allowed to be the same or not – or they may assume that they *have* to be. Depending on how learners choose to answer this, the constraints will be different. It is probably more interesting if different learners are abiding by different laws but such an arrangement might be difficult to work with, so by all means be dictatorial about it if you wish!

Plenary (25 min)

Learners may spot patterns in cases such as: $3 + 5 = 2 \times 4$, $6 + 8 = 2 \times 7$; i.e., that the right-hand side is twice the mean or median of the two numbers on the left. This could be proved in several ways, such as pictorially or with algebra: $(n - 1) + (n + 1) = 2n$.

The four numbers can't be *consecutive*, since if you write $(n - 1) + n = (n + 1)(n + 2)$ and expand and simplify you end up with the quadratic equation $n^2 + n + 3 = 0$, which has no real roots, since '$b^2 - 4ac$' is -11, which is negative. Learners may find other explanations to back up their gut feeling that it cannot be done.

Learners may be familiar with the fact that $2 + 2 = 2 \times 2$ and may also notice that $0 + 0 = 0 \times 0$. *Are there any more? What about if you use negative numbers?* Using algebra, $a + a = a^2$, so $a^2 - 2a = 0$ and $a(a - 2) = 0$, so $a = 0$ or 2 *only*, which proves that $2 + 2 = 2 \times 2$ and $0 + 0 = 0 \times 0$ are the only possible solutions. This shows the power of algebra not only to find solutions but to find *all the possible solutions* and rule out the possibility of any more. This is in contrast to finding solutions by inspection (or 'trial and improvement'), which may not close the door on other possible answers.

For $\square + \square + \square = \square \times \square \times \square$, similar algebra to that used above gives $a = 0$ or $\sqrt{3}$ or $-\sqrt{3}$, so the only possibilities are: $0 + 0 + 0 = 0 \times 0 \times 0$, $\sqrt{3} + \sqrt{3} + \sqrt{3} = \sqrt{3} \times \sqrt{3} \times \sqrt{3} = 3\sqrt{3}$ and $(-\sqrt{3}) + (-\sqrt{3}) + (-\sqrt{3}) = (-\sqrt{3}) \times (-\sqrt{3}) \times (-\sqrt{3}) = (-3\sqrt{3})$. So this time there are three possible solutions.

For $\square + \lozenge = \square \times \lozenge$, we have $a + b = ab$, so $ab - a = b$ and $a(b - 1) = b$. So $a=\frac{b}{b-1}$, $b \neq 1$, which means that $a=1+\frac{1}{b-1}$, which is never an integer unless $b - 1 = \pm 1$, so there are no solutions other than $a = b = 2$ or $a = b = 0$.

For □ − ◊ = □ × ◊, we have $a - b = ab$, so in a similar way $a = \frac{1}{1-b} - 1$, which is never an integer unless $1 - b = \pm 1$, so there are no solutions other than $a = -2$ and $b = 2$ or $a = b = 0$.

Where the numbers are restricted to positive integers, the only solutions to 'sum = product' for two, three and four numbers are:

$2 + 2 = 2 \times 2$

$1 + 2 + 3 = 1 \times 2 \times 3 = 6$

$1 + 1 + 2 + 4 = 1 \times 1 \times 2 \times 4 = 8$

For five numbers, there are three solutions:

$1 + 1 + 1 + 2 + 5 = 1 \times 1 \times 1 \times 2 \times 5 = 10$

$1 + 1 + 1 + 3 + 3 = 1 \times 1 \times 1 \times 3 \times 3 = 9$

$1 + 1 + 2 + 2 + 2 = 1 \times 1 \times 2 \times 2 \times 2 = 8$

Homework (5 min)

Learners could be asked to make up two mathematical problems, one of which is possible and one of which is impossible. *Try to make them so that it is not obvious without doing some work which is which.* This can be quite difficult!

To make it harder

There should be plenty of scope for learners to investigate avenues that are appropriate to their current skills. Problems such as □^{2} = 2□; i.e., $x^2 = 2x$, generalizing to $x^n = nx$, may be suitable for those requiring additional challenges.

Investigating $y = x^x$ could also be interesting.

To make it easier

Finding examples with small positive integers should be accessible to all learners. Calculators may support those with weak numeracy and allow them to consider generalities alongside developing their numerical skills.

Equality

Look at this equation:

$$\square + \square = \square \times \square$$

Put numbers in place of the four □'s.

Try to find as many examples as you can.

Can the four numbers, left to right, be *consecutive* (go up in ones)?

If they can, what are all the possibilities?

If they can't, why is it impossible?

Can the four numbers all be *the same number*?

If they can, what are all the possibilities?

If they can't, why is it impossible?

Can you do it using just *two different numbers*?

If you can, what are all the possibilities?

If you can't, why is it impossible?

What questions can you ask and answer about these situations?

$$\square - \square = \square \times \square$$

$$\square + \square + \square = \square \times \square \times \square$$

$$\square + \lozenge = \square \times \lozenge$$

What other situations can you think of?

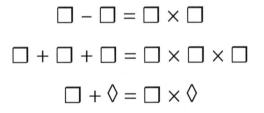

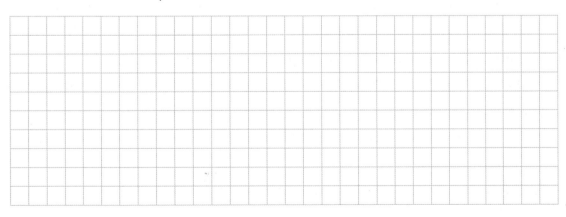

Indices

Introduction

It can be easy to learn the so-called 'rules of indices' in a very instrumental way, and perhaps be quite good at answering questions similar to those you have been drilled in, without necessarily having much sense of what it all means. For example, a learner who completes question after question writing things like $3a^2 \times 5a^6 = 8a^{12}$ has presumably misremembered which bit to add and which bit to multiply ($3 + 5 = 8$ and $2 \times 6 = 12$, instead of $3 \times 5 = 15$ and $2 + 6 = 8$, giving the correct answer $15a^8$). Although it may enable them to correct the exercise, reminding learners that it is 'the other way round' does not lead them towards any real learning. The intention of this lesson is to work on the understanding and explaining side of simplifying indices, particularly by using numbers and letters interchangeably.

Aims and Outcomes

- understand and use index rules to simplify algebraic expressions

Lesson Starter (20 min)

You may wish to have the problems below prepared on the board, or have the class do something else while you write them out.

What do these equal?

$\frac{2 \times 151}{151}$ $\frac{2 \times 151 \times 151}{151 \times 151}$ $\frac{2 \times 151 \times 151 \times 151}{151 \times 151 \times 151}$ $\frac{2 \times 151 \times 151 \times 151 \times 151}{151 \times 151 \times 151 \times 151}$

It is interesting to see whether learners reach for a calculator. If they use a calculator on the first two, say, do they continue to use it on the third and fourth or do they observe a repeating structure?

They all equal 2, because the equal numbers of 151s on the top and the bottom cancel out in each case. However, it would be just as correct to say that they equal $\frac{2 \times 151 \times 151 \times 151 \times 151 \times 151}{151 \times 151 \times 151 \times 151 \times 151}$, say, by extending the pattern, which would be an interesting answer.

In discussion, learners will find that they need to distinguish 'the number' (i.e., the base) from 'the number of occurrences of the number', and some may even suggest writing, say, the fourth one as $\frac{2 \times 151^4}{151^4}$, where the index (4, here) counts the number of occurrences of 151 multiplied together.

What do these equal?

$\frac{47 \times 83 \times 151}{47 \times 151}$ $\frac{47 \times 83 \times 83 \times 151}{47 \times 151 \times 83 \times 47}$ $\frac{47 \times 83 \times 151 \times 83 \times 83}{47 \times 151}$ $\frac{47 \times 83 \times 151 \times 47 \times 151}{47 \times 151 \times 47 \times 47 \times 47 \times 47 \times 83}$

They equal 83, $\frac{83}{47}$ (there is no need to convert this to a decimal or a mixed number unless learners wish to), 83^3 (let's not worry about working that out just for the moment) and $\frac{151}{47 \times 47 \times 47}$ or $\frac{151}{47^3}$.

The complexity of the final one may push learners into going through each different base number systematically, counting up the number of occurrences on the top and the bottom.

Learners may wish to get 'an answer' (i.e., a single number), but you can casually state that you're only interested for now in how many of each number remain – i.e., in *simplifying* rather than *evaluating*. (This might be seen as being interested in the *calculation* that you *would* do rather than the final value that you would obtain.)

How did you do it? What did you focus on? Where did you start? Why?

How do you work out what's left?

The difference between the number of occurrences on the top and on the bottom is likely to be the key.

When does a number completely disappear? When a factor appears an equal number of times on the top and on the bottom.

Make up two for the person next to you.

Main Lesson (20 min)

Give out the Task Sheet and let learners think about the different quantities. In parts A and B, you could encourage learners to cancel factors in the numerator with factors in the denominator. If they are stuck, rather than telling them how to get the answer you could ask learners to replace the *d*'s with threes, say, the *e*'s with fives and the *f*'s with sevens (or other suitable co-prime numbers) and then try. This can be a very useful strategy whenever trying to simplify algebra, so is a useful learning point alongside the goal of becoming confident with indices. *When something is too hard, make it simpler, solve it, and then put the complexity back in and try again.*

In the part C, it would be good to discourage an excessive reliance on calculating the values (especially by using a calculator). It is a very powerful mathematical idea to be able to say that two things are definitely exactly equal without necessarily knowing (or even caring) what the value (even approximately) is of either! For example, $5^{59} \times 5^{154} = 5^{213}$.

Plenary (15 min)

The answers to part A are:

1. df 2. de 3. f 4. ef 5. de 6. d

Questions 2 and 5 have the same answer because the expression in 5 is identical to that in 2, just written using indices.

The answers to part B are:

1. $\frac{de}{4}$ 2. $\frac{4}{f}$ 3. 4 4. $\frac{2e^3}{fd}$ 5. $12de^2$ 6. $\frac{2d^2}{3e}$

The answer is 'just a number' in question 3 because the *e*'s, *f*'s and *d*'s exactly cancel out (the e^2 on the bottom is exactly the same as the $e \times e$ on the top, for instance).

For the final section, part C, the joining lines should be as follows:

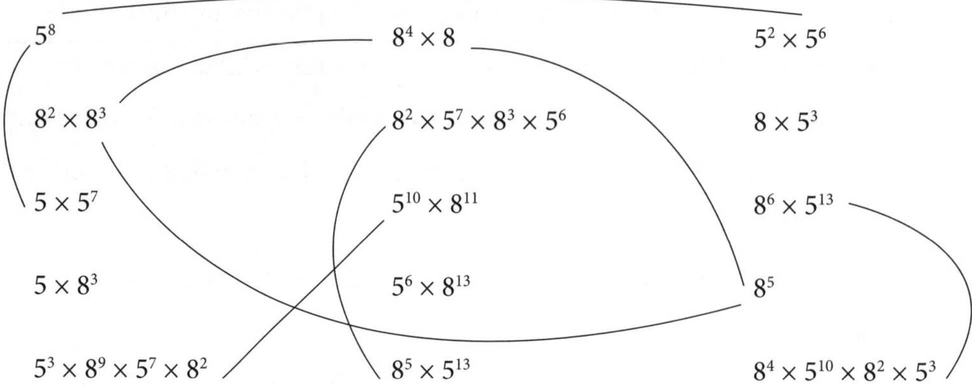

A common problem is realizing/believing that order doesn't matter in multiplication, even when there are more than two numbers. Learners may be happy that $7 \times 4 = 4 \times 7$ but less sure that $3 \times 4 \times 5 = 3 \times 5 \times 4 = 4 \times 5 \times 3 = 4 \times 3 \times 5 = 5 \times 3 \times 4 = 5 \times 4 \times 3$. So it may take some time before learners are confident that $e \times f \times e = e^2 f$ or that $5e \times 6e = 5 \times 6 \times e^2 = 30e^2$.

You might try to encourage the use of the mathematical terms 'numerator' and 'denominator' during whole-class discussion, perhaps mixing that with the more immediate 'top' and 'bottom' used here. It is good for learners to become familiar with technical words, so long as that does not present too much of a barrier to participating in this discussion.

At the end you may want to take the opportunity to collect and generalize 'rules' such as $a^g \times a^h = a^{g+h}$, $a^g \div a^h = a^{g-h}$, $a^0 = 1$, etc.

Homework (5 min)

Find out what the word 'zenzizenzizenzic' means.

It is mainly 'famous' for having more letter z's than any other word in the English language! But it is also an obsolete word for the eighth power. The others in the sequence are *square* (second power), *cube* (third), *zenzizenzic* (or *biquadrate*) (fourth), *surfolide* (fifth), *zenzicube* (sixth) and *second surfolide* (seventh). Only 'square' and 'cube' are commonly used today – thankfully!

To make it harder

Learners who find this fairly easy could be challenged to construct a series of quotients of increasing complexity, each of which simplifies (with an increasing level of surprise!) to something like '*it*', say. (*See if you can make* 'it'*!*)

For example, it could begin: $\frac{t \times i \times t \times i \times i}{i \times i \times t}, \frac{t^2 \times i^4}{i^3 \times t}, \ldots$

To make it easier

Learners daunted by the abstract nature of multiplying letters, may prefer to work more with numbers initially, finding ten products or quotients that simplify to five, for instance, or using powers of 10 to make the calculations easier to begin with; for example, $\frac{10 \times 10 \times 10}{10 \times 10}$.

Indices

A. Simplify these:

1. $\dfrac{d\times e\times f\times e\times f\times f}{e\times f\times f\times e}$

2. $\dfrac{d\times e\times f\times f\times e}{f\times e\times f}$

3. $\dfrac{d\times e\times f\times e\times f\times f}{e\times f\times f\times e\times d}$

4. $\dfrac{d\times e\times f\times e\times f\times f}{e\times f\times f\times d}$

5. $\dfrac{d\times e^2\times f^2}{f^2\times e}$

6. $\dfrac{d\times e\times f\times e\times f\times f}{e\times f\times f\times e\times f}$

Which two answers are the same? Why?

B. Simplify these:

1. $\dfrac{2\times d\times e\times d\times f\times e}{8\times e\times f\times d}$

2. $\dfrac{8\times e\times d^3\times f\times e}{2\times e\times f\times d^3\times f\times e}$

3. $\dfrac{8\times e\times d\times f\times e}{e^2\times f\times d\times 2}$

4. $\dfrac{2\times e\times d\times 4\times e^3}{4\times e\times f\times d^2}$

5. $\dfrac{2e\times 3d^3\times 4e^2}{2\times 2d^2}$

6. $\dfrac{2e^3\times 3d^3e}{e^5\times 9d}$

One of these answers is just a number (no letters). Why does that happen?

C. Join up with a line any of the expressions that you think have the same value.

5^8	$8^4\times 8$	$5^2\times 5^6$
$8^2\times 8^3$	$8^2\times 5^7\times 8^3\times 5^6$	8×5^3
5×5^7	$5^{10}\times 8^{11}$	$8^6\times 5^{13}$
5×8^3	$5^6\times 8^{13}$	8^5
$5^3\times 8^9\times 5^7\times 8^2$	$8^5\times 5^{13}$	$8^4\times 5^{10}\times 8^2\times 5^3$

Explain why you think they are the same.

When you finish, if some expressions are not connected to any others, make up ones that connect with them.

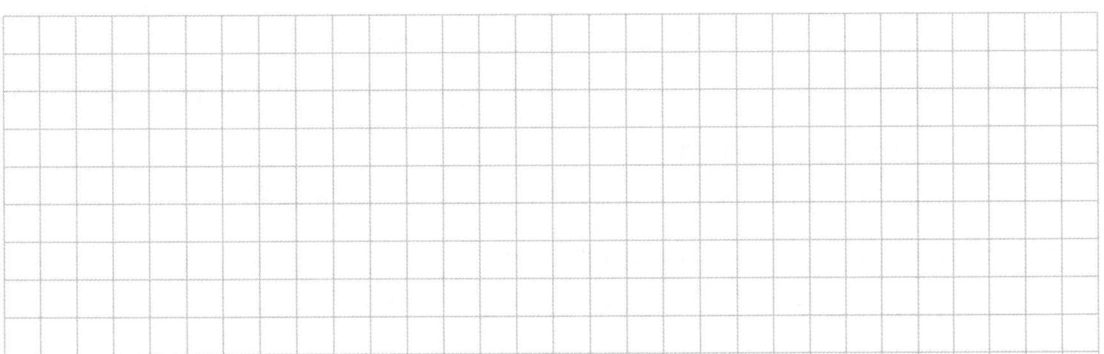

30 Inverse Functions

Introduction

'Doing and undoing' is a key mathematical idea. In life it is often harder to *undo* things than it is to *do* them in the first place: it is easier to get your room into a mess than it is to tidy it up! In mathematics, inverse operations are generally harder and more interesting than the original operations. Subtraction is harder than addition, division is harder than multiplication, square rooting is harder than squaring, factorizing is harder than expanding, integrating is harder than differentiating, etc. Functions, in general, are a big idea in pure mathematics. You can even consider 'dividing *into* something' or 'taking away *from* something' as functions and so treat $f(x) = \frac{10}{x}$ or $g(x) = 10 - x$, for instance, as one-step functions as well. The notation is often problematic; for example, writing f^{-1} to mean 'the inverse function of f' rather than '$\frac{1}{f}$'. Other notations, such as $f: x \rightarrow 3x - 2$ or the := symbol ('set equal') are also sometimes used. In more advanced work it becomes important to view functions as *objects* rather than *processes*: objects can have things *done* to them, like differentiation, for example. (See also Lesson 23.)

Aims and Outcomes

- find the inverses of one- and two-step functions
- understand the idea of an inverse function in algebra

Lesson Starter (10 min)

Ask for two volunteers. Give the first one a cheap tube of toothpaste and a plate, then time how quickly they can squeeze all the toothpaste out of the tube onto the plate. Then give the second volunteer a teaspoon and ask them what they think their task is going to be! Time how quickly they can put it all back in again.

'It is generally harder to undo things than it is to do them in the first place.'

Do you agree or disagree with this statement? Why? Can you think of examples?

Computer software, with its highly convenient 'undo' feature, does buck this trend slightly, but in the real world it is hard to unscramble an egg or put a jigsaw back together or make up with someone you have hastily offended, etc.

Can you think of mathematical *examples of 'doing and undoing'? (Think about the order in which you may learn different topics in school.)* You can often 'undo' transformations just as easily as they were 'done' in the first place (e.g., a reverse translation, rotation or reflection) but with numerical and algebraic processes going back is often much harder.

Main Lesson (25 min)

When you get dressed, you have to put on your socks first and then your shoes. What happens when you get undressed*?*

Things have to happen in the reverse order, like loading and unloading a lorry: you put on *first* the things you want to unload *last*, at the end of the day, and the last things you load on are the things you want to deliver at your first stop.

Give learners the Task Sheet. The operations g and h at the top are 'put on socks' and 'put on shoes' respectively, so g^{-1} and h^{-1} are 'take off socks' and 'take off shoes' respectively.

Think of examples of mathematical functions g and h. You could introduce the $g^{-1}(x)$ notation if learners are unfamiliar with that and you might wish, either formally or informally, to develop the idea that $(fg)^{-1}(x) = g^{-1}(f^{-1}(x))$.

Then invite learners to contribute to a list on the board such as: $g(x) = 5x$, $h(x) = \frac{5}{x}$, $i(x) = x + 5$, $j(x) = x - 5$, $k(x) = 5 - x$, $l(x) = \frac{x}{5}$, etc.

Then ask learners to choose pairs of these to combine, both ways around, on the sheet, constructing composite functions and finding their inverses. For example, using $g(x) = 5x$ and $h(x) = \frac{5}{x}$, on the first line we can construct $gh(x)$ by operating with h first followed by g, and then on the second line we can construct $(gh)^{-1}(x)$ by operating first with g^{-1} and then with h^{-1}.

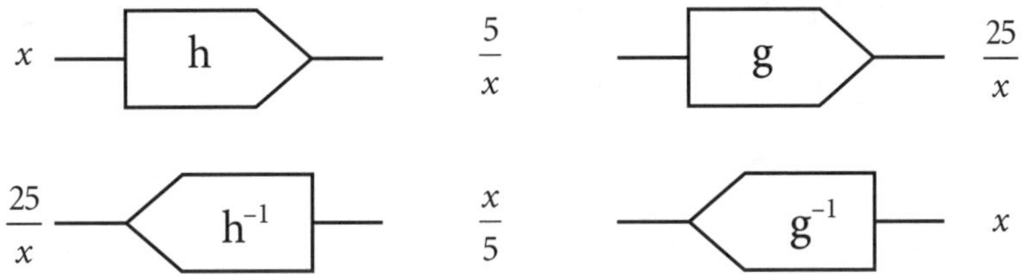

x → [h] → $\frac{5}{x}$ → [g] → $\frac{25}{x}$

$\frac{25}{x}$ ← [h^{-1}] ← $\frac{x}{5}$ ← [g^{-1}] ← x

So in this case, $(gh)^{-1}(x) = gh(x) = \frac{25}{x}$ (gh is a *self-inverse* function) and $(gh)^{-1}(x) = h^{-1}(g^{-1}(x))$.

Encourage learners to complete more examples and look for patterns.

Plenary (20 min)

You may not feel a need to push symbolism such as $(fg)^{-1}(x) = g^{-1}(f^{-1}(x))$ too much, but an informal sense that 'to reverse a combination of steps you need to reverse each of them separately *and in the reverse order*' (however expressed) may be helpful. And the lesson should provide plenty of opportunity for learners to practise examples and give explanations to one another.

Learners who have worked on the more difficult differentiation material below could also describe what they have done and offer some of their best constructions.

Homework (5 min)

Draw graphs of the functions used today and their inverses and look for a connection between the graphs.

A graph and its inverse function are reflections of each other in the line $y = x$, since an inverse function corresponds to swapping the input (x) and output (y) values the other way round.

What will happen if a graph is symmetrical in the line $y = x$*?*

This happens for *self-inverse* functions such as $f(x) = x$, $f(x) = -x$ and $f(x) = \frac{1}{x}$. Learners could try to find other self-inverse functions.

To make it harder

Learners who are confident with this work could construct problems in which a composite function $fg(x)$ is given, and possible pairs of functions f and g are to be found. Or in which $fg(x)$ is given along with *either* $f(x)$ *or* $g(x)$, and the other one has to be found. For example, 'If $fg(x) = x + 5$ and $f(x) = 2x$, what is $g(x)$?' (The answer is $g(x) = \frac{x+5}{2}$.)

Or other combinations could be given, such as $fg(x)$ and $g^{-1}(x)$, and the question asks for $(fg)^{-1}(x)$ or $f(x)$, etc.

Learners who are very confident could consider a composition of *three* functions $fgh(x)$ and find an expression for $(fgh)^{-1}(x)$ in terms of the inverse of each separate function.

The answer is $(fgh)^{-1}(x) = h^{-1}g^{-1}f^{-1}(x)$.

Keen learners could also find out about the scientific concept of *entropy* and how it describes why some physical processes, like an explosion, for example, are very hard to reverse!

To make it easier

Making sure that each individual function used is one-step (e.g., $f(x) = x + 10$ or $g(x) = 3x$) may help learners who are having difficulties initially.

Inverse Functions

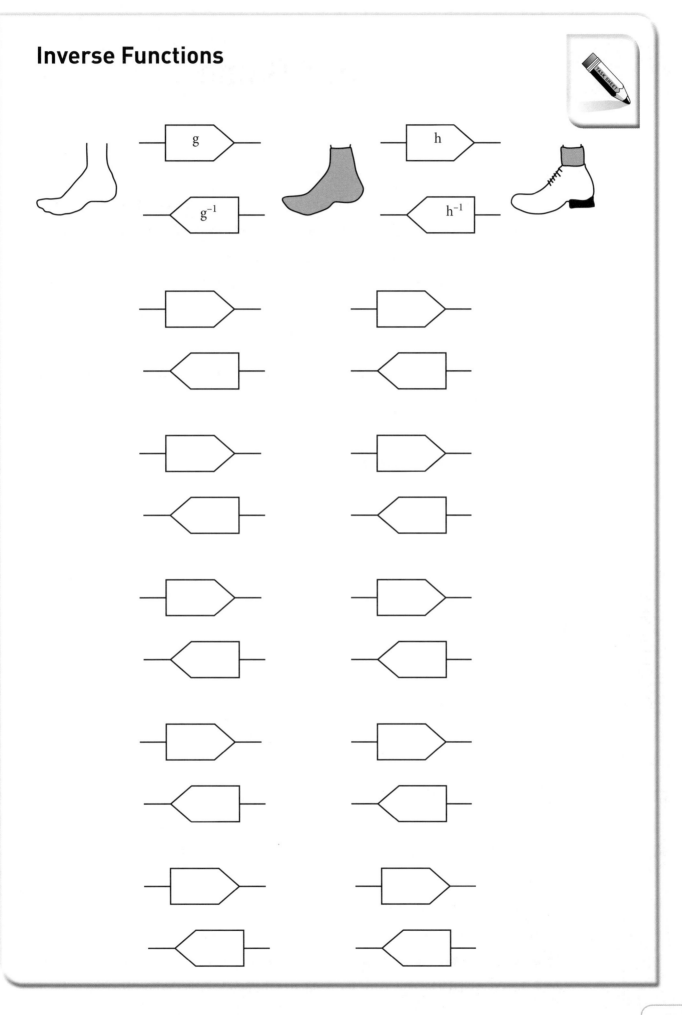

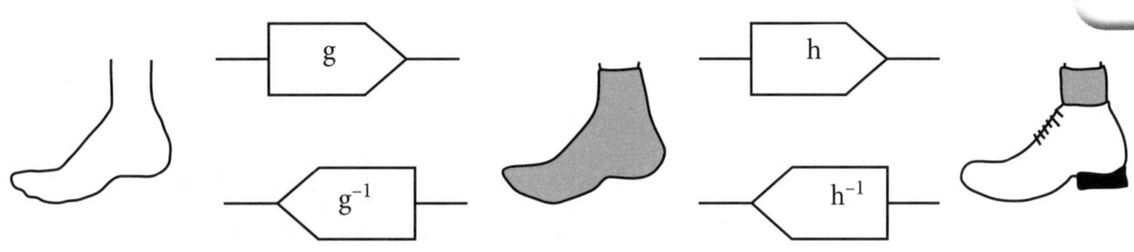

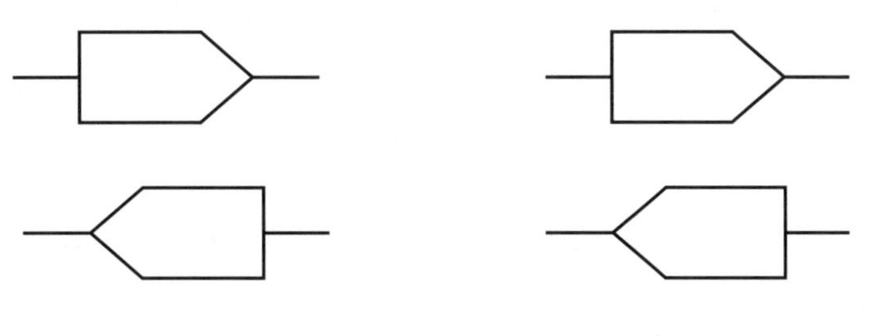

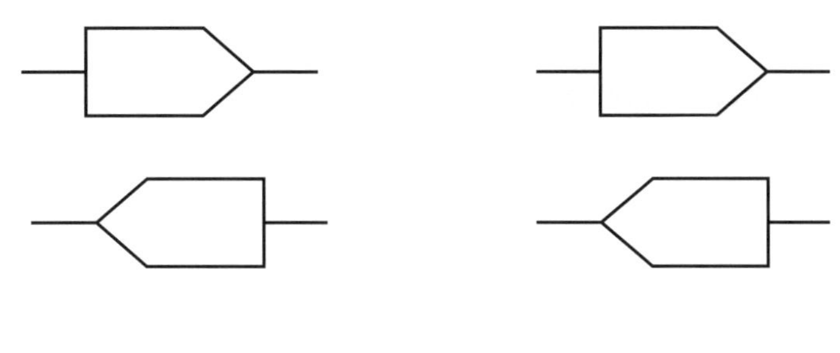

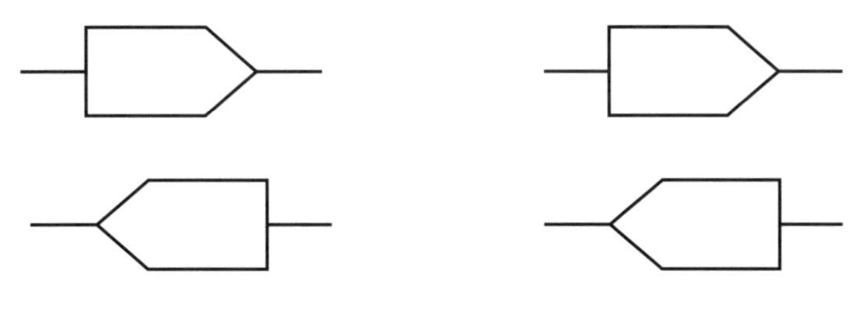

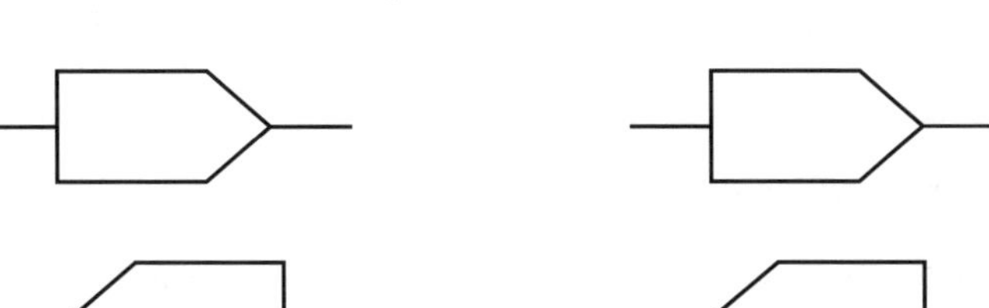

31

Kim's Game

Introduction

This lesson harnesses a well-known children's game, exploiting it as a context for working with directed numbers. When asked for strategies to help with playing Kim's Game, learners usually say that they look for things in common among the objects or try to connect them mentally in some way. When *numbers* are the objects, this turns out to be particularly easy, although this is not always obvious when people are initially confronted with the game, as in the starter below.

Aims and Outcomes

- work on numerical and algebraic problems related to addition and subtraction of directed quantities

Lesson Starter (20 min)

Write a collection of directed numbers on the board, or show them on a screen; for example:

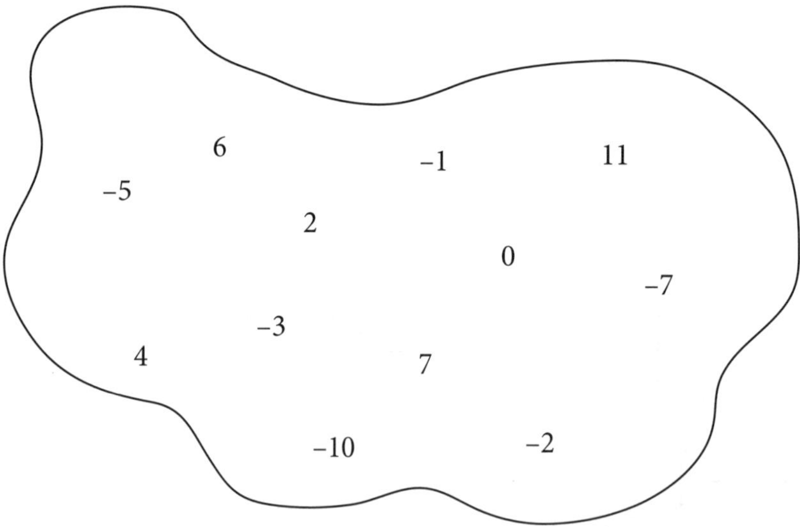

You have one minute to try to remember them. Then I am going to rub out one of the numbers and you have to say which number is missing. (Obviously, learners are not allowed to have pens and paper!)

Close your eyes. (Rub out a number.) *Open your eyes. Which number is missing?* (Or if using an electronic whiteboard you could blank the screen, delete one, and then show the screen again.)

Replace the number (with a different one, perhaps?) and repeat the process.

Does it get easier the more times you do it, or do you get more confused?

Can anyone think of any strategies for making this easier? Learners could discuss this in pairs.

Learners may find it helpful to use the *position* of the numbers on the board/screen to aid their recall. They may try pairing up the numbers or it may occur to someone to *find the sum*. Then, if initially the total is t, and after removing one number the new total is n, then the missing one must be $t - n$. Doing this computation mentally may be difficult if either t or (especially) n is negative.

Main Lesson (20 min)

Give learners the Task Sheet and let them try the game in pairs, with or without the 'sum the numbers' method, depending on whether this has emerged publicly in the lesson yet or not.

Learners might then construct other games, based on larger numbers, fractions, decimals or algebraic expressions such as $5a - 3b$, $b - a$, etc., again utilizing the idea of the various elements having a convenient sum.

Plenary (15 min)

Encourage learners to discuss their strategies and to share their different constructions. The idea of using the sum of the elements may be likened to spotting which piece of a jigsaw is missing: if all the pieces are jumbled up in random places, this could be very hard, but once the jigsaw is assembled the missing piece stands out clearly!

Homework (5 min)

Make a twelve-piece Kim's Game puzzle according to some theme, such as 'directed numbers' or 'collecting terms', etc. Perhaps learners could make 'easy' or 'hard' versions, justifying the difficulty level that they think is appropriate.

Removal of what terms make the trickiest puzzles? Why?

To make it harder

Learners who want an extra challenge could explore the situation when *two* items are removed, either in succession (without replacement) or together. What strategies can they develop for this scenario?

They may also like to explore magic squares containing directed numbers.

For example:

−1	9	−5
−3	1	5
7	−7	3

What makes this a magic square?

How many numbers can you delete so that someone else can still work out what they are? Why? Does it matter which *numbers you delete? Why / why not?*

What other magic squares can you construct?

Find out about redundancy *in information theory and* checksums *used for error correction.*

To make it easier

Learners who find this hard could begin with three 'objects' and examine what happens to the total when each, in turn, is removed. Alternatively, they could work with a small collection of positive integers, looking for which is missing when one is removed.

Kim's Game

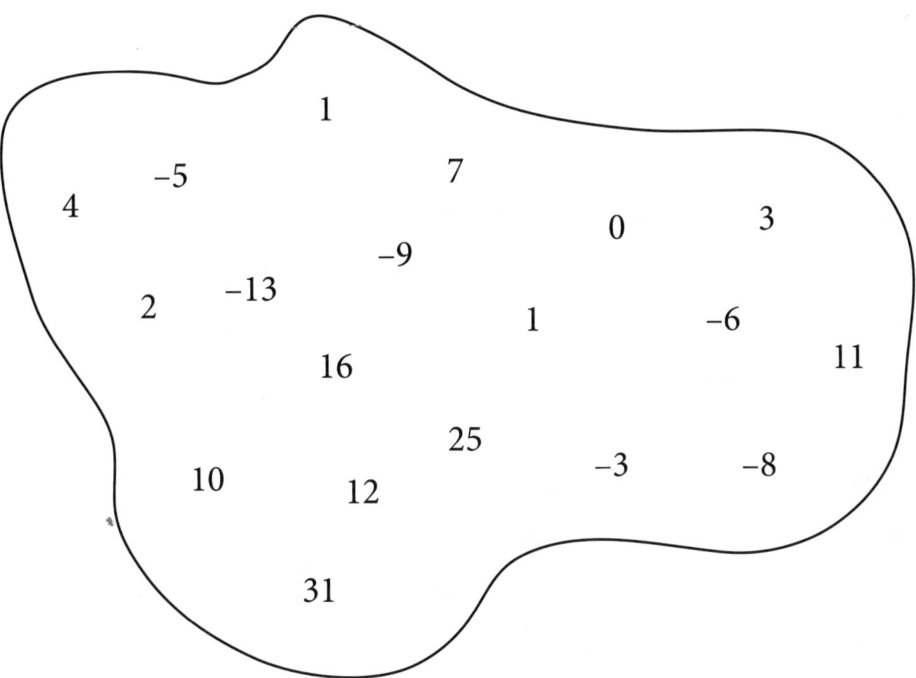

Study the diagram for one minute.

Then close your eyes.

A friend will place their finger over one of the numbers.

How quickly can you say which number is hidden?

Try it a few more times.

Does it get easier?

What strategies can you use to make this easier?

Invent a similar game and work out a strategy for playing it.

You could use numbers or algebraic expressions.

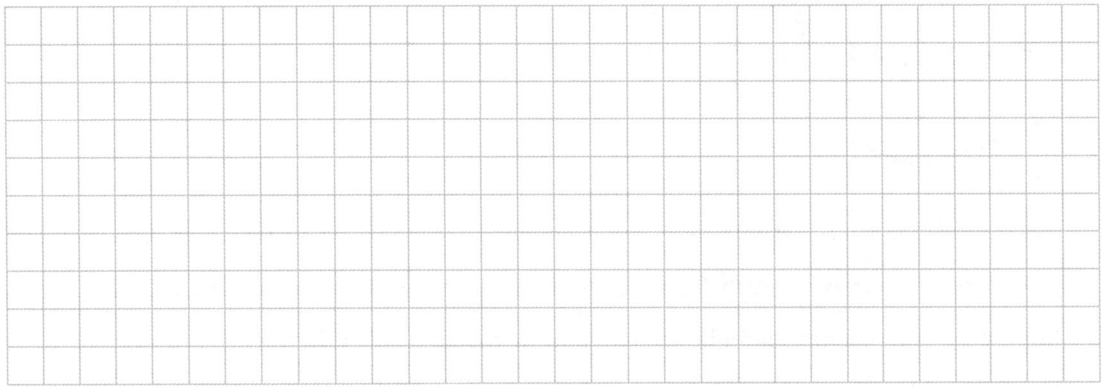

32

Many Faces

Introduction

Having an ability to walk around a 'mathematical object' mentally and view it from several different angles can be very useful. Equivalence is a big idea in mathematics: learners need to understand about equivalent expressions like $3x - x$ and $2x$, equivalent ratios and equivalent fractions, and so on. They can see equivalence as different ways of looking at the same thing. In the classroom, seeking equivalences can help to get away from the idea that maths is all about getting the one right answer that is in the teacher's mind or the back of the textbook. Like the story of the blind men and the elephant, where each man felt a different portion of the elephant and got a different impression of what it was like, different learners can bring different perspectives to bear and each have something of value to contribute. Competent learners can sometimes be reluctant to see things in another way when they feel that they can 'already do it'. But they might be persuaded that the best mathematicians are the ones who can look at things successfully in a number of ways and tune in to different people's ways of seeing and that different perspectives have different advantages at different times.

Aims and Outcomes

- examine multiple representations of algebraic expressions
- work on simplifying algebraic expressions as a means of finding equivalence

Lesson Starter (10 min)

Look at this drawing of a cube:

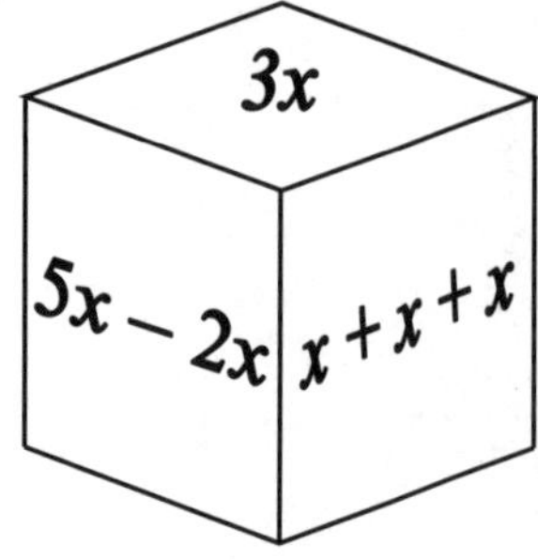

You can see three faces of this cube. What do you think might be on the other three faces? Why? (Learners may be momentarily fazed by the thought of opposite faces on a die adding up to seven, but if this is a problem you might need to indicate that that is not the particular game being played here!) Possible answers would be $3 \times x$ or $2x + x$ or $\sqrt{9x^2}$, etc.

The idea for today's lesson is that the different faces of the cube each contain expressions that are in some sense 'the same' – *they equal the same amount, or are equivalent to each other. They are different ways of viewing the same algebraic expression.*

Main Lesson (20 min)

Give out the Task Sheet and encourage learners to find multiple ways of representing $12x$. They might be encouraged to try to think of something no one else in the room is likely to think of, or of something surprising, clever or unusual. 'Aim to impress' could be a helpful direction.

Plenary (25 min)

This is likely to focus on learners convincing one another that things that don't *look* equal *are* actually equal. How intricately can someone disguise $12x$? Learners sometimes decide to make a highly complex component and multiply it by a (possibly disguised) zero! For example, one complicated possibility might be $\frac{14x^5(x-2)(5^0-1)}{3x^{(17-\sqrt{2})}}+\frac{3x^7(3^3+1)}{(2^3-1)x^6}$, where the entire first term is 'killed' by the $(5^0 - 1)$ factor in the numerator, which equals zero. Learners can sometimes really enjoy making up these horrendous-looking examples and then explaining them away to others! Instead of 'Book 4' on the cover of their fourth writing books, in one class some learners, began putting 'Book' followed by some highly complicated calculation that came to four. Inevitably there will be some mistakes, but provided they are handled sensitively then the exercise can be a lot of fun.

Homework (5 min)

Make nets for three cubes displaying six algebraic equivalences for each one. Explain underneath how you know that the various expressions really are equivalent. (Learners needn't worry about the orientation of the writing on the six faces.)

To make it harder

Learners who have come across trigonometric identities before might be challenged to construct a cube, for example, for $\cos 2x$, with possible answers such as $\cos^2x - \sin^2x$, $2\cos^2x - 1$, $1 - 2\sin^2x$, $\pm\sqrt{\frac{1}{2}(1+\cos 4x)}$, $\cos(x + x)$, etc.

Confident learners might be asked to consider whether $\frac{x^2}{x}$, for example, is equivalent to x? *What about if x might equal zero?* This is a tricky area, and learners might explore graphs such as $y = \frac{x^2}{x}$, which is the same as the graph of $y = x$ but with the point (0, 0) missing (i.e., a graph with a hole in it!). Graph-drawing software may cloud the issue, as it will not show up these sorts of problems. Learners could find out more about 'restricted domains'.

Other challenges might be to work with other regular polyhedra. For example, could anyone do an icosahedron for x^{20} (see over the page)?

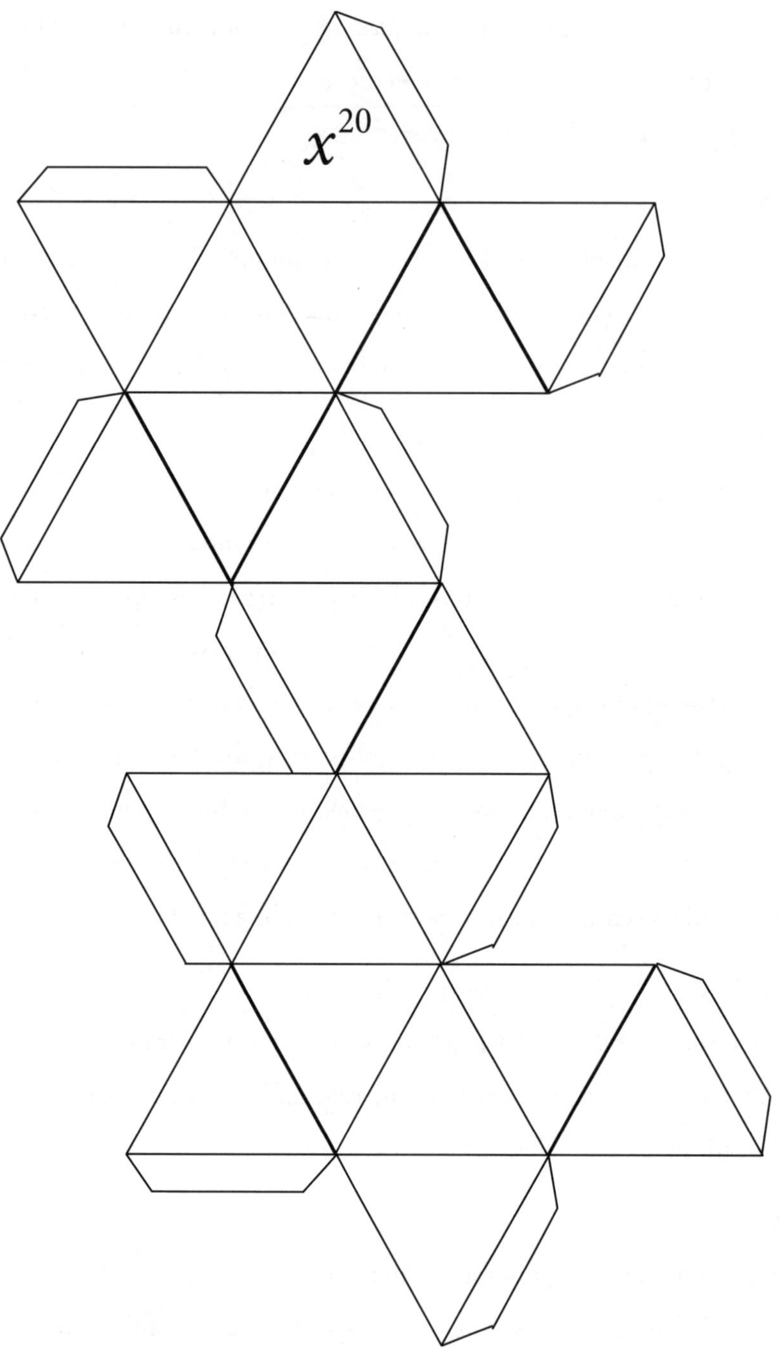

To make it easier

Learners who find this difficult could spend more time initially generating multiple examples of less complicated mathematical objects.

Many Faces

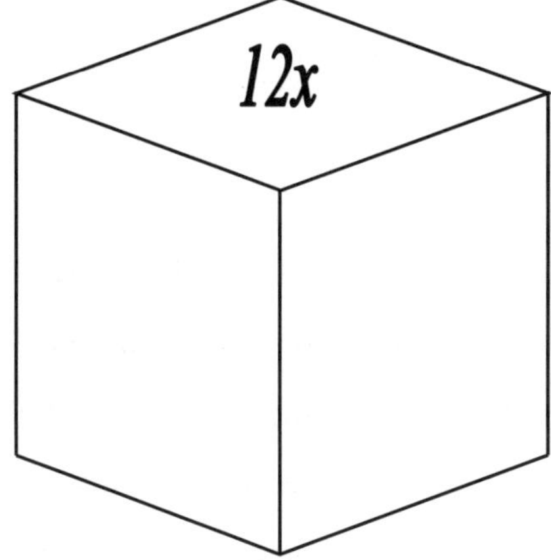

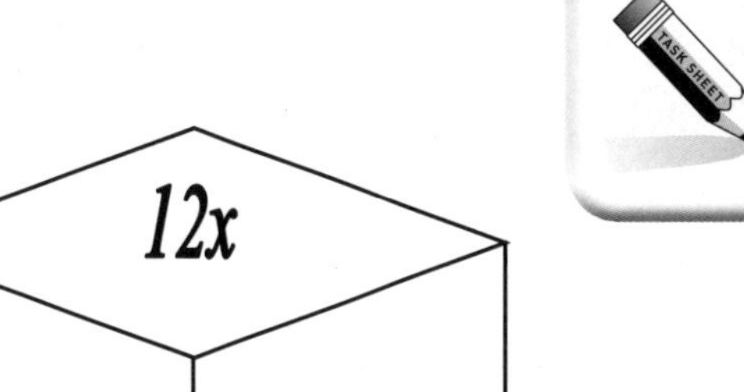

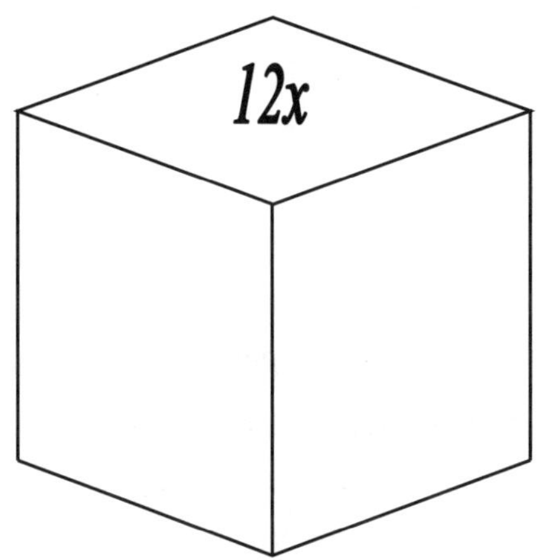

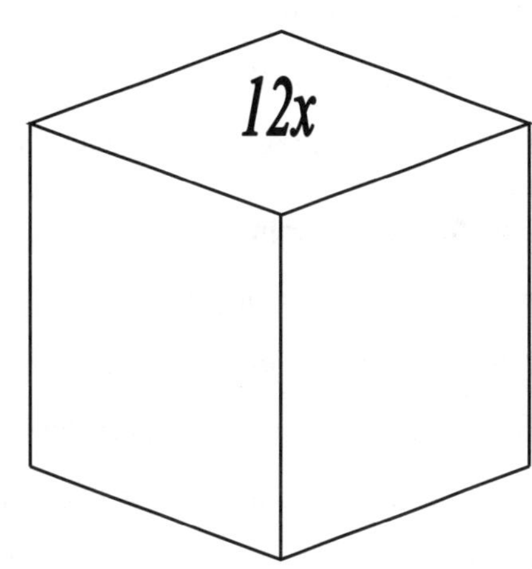

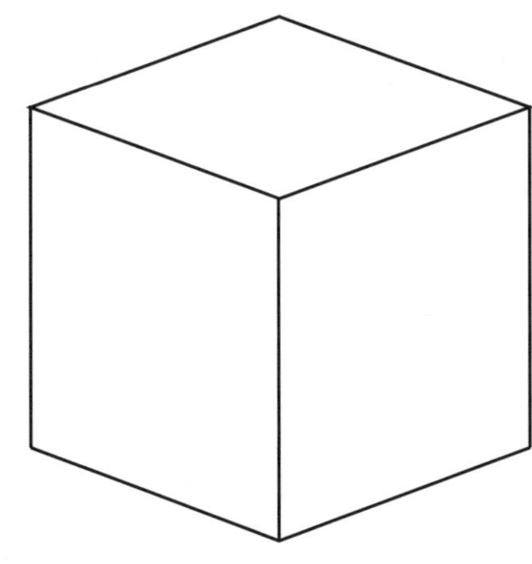

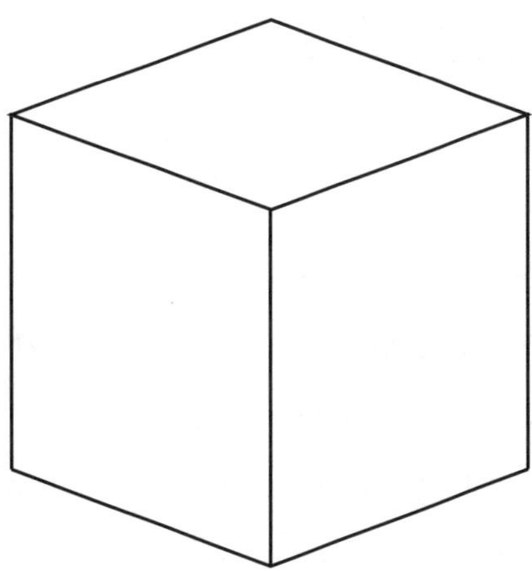

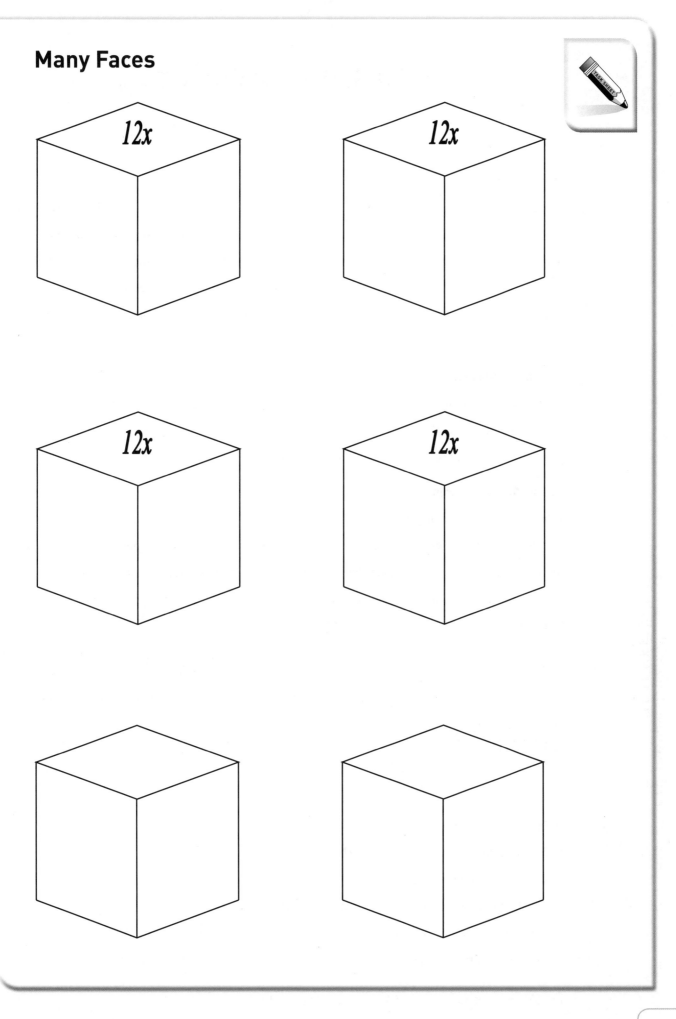

33 Maximum Product

Introduction

Recreational mathematics is full of digit-related problems. In some cases, expressing a two-digit number, say, as $28 = 2 \times 10 + 8$ or, more generally, 'ab' $= 10a + b$, leads to elegant solutions. The problem behind this lesson is a little different in that it calls for good estimation skills and gives plenty of opportunity to practise multiplication techniques while something a bit more interesting is going on. The better learners' number sense is, the fewer calculations they will have to do – a convenient bit of self-differentiation.

Aims and Outcomes

- practise multiplication methods
- use estimation to make sensible choices in problem solving
- use logical reasoning to find a maximal solution

Lesson Starter (10 min)

Which do you think is bigger, 21×3 or 31×2? Why?

Obviously you can just work them out and see that $63 > 62$, but can you explain in words why the same digits in different places make different answers and which one you would expect to be bigger?

This is quite hard. Rectangle area diagrams, such as the following, to represent multiplication, may be helpful:

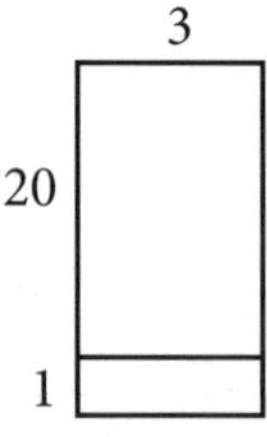

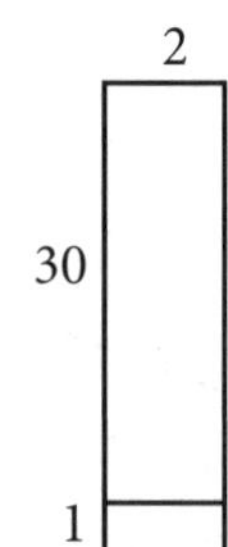

The top rectangles in each drawing are both of the same area (60), but the bottom rectangle is 3 in the left-hand drawing but only 2 in the right-hand one.

Main Lesson (25 min)

What about 32×4 versus 42×3? Which wins this time? Why?

Can you extend this pattern?

If you let the three digits be a, $a + 1$ and $a + 2$, then the two products come to $11a^2 + 31a + 20$ and $11a^2 + 32a + 20$, respectively, so the first one is therefore a more than the second one each time.

What other products can you make from the digits 1, 2 and 3, using each digit once?

1×23 $\quad$ 1×32 $\quad$ 2×13 $\quad$ (2×31) $\quad$ 3×12 $\quad$ (3×21)

Listing these systematically helps learners to avoid repeats or omissions.

Can you see straight away that any of these products are obviously bigger or smaller than any of the others, without working them out?

None of them beats $21 \times 3 = 63$, so that is the largest product possible using these three digits.

What if you have the numbers 1, 2, 3 and 4; still using each digit once?

Give out the Task Sheet and encourage learners to try to find the maximum possible product with 1, 2, 3 and 4. Then try increasing the number of digits involved, up to 1 to 9 eventually. Learners should be encouraged to see what patterns develop and to try to explain them.

Plenary (20 min)

The maximum possible products are:

123	$21 \times 3 = 63$
1234	$41 \times 32 = 1312$
12345	$431 \times 52 = 22\,412$
123456	$631 \times 542 = 342\,002$
1234567	$6531 \times 742 = 4\,846\,002$
12345678	$8531 \times 7642 = 65\,193\,902$
123456789	$87531 \times 9642 = 843\,973\,902$

There are various principles that might emerge, rather than a neat algebraic formula.

1. The two numbers should be of similar size (i.e., the same number of digits or only one different).
2. The values of the digits in each number must decrease from left to right.
3. The leading digits must be the two largest digits.
4. If the two numbers are of different lengths, the *largest* digit is most effective at the start of the *smaller* number.
5. Fill up the remaining digits in decreasing order of size, alternating between the two numbers, beginning with the one with the smaller leading digit.

You can illustrate the above algorithm for the digits 1 to 7 as follows:

Since we have an odd number of digits, the product must be 4-digit × 3-digit.

The 7 is more useful at the start of the three-digit number, so the next largest digit, the 6, must go at the beginning of the four-digit number.

So we have: 6 _ _ _ × 7 _ _.

Place the 5 next to the 6 (so that it multiplies the bigger 7 rather than the smaller 6):

6 5 _ _ × 7 _ _

Alternate the remaining digits between the two numbers:

$$6\,5\,3\,1 \times 7\,4\,2 = 4\,846\,002$$

Learners may not get all the way to the very best possible solutions, but they should be able to produce some sensible strategies and make some correct deductions about them. They could use logical reasoning to say that one thing is definitely going to be greater than something else.

Homework (5 min)

Learners could try to use the digits 1 to 9, once each, to make a fraction equal to $\frac{1}{2}$. Then try to make $\frac{1}{3}$, again using all the digits 1 to 9 once each. All fractions up to $\frac{1}{9}$ are possible. There are several possible answers, such as: $\frac{6729}{13458} = \frac{6792}{13584} = \frac{7329}{14658} = \frac{9273}{18546} = \frac{9327}{18654} = \frac{1}{2}$. Possible answers for the others are:

$\frac{5823}{17469} = \frac{5832}{17496} = \frac{1}{3}$

$\frac{3942}{15768} = \frac{4392}{17568} = \frac{5796}{23184} = \frac{7956}{31824} = \frac{1}{4}$

$\frac{2697}{13485} = \frac{1}{5}$, $\frac{2943}{17658} = \frac{4653}{27918} = \frac{5697}{34182} = \frac{1}{6}$

$\frac{2394}{16758} = \frac{2637}{18459} = \frac{4527}{31689} = \frac{1}{7}$

$\frac{3187}{25496} = \frac{4589}{36712} = \frac{4591}{36728} = \frac{6789}{54312} = \frac{1}{8}$

$\frac{6381}{57429} = \frac{6471}{58239} = \frac{1}{9}$

(With thanks to Dodd, P. (1998), *Some Puzzles – A Mathematical Resource Book*. UK: Dodd.)

To make it harder

Learners who cope well with this could be invited to pose their own digit-related problems, such as trying to make four square numbers from the digits 1 to 9, again using each digit once each.

In this case there are exactly five possible solutions:

1, 4, 9, 872356

4, 25, 81, 7396

9, 81, 324, 576

1, 36, 529, 784

9, 25, 361, 784

Another possible extension task would be to use the digits 1 to 9, once each, to make *two* products that have the same answer. A suitable 'clue', if necessary, would be to give one possible product: 3634. The multiplications would be $158 \times 23 = 79 \times 46 = 3634$.

To make it easier

A good way to keep the task manageable initially is to restrict the number of digits used.

Maximum Product

1 2 3 4 5 6 7 8 9

Using the digits 1 to 4, once each, form two numbers with the *maximum possible product*.

Then try using the digits 1 to 5, and so on.

Eventually, try using *all nine digits*.

What is the *maximum possible product* of two numbers together using all the digits 1 to 9?

This time, using the digits 1 to 9, once each, form two numbers with the *minimum possible product*.

Which do you think is easier, finding *maximum* products or *minimum* products? Why?

34 Monkeying Around

Introduction

When you ask learners to tell you the biggest number they know, you are likely to hear words like 'billion' and 'trillion' and even 'zillion' or 'gazillion', but learners don't always have much sense of their precise meanings– presuming that they have one! *Fermi problems*, in which learners make rough estimates of the orders of magnitude of different quantities, can lead to valuable practice in handling units, as well as logical thinking and estimation skills that are helpful in daily life, not to mention in checking that examination questions have probably been answered correctly!

Aims and Outcomes

- convert between different metric, imperial and other units
- estimate quantities by doing approximate calculations
- use standard form to represent very large or very small numbers

Lesson Starter (15 min)

Hold up an ordinary piece of A4 paper. *I want to fold this piece of paper in half, and half again, and so on.* (Do it, folding, say, four times.)

I'll give a merit (or whatever rewards system you operate) *for every fold you can do past fold eight.* Get learners to try it: they can start with a new piece of paper if they prefer.

They won't be able to fold more than seven or eight times. It is possible to fold a large enough sheet of paper up to 12 times, but in normal circumstances seven or eight times is the practical limit. If learners think that the 'seven or eight times rule' is a myth, they are welcome to try to prove it by folding more times! There will need to be rules about no *un*folding, of course (!), about folding the *whole thing* in half, not just part of it, and about keeping the folding going in the same direction each time. Negotiating the 'rules' is part of the fun.

If you could *fold the paper 100 times, how thick would it get?*

Learners may think that the answer is 100 times the thickness of the paper, but some thought shows that it is actually 2^{100} times the thickness of the paper, say 0.1 mm. This would make 1.3×10^{23} km – about 100 000 times the diameter of the Milky Way! For comparison, lower estimates for the size of the visible universe begin at around 8.8×10^{23} km!

Learners could see what difference making only 50 folds has. This time, $2^{50} \times 0.1$ mm $= 1.1 \times 10^{8}$ km, which is around one astronomical unit, the mean distance from the earth to the sun. Learners may also like to think about the *width* of this resulting stack of paper – slimmer than the estimated diameter of a proton!

Main Lesson (20 min)

Give out the Task Sheet and perhaps suggest that different learners (or groups of learners) begin at different places, so that at least one person tries each problem.

Commonly, learners will complain that they can't do a particular problem because they don't have the necessary information. Of course, one approach would be to go searching for the required numbers, perhaps on the internet, but alternatively it is possible to encourage learners to estimate (or guesstimate, if necessary) any numbers that they feel they need. This can help to make them more independent and cultivate greater initiative and a 'can do' attitude!

Plenary (20 min)

Learners could present their calculations on the board, under the scrutiny of their peers.

Where will you be in 1000 seconds?, etc.

One thousand seconds is $16\frac{2}{3}$ minutes, so learners may still be in their mathematics lesson (if they're lucky!), or in the lunch queue, etc., depending on the time of day.

One million seconds is about $11\frac{1}{2}$ days.

One billion seconds is about 32 years.

One trillion seconds is about 32 000 years!

How long would it take to count/write/type to 1 000 000?, etc.

Taking an average of three seconds to say each number would mean a total time of 3 000 000 seconds, which is about 35 days (assuming no sleep, etc.!). To count to one billion would take 1000-times longer – more, because you would need more than three seconds to say most of the numbers. This gives about 100 years! (If learners begin now they might just manage it before they die if they are lucky. The teacher is probably too old to make it now!) To count to one trillion would take over 100 000 years. This can be a helpful way to visualize the sizes of these huge numbers: 'a million in a month, a billion in a lifetime!'

What is the total of all the numbers from 1 to 1 000 000?

This is similar to the well-known 'Gauss-as-a-child' problem, where his teacher is said to have asked him to add up all the numbers from 1 to 100. There are many possible approaches, such as $\frac{1\,000\,000 \times 1\,000\,001}{2}$. Learners could be encouraged to estimate the rough size first.

What is the total of all the digits in all the numbers from 1 to 1 000 000? Why?

One way is to pair them up:

0	999 999
1	999 998
2	999 997

…

9 999 990

10 999 989

...

48 737 951 262

...

499 999 500 000

Then you have 500 000 pairs, each pair having a sum of 6×9, along with 1 000 000 left on its own, giving a total of $500\,000 \times 54 + 1 = 27\,000\,001$. In general, the sum of the digits in the integers from 1 to 10 is therefore $\frac{9n(10^n)}{2}+1$.

An extension to this would be to ask how many 1s, 2s, etc., there are when all the numbers from 1 to 1000 are written down. Alternatively, if a number from 1 to 1000 is chosen at random, what is the probability that it contains a 2, for example?

The first question is easier, because we just have to consider making three-digit numbers containing a 2. There are 10×10 possibilities for the remaining 2 digits, and the 2 can go in any of three positions (first digit, second digit or third digit), so there must be 300 possible occurrences of the number 2 (since 1000 doesn't contain a 2). This works because numbers like 262, for instance, are counted twice, so we are counting the total number of 2s, and there will be fewer actual numbers than this.

To find the number of numbers containing *at least one 2*, which is necessary for the second question, we can think about how many numbers from 1 to 1000 *don't* contain a 2. There are nine possibilities (0, 1, 3, 4, 5, 6, 7, 8 and 9) for each digit, so there will be 9^3 three-digit numbers, along with 1000 itself (which doesn't contain a 2), making $9^3 + 1 = 730$. So the number of numbers that *do* contain a 2 will be $1000 - 730 = 270$.

We can link these two answers together, because 27 of these 270 numbers will contain *two* 2s, because the third digit can be any of the nine numbers 0, 1, 3, 4, 5, 6, 7, 8 or 9, and each of these numbers (e.g., 262) can be written in three ways (e.g., 262, 622 and 226). So to find the number of 2s in all the numbers we need to add 27 to our total, making 297, and we also need to add three more to account for the number 222, which has three 2s, bringing the total to 300, as before.

This will be the same for all the other digits as well, except for 1 and 0. For 1, because 1000 contains a 1, the number of digit 1s will be one more (301) and the number of numbers containing a 1 will be $270 + 1 = 271$. Zero is problematic, because we probably wouldn't count leading 0s, so there are only 192 of them.

Homework (5 min)

Find out who Britney Gallivan is and what she did that was famous.

She was the first person to fold a strip of paper 9, 10, 11 and 12 times – something that was previously thought to be impossible.

To make it harder

A task for learners who want an extra challenge could be the following:

Have you ever heard anyone say this: 'If you have an infinite number of monkeys sitting at an infinite number of typewriters, eventually, by chance, they will type out the complete works of Shakespeare'? What point do you think is being made? Do you agree with it? Why / why not?

'Infinite' is hard to handle, but the age of the universe is thought to be about 14 billion years, so you could suppose that you had an average school full of monkeys available (say 1000?) and that a typewriter has around 50 keys. *How often might a monkey be able to press a key? Try working out the probability of getting the first 100 characters of* Hamlet *correct.*

Each time a key is struck at random, the probability of getting the right character is $\frac{1}{50}$, so (assuming the events are independent) the probability of getting 100 correct characters one after the other is $\left(\frac{1}{50}\right)^{100}$. If the monkeys strike keys on average once a second, that gives them about 4×10^{17} goes (given the age of the universe) so the expected number of 'successes' would be $(4 \times 10^{17}) \times \left(\frac{1}{50}\right)^{100} \times 1000 = \frac{4\times10^{20}}{50^{100}} = \frac{4\times10^{20}}{5^{100}\times10^{100}} \approx \frac{1}{5^{99}\times10^{80}}$, which is practically never! And that's just for the first 100 characters of one particular play! But then 1000 monkeys is a far cry from an infinite number of monkeys, you might say . . .

To make it easier

Using smaller numbers (such as 50 or 100) can be a more accessible start for learners who find 1 000 000 too daunting initially.

One Million = 1 000 000

Where will you be in 1000 seconds?

… in 1 000 000 seconds?

… in 1 000 000 000 seconds?

… in 1 000 000 000 000 seconds?

Why?

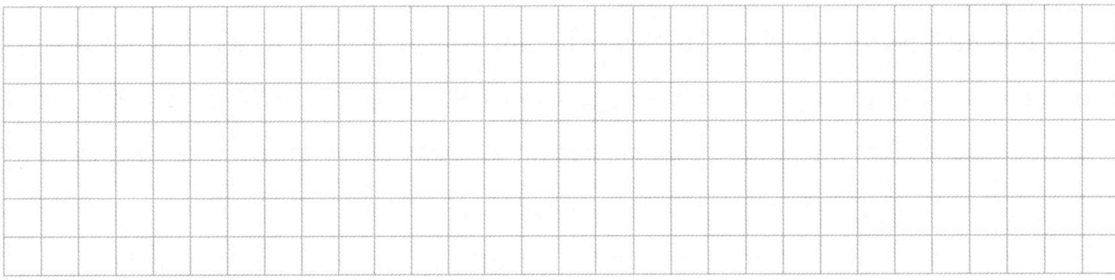

How long would it take to count to one million? Why?

Could someone do it in their lifetime? Why / why not?

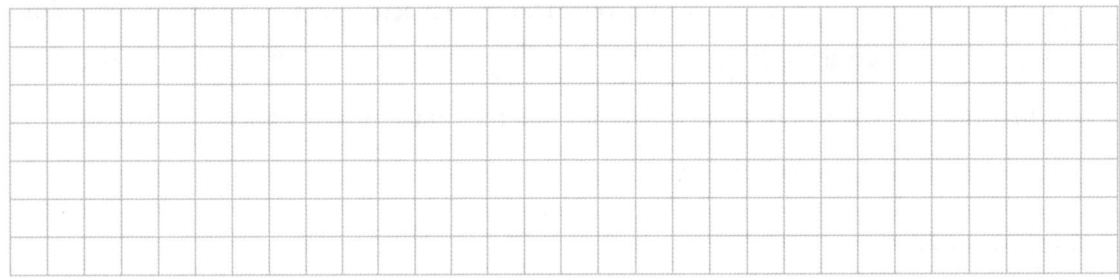

How long would it take to count to one billion? Why?

How long would it take to count to one trillion?

How long would it take to write or type all the integers from 1 to 1 000 000? Why?

What is the total of all the integers from 1 to 1 000 000? Why?

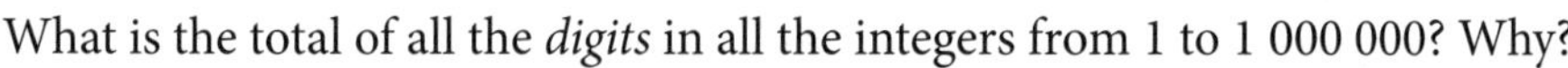
What is the total of all the *digits* in all the integers from 1 to 1 000 000? Why?

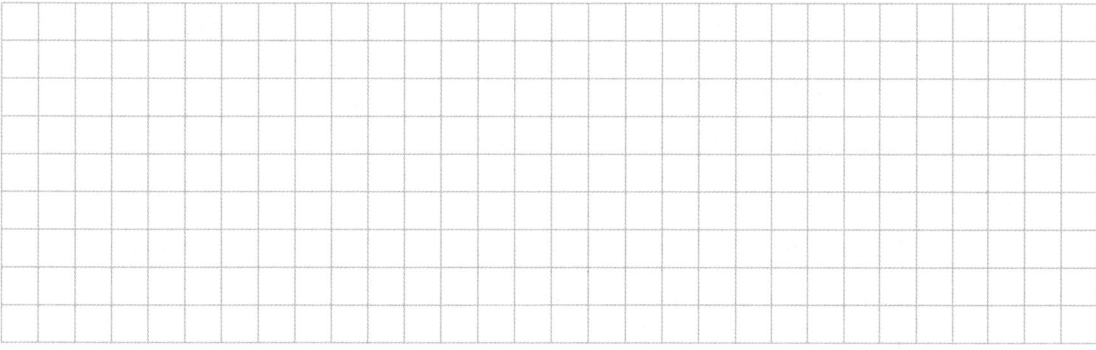

What other 'million' questions can you ask and answer?

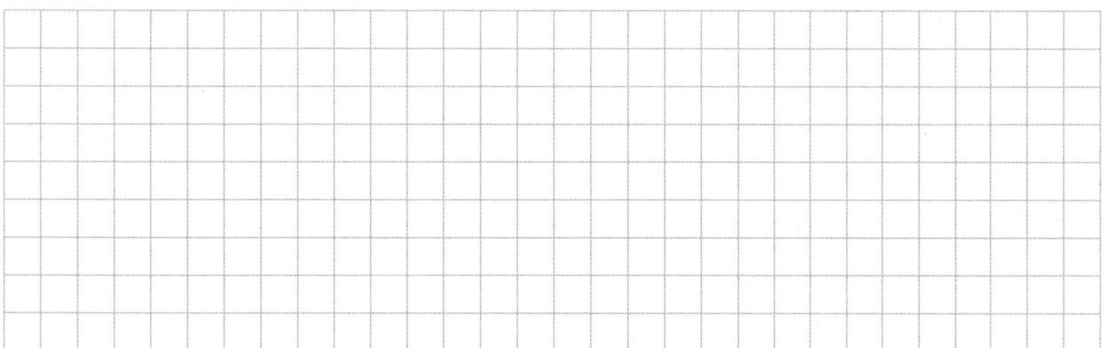

35 Odd Ones Out

Introduction

Simple-minded 'what's the odd one out?'-type questions are more psychological than mathematical. It comes down to trying to think how the person asking the question is most likely to be thinking. In the classroom this tends to lead to 'guess what's in the teacher's mind' and overly simplistic thinking. It also propagates the idea that there is always one right answer and that 'thinking outside the box' is bad. Instead, accepting that any member of a set of numbers could be the odd one out opens up many possibilities for creative mathematical thinking, which is what this lesson seeks to exploit.

Aims and Outcomes

- construct examples of mathematical objects which satisfy certain conditions
- find exceptions to general rules and anomalies within patterns

Lesson Starter (10 min)

Look at these numbers: 2, 3, 4, 5. Which one could be the 'odd one out' and why?

Try to think of a reason why each number could be the odd one out.

Learners can be very inventive when presented with this sort of task, so allow plenty of time for different kinds of answers to develop.

Possible answers (previously given by learners) include:

2 because it's the only even prime

2 because it's the only one for which you can't draw a polygon with that many sides

3 because it's the only non-factor of 20

3 because it's the only multiple of 3

3 because it's the only number with a reciprocal with a recurring decimal expansion

4 because it's the only numeral that can be written with straight line segments only

4 because it's the only square number

4 because it's the only composite (i.e., non-prime) number

5 because it's the only number that increases when rounded to the nearest 10

5 because it's the only number which is the sum of two of the others

5 because it's the only number you can write in Roman numerals without taking your pen off the paper

Main Lesson (25 min)

The mathematical objects don't have to be numbers – mathematics is more than just numeracy or arithmetic. What else do we work with in mathematics?

Learners might suggest shapes, algebraic expressions, functions, fractions, graphs, etc.

Give out the Task Sheet. You could ask different learners to work with different categories of object, for example:

four equations of straight-line graphs

four fractions

four surds

four triangles

four …

There should be plenty of challenge associated with choosing suitable sets of objects such that any one of them could be considered to be the odd one out without requiring reasons that are too contrived. Learners could try to order their sets of objects according to some notion of difficulty.

Plenary (20 min)

If each group puts their best two examples onto a sheet of paper, these could be passed around, each group passing on theirs to the next group in a cycle, so that everyone gets to try everyone else's problems. Then discussion could relate to which ones were easier or harder and why. Were there any disagreements about whether reasons were valid? Were highly contrived reasons thought to be acceptable? Why / why not?

Homework (5 min)

Learners could make a poster illustrating their four objects and why each one could be the odd one out.

They could also look for odd-one-out puzzles in books or on the internet and try to find alternative answers. Can they see any that could be genuinely misinterpreted? They could try to construct some deliberately ambiguous ones that have more than one reasonable answer.

To make it harder

This is a task that self-differentiates well, with more ambitious learners choosing to handle more complicated objects, or increasing the number of objects to five or more.

For example, which is the odd one out here?

$f(x) = x^3$ $\qquad f(x) = \frac{x}{x^2 - 1}$ $\qquad f(x) = \frac{1}{x}$ $\qquad f(x) = 3x - 1$ $\qquad f(x) = \frac{1}{x^2}$

Or here?

$f(x) = \sin x$ $f(x) = \cos x$ $f(x) = \tan x$ $f(x) = \sin^2 x$ $f(x) = \cos^2 x$

To make it easier

Learners could stay with positive integers as their objects and still have plenty to think about.

Odd Ones Out

Put four 'things' (e.g., numbers, expressions, statements or shapes) in the four boxes.

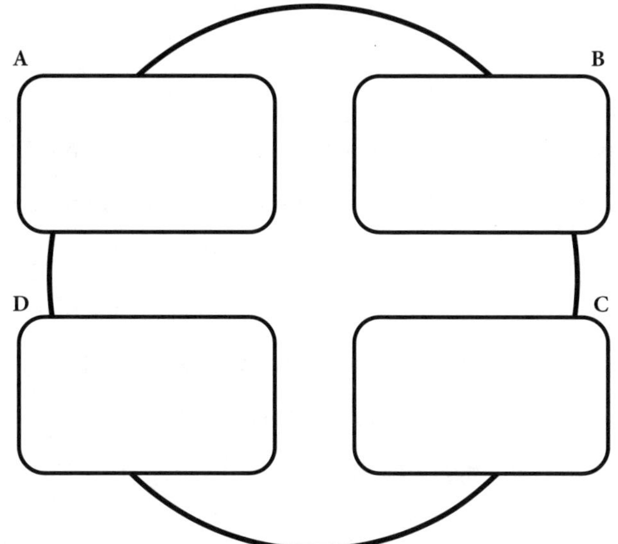

Find a reason why *each one* could be the odd one out.

Reason for **A** being the odd one out:

Reason for **B** being the odd one out:

Reason for **C** being the odd one out:

Reason for **D** being the odd one out:

36 Ordering Fractions

Introduction

Learners will have worked previously with visual representations of fractions, such as portions of shapes, fraction 'walls', pizzas/cake, discrete examples concerning sweets, etc. They may be less used to thinking of fractions as just numbers on a number line. Initially they may be uncomfortable talking about three-quarters, for example, as a number – they may want to ask 'three-quarters of what?' To answer 'three-quarters of one' might just compound the problem. If learners are happy that $\frac{3}{4} = 0.75$ then they may feel that 0.75 doesn't have to be 0.75 'of' anything, so perhaps $\frac{3}{4}$ doesn't have to be either. Fractions are just numbers.

Aims and Outcomes

- add and subtract fractions by using a common denominator
- add and subtract mixed numbers
- compare the sizes of fractions using a common denominator

Lesson Starter (15 min)

Draw the following line on the board (or use whiteboard software or a physical washing line, etc.):

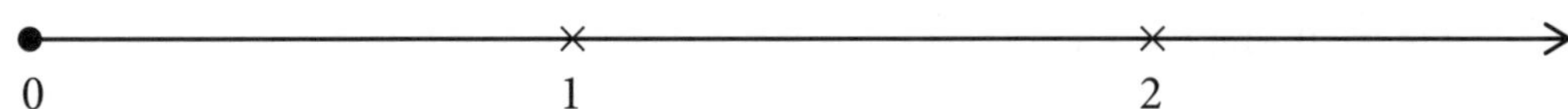

Think of a fraction *that goes somewhere along this line and come and mark it on the board.*

How do you know it goes there? Can you convince us? Do you agree with so-and-so's position? Why / why not? Does this one need moving a bit? Why? etc.

If learners offer decimals instead of fractions, see if the class can convert them into fractions.

Learners may need encouragement to find fractions that will go in particular gaps or, perhaps, anywhere greater than 1. Some learners may want to put $\frac{1}{2}$ at the midpoint of the whole line. If disagreements arise, they should be resolved by learners defending their views and explaining rather than by the teacher 'pulling rank'. The only rule is that it has to make sense.

Main Lesson (25 min)

With several fractions, such as $\frac{2}{3}$, $1\frac{1}{4}$ and $1\frac{4}{5}$, on the board, start asking questions like these (using whatever fractions are on the board at this stage):

Which fraction is closer to $1\frac{1}{4}$*? Is it* $\frac{2}{3}$ *or* $1\frac{4}{5}$*?* (Suggest fractions either side.) *Why?*

Which two fractions are $\frac{11}{20}$ apart?
Which fraction is $\frac{1}{4}$ more/less than $\frac{2}{3}$?
What other questions like this can you ask?

Different strategies may become apparent, such as finding equivalent fractions with a common denominator, or converting to decimals – which can be thought of as a bit like finding a common denominator of 1. Learners may be more comfortable treating the fractions as fractions *of* some convenient number, such as 60, which might be a reason for doing it initially and then trying to avoid it later. If learners are working in groups, they may be able to compare each other's approaches.

Give learners the Task Sheet and ask them to work on the questions.

Plenary (15 min)

Which methods did you find most useful? When? Why?

When is converting to decimals helpful/unhelpful? Why?

Which sorts of problems were easiest/hardest to do? Why do you think that was?

How can you make a harder problem easier or an easier problem harder? Can you give an example?

The fractions in order are: $\frac{2}{5}$, $\frac{3}{4}$, $\frac{4}{5}$, $1\frac{1}{3}$, $1\frac{1}{2}$, $2\frac{1}{4}$.

The pair with the biggest gap is obviously the first and the last ($\frac{2}{5}$ and $2\frac{1}{4}$), but if the question is interpreted as the *consecutive* pair with the biggest gap then it is $1\frac{1}{2}$ and $2\frac{1}{4}$, which are $\frac{3}{4}$ apart.

The pair closest together is $\frac{3}{4}$ and $\frac{4}{5}$, which have a gap of $\frac{1}{20}$.

The two with the biggest total will be the largest two: $1\frac{1}{2} + 2\frac{1}{4} = 3\frac{3}{4}$.

Homework (5 min)

Repeat the exercise on the Task Sheet choosing a *different* set of six fractions, either an easier six or a harder six, depending on what learners are comfortable with.

What other questions can learners ask about their set of fractions?

Do some sets of fractions seem to lead to more questions than others? Why?

To make it harder

Harder numbers will make the procedures more difficult. Venturing left of the zero mark will allow able learners to work with directed fractions and to invent quite challenging problems. Learners familiar with Pythagoras' Theorem could try to find the distance from $(\frac{3}{4}, \frac{2}{5})$ to $(1\frac{4}{5}, 2\frac{2}{3})$ and other similar problems.

The distance would be $\sqrt{\left(1\frac{4}{5}-\frac{3}{4}\right)^2+\left(2\frac{2}{3}-\frac{2}{5}\right)^2}=\sqrt{\left(\frac{21}{20}\right)^2+\left(\frac{34}{15}\right)^2}$ = 2.50 (correct to 2 significant figures). Quite a lot of different operations are necessary here, so problems such as this can be demanding. Learners could estimate approximate answers by visualizing the points to make sure that their final numbers are reasonable.

To make it easier

Learners experiencing difficulties might be happier sticking to fractions of the family $\frac{a}{2^b}$ (where a and b are small positive integers); i.e.: $\frac{1}{2}$, $\frac{1}{4}$, $\frac{3}{4}$, $\frac{1}{8}$, $\frac{3}{8}$, $\frac{5}{8}$, $\frac{7}{8}$, etc.

Fractions

As accurately as you can, mark these six fractions on the number line below:

$\frac{2}{5}$ $\quad 2\frac{1}{4}$ $\quad 1\frac{1}{2}$ $\quad 1\frac{1}{3}$ $\quad \frac{4}{5}$ $\quad \frac{3}{4}$

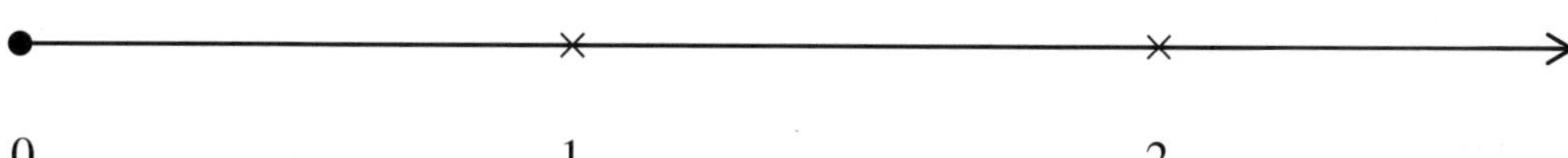

Use these six fractions for the rest of the questions on this sheet.

Explain how you decided on the positions above.

Are there any you are less sure about? Why?

Which pair of these fractions has the *biggest gap* between them?

How do you know?

Which pair of these fractions has the *smallest gap* between them?

How can you be sure?

Which pair of these fractions has the biggest *total*?

How do you know?

Choose any *three* of these fractions and work out their *total*.

Which set of three fractions do you think is *easiest*? Why?

Which set of three fractions do you think is *hardest*? Why?

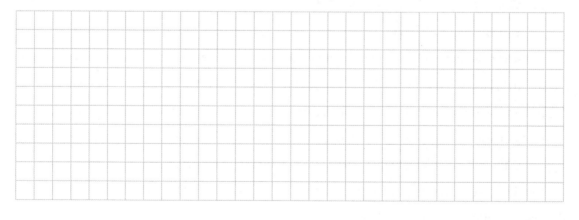

37

Percentage Increases and Decreases

Introduction

The topic of percentage increase and decrease is ripe for misconceptions, conundrums and paradoxes, and it is an important area to be comfortable with in daily life, given the prevalence of percentage-off offers and interest rates. Learners normally initially encounter percentages in school by finding 10 per cent or 1 per cent of an amount by dividing by 10 or 100, so it is natural to think of percentage increases or decreases as the addition or subtraction of a certain amount. This lesson may be an opportunity for some learners to move to a scale-factor (multiplier) approach, which can be much more helpful when thinking about repeated percentage change, such as five years of 2 per cent per annum interest involving multiplication by a factor of 1.02^5.

Aims and Outcomes

- understand and calculate percentage increase and decrease
- understand and calculate repeated percentage change

Lesson Starter (15 min)

A woman takes her friends out for a special dinner and spends £80. She pays a 10 per cent service charge but she's also got a 20 per cent off coupon. Should she get the 20 per cent off first and then pay the 10 per cent or should she pay the 10 per cent first and then get the 20 per cent off? Which way do you think will lead to the smaller total bill? Why?

Learners frequently argue a great deal over this. If you pay the 10 per cent charge first, your 20 per cent reduction will be of a bigger amount, so you get more off, but you were paying more in the first place. On the other hand, if you get the 20 per cent off first, your service charge will be 10 per cent of a smaller amount. In fact, these two factors exactly cancel out. If the bill is £80, in the first scenario she will pay $80 \times 1.1 \times 0.8 =$ £70.40 and in the second case she will pay $80 \times 0.8 \times 1.1 =$ £70.40, so it doesn't matter, at least as far as the customer's payment is concerned – although it could be that the serving staff would get £8 rather than £6.40, if their 10 per cent were worked out first, which the customer might or might not prefer!

Main Lesson (20 min)

Give out the Task Sheet and encourage learners to involve themselves in both tasks. You might want to discuss the first one briefly before they work on the carpet advertisement.

Plenary (20)

You could have two separate plenaries to discuss the two tasks, or combine both into one.

50 per cent off

The cartoon man thinks that two lots of 50 per cent reduction will be 100 per cent reduction and he will have nothing to pay! Really, if a price were reduced by 50 per cent twice that would be equivalent to paying 25 per cent (75 per cent off), but actually he will get 50 per cent off both items, so it will still be 50 per cent off – equivalent to buying one and getting one free. As people say: 'If something seems too good to be true, it probably is!'

The carpet advertisement

Learners may be surprised that '50 per cent off then another 20 per cent off' is exactly equivalent to '20 per cent off then another 50 per cent off'. If they feel that these should lead to different outcomes, you could ask them which they think would be a bigger reduction and why. Seeing percentage reductions multiplicatively (rather than as subtractions) makes it easier to see that because multiplication is commutative it doesn't matter whether we do $\times 0.5 \times 0.8$ or $\times 0.8 \times 0.5$.

$$£300 \rightarrow £150 \rightarrow £120$$

This is £180 off altogether, which, expressed as a percentage of the original £300, is 60 per cent off. '50 per cent followed by 20 per cent' sounds more like 70 per cent than 60 per cent, so there is a tendency for the advertisement to *exaggerate* the reduction.

More generally, $0.5 \times 0.8 = 0.4$, so the offer is equivalent to 60 per cent off regardless of the starting price.

A 50 per cent reduction followed by a 40 per cent reduction is equivalent to 70 per cent off because $0.5 \times 0.6 = 0.3$.

A 50 per cent reduction followed by a 60 per cent reduction is equivalent to 80 per cent off because $0.5 \times 0.4 = 0.2$.

In general, for a p% overall percentage decrease, you need a 50 per cent decrease followed by a $(2p - 100)$% decrease. This will be negative if $p < 50$, because the overall percentage decrease cannot be smaller than the 50 per cent decrease that we have at the first stage!

Generalizing further, an a% decrease followed by a b% decrease is equivalent to a $\left(a+b-\frac{ab}{100}\right)\%$ decrease.

Homework (5 min)

Look for (and bring in to school if possible) advertisements quoting percentages in some way. Do you think the advertisements present the offers fairly and clearly? Why / why not?

To make it harder

Learners who are comfortable with percentage changes could try to find out how many 10 per cent reductions are necessary to reduce something to half its original value. This is equivalent to solving the equation $0.9^x = 0.5$, which can be done by trial and improvement or, if learners know about them, by logarithms. The answer is $x = 6.58$ (correct to 2 decimal places), so seven 10 per cent reductions would be necessary. Learners could invent similar problems, such as 'How many 50 per cent reductions are needed to decimate (i.e., reduce to one-tenth of its original value) something?' (The answer is four.)

To make it easier

Working with 10 per cent off may be helpful for those who find percentages difficult to access. *What happens if you do 10 per cent off and then another 10 per cent off – is it the same as 20 per cent off? Why / why not?*

Ten per cent off, followed by another 10 per cent off, is only 19 per cent off, because the second 10 per cent is smaller than the first 10 per cent, since it is 10 per cent of a smaller amount. The reverse of this situation, with percentage increases, is the idea behind compound interest.

Multipliers and What They Do!

multiplier	what it does
0.00	100% decrease (all gone!)
0.05	95% decrease
0.10	90% decrease
0.15	85% decrease
0.20	80% decrease
0.25	75% decrease
0.30	70% decrease
0.35	65% decrease
0.40	60% decrease
0.45	55% decrease
0.50	50% decrease
0.55	45% decrease
0.60	40% decrease
0.65	35% decrease
0.70	30% decrease
0.75	25% decrease
0.80	20% decrease
0.85	15% decrease
0.90	10% decrease
0.95	5% decrease
1.00	stays the same (no change!)
1.05	5% increase
1.10	10% increase
1.15	15% increase
1.20	20% increase
1.25	25% increase
1.30	30% increase
1.35	35% increase
1.40	40% increase
1.45	45% increase
1.50	50% increase
1.55	55% increase
1.60	60% increase
1.65	65% increase
1.70	70% increase
1.75	75% increase
1.80	80% increase
1.85	85% increase
1.90	90% increase
1.95	95% increase
2.00	100% increase (doubles it!)
2.05	105% increase

(Obviously the in-between values work in the same way.)

Percentages

© Megan Gay

SALE

50% off

Why does she think that?

Is she right? Why / why not?

Is it true to say that 2 × 50% = 100%? Why / why not?

This is a real advertisement for a sale at a carpet company:

Start with a carpet costing £300.

How much does it cost after '50% off'?

How much does it cost after 'an extra 20% off' this?

How much 'percentage off' is the final amount from the original £300?

Now change the advertisement.

Keep the 50% decrease but change the 20% to something else and see what happens to the overall percentage decrease.

Work out what the 20% has to change to so that the overall percentage decrease is 70%.

Find a connection between the value for the 20% (the decrease in the second step) and the overall percentage decrease. (Keep the 50% the same.)

Find a pair of percentage decreases which overall make a percentage decrease of 80%.

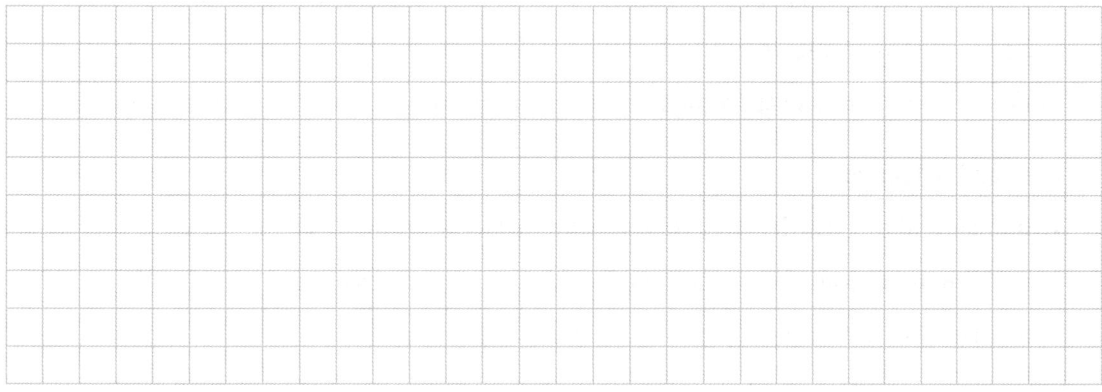

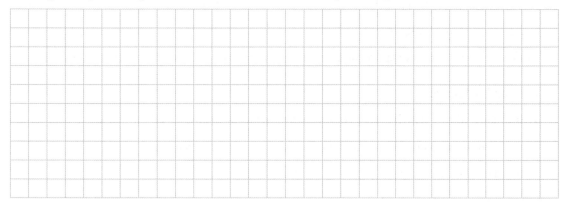

Generalize as far as you can.

Why do you think the company chose to advertise their offer in this way?

Did you notice the tiny words 'up to' over the large '50%'?

What is your opinion about this advertisement?

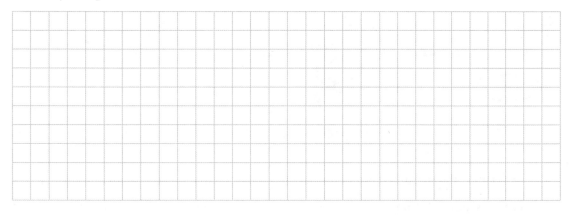

With thanks to the carpet company, who wish to remain anonymous, for permission to reproduce their advertisement.

38 Pint Cone

Introduction

It is well known that people tend to underestimate volumes, yet it still may seem unlikely that a cone (with a lid) made from a single sheet of (waterproof!) A4 paper could hold a pint of liquid. Textbooks frequently ask learners to calculate volumes and surface areas of various arbitrary solids without necessarily helping them to gain a sense of how big or small the answers should be. This makes it very hard for learners to tell whether the final answer is about the right size. 3D practical work can help learners to appreciate how much, for instance, 500 cm^3 of volume 'feels like'.

Aims and Outcomes

- estimate and calculate lengths, volumes and surface areas in 3D solids
- use formulae for calculating the volume and surface area of a cone
- use mathematical reasoning to solve a maximization problem

Lesson Starter (10 min)

You could begin with some mental imagery: *What do you get if you unravel a cone?* (This is not meant to sound like a joke!) *Imagine slicing from the vertex to the bottom and opening out the surface.* Another way to phrase the question is to ask: *What is the net of a cone? Can you describe the shape/draw it/name it?*

You end up with a *sector* of a circle, plus a whole circle for the base, if you're including that.

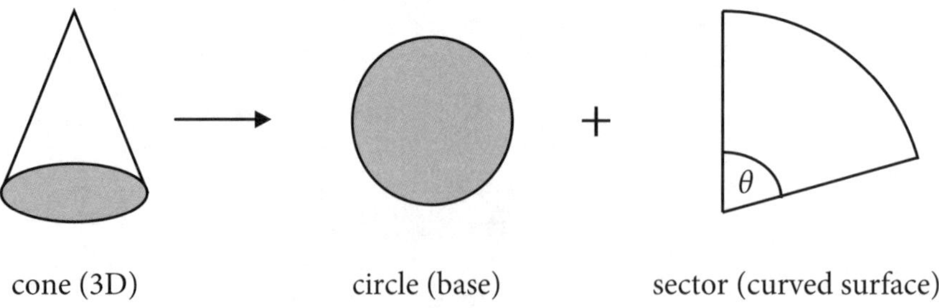

cone (3D) circle (base) sector (curved surface)

To fit together, the circumference of the base has to be equal to the arc length of the sector.

Learners may feel strongly that the sector is in fact a triangle or that the angle θ must be a certain value, such as 60° or 90°, or that *two* pieces are necessary ('front' and 'back'), or perhaps that the curved surface will be impossible to lay out flat (like that of a sphere, for instance). These misconceptions will be addressed as the lesson proceeds, so it is not necessary to try to win the arguments at this stage! It can be quite counterintuitive that a cone has a flat circular bottom that can stand on a table and yet its circumference fits exactly against an arc from a sector of another (larger) circle.

Main Lesson (25 min)

Give out the Task Sheet and encourage learners to work on the problem. Scissors, compasses, etc., may or may not be helpful. Some learners, or groups of learners, might challenge themselves to try to do it solely from sketches, with no accurate drawing or measurement. They would need to know that A4 paper is 21 cm by 29.7 cm. A compromise is to use paper and scissors to get a feel for the problem, but to avoid trying to make accurate cones and use calculation instead.

Plenary (20 min)

Taking the 21 cm side as the radius of a sector with $\theta = 90°$ gives a base circumference of $\frac{21\pi}{2}$, meaning that the base radius must be 5.25 cm. A circle with this radius (shaded below) will comfortably fit into the space left on the A4 sheet:

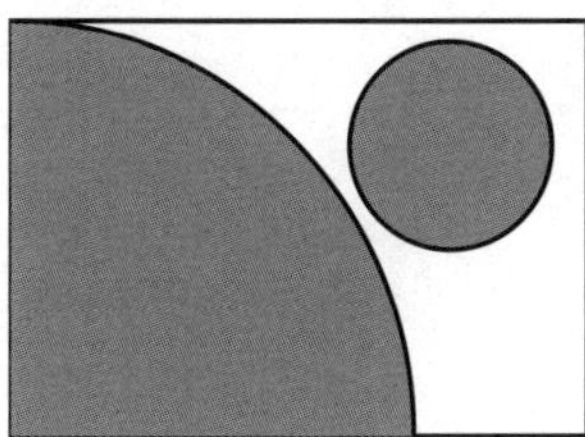

Using Pythagoras' Theorem, the height of the cone is $\frac{21\sqrt{15}}{4}$ cm, giving a volume of 586.9 cm^3, correct to 1 decimal place – a little more than one pint (568 ml). Other answers are possible. *Is there any advantage to using a smaller* θ *and bigger* r*? Why / why not?*

Homework (5 min)

Learners could try to find the *cylinder* with the largest possible volume they can cut out from a piece of A4 paper. *Which way round do you think it is better to make the cylinder? Long and thin or short and fat? Does it make a difference if circular ends have to be cut out as well?*

If learners roll the A4 paper 'long ways', then the 21 cm side becomes the circumference of the end of the cylinder (radius r, height h), giving a volume of $\pi r^2 h = \pi\left(\frac{21}{2\pi}\right)^2\left(21\sqrt{2}\right) = \frac{21^3\sqrt{2}}{4\pi} = 1042.229$ cm^3 (correct to 3 decimal places), whereas if they roll the paper 'short ways', then it is the 29.7 cm side that becomes the circumference of the end of the cylinder, giving a volume of $\pi\left(\frac{21\sqrt{2}}{2\pi}\right)^2 21 = \frac{21^3}{2\pi}$ = 1473.934 cm^3 (correct to 3 decimal places). So the short fat cylinder has an almost 50 per cent larger volume than the tall thin one.

To make it harder

Learners who manage this task quickly could consider volume and area scale factors. For example, how large a piece of paper would be necessary to make a *two*-pint cone? How large a volume of cone could be made from an *A3* piece of paper?

A two-pint cone would need a scaling up by a linear scale factor of $\sqrt[3]{2}$, or about a 25 per cent increase. A3 paper has twice the area of A4 paper, so could produce a cone with volume $\left(\sqrt{2}\right)^3 = 2\sqrt{2}$ times bigger, about a 180 per cent increase.

To make it easier

Learners who find this hard could spend longer making and calculating the volume for a few specific cones.

Pint Cone

What is the largest volume cone you can make out of one sheet of A4 paper?

What if you have to include a circular 'top' as well (shaded below)?

Can you make a cone that will hold *one pint* (568 ml)? Why / why not?

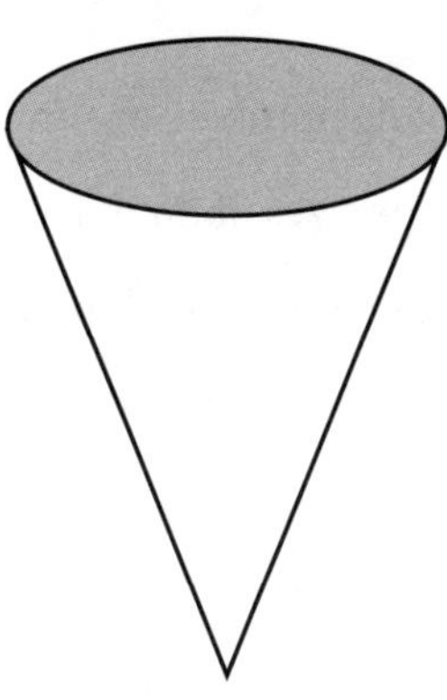

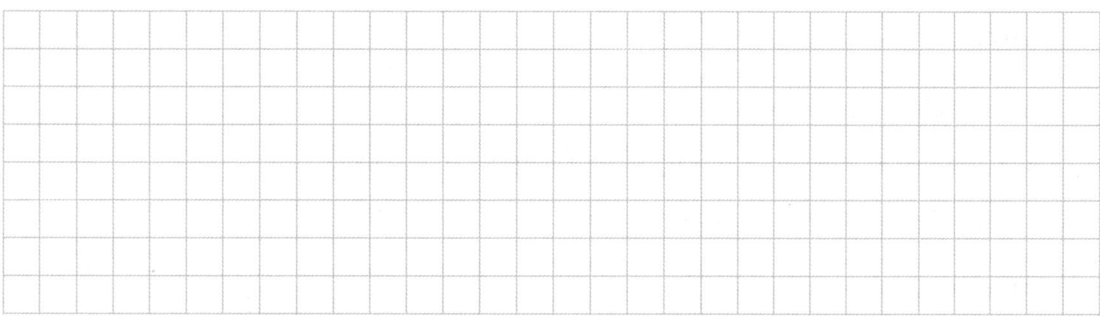

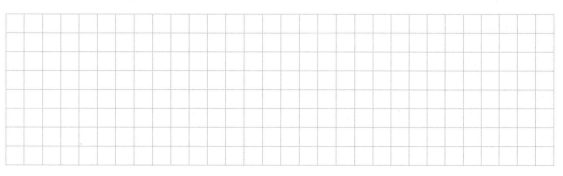

What flat shapes do you get if you unravel a cone?

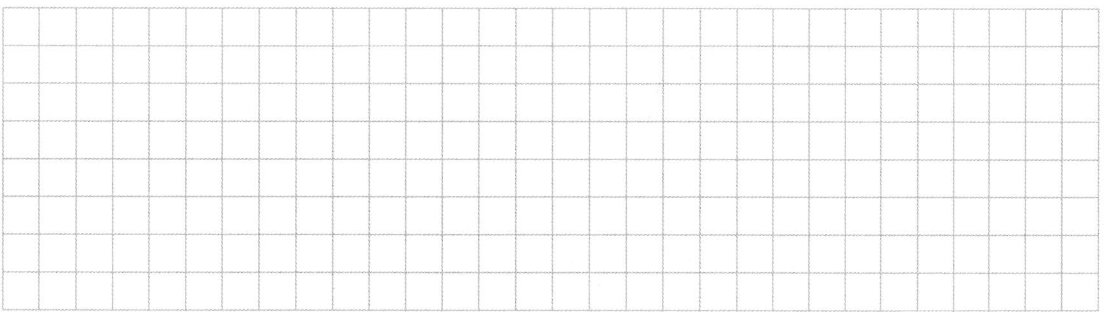

What measurements will these pieces need to make a cone with the biggest possible volume? Why?

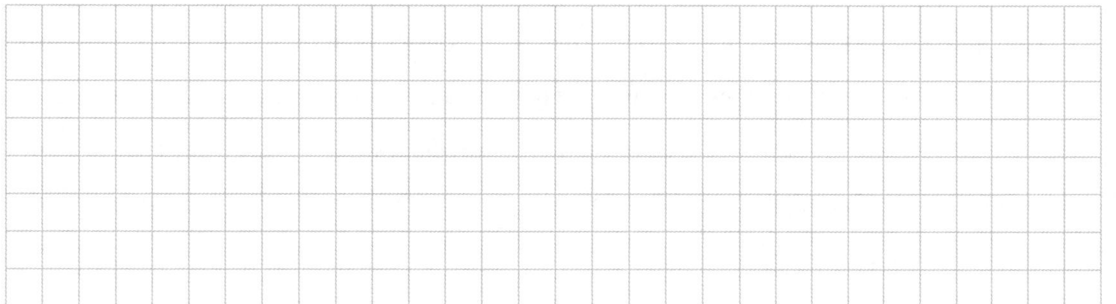

39 Polygon Areas

Introduction

It is possible for learners to work through routine exercises on area, multiplying numbers together or substituting into formulae without much sense of what area *is* or whether the sizes of their answers are reasonable. Textbook questions frequently present a lot of very similar-looking rectangles or triangles, for example, with highly varying dimensions (by factors of 10 or 100, perhaps) marked on the sides. People often find it very difficult to estimate the area of a shape by looking – much harder than estimating length. In this lesson, by using quite complicated shapes, and allowing for different methods, learners are encouraged to develop more of a feel for how small an area such as 10 cm^2, say, is.

Aims and Outcomes

- find the area of polygons made up from triangles and rectangles
- find the area of triangles given two sides and an included angle

Lesson Starter (10 min)

Display or draw the shape below.

Say what you see. You could do this in groups, pairs or whole-class.

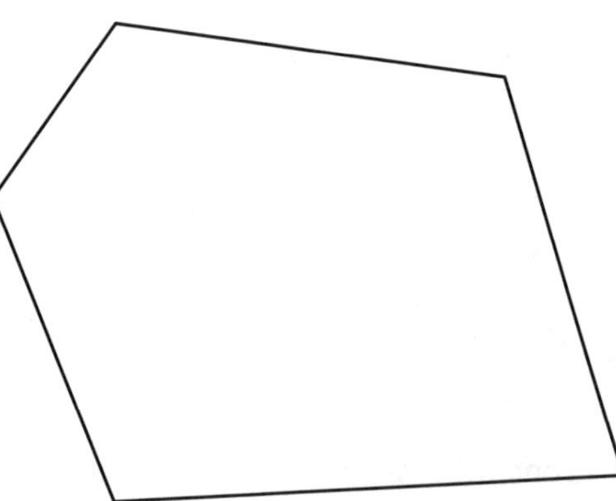

Many different observations are possible, such as 'A house blown over in the wind!' or regarding relationships between the sides or angles. Maybe it's a 2D projection of a 3D shape? Encourage clarity in learners' descriptions: *Did you understand what so-and-so just said? Can you put it in your own words?* You might also wish to take the opportunity to use and encourage learners to use correct mathematical vocabulary.

Main Lesson (25 min)

What do we mean in maths by 'area'*? Would it be possible to work it out for this shape* (the polygon used in the starter)? *Perimeter* would be pretty easy with a ruler, but area is much harder. Ask learners, perhaps in groups or pairs, to think about their strategies.

Then give out the Task Sheet and let learners work individually or in groups. You might want to mention that the shapes are drawn accurately, especially if learners have recently been working on tasks involving 'mathematical sketches'. Learners could estimate the areas first, or at least attempt to order the shapes by area, before they begin any calculations.

Some might begin with angles, lengths and perimeter. Others might go straight to area.

Possible approaches could include:

- tracing onto squared paper and counting squares and part-squares
- imposing a rectangle (or some other convenient shape) on top so that the 'stick-out' bits and 'stick-in' bits roughly cancel each other out
- distorting the shape so that some sides are parallel, so making it easier to work with (but will that affect the area, and if so how?)
- enclosing the shape in a rectangle (or rectilinear shape) and subtracting the areas of the shapes around the edge
- dividing the shape into triangles and using area $= \frac{1}{2}ab\sin C$, if learners know that formula. (In how many different ways can this be done? Why? Are the answers the same?)

Do any of the learners notice that one of the shapes on the Task Sheet can be made by combining three of the others?

Plenary (20 min)

Compare answers and discuss different approaches. *Which ideas generalize well to other shapes and which seem more like specific 'tricks' for a particular one?*

The order of the shapes by area, along with approximate values, is:

shape	C	D	B	F	E	A
area (cm^2)	3	8	9	20	21	33

Of course, if you photocopy the task sheet onto A3 paper, then all these values will be doubled.

Shape *F* is composed of shapes *B*, *C* and *D* glued together (without any overlaps), so its area is the sum of the areas of those three shapes.

Homework (5 min)

Draw your own shape and find its area. Try to make it at least as challenging as the one we started with. You could try to make an 'easy-if-you-know-how' shape that isn't obvious at first sight. Learners could make posters illustrating their method of calculating the area.

To make it harder

More challenging shapes are easy to make. Rather than it becoming the teacher's task to invent complex shapes, learners could be asked to come up with a sequence of progressively more difficult shapes, with solutions, and to justify their ordering of difficulty. The shapes should still be polygons, but might have various shaped holes missing, for example.

Learners seeking an extra challenge might consider how accurately they can state their final answers. If they have worked out the same shape in more than one way, which method do they think is the most reliable and why?

Confident learners might be encouraged to find out what *Bretschneider's Formula* is and to try it out on some shapes. Heron's formula would be a simpler alternative.

To make it easier

An easier starting point would be a non-right-angled triangle, which learners could perhaps divide into two right-angled triangles to find the area.

Areas

(These shapes *are* drawn accurately.)

What mathematical things can you say about each of these shapes?

How accurately can you work out their areas?

Which do you think are easier and which harder? Why?

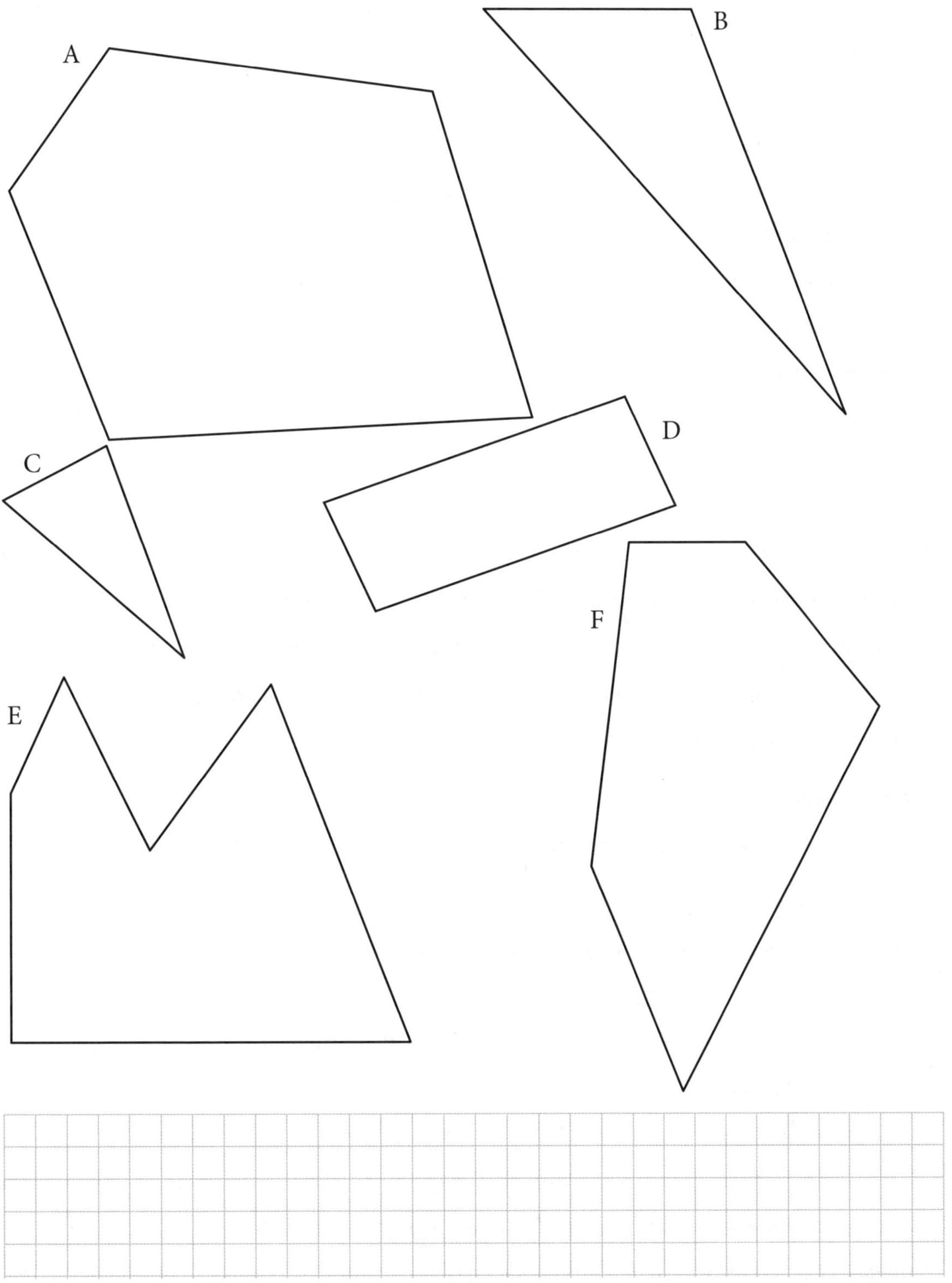

40 Prime Numbers

Introduction

The most common definition of a prime number used in school seems to be 'an integer whose only factors are one and itself', which unfortunately leaves open the question of whether one is itself a prime number. Until the nineteenth century most mathematicians regarded one as a prime number – Henri Lebesgue (1875–1941) is often said to be the last professional mathematician to call one prime – so it is a little unfair to regard learners as silly for thinking this today, or for questioning why we do not now regard one as a prime number – it is still a good question. Some people get around the problem by defining a prime number as 'a positive integer with exactly two factors', so that one, with only one factor, doesn't have enough factors to be a prime number. Sometimes teachers say that one is a square number and that square numbers are never prime, but a better answer is to talk about *unique factorization* – the idea that any number can be expressed as a product of powers of prime numbers in *only one way*. So 175, for example, is $5^2 \times 7$ and, other than reordering the factors (7×5^2 or $5 \times 7 \times 5$), there is no other possible way of factorizing it into primes. This turns out to be really useful, and allowing 1 to count as a prime number would mess this up, because you could write $175 = 1 \times 5^2 \times 7$ or $1^{38} \times 5^2 \times 7$, etc., and there would be infinitely many possible prime factorizations, which would be inconvenient. This is helpful because it links to a topic (prime factorization), which exposes the power of prime numbers as the building blocks of all numbers, somewhat like the periodic table of the elements in chemistry. Multiplicatively, 1 is not a useful building block!

Aims and Outcomes

- appreciate the wonder of prime numbers, the building blocks of all the integers

Lesson Starter (10 min)

What is a prime number? Can you give some examples?

Is 1 a prime number? Why / why not? (See above.)

How many prime numbers are there? Do you think that they go on forever? Why / why not?

You could mention *Euclid's proof*:

Imagine that you think you have all the prime numbers that there are and you write them down in a list. This is supposed to be a complete list of all the prime numbers – there aren't any others. Multiply all these numbers together and add one. Then think about this number that you get. None of your prime numbers on your list will go into this number. (Why not? Because dividing by any of these numbers will leave a remainder of 1.) So either this resulting number is prime itself, or there must be at least two other prime numbers that go into it which are not on our list. Either way, there are more prime numbers than we had at the beginning. In other words, however many prime numbers you have, there will always be more. So the prime numbers must go on forever.

See if learners can express this in their own words. A common error is to think that 'the product plus one' has to be prime, but this is not necessarily the case. The first occasion where you get a non-prime is $2 \times 3 \times 5 \times 7 \times 11 \times 13 + 1 = 30\,031$, because $30\,031 = 59 \times 509$.

Main Lesson (25 min)

Give learners the Task Sheet and invite them to colour in:

- all the multiples of two, except two
- all the multiples of three, except three

Do we need to do the multiples of four? Why not?

They are all already coloured in, since all multiples of four are necessarily multiples of two.

- all the multiples of five, except five
- . . . and so on, until only prime numbers are left.

Learners need to colour in only multiples of primes (except the first multiple, in each case).

At what stage will you be able to stop? Why?

This process is known as the *Sieve of Eratosthenes.*

Exploring *Bertrand's postulate* (actually, now a theorem, since it was proved by Chebyshev, so it is sometimes called the *Bertrand–Chebyshev Theorem*) can be an interesting task to pursue. The idea is to think of any integer greater than 1 and double it. The theorem says than in between these two numbers there will be *at least one prime.* For example, if you choose 10, double 10 is 20, and in between 10 and 20 there are four prime numbers (11, 13, 17 and 19), so at least one.

Another avenue to explore would be Goldbach's conjecture, still unproved and considered one of the big unsolved problems in mathematics. It says that every integer greater than 2 can be made by adding up exactly two prime numbers. For example, if you pick 10 you can make it from $3 + 7$. A good task is to write out 'Goldbach partitions' for the positive integers up to 20, say.

Plenary (20 min)

The missing primes from the list are: 11, 13, 17, 19, 23, 29, 31, 37, 41, 43, 47, 53, 59, 61, 67, 71, 73, 79, 83, 89, 97, 101, 103, 107, 109 and 113.

Can you explain in words what is special about the prime numbers?

Where do the prime numbers come in the table? Why?

All positive integers can be thought of as either $6n$, $6n + 1$, $6n + 2$, $6n + 3$, $6n + 4$ or $6n + 5$ (why not $6n + 6$?), where n is any positive integer. *Try to factorize these. Which ones factorize?* E.g., $6n + 2 = 2(3n + 1)$. So (apart from 2 and 3) prime numbers are always one more or one less than a multiple of six, so they have to come in either the fourth or the sixth columns of our table.

Homework (5 min)

Have a look at http://ptolemy.co.uk/primitives/primitives-application. Can you predict the next drawing? For which of the drawings is there more than one possibility? Why?

To make it harder

Keen learners could find out about the *Twin Prime Conjecture. Why is it called a 'conjecture' rather than a 'theorem'?* Because it has *still* not been proved to be true.

Find out how many digits the largest known prime number has. About 12 million, at the time of writing.

To make it easier

Counters or cubes could be a support to learners who are unsure about integers and their factors.

Prime Numbers

(2)	(3)	4	(5)	6	(7)
8	9	10	11	12	13
14	15	16	17	18	19
20	21	22	23	24	25
26	27	28	29	30	31
32	33	34	35	36	37
38	39	40	41	42	43
44	45	46	47	48	49
50	51	52	53	54	55
56	57	58	59	60	61
62	63	64	65	66	67
68	69	70	71	72	73
74	75	76	77	78	79
80	81	82	83	84	85
86	87	88	89	90	91
92	93	94	95	96	97
98	99	100	101	102	103
104	105	106	107	108	109
110	111	112	113	114	115
116	117	118	119	120	121

Use the chart to complete this list of the first 100 prime numbers.

2		179	283	419
3		181	293	421
5		191	307	431
7		193	311	433
		197	313	439
		199	317	443
		211	331	449
		223	337	457
		227	347	461
		229	349	463
	127	233	353	467
	131	239	359	479
	137	241	367	487
	139	251	373	491
	149	257	379	499
	151	263	383	503
	157	269	389	509
	163	271	397	521
	167	277	401	523
	173	281	409	541

What patterns do you notice in the table? Can you explain them?

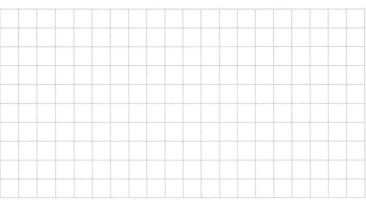

41 Prime-Generating Formulae

Introduction

Mathematics teachers often want their learners to develop accuracy, speed and fluency in substituting numbers into algebraic expressions without having to ask them to plough through pages of mindless practice exercises in which they effectively substitute random numbers into random formulae. Such tasks can contribute to the 'it's all pointless' feeling many learners develop towards their mathematics. One solution is to generate tables of y-values for a range of x-values, according to some suitable formula, and plot the coordinates on a graph. One advantage of this is that rogue points often stand out and can prompt some self-checking and correction. However, this can also be a drawback: if learners always have this backup, then they may not develop the carefulness that they need. So this lesson aims to promote carefulness and attention to detail by exploring the limits of prime-generating formulae. Being just one number out, say, will usually change a prime into a non-prime (with the exception of two and three), although not necessarily vice versa! All values should come out as integers, which avoids the issue of rounding. There is also opportunity here for learners to grow in their familiarity with the prime numbers by constantly consulting the table provided to see whether or not their values are prime.

Aims and Outcomes

- accurately substitute values into polynomial expressions
- appreciate the difficulty of finding prime numbers
- develop familiarity with prime numbers

Lesson Starter (10 min)

Which numbers can you make by multiplying prime numbers together? Suppose you can use as many of each prime number as you want, but no other numbers, and you're not allowed to add, subtract, etc., only multiply. For example, you can make 18 by doing $2 \times 3 \times 3$. Which numbers can you make this way and which can't you?

Many learners are very surprised that you can make all the integers just out of prime numbers. All integers can be decomposed into their prime factors; therefore, we can build any number by multiplying together the right combination of prime numbers. They may think that they have found exceptions, either because they have not spotted the prime factors or because they fail to recognize a number as a prime number, and this can lead to fruitful discussion. If we didn't have a five, say, then that would be a big problem, because there would be a whole collection of numbers we couldn't make (i.e., the multiples of five), but if we didn't have a six, that would be all right, because we can make 6 from 2 × 3. So we could live without the *composite* numbers (non-primes), but we really need the primes! This is like saying that if we had no water (H_2O) then we could make some from hydrogen (H) and oxygen (O), but if we had no hydrogen then we would be stuck, because we can't use chemistry to make that out of other elements. The relationship between elements and compounds in science is a little like that between primes and composites in mathematics, although not quite, since ordinary hydrogen is H_2, containing two atoms of hydrogen, yet it is still an element. And there are only 100 or so known elements, rather than infinitely many. Also, of course, modern physics explains how an element can be converted into a different element in nuclear processes.

Main Lesson (25 min)

Do you know a formula for odd numbers? Or for even numbers? Square numbers? Triangle numbers? Prime numbers? Any other sort of numbers?

The first three are fairly easy ($2n - 1$, $2n$ and n^2 would be possible answers, where n is any integer), and some learners may know that triangle numbers are $\frac{1}{2}n^2 + \frac{1}{2}n$ or $\frac{1}{2}n(n + 1)$, but prime numbers are a different matter. Christian Goldbach (1690–1764) showed that no polynomial formula with integer coefficients can give a prime number for *all* integer values, and Adrien-Marie Legendre (1752–1833) proved that there is no rational algebraic function that always gives prime numbers. In other words, there is no simple formula that will give you prime numbers for every number you care to substitute in.

Here's a possible candidate for a prime-generating formula: $\frac{1}{2}n^2 - \frac{1}{2}n + 2$.

How can we check how good it is?

Substitute $n = 1, 2, 3, 4, \ldots$ *and you get 2, 3, 5, (looking good so far) 8 (oh dear!).*

If you substitute $n = 0$ *you get the same value (2) as with* $n = 1$.

What happens with negative integer n?

Give out the Task Sheet and encourage learners to work on the formulae. Different groups could take responsibility for different formulae. It would be possible to use a spreadsheet to speed up the work, but if your aim is for learners to practise substituting accurately into quadratic expressions by hand, then spreadsheets might need to be used strategically, if at all.

Plenary (20 min)

Formula	Generates prime numbers for values
$n^2 + n + 41$ (Euler)	$n = 0$ to 39
$n^2 - n + 41$ (Legendre)	$n = 0$ to 40 (but $n = 0$ and $n = 1$ give the same prime)
$n^2 - 79n + 1601$	$n = 0$ to 79 (but n and $79 - n$ give the same primes)
$n^3 + n^2 + 17$	$n = 0$ to 10
$2n^2 + 11$	$n = 0$ to 10
$2n^2 + 29$ (Legendre)	$n = 0$ to 28
$4n^2 + 4n + 59$	$n = 0$ to 13
$n^2 + n + 17$	$n = 0$ to 15

Share results and see how learners rate the different formulae. *Is it generally true that the simpler, easier formulae work for fewer values of* n*? Which ones give a good ratio of quantity of primes to 'effort'? Could you place them in order?*

In the table below, the **bold** numbers indicate primes. In the $n^2 - 79n + 1601$ column, the numbers continue for $n > 41$ back up again in the same pattern.

For more information, see www.maa.org/editorial/mathgames/mathgames_07_17_06.html.

n	$n^2 + n + 41$	$n^2 - 79n + 1601$	$n^3 + n^2 + 17$	$2n^2 + 11$	$2n^2 + 29$	$4n^2 + 4n + 59$	$n^2 + n + 17$
0	**41**	**1601**	**17**	**11**	**29**	**59**	**17**
1	**43**	**1523**	**19**	**13**	**31**	**67**	**19**
2	**47**	**1447**	**29**	**19**	**37**	**83**	**23**
3	**53**	**1373**	**53**	**29**	**47**	**107**	**29**
4	**61**	**1301**	**97**	**43**	**61**	**139**	**37**
5	**71**	**1231**	**167**	**61**	**79**	**179**	**47**
6	**83**	**1163**	**269**	**83**	**101**	**227**	**59**
7	**97**	**1097**	**409**	**109**	**127**	**283**	**73**
8	**113**	**1033**	**593**	**139**	**157**	**347**	**89**
9	**131**	**971**	**827**	**173**	**191**	**419**	**107**
10	**151**	**911**	**1117**	**211**	**229**	**499**	**127**
11	**173**	**853**	1469	253	**271**	**587**	**149**
12	**197**	**797**	1889	299	**317**	**683**	**173**
13	**223**	**743**	2383	349	**367**	**787**	**199**
14	**251**	**691**	2957	403	**421**	899	**227**
15	**281**	**641**	3617	461	**479**	1019	**257**
16	**313**	**593**	4369	523	**541**	1147	289
17	**347**	**547**	5219	589	**607**	1283	323
18	**383**	**503**	6173	659	**677**	1427	359
19	**421**	**461**	7237	733	**751**	1579	397
20	**461**	**421**	8417	811	**829**	1739	437
21	**503**	**383**	9719	893	**911**	1907	479
22	**547**	**347**	11 149	979	**997**	2083	523
23	**593**	**313**	12 713	1069	**1087**	2267	569
24	**641**	**281**	14 417	1163	**1181**	2459	617
25	**691**	**251**	16 267	1261	**1279**	2659	667
26	**743**	**223**	18 269	1363	**1381**	2867	719
27	**797**	**197**	20 429	1469	**1487**	3083	773
28	**853**	**173**	22 753	1579	**1597**	3307	829
29	**911**	**151**	25 247	1693	1711	3539	887
30	**971**	**131**	27 917	1811	1829	3779	947
31	**1033**	**113**	30 769	1933	1951	4027	1 009
32	**1097**	**97**	33 809	2059	2077	4283	1073
33	**1163**	**83**	37 043	2189	2207	4547	1139
34	**1231**	**71**	40 477	2323	2341	4819	1207
35	**1301**	**61**	44 117	2461	2479	5099	1277

n	$n^2 + n + 41$	$n^2 - 79n + 1601$	$n^3 + n^2 + 17$	$2n^2 + 11$	$2n^2 + 29$	$4n^2 + 4n + 59$	$n^2 + n + 17$
36	**1373**	**53**	47 969	2603	2621	5387	1349
37	**1447**	**47**	52 039	2749	2767	5683	1423
38	**1523**	**43**	56 333	2899	2917	5987	1499
39	**1601**	**41**	60 857	3053	3071	6299	1577
40	1681	**41**	65 617	3211	3229	6619	1657
41	1763	**43**	70 619	3373	3391	6947	1739

Homework (5 min)

Learners could write about the pros and cons of the different formulae and the different n-values for which they work. They could find out about other prime-generating formulae and, if they wish, try their hand at inventing some of their own! Some formulae are very complicated. The best-known *linear* one is $81\,737\,658\,082\,080n + 6\,171\,054\,912\,832\,631$, which is prime for all values of n from 0 to 24 – but this would be hard to check! There are some records for 'primes in arithmetic progression' (i.e., primes spaced at equal intervals) at http://users.cybercity.dk/~dsl522332/math/aprecords.htm.

To make it harder

Confident learners could try substituting *negative* integer values of n. They could also attempt to sketch the graphs of some of these functions, perhaps considering other curves that would pass through the same integer points.

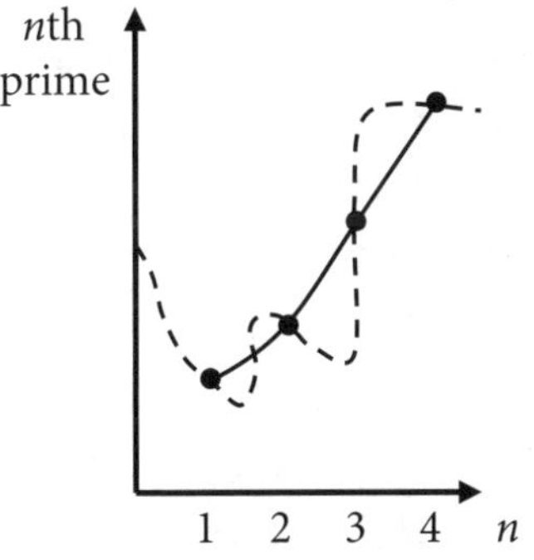

*What different curves would pass through the points at (1, **2**), (2, **3**), (3, **5**) and (4, **7**)?*

A shorter extension task would be the following: Extend the list of primes to the next couple of lines. Is this year a prime year? When is the next prime year?

To make it easier

Learners who find the substitution hard could be advised to use the table function on a 'mathematical' calculator (or a spreadsheet) to check their calculations.

Prime-Generating Formulae

The first 480 prime numbers are:

2	3	5	7	11	13	17	19	23	29	31	37
41	43	47	53	59	61	67	71	73	79	83	89
97	101	103	107	109	113	127	131	137	139	149	151
157	163	167	173	179	181	191	193	197	199	211	223
227	229	233	239	241	251	257	263	269	271	277	281
283	293	307	311	313	317	331	337	347	349	353	359
367	373	379	383	389	397	401	409	419	421	431	433
439	443	449	457	461	463	467	479	487	491	499	503
509	521	523	541	547	557	563	569	571	577	587	593
599	601	607	613	617	619	631	641	643	647	653	659
661	673	677	683	691	701	709	719	727	733	739	743
751	757	761	769	773	787	797	809	811	821	823	827
829	839	853	857	859	863	877	881	883	887	907	911
919	929	937	941	947	953	967	971	977	983	991	997
1009	1013	1019	1021	1031	1033	1039	1049	1051	1061	1063	1069
1087	1091	1093	1097	1103	1109	1117	1123	1129	1151	1153	1163
1171	1181	1187	1193	1201	1213	1217	1223	1229	1231	1237	1249
1259	1277	1279	1283	1289	1291	1297	1301	1303	1307	1319	1321
1327	1361	1367	1373	1381	1399	1409	1423	1427	1429	1433	1439
1447	1451	1453	1459	1471	1481	1483	1487	1489	1493	1499	1511
1523	1531	1543	1549	1553	1559	1567	1571	1579	1583	1597	1601
1607	1609	1613	1619	1621	1627	1637	1657	1663	1667	1669	1693
1697	1699	1709	1721	1723	1733	1741	1747	1753	1759	1777	1783
1787	1789	1801	1811	1823	1831	1847	1861	1867	1871	1873	1877
1879	1889	1901	1907	1913	1931	1933	1949	1951	1973	1979	1987
1993	1997	1999	2003	2011	2017	2027	2029	2039	2053	2063	2069
2081	2083	2087	2089	2099	2111	2113	2129	2131	2137	2141	2143
2153	2161	2179	2203	2207	2213	2221	2237	2239	2243	2251	2267
2269	2273	2281	2287	2293	2297	2309	2311	2333	2339	2341	2347
2351	2357	2371	2377	2381	2383	2389	2393	2399	2411	2417	2423
2437	2441	2447	2459	2467	2473	2477	2503	2521	2531	2539	2543
2549	2551	2557	2579	2591	2593	2609	2617	2621	2633	2647	2657
2659	2663	2671	2677	2683	2687	2689	2693	2699	2707	2711	2713
2719	2729	2731	2741	2749	2753	2767	2777	2789	2791	2797	2801
2803	2819	2833	2837	2843	2851	2857	2861	2879	2887	2897	2903
2909	2917	2927	2939	2953	2957	2963	2969	2971	2999	3001	3011
3019	3023	3037	3041	3049	3061	3067	3079	3083	3089	3109	3119
3121	3137	3163	3167	3169	3181	3187	3191	3203	3209	3217	3221
3229	3251	3253	3257	3259	3271	3299	3301	3307	3313	3319	3323
3329	3331	3343	3347	3359	3361	3371	3373	3389	3391	3407	3413

There is no simple formula that will generate prime numbers for *all* integer values of n.

Try these formulae below for different integer values of n.

(The names in brackets are the original inventor/discoverer where known.)

Which values of n give prime numbers and which don't?

For each formula, try to find the longest sequence of consecutive integer values of n that generates an unbroken list of primes.

$n^2 + n + 41$ (Euler)

$2n^2 + 29$ (Legendre)

$n^2 - n + 41$ (Legendre)

$n^3 + n^2 + 17$

$2n^2 + 11$

$n^2 - 79n + 1601$

$n^2 + n + 17$

$4n^2 + 4n + 59$

Which formulae do you think are best? Why?

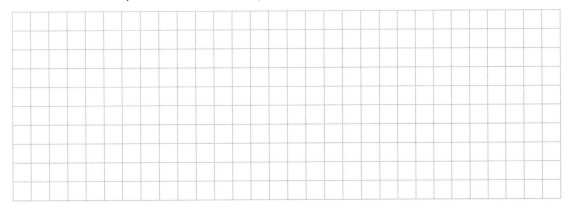

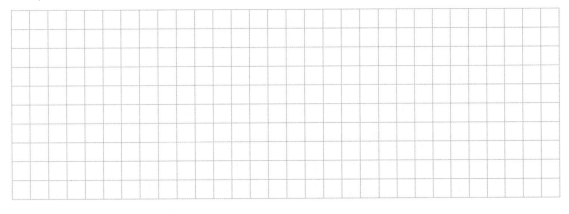

Can you think of other ones?

42 Probability Pi

Introduction

The number pi (π) often fascinates children and adults alike. If you print off a section of it and put it on the wall all the way round the classroom it cannot fail to become a talking point. You may be surprised how many digits of it some of your learners will remember, without explicitly trying (peripheral learning), and while this may be of questionable value itself it may provoke all kinds of thoughts about infinity, irrational numbers, circles, fractions and decimals. This lesson explores π by drawing 'pie' charts to show the relative frequencies of the digits in the number.

Aims and Outcomes

- draw pie charts, calculating the appropriate angles from a frequency table
- understand the nature of randomness in the digits of π

Lesson Starter (5 min)

Can you give us an example of a 'random number'? Explain why you chose your number.

Do you agree that so-and-so's number is 'random'? Why? Have any two people chosen the same 'random' number? Is this likely? Why / why not?

Does your calculator generate random numbers? Have you any idea how it does it? How could you check that the numbers really are 'random'?

Randomness is notoriously difficult to define or measure. Is '7' a random number? This is probably a meaningless question unless there is some shared sense of what we might mean by this or in what context the 7 could arise. Many people find the static nature of, say, tables of random numbers, problematic, and cannot accept that the digits in a number such as π can be random, when they are completely unchanging.

Main Lesson (25 min)

Give out the Task Sheet. The early part invites learners to explore what they understand by the idea of 'random digits'. Then ask different groups of learners to work with different sections (different rows, perhaps) of the π digits given, and count up the frequency of each digit, 0 to 9. They can then draw pie charts to illustrate the relative proportions of different digits in π up to different numbers of decimal places.

Plenary (25 min)

Here are the results for the first 1 000 digits:

Digit	Frequency	Angle (°)
0	93	33
1	116	42
2	103	37
3	103	37
4	93	33
5	97	35
6	94	34
7	95	34
8	101	36
9	105	38
Total	1000	360

(It is possible to obtain this data easily using a word-processing package, pasting in the first 1000 or so digits of π from the internet and using a 'search and replace' feature to swap all occurrences of '0' for the letter 'a', all occurrences of '1' for the letter 'b', and so on, recording the number of replacements made each time.)

There is plenty of opportunity to talk about what learners regard as 'significant' differences.

How can the digits be 'random' if they can be calculated precisely and are always exactly the same? Sometimes the word 'pseudorandom' is used because of this. A decimal expansion is called 'normal' if each digit appears approximately one-tenth of the time (in the long run). No one has proved yet whether numbers like π, e and $\sqrt{2}$ are normal or not, although, for instance, the first 30 million digits of π are very uniformly distributed, and it seems likely that it is normal. (See http://news.bbc.co.uk/1/hi/sci/tech/2146295.stm for more information.)

Of course, a number could pass the test for normal (e.g., $0.\dot{0}12345678\dot{9}$ would pass it [almost] perfectly!) without being 'random' in the slightest!

Learners may comment on the fact that the sectors in their pie charts are so close to equal that drawing a pie chart with ten almost equal sectors does not communicate much. On the other hand, they might feel that it shows very well the symmetry in the distribution of digits.

Homework (5 min)

Draw pie charts to show the proportions of each digit in the decimal expansions of rational numbers such as $\frac{1}{7}$*, etc. What patterns do you find? Can you explain them?*

To make it harder

Learners who finish this work could try π in *other bases* or other irrational numbers, such as e or $\sqrt{2}$. There are plenty of irrational numbers which are definitely *not* normal; for example, 0.101001000100001 … Pseudorandom number generators are important in cryptography – and learners could find out more about this.

To make it easier

Those who find this work difficult could begin by drawing bar charts or vertical line graphs and think about the pros and cons of different graphical representations.

'Pi' Chart

Here are the first 1000 digits of the number π. (The digits go on forever.)

3.1415926535897932384626433832795028841971693993751058209749445923078164062862089986
2803482534211706798214808651328230664709384460955058223172535940812848111745028410270
1938521105559644622948954930381964428810975665933446128475648233786783165271201909
1456485669234603486104543266482133936072602491412737245870066063155881748815209209628
2925409171536436789259036001133053054882046652138414695194151160943305727036575959 19
5309218611738193261179310511854807446237996274956735188575272489122793818301194912 98
3367336244065664308602139494639522473719070217986094370277053921717629317675238467 48
1846766940513200056812714526356082778577134275778960917363717872146844090122495343 01
4654958537105079227968925892354201995611212902196086403441815981362977477130996051 87
0721134999999837297804995105973173281609631859502445945534690830264252230825334468 50
3526193118817101000313783875288658753320838142061717766914730359825349042875546873 11
59562863882353787593751957781857780532171226806613001927876611195909216420198 …

Do you think that the digits *look* 'random'?

What do you think that it means to say that the digits are 'random'?

How could you *test* whether the digits are random?

One way to begin is to look at *digit frequency*.

Look at either the first 50 digits, or the first 100, or the first 150, etc., depending on what other people are doing, and count up how many of each digit there are.

Put your results into this table and consider drawing a pie chart to show the relative frequency of each digit.

Digit	**Frequency**	**Angle (°)**
0		
1		
2		
3		
4		
5		
6		
7		
8		
9		
Total		360

What does this tell you about the digits of pi?

43 Properties of Circles

Introduction

Circles are ubiquitous yet possess fascinating properties and link to all sorts of interesting mathematics. A circle can be defined as the locus of all points in two dimensions that are a fixed distance from a certain fixed point. Points *inside* the circle are *closer* to the fixed point; points *outside* the circle are *further away*. So the circle represents the boundary between these two regions, one of finite area and one of infinite. The word 'circle' is sometimes used to refer to the entire interior 2D region; for instance, when someone says 'the area of a circle' they are not referring to a one-dimensional curve (with zero area) – others prefer to say 'disc'. This lesson looks at what makes the centre of a circle special by asking learners to find methods of locating it for a given circle.

Aims and Outcomes

- engage with ideas of proof in a geometrical context
- use circle theorems and other circle facts to find the centre of a circle

Lesson Starter (10 min)

Does anyone think they know what a circle is?! (You could do this with the whole-class or learners could discuss it in groups or pairs.)

Obviously, learners 'know' but can they articulate it? In a friendly way, the teacher tries deliberately (perhaps humorously) to misunderstand, perhaps by drawing shapes such as these on the board when they would seem to be included in the definitions offered by learners, for example:

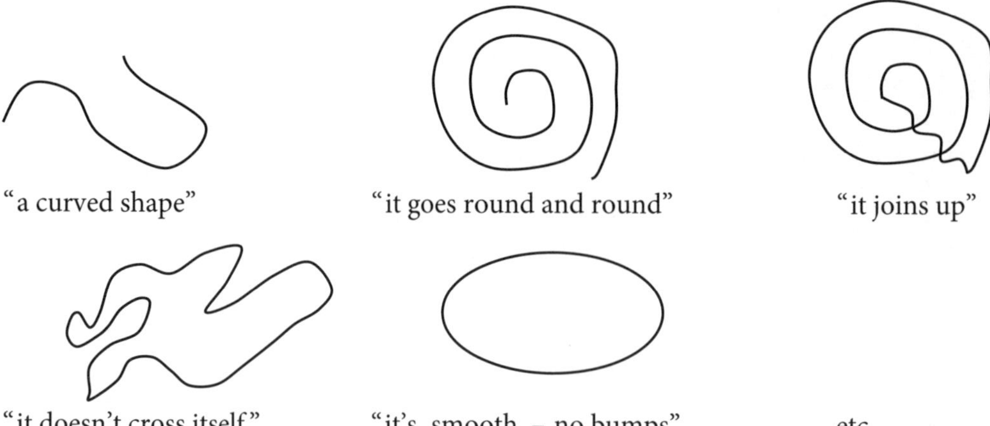
"a curved shape"
"it goes round and round"
"it joins up"
"it doesn't cross itself"
"it's smooth – no bumps"
etc.

This can lead to a definition relating to all points being a fixed distance from a fixed point. Often it is easier to describe how to make something rather than what it is, so if learners are stuck you could suggest that they try to describe 'what you do' to get a circle.

How would you check *that something is circular?*

Measuring the width all the way round isn't enough – as there are 'curves of constant width' which are not circles. (*Can you draw one? How?*)

How many sides *has a circle got?*

One (curved) side? Two sides (an inside and an outside)? Infinitely many (a regular n*-gon, with* $n \to \infty$*)?* Or are there other answers?

Main Lesson (25 min)

Give out the Task Sheet. *Your task is to work out a way of finding the* centre *of a circle.*

Suppose you want to be really *accurate. Sometimes it really matters; for example, in engineering if you are going to spin a disc at high speed, being slightly off centre could be dangerous.*

Learners may suggest approximate strategies. Try to get learners to unpack answers like 'go across to the middle' or 'go exactly half way down'.

Learners may suggest folding the circle into quarters (or in half twice, unfolding in between).

What if you can't fold the circle? Say it's made of something rigid, such as metal.

One idea is to cut out the circle from a piece of card and hang it up from a point on the circumference. The centre must lie vertically below the hanging point (if the cardboard is uniform). Draw in the vertical line (a weight on a piece of string would help) and repeat once or twice more. Where the lines intersect should be the centre.

Another method involves using callipers to inscribe the circle in smallest possible square, then marking in the diagonals of the square to give the centre of the circle where they intersect.

Plenary (20 min)

Learners could use *Thales' theorem* (the angle in a semicircle is 90°) and a set-square to find a diameter by simply placing the set-square with the right angle on the circumference and joining the points where the sides of the triangle intersect the circumference of the circle.

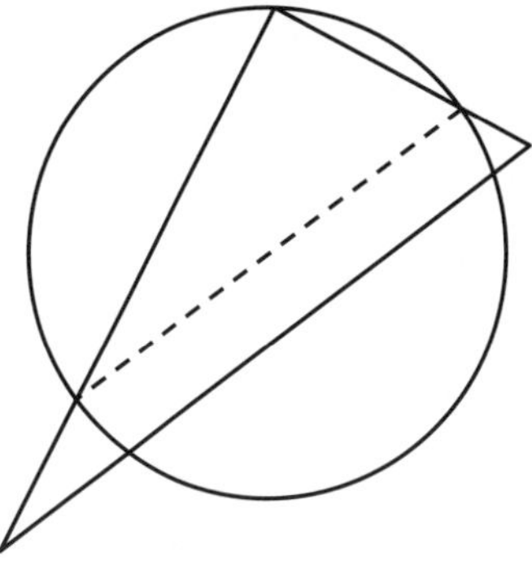

The dashed line shows a diameter.

Doing this at another position gives another diameter, and the intersection of the two diameters must be the centre of the circle. (Learners sometimes ask what use a set-square ever is, so this would be an example.)

Could you do it with a set-square that was set to 100° instead of 90°? How?

(Yes, if you had another set-square that was 'set' to either 50° or 200°, using the fact that the angle subtended by an arc at the centre of a circle is twice that subtended by the same arc at the circumference. With a 90° set-square, a ruler effectively functions as a 180° set-square!)

A more common method would be to draw any chord and construct the perpendicular bisector. Then do the same with another (non-parallel) chord. The intersection of the perpendicular bisectors must be the centre of the circle. *Why?*

Homework (5 min)

Imagine a world without circles. What would it be like? What circles are there in nature? Do you think that there are any living things that use wheels to move around? Why / why not? Find out about this.

To make it harder

Learners who finish early could think about the following problems:

Does a triangle have a 'centre'? Why / why not? Think about different sorts of triangle. Find out about the circumcentre, centroid, incentre, excentres, orthocentre and nine-point centre.

Make up a definition for the centre of other shapes. Do you think that these definitions could be useful? Why?

To make it easier

All learners should be able to think about ways of locating the centre of a circle – approximately, if not 'exact in principle'.

The Centre of a Circle

Find the centre of this circle. Be as accurate as you can. Use whatever method you like.

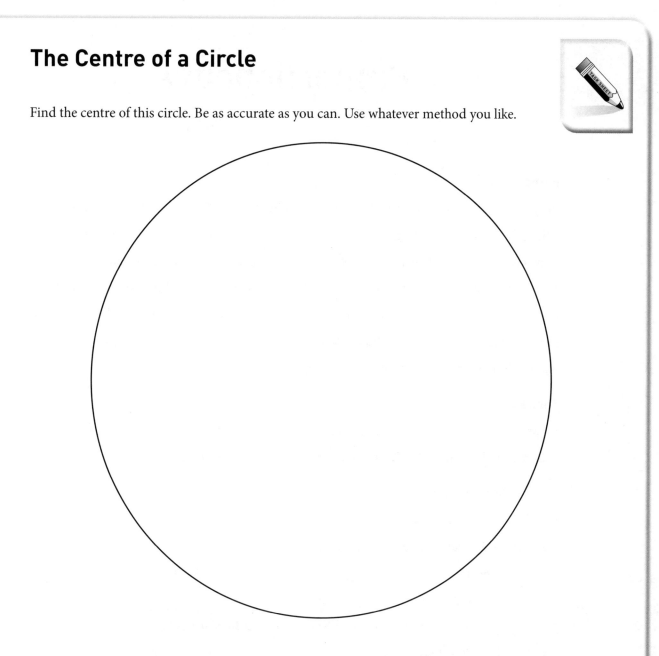

When you have located the centre, use compasses to draw a series of *concentric circles* (circles with the same centre but different radii).

It won't look right unless you are pretty accurate about the position of the centre!

How many different exact methods can you find for locating the centre of a circle?

What advantages or disadvantages do they have?

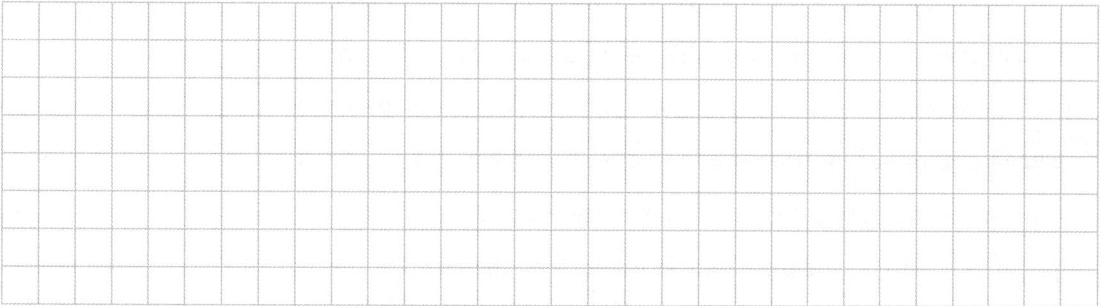

44

Proportionality

Introduction

Proportionality is a key idea in mathematics, touching areas as diverse as percentages, trigonometry, enlargement and 2D and 3D geometry. Failing to understand proportionality can have a disproportionately large effect! Many misconceptions, apparent paradoxes and counterintuitive results are a consequence of thinking that 'everything is linear'. Direct proportionality ($y \propto x$) is indeed a linear relationship – a straight-line graph through the origin, usually with positive gradient – but *inverse* proportionality is *not* simply a straight line with negative gradient but a *curve*. This difference lies behind the Starter problem below.

Aims and Outcomes

- appreciate that not all mathematical relationships are linear
- understand different possible kinds of proportional relationships between quantities

Lesson Starter (20 min)

Craig wants to work out 360 ÷ 15.

He says: *'15 is half way between 10 and 20.*

360 ÷ 10 = 36

360 ÷ 20 = 18

So 360 ÷ 15 must be half way between 36 and 18, which is 27.

So 360 ÷ 15 = 27.'

What do you think of Craig's answer and his method? Do you agree that 27 is half way between 18 and 36? Why / why not?

His answer is too big – it should be 24 – but his method may seem plausible to many learners.

When does this sort of method work and when doesn't it? Why?

For example, 360 × 15 *is* half way between 360 × 10 and 360 × 20.

For example, 360×15^2 is *not* half way between 360×10^2 and 360×20^2.

Learners may be quite surprised that this sort of approach sometimes fails, since such methods often can be relied on. They may find it hard at this stage to say what is wrong, and after some discussion you may prefer to leave this and return to it later. If learners are familiar with the reciprocal graph $y = \frac{1}{x}$, and maybe the parabola $y = x^2$, then the fact that these graphs are curves rather than straight lines may be helpful. At the very least, learners may be encouraged to be a little wary of using 'short cuts' in arithmetic without understanding why they are supposed to work.

Main Lesson (20 min)

Give out the Task Sheet. Try to be accepting of any patterns that learners notice, especially initially, even if they are 'down the columns' patterns rather than the more sought-after horizontal connections made by comparisons with the x-column. Try to encourage learners to communicate what they notice as clearly as they can: this can be the hardest aspect of the task, and can be very valuable.

Plenary (15 min)

If you have a data projector, it is easy to have a spreadsheet open and quickly generate columns of numbers according to whatever rule you want. This can be helpful if learners refer to columns of numbers that are not on the sheet but which they are constructing in order to illustrate a point that they are making.

The formulae used for columns a to f are: $a = 4x$, $b = 7x$, $c = 0.2x$, $d = \frac{48}{x}$, $e = 3x^2$ and $f = \frac{360}{x^2}$, so a, b and c are examples of direct proportionality, d is inverse proportionality and e and f are more complicated examples involving the square of x. It is less important that learners identify these precise relations than that they appreciate the different *kinds* of connections between the variables.

Helpful questions can be: *What happens to the* a*-number when you double the* x*-number?* (E.g., looking at $x = 6$ and $x = 12$.) Or: *What happens to the* d*-number when you divide the* x*-number by three?* (E.g., looking at $x = 15$ and $x = 5$.), etc. Learners can be adept at finding numerous numerical connections. They may be surprised that if you have an equation such as $b = 7x$ and you double x, b only *doubles* – it doesn't get seven times bigger. Algebraically, $7(2x) = 2(7x) = 2b$.

It may be a good time to introduce proportionality notation (the 'fish' symbol: $\propto$, which is not *quite* the same as a Greek alpha: α) and terms like 'direct proportionality' and 'inverse proportionality'. You may also wish to begin working on proportionality problems of the following kind, with learners imagining (or constructing) the corresponding columns of numbers. For instance, y *is inversely proportional to* x*. When* x *is 6,* y *is 8. What is* y *when* x *is 10?* The answer is $y = 4.8$.

Homework (5 min)

Construct a table of numbers containing proportional, inversely proportional and other relationships. Can you make all the numbers integers? Why / why not? More adventurous learners can make this into quite a demanding task. They should write down the connections between the variables either as proportionalities or as equations.

Another possibility would be the following problem, which also exhibits a lack of linearity that learners may find surprising:

Think about this statement: 'Because 30 is nearer to 25 than to 36, $\sqrt{30}$ must be nearer to 5 than to 6.'

Is $\sqrt{30}$ nearer to 5 than to 6?

Make up some more statements like this. Check them to see if the conclusions are true. Will this sort of reasoning always work?

Although $\sqrt{30}$ is nearer to 5 than to 6, the reasoning is false, and it is occasionally (mis)used when finding square roots by trial and improvement. For example, although 30.4 is nearer to 5^2 than to 6^2, $\sqrt{30.4}$ is 5.5136 (correct to 5 significant figures), so is nearer to 6 than to 5. In general x will be nearer to b than to a (where $b > a$), even though x^2 is nearer to a^2 than to b^2, if $\left(\frac{a+b}{2}\right)^2 < x^2 < \frac{a^2+b^2}{2}$. Since $25 < 30 < 36$, it is correct to say that $\sqrt{25} < \sqrt{30} < \sqrt{36}$; it is just wrong to assume that the $y = x^2$ curve is a straight line and that the square roots will be evenly spaced.

To make it harder

A possible question for someone who finishes early might be:

'On a summer's day, the temperature was 25°C. Back in the winter, I remember when it was 5°C. So today is five times hotter than then.' Why is this silly?

This is wrong because, among other reasons, the Celsius temperature scale doesn't have its zero at the lowest possible temperature, 'absolute zero', –273°C. The temperature of 0°C is an arbitrary point to do with the properties of melting ice. The temperature of 2°C is only slightly hotter than 1°C – certainly not 'twice as hot', whatever that means!

What other examples can you think of that are like this? E.g., shoe sizes, etc.

Extrapolating is often more dangerous than *interpolating*, even when relationships are linear, over a certain range. Again, learners could be invited to think of or research examples of this.

To make it easier

Learners who find the relationships hard to appreciate might find it helpful to look at the graphs. Drawing the graphs by hand could be valuable, but using software would obviously be much quicker.

Proportionality

x	a	b	c	d	e	f
1	4	7	0.2	48	3	360
2	8	14	0.4	24	12	90
3	12	21	0.6	16	27	40
4	16	28	0.8	12	48	22.5
5	20	35	1.0	9.6	75	14.4
6	24	42	1.2	8	108	10
7	28	49	1.4	6.85714286	147	7.34693878
8	32	56	1.6	6	192	5.625
9	36	63	1.8	5.33333333	243	4.44444444
10	40	70	2.0	4.8	300	3.6
11	44	77	2.2	4.36363636	363	2.97520661
12	48	84	2.4	4	432	2.5
13	52	91	2.6	3.69230769	507	2.13017751
14	56	98	2.8	3.42857143	588	1.83673469
15	60	105	3.0	3.2	675	1.6
16	64	112	3.2	3	768	1.40625
17	68	119	3.4	2.82352941	867	1.24567474
18	72	126	3.6	2.66666667	972	1.11111111
19	76	133	3.8	2.52631579	1083	0.99722992
20	80	140	4.0	2.4	1200	0.9

Look at the columns of numbers. (Some of the numbers have been rounded.)

What patterns can you see down the columns?

What patterns can you see connecting the x-numbers to each of the other columns?

Column	Connection with *x*-numbers
a	
b	
c	
d	
e	
f	

45 Pythagoras' Theorem

Introduction

Pythagoras' Theorem is a beautiful result. People have been captivated by it for so long that there are now literally thousands of proofs, some so elegantly visual that they need no accompanying explanation (see, for instance, Nelsen, R. B. [1997 and 2001], *Proofs Without Words* [vols 1 and 2], Washington, DC: The Mathematical Association of America). When learners using the Theorem make errors such as 'cancelling the squares', effectively converting $a^2 + b^2 = c^2$ into an impossible $a + b = c$, it suggests that they may have little appreciation of the origin of the Theorem or its connection with area. (How can the sum of the two legs of a right-angled triangle be the same distance as the hypotenuse, when the hypotenuse is clearly the shortest possible distance between the two acute vertices?) This lesson focuses on the *proof* of Pythagoras' Theorem rather than on using it to calculate the lengths of sides in right-angled triangles, since this can often receive less emphasis in the classroom than it deserves.

Aims and Outcomes

- understand and prove Pythagoras' Theorem

Lesson Starter (20 min)

Is this a regular octagon? Why / why not?

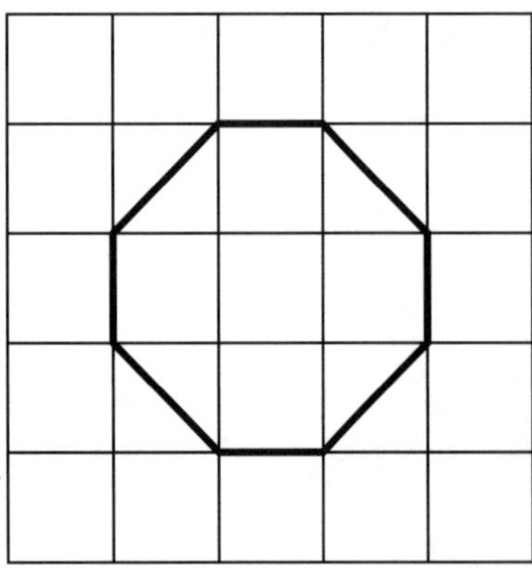

What does 'regular' mean? All vertices need to have the same angle and all sides the same length. This octagon satisfies the former (all the angles are 135°) but not the latter, since the four slanting diagonal sides are longer than the other four (two vertical and two horizontal) sides. The diagonal of a square is longer than the sides.

Is this an equilateral triangle? Why / why not?

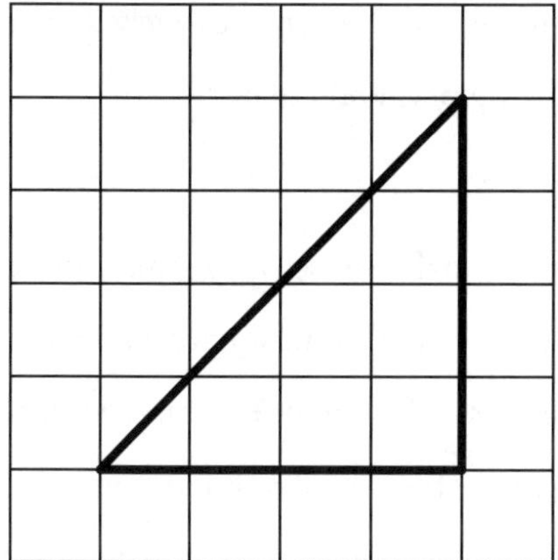

This one is a bit more obvious, because clearly it is right-angled, and therefore cannot be equilateral, since in an equilateral triangle all the angles must be 60°. Again, the diagonal ('hypotenuse') is longer than the 'legs', and perhaps this example helps learners to see why, if they are sceptical.

How much longer is a diagonal of a square than the side of the square? Measurement may suggest that it is 1.5 times as long, but this is slightly too much.

Is this an equilateral triangle? Why / why not?

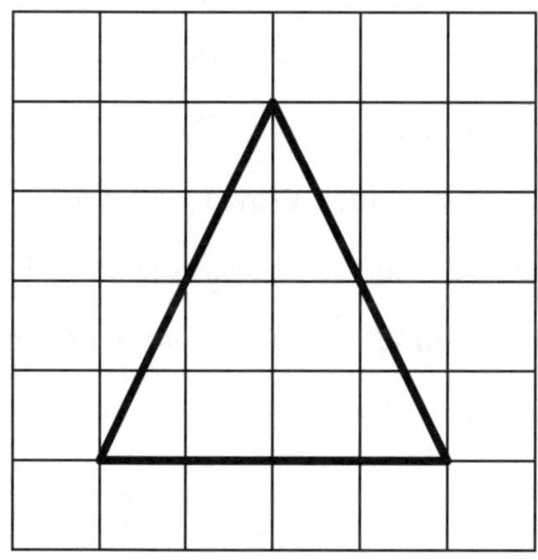

This one looks a bit more like it might be, and this time there are no right angles, but still the answer is no. The base of the triangle is four units, and so is the height, but the *slanting* sides must be *longer* than four – see the picture below:

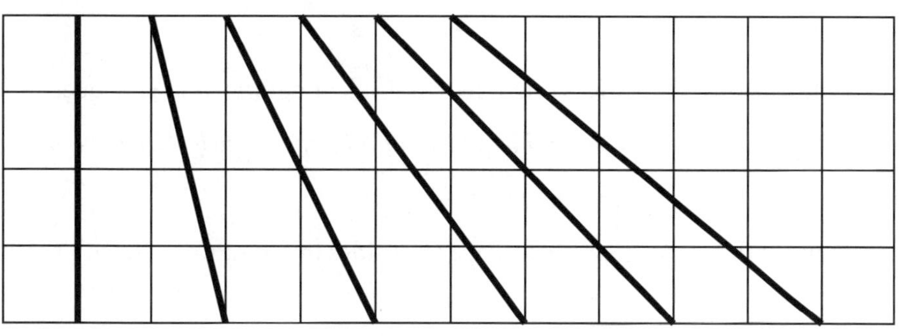

The shortest route from the top of this diagram to the bottom is to travel at right angles (i.e., the left-hand line segment). Each of the other line segments must be progressively longer as you move to the right, since they deviate increasingly from being perpendicular.

Main Lesson (20 min)

Give learners the Task Sheet and encourage them to make sense of the questions and prompts, perhaps in pairs. Initially they should see that the diagonal of a unit square has length $\sqrt{2}$ and then, in general, see their way through the proof of Pythagoras' Theorem. Encourage learners to explain what they understand at each stage. They could make their own version out of coloured paper where they can slide the pieces around physically. Or they could make it using the drawing tools in a word-processing package – clicking and dragging the pieces into place.

Plenary (15 min)

In part A, because the big tilted square is made up of four right-angled triangles, each of area $\frac{1}{2}$ of the original 1×1 square, its area must be $4 \times \frac{1}{2} = 2$. That means that its side lengths must be exactly $\sqrt{2}$ – a little *less* than 1.5.

In part B, the white space in the left-hand diagram is a square with side length c, so the area is c^2. In the right-hand diagram this same white space is arranged differently, being made up of a small square of area a^2 and a larger square of area b^2. The total area of the white space hasn't changed, since the four triangles have just been shifted around, so $a^2 + b^2 = c^2$: Pythagoras' Theorem. This works as a proof, because a, b and c can take any positive values, provided that $a + b < c$. Learners might be encouraged to visualize mentally what happens to the diagrams as these lengths vary, a increasing until it is equal to b (isosceles triangle and symmetrical tilted square, like in the diagram in part A) and then on so that a becomes greater than b. Dynamic illustrations of this kind of thing are available on the internet.

Homework (5 min)

Learners could be asked to research three interesting facts about Pythagoras – he had some unusual beliefs and practices – and/or to find a different proof of the Theorem that they can understand and bring it in and explain it during the next lesson. (See also the homework for Lesson 55.)

To make it harder

Learners confident with these ideas might like to think about the following question:

If you fold off a square from the end of a piece of A4 paper, which is longer – the diagonal of the square or the longer side of the original piece of paper?

In fact they are the same, because A4 paper has sides in the ratio $1 : \sqrt{2}$, with the smaller side of length 21 cm.

How long will the diagonal of a sheet of A4 paper be?

Using Pythagoras' Theorem, the diagonal will be $\sqrt{3}$ units long or $21\sqrt{3}$ cm = 36.4 cm (correct to 1 decimal place).

To make it easier

Learners finding these ideas difficult may be helped by cutting out the shapes and moving them around. They may also find that dissecting the square at the top of the Task Sheet, using scissors, helps them to find its area.

Pythagoras' Theorem

A. Below on the left is a square with side length one unit.

How long do you think the thick diagonal line is?

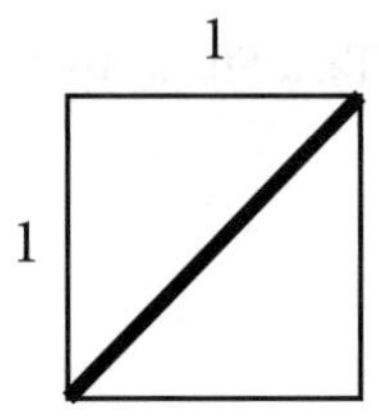

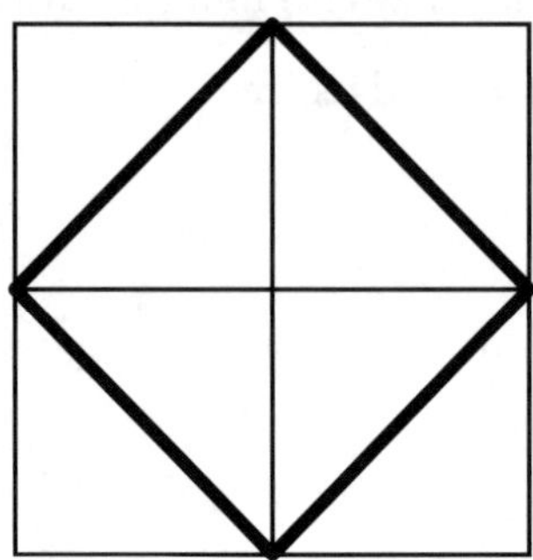

Now look at the diagram on the right.

Can you see the left-hand diagram 'inside' this one?

Look at the big tilted square (with thick sides), split into four right-angled triangles.

Work out the area of this big tilted square.

How long must the thick diagonal line be?

B. The left-hand diagram shows four congruent right-angled triangles placed into the corners of a large square. The white space left inside makes another, smaller square, which is tilted.

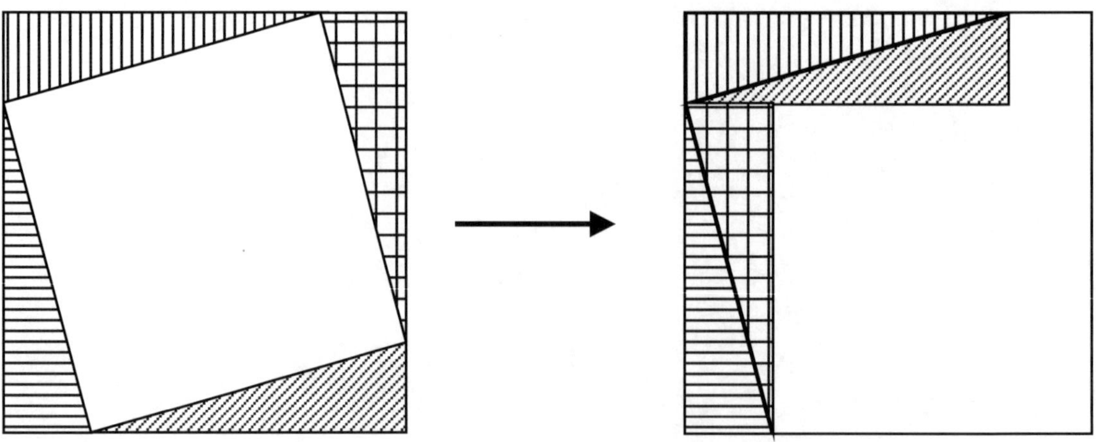

Try to imagine how two of the triangles (the two on the right of the left drawing) can slide (translate), without changing size, to give the picture on the right. Can you visualize the movement?

In the first diagram, label the lengths of the sides of the triangles a, b and c, in increasing order of size, so $a < b < c$.

Find where a, b and c should go in the second diagram and label them clearly everywhere they occur.

How can you be sure that the tilted white square is actually a square?

What is the area of the tilted white square in the first diagram?

Work out the area of the white space in the second diagram?

What does this prove? Why?

46 Quadratic Probabilities

Introduction

The quadratic formula $x = \frac{-b \pm \sqrt{b^2 - 4ac}}{2a}$ for the solutions to the general quadratic equation $ax^2 + bx + c = 0$ (where $a \neq 0$) is often problematic for learners to use if any of the coefficients (but especially b) are negative. Learners often like the apparent simplicity of what is sometimes rather grandly referred to as 'the formula' in comparison to other methods for solving quadratic equations. However, they are not always precise enough with their substituting to obtain accurate answers reliably, so this lesson gives plenty of opportunity for practice while underlining the importance of knowing which number is a, b or c! The theme is the property of the *discriminant* ($b^2 - 4ac$) part of the formula in 'discriminating' among the possibilities of 2, 1 or 0 solutions.

Aims and Outcomes

- practise using the quadratic formula to solve quadratic equations
- understand the role of the discriminant in determining the number of solutions of a quadratic equation

Lesson Starter (15 min)

What do you see when you look at this?

$$\frac{-5 \pm \sqrt{5^2 - 4 \times 3 \times 2}}{2 \times 3}$$

Learners could work it out ($-\frac{2}{3}$ or -1).

Where do you think it might have come from?

It is likely to be reminiscent of the quadratic formula $x = \frac{-b \pm \sqrt{b^2 - 4ac}}{2a}$.

Find an equation for which these are the solutions. And another one. And another one.

For example, $3x^2 + 5x + 2 = 0$ or $6x^2 + 10x + 4 = 0$ or $(x + \frac{2}{3})(x + 1) = 0$ or $(3x + 2)(x + 1) = 0$ or $\left(x - \frac{-5 + \sqrt{5^2 - 4 \times 3 \times 2}}{2 \times 3}\right)\left(x - \frac{-5 - \sqrt{5^2 - 4 \times 3 \times 2}}{2 \times 3}\right) = 0$, etc.

Invent a harder problem, like this for example: $\frac{6 \pm \sqrt{(-6)^2 - 1 \times 4 \times 5}}{5 \times 2}$. *(How do you decide what 'a' is? Here, a = 5, b = −6 and c = 1 would be one possibility, but you can always scale all three coefficients by any non-zero constant.)*

What about $\frac{4 \pm \sqrt{40}}{6}$*? Is there enough information?*

Yes, because the 6 in the denominator tells you that $2a = 6$, so $a = 3$, and the 4 in the numerator means that $4 = -b$, so $b = -4$, so since $b^2 - 4ac = 40$ it follows that $16 - 12c = 40$ and so $c = -2$. (As before, a, b and c could be any non-zero multiple of these values, such as -6, 8, 4, etc.)

Will this always be possible for any $\frac{p \pm \sqrt{q}}{r}$ *where* r ≠ 0?

Yes, because a similar process will give $a = \frac{kr}{2}$, $b = -kp$ and $c = \frac{k(p^2 - q)}{2r}$, where k is a non-zero constant.

Main Lesson (25 min)

Somebody give us three numbers, please.

However 'random' the numbers are, insert them as a, b and c into $ax^2 + bx + c = 0$, so writing something like $27x^2 - 52\frac{1}{2}x + 31\pi = 0$.

How would we work out x? Learners may suggest trial and improvement, factorizing or drawing a graph, etc., but using 'the formula' is going to be easiest here.

Your example may or may not have solutions. If it does, you could ask:

If we keep repeating this game (of choosing three random numbers, making the corresponding quadratic equation and trying to solve it) are we going to have any problems? Why / why not?

On the other hand, if the equation you have obtained doesn't have any solutions, try to examine why not.

Evaluate $b^2 - 4ac$ (the discriminant) and discuss what will happen in the quadratic formula if $b^2 - 4ac$ is greater than zero (two solutions), less than zero (no real solutions) or equal to zero (one repeated solution).

Give out the Task Sheet and let learners work on the tasks. Logical systematic thinking is needed, and an exhaustive search through all possible examples.

Plenary (15 min)

How did you make sure you had checked all *the possibilities?*

What order did you do them in? Why?

Did anything surprise you?

Learners may be surprised that a quadratic with no solutions is not a strange oddity, as it might be in the mathematics classroom – the 'majority' of randomly-generated equations in Task 1 are like this!

Task 1 (repeats allowed)

a	b	c	$b^2 - 4ac$	x_1	x_2
1	1	1	–3	no solutions	
1	1	2	–7	no solutions	
1	1	3	–11	no solutions	
1	2	1	0	–1	–1
1	2	2	–4	no solutions	
1	2	3	–8	no solutions	
1	3	1	5	$\frac{-3+\sqrt{5}}{2}$	$\frac{-3-\sqrt{5}}{2}$

a	*b*	*c*	$b^2 - 4ac$	x_1	x_2
1	3	2	1	−1	−2
1	3	3	−3	no solutions	
2	1	1	−7	no solutions	
2	1	2	−15	no solutions	
2	1	3	−23	no solutions	
2	2	1	−4	no solutions	
2	2	2	−12	no solutions	
2	2	3	−20	no solutions	
2	3	1	1	$-\frac{1}{2}$	−1
2	3	2	−7	no solutions	
2	3	3	−15	no solutions	
3	1	1	−11	no solutions	
3	1	2	−23	no solutions	
3	1	3	−35	no solutions	
3	2	1	−8	no solutions	
3	2	2	−20	no solutions	
3	2	3	−32	no solutions	
3	3	1	−3	no solutions	
3	3	2	−15	no solutions	
3	3	3	−27	no solutions	

The answers are: (a) $\frac{1}{9}$, (b) $\frac{1}{27}$, (c) $\frac{23}{27}$.

Task 2 (no repeats)

a	*b*	*c*	$b^2 - 4ac$	x_1	x_2
1	2	3	−8	no solutions	
1	3	2	1	−1	−2
2	1	3	−23	no solutions	
2	3	1	1	$-\frac{1}{2}$	−1
3	1	2	−23	no solutions	
3	2	1	−8	no solutions	

The answers are: (a) $\frac{1}{3}$, (b) 0, (c) $\frac{2}{3}$.

Task 3 (one negative)

a	*b*	*c*	$b^2 - 4ac$	x_1	x_2
−1	2	3	16	−1	3
−1	3	2	17	$\frac{3-\sqrt{17}}{2}$	$\frac{3+\sqrt{17}}{2}$
−2	1	3	25	−1	$\frac{3}{2}$

a	b	c	$b^2 - 4ac$	x_1	x_2
−2	3	1	17	$\frac{3-\sqrt{17}}{4}$	$\frac{3+\sqrt{17}}{4}$
−3	1	2	25	$-\frac{2}{3}$	1
−3	2	1	16	$-\frac{1}{3}$	1
1	−2	3	−8	no solutions	
1	−3	2	1	2	1
2	−1	3	−23	no solutions	
2	−3	1	1	1	$\frac{1}{2}$
3	−1	2	−23	no solutions	
3	−2	1	−8	no solutions	
1	2	−3	16	1	−3
1	3	−2	17	$\frac{\sqrt{17}-3}{2}$	$\frac{-\sqrt{17}-3}{2}$
2	1	−3	25	1	$-\frac{3}{2}$
2	3	−1	17	$\frac{\sqrt{17}-3}{4}$	$\frac{-\sqrt{17}-3}{4}$
3	1	−2	25	$\frac{2}{3}$	−1
3	2	−1	16	$\frac{1}{3}$	−1

The answers are: (a) $\frac{7}{9}$, (b) 0, (c) $\frac{2}{9}$.

One negative value makes it far more likely that '$4ac$' is going to be negative, guaranteeing that the discriminant will be positive.

Homework (5 min)

Pick a different three numbers (all different) and make all six possible equations. Solve each one if possible, and if not explain why they cannot be solved.

To make it harder

Learners could try arranging coefficients 1, 2 and 3 so that:

- the *sum* of the roots is the *maximum* possible
- the *product* of the roots is the *maximum* possible
- the *difference* between the roots is the *maximum* possible
- *one* of the roots is as *large* as possible

Suppose that while you were asleep last night someone went and changed the quadratic formula – every occurrence of it, everywhere, in every book! Would you be able to tell? Why? Which changes can you tell are wrong and which can't you tell easily? (Suppose that you don't actually remember the formula itself.)

Learners may not know how to complete the square to re-derive the formula, but they may still be able to find errors in formulae that are 'close' to being correct. They could do this by using the formula on a quadratic equation that they can solve in some other way; for example, graphically or by factorizing. Also, they may realize that in $ax^2 + bx + c = 0$, if a, b and c are all multiplied by any non-zero constant then the solutions of the equation will not change. This means that the quadratic formula must be 'dimensionally sound', so $\frac{-b \pm \sqrt{b-4ac}}{2a}$, with b under the square root rather than b^2, must be incorrect. They may also spot things like the fact that $\frac{-b+\sqrt{b^2-4ac}}{2a}$, with + instead of the ± symbol, would give only one solution, or that $\frac{-b \pm \sqrt{b^2-4ac}}{2b}$, with a b in the denominator, would be undefined when $b = 0$, which should not happen, since we know that a difference of two squares will factorize. They may realize that $\frac{\pm\sqrt{b^2-4ac}}{2a}$ would mean that the two solutions to any quadratic equation would always have to be of the same magnitude and opposite sign, which is clearly not the case – and so on. Learners could make a poster of 'wrong formulae', annotated with explanations of why the formulae cannot be right – perhaps with the correct formula prominently positioned in the centre.

Keen learners might also like to find out about what 'complex numbers' are and how they can arise from the solutions to quadratic equations.

To make it easier

All learners who can solve quadratic equations using the formula should be able to begin the task, provided that they are encouraged to choose 'nice' enough numbers initially for a, b and c.

Quadratic Probabilities

The solutions to $ax^2 + bx + c = 0$ are $x = \frac{-b \pm \sqrt{b^2 - 4ac}}{2a}$, provided that $a \neq 0$.

Task 1

If a, b and c must be 1, 2 or 3 (repeats allowed), and a random quadratic equation is generated, what is the probability that:

a. the equation has *two distinct real roots*?

b. the equation has *one repeated root*?

c. the equation has *no real roots*?

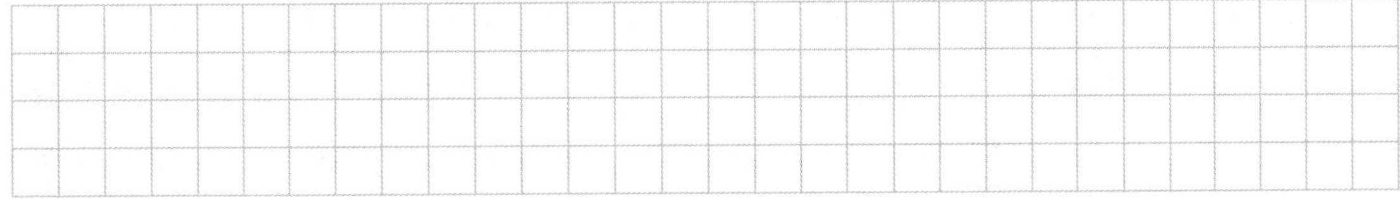

Task 2

This time, a, b and c are chosen at random from the following cards, without replacement (i.e., no repeats):

1

3

What is the probability that:

a. the equation has *two distinct real roots*?

b. the equation has *one repeated root*?

c. the equation has *no real roots*?

Task 3

What difference does it make if you have *exactly one* negative sign (for one of a or b or c)?

47 Quadratics in Disguise

Introduction

When is a quadratic equation not a quadratic equation? Experienced equation solvers will spot when an equation is equivalent by some transformation to a quadratic equation. This means that while they are proceeding step by step with their algebra they have a sense of the bigger picture and are anticipating subsequent steps. This fluency makes for confidence and self-checking and a sense of satisfaction about what is going on. Learners frequently find it very hard to see the wider picture, and switching places with the question writer, and seeking to construct problems with certain kinds of solutions, can be a very worthwhile experience. This lesson gives learners the opportunity to construct and solve quadratic equations in disguise that are guaranteed by them to have rational (and often integer) solutions.

Aims and Outcomes

- manipulate algebraic expressions and substitute numbers for letters and vice versa
- solve quadratic equations by rearranging and factorizing

Lesson Starter (15 min)

Is it easier to make up questions or to answer them? What do you think? Is it easier to be a teacher or a learner?! Perhaps it depends on the question or the lesson: think of some examples each way.

For example, simultaneous equations are often much easier to make up than they are to solve, because you can start with the values of x and y at the beginning. (If you decide that x is going to be 37 and y is going to be 183 then you can easily write down $42x + 51y = 10\,887$ and $27x - 68y = -11\,445$, and it would be much more work for someone else to solve these than it was for you to make them up!)

Try to think of some questions that would be harder to make up than to answer.

Constructing non-calculator questions so that they turn out nicely can be difficult, or fractions questions so that you end up with lots of things cancelling neatly. Dividing a quantity in a certain ratio so that you end up with friendly amounts, angle-chasing questions that aren't too obvious and quadratics that factorize would be other possible examples. Learners are likely to be influenced by whatever work you happen to have been doing recently. Of course, some things, like simultaneous equations, can become harder to set up if you are trying to test specific skills and make the work turn out in a certain way.

Main Lesson (20 min)

Can you solve this equation? $x(x - 2) = 8$

Expanding and rearranging gives $x^2 - 2x - 8 = 0$, which factorizes to $(x - 4)(x + 2) = 0$, so $x = -2$ or 4. (Learners may easily spot that $x = 4$ is a solution, since $4 \times 2 = 8$, but they are less likely to notice that $-2 \times -4 = 8$ gives the other solution.)

Give learners the Task Sheet and encourage them to make up 'quadratics in disguise' that end up giving integer (or at least rational) answers, like this. Learners may begin by deciding what one of the x values is going to be and constructing the equation around this (e.g., set $x = 7$ and write $x(x + 3)$, which must equal 70, and then solve $x(x + 3) = 70$ to check and to find out what the other solution is [$x = -10$]). Alternatively, they may begin with a factorized form such as $(x + 5)(x - 3)$, and expand and rearrange to construct an equation such as $x^2 + 2x = 15$. Perhaps try it both ways?

Plenary (20 min)

The solutions are:

1. $x = -4$ or 3
2. $x = -9$ or 1
3. $x = \pm 4$

The first method (described above) is certainly easier for creating problems like that in Question 3. Begin with a pair of equal products, such as $5 \times 6 = 2 \times 15$. Then choose one of the values for x (say, 4) and construct expressions equal to 5, 6, 2 and 15: $(x + 1)$, $(x + 2)$, $(x - 2)$ and $(2x + 7)$. There is a lot of freedom here. Then substitute in and you have your equation, but you need to solve it to find out what the *other* value of x is ($x = -4$ here). The second solution will not necessarily be an integer – it could be any rational number, and you might choose to accept that or to have a second attempt if it doesn't come out as an integer. The second root cannot be irrational, because irrational roots of quadratics always come in pairs, so if one is rational then the other must be.

For the second section, there are many possibilities, such as $\frac{x+3}{x-1} = \frac{2x+1}{x+2}$ (which has solutions $x = -1$ or 7). In general, you can begin with two equivalent fractions (e.g., $\frac{3}{6} = \frac{2}{4}$). Then choose a rational value for x (e.g., 5). (Of course, as above, x will have *two* values, but the second one will turn up at the end as a surprise. But if one of the x values is rational, then the other one has to be, so it will be all right whatever it is.) Then construct four expressions involving x (which is 5 here) for the four numbers (3, 6, 2 and 4) in the equivalent fractions and substitute them for the numbers; i.e., $\frac{2x-7}{x+1} = \frac{x-3}{x-1}$. Working it through from here gives you the solutions $x = 2$ or 5.

Homework (5 min)

Depending on what point has been reached in the lesson it may seem appropriate to set one or more equation constructions for homework, perhaps along with a written explanation of how each equation was produced and its solution.

To make it harder

Learners who make expert progress with this might like to contemplate the following problem:

Simplify $(x - a)(x - b)(x - c) \ldots (x - z)$.

The answer is zero, because one of the brackets is $(x - x)$, and this kills the whole product.

They also might like to construct other classes of 'disguised quadratics' than those exemplified on the sheet.

To make it easier

Learners who are not confident solving 'undisguised' quadratic equations might be advised to practise these first.

Quadratics in Disguise

Solve these three equations.

Make up another 'quadratic equation in disguise' similar to each one of them. Make sure that the solutions are integers.

1. $\frac{12}{x} = x + 1$
2. $(3x - 2)(x + 7) = (2x - 1)(x + 5) + 2x$
3. $(2x + 7)(x - 2) = (x + 1)(x + 2)$

Now look at this equation:

$$\frac{x + \square}{x - \square} = \frac{\square x + \square}{x + \square}$$

Put positive integers in each of these boxes so that all the solutions (possible values of x) are rational.

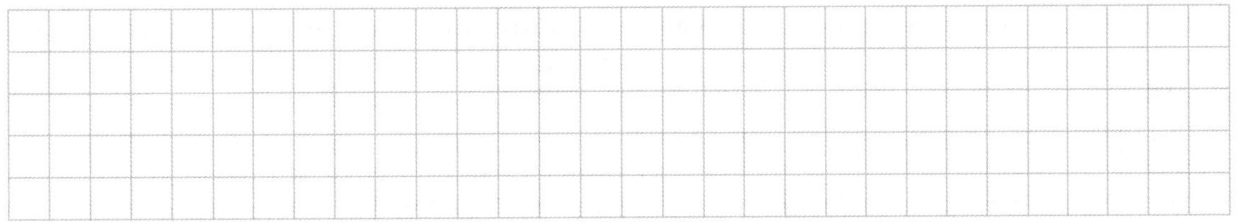

Keep three plus signs and one minus sign, but have the minus sign in a different place.

Again, find positive integers that you can put in these boxes so that the solutions (possible values of x) are rational.

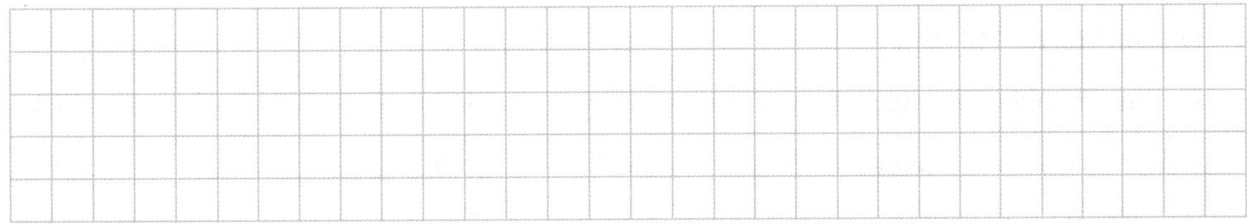

Try to write down how you would explain to someone else how to do this.

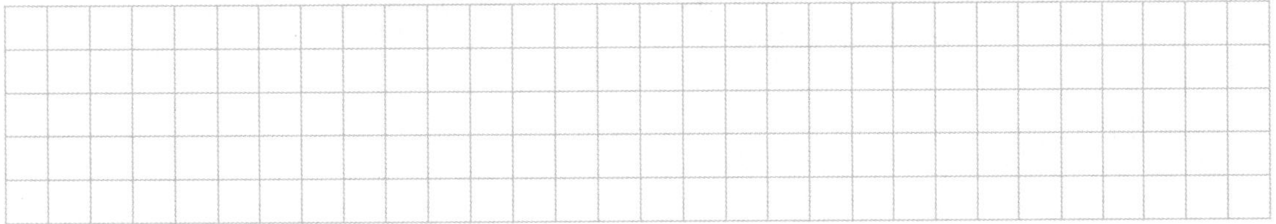

48 Radical Equations

Introduction

In the secondary school curriculum there is a progression from solving simple linear equations such as $5x - 2 = 13$, through similar equations with non-integer and negative solutions to ones with the unknown appearing on both sides, through equations with brackets and fractions to simultaneous and quadratic equations. But there are alternative routes. If a learner can solve $\frac{x}{2} + 9 = 41$ by performing a sequence of operations to both sides of the equation, there is no reason why they could not progress next to tackling non-linear equations such as $\frac{2}{x} + 9 = 41$ or $\sqrt{x} + 9 = 41$ or $x^2 + 9 = 41$ in similar ways. In this lesson, the idea is to work on indices by solving *radical* equations – equations which learners would not normally meet at this level but which provide a context for practising 'the rules of indices', not least by substituting the final answer(s) back into the original equations. The word 'radical' refers to roots. You might wish to avoid calculator use throughout, since modern calculators can be very sophisticated in their handling of complicated indices. Alternatively, learners could be expected to use the technology intelligently for assisting and checking rather than finding the answers, which obviously takes away the purpose of the task.

Aims and Outcomes

- practise applying the laws of indices to numbers and algebra
- use a balancing strategy to solve unfamiliar equations

Lesson Starter (10 min)

If your school has a system of merits or awards, you could put something like this onto the board as learners enter the room. Deliberately make it un-straightforward, and be careful to check that it won't bankrupt you!

I promise to give $\left(\frac{1}{27^{-\frac{2}{3}}}\right)^{\frac{1}{2}} - (5^2 - 3^2)^{\frac{1}{4}} - 7^0$ *merits to every person who can work this out.*

Signed ....

Learners may initially be intimidated by the complexity. Those who opt for calculators may not have as much of an advantage as they think, unless they are very careful and competent with the keys. It is likely that several different answers will be obtained, leading to fruitful discussion.

What did you get? Where did you start? Why do you think your answer is correct? Since $27^{-\frac{2}{3}} = \frac{1}{9}$, the expression reduces to $3 - 2 - 1 = 0$, as learners might have anticipated!

Main Lesson (25 min)

Have learners ever seen *equations* with indices that are negative or fractions? E.g.,

$$5x^{\frac{1}{2}}-2=43.$$

Adding 2 to both sides and dividing both sides by 5 makes this equivalent to

$$x^{\frac{1}{2}}=9.$$

So $x = 81$ (not 3, of course – a common error!) by squaring both sides.

Learners can check on a calculator by substituting in.

Invite learners to make up some equations like this that have integer solutions.

Give out the Task Sheet and allow learners work on solving the radical equations.

Plenary (20 min)

The solutions are 512 (not 2!), 16, 4, 5, 8 and 16. With practice, some learners may be almost able to 'look and say' the solutions without writing anything down.

It would be good to share some of the equations that learners have constructed (such as 'the one you're most pleased with' or 'your hardest equation') and challenge the class to solve it together or in pairs.

Homework (5 min)

Construct a pair of 'simultaneous radical equations' or construct some 'radical inequalities' to solve, in the same way as you might solve more normal versions of these. For example,

$$5x^{\frac{1}{3}}-2y^{\frac{1}{2}}=4$$

$$3x^{\frac{1}{3}}+y^{\frac{1}{2}}=9$$

have the solution x = 8 *and* y = 9. *And* $x^{-\frac{3}{4}}>64$ *has the solution* $x<\frac{1}{256}$ *(note the direction of the inequality sign). Remember that taking the reciprocal of both sides of an inequality – if that step features in your solution, which it needn't necessarily– generally means reversing the direction of the inequality sign: for example, 3 < 5, but* $\frac{1}{3}>\frac{1}{5}$. *But this needs care if one side is negative, since –3 < 5 but* $-\frac{1}{3}<\frac{1}{5}$ *(with the inequality sign the same way round).*

To make it harder

For those who want a more demanding equation, they could try to solve $x^{\frac{2}{3}}+3=4x^{\frac{1}{3}}$. It will be tempting to try to subtract the indices (i.e., to subtract $x^{\frac{1}{3}}$ from both sides, or to divide both sides by this), but the key observation is that $x^{\frac{2}{3}}=\left(x^{\frac{1}{3}}\right)^2$, so this is a quadratic in $x^{\frac{1}{3}}$. This may be handled more easily by letting $y = x^{\frac{1}{3}}$ so that the equation becomes $y^2 + 3 = 4y$ or $y^2 - 4y + 3 = 0$, which factorizes to $(y - 1)(y - 3) = 0$, giving $x^{\frac{1}{3}} = 1$ or $x^{\frac{1}{3}} = 3$, so $x = 1$ or 27 (learners can check these solutions in the original equation). Learners may spot that $x = 1$ is a solution but are less likely to notice $x = 27$, or to be able to justify why there might be only two solutions, so the method outlined has important advantages over an inspection approach that could find *some* solutions but not necessarily *all* the solutions. A similar-looking equation such as $x^{\frac{1}{2}} = 3x^{\frac{1}{4}} + 4$, which, by the same sort of method, gives $x^{\frac{1}{4}} = 4$ or -1, has only *one* solution ($x = 256$), since $x^{\frac{1}{4}} \geq 0$ for all values of x.

To make it easier

Learners who find this work very challenging might be encouraged to devise equations which require *only one step* for their solution.

Radical Equations

All of these equations below have integer solutions.

Solve them.

$2x^{\frac{1}{3}} - 6 = 10$

$2x^{\frac{3}{2}} + 6 = x^{\frac{3}{2}} + 70$

$x^{-2} = \frac{1}{16}$

$15x^{-1} = 3$

$10x^{-\frac{1}{3}} + 1 = 6$

$3x^{\frac{1}{4}} + 5 = 11$

Make up some different equations like these – the solutions must be integers.

Try to make some of them look complicated.

Can you grade your questions according to how hard you think they are?

Do other people agree with your grading?

See if other people can solve your equations. Make sure that *you* know what the answers are!

49 Randomness

Introduction

Please note that for this lesson the homework comes first, in advance of the lesson (see below).

Many learners will happily say that the probability of a fair coin coming up heads is one half, but appreciating the way in which randomness works in practice may be much more subtle. If you throw that coin 100 times what will happen? Learners are frequently confused about how likely they are to get exactly 50 heads, whether this is more or less likely than 49 heads, etc. In fact, 50 heads is the most likely number of heads to get (the mode), and also the mean number of heads in the long run (if you keep throwing the coin 100 times), but the probability of 50 heads is only 0.0796, which is only marginally greater than the probability of getting 49 heads, which is 0.0780 (correct to 3 significant figures). (This is because there are $\frac{51}{50}$ times as many ways of getting 50 heads as there are of getting 49 heads. The number of ways of getting no heads is just one, of course: TTTTT … TTTTT.) Philosophical issues, such as determinism, are likely to come up in discussion, because learners may feel that the roll of a dice or a coin depends solely on physical laws that in principle are predictable. Does this mean that nothing can be truly random? It is quite hard to define what exactly we mean by 'random'.

Aims and Outcomes

- examine the nature of randomness when throwing a fair coin
- understand what it means to say that 'the probability equals one half'

Homework (5 min)

Give learners the top portion of the Task Sheet for them to complete at home in advance of the lesson. It would be hard to do this part in the classroom, as it would be difficult to conceal which learners were throwing the coin and which were concocting the results, as throwing a coin is generally a noisy and obvious business! So preparing this beforehand is quite helpful. Allow yourself enough time to collate the results, either typing them up into a spreadsheet (a learner might be willing to do this?) or photocopying the returned slips of paper (by reducing the size you should be able to fit them all onto two sides of A4). If you simply do not have time for all this, then you can just use the results from my class (I selected 20 sets of results, for convenience) at the bottom of the Task Sheet, though learners are likely to be more engaged in the activity if it is each other's results that are being discussed. Although about half the class will have a different homework task from the other half, it is hard to say which has the greater job!

Lesson Starter (10 min)

Do you think it is possible to control what number comes up when you throw a die? Why / why not?

There are videos on the internet of 'controlled throws' where, with a great deal of practice, someone can have a high probability of getting the number they want, by controlling the way the die spins and rolls before it lands. A quick search, for example on youtube.com, will pull up some quite impressive video clips of these. Just watching without comment can be very engaging. (Remember to check video clips all the way through for suitability beforehand.) Realizing that some people can do this can be worrying for anyone contemplating any serious gambling!

Main Lesson (25 min)

Distribute the results from everyone's homework (see above) and encourage learners to make conjectures about which results are genuine and which are fake. This is a good task to do in groups, because different opinions are likely to emerge and provoke learners into greater thought than if they were working alone.

Plenary (20 min)

The answers (according to the participants!) were:

Name	Genuine/fake
Jack	G
Selina	F
Priya	F
Bella	F
Ryan	G
Ed	F
Dom	F
Deesha	F
Manpal	G
Hannah	G
Ben	F
Kiran	G
Kate	F
Ani	G
Ellie	G
Megan	G
George	F
Oli	G
Abi	F
Tom	F

Typically, learners use many different strategies:

- frequency tests – roughly ten heads and ten tails?
- looking for runs of heads or tails – learners would probably not think to allow five heads in a row, for instance, yet the probability of something like that happening by chance is not as small as many people might think
- counting the number of *switches* from heads to tails and vice versa

'Random' things don't always look all that random. Some people see a connection here with the argument from design for the creation of the universe. Random processes (especially when there is some kind of feedback involved) can lead to very ordered-looking results.

How did we know that the coins were 'fair' in the first place? Perhaps instead we should use results such as these to make conjectures about whether the coins could be considered to be 'fair'?

Learners can reveal whether their results were concocted or genuine. But do we trust learners who were perhaps feeling lazy and so made up the results even though they claimed to have thrown the coin? What proportion of the class claim to have faked their results? It should be about 50 per cent! If suspicion does end up falling on anyone in particular, remember that 'anything can happen' when you throw a coin, so we can never be sure!

To make it harder

Keen learners might like to find out what *Penney's Game* is and how to win it. They might also like to look into whether the digits in a number like pi are 'random' (see Lesson 42).

To make it easier

All learners are likely to be able to have an opinion about whose results are real and whose are not.

Randomness

The Rules

Throw a fair coin once.

- If it comes up *heads*, throw it 20 more times, recording, in order, whether you get heads (H) or tails (T) each time.
- If it comes up *tails*, don't throw the coin any more, but *make up* 20 results that you think look as realistic as possible.

Name: ______________________________

Here are my 'results':

Results

Here are some results from another class:

Whose results do you think are genuine and whose do you think are made up? Why?

Name	1	2	3	4	5	6	7	8	9	10	11	12	13	14	15	16	17	18	19	20	Genuine/ Fake?
Jack	H	H	T	H	H	T	T	T	H	H	T	T	H	H	T	H	T	H	H	T	
Selina	H	T	T	H	T	H	H	T	T	H	T	H	T	T	T	T	H	T	H	T	
Priya	H	T	T	T	H	H	T	H	H	H	H	T	T	T	H	H	H	H	T	H	
Bella	T	H	T	T	T	H	H	T	H	T	T	H	T	T	T	T	H	T	H	H	
Ryan	T	H	H	T	H	H	H	T	H	T	T	T	T	H	H	H	H	T	T	H	
Ed	H	H	T	H	T	H	H	T	T	T	H	H	T	H	T	H	T	T	T	T	
Dom	T	T	T	H	H	T	H	T	T	T	H	T	H	H	T	T	H	T	H	T	
Deesha	T	H	T	H	H	T	H	T	H	H	H	T	T	H	T	T	T	T	H	H	
Manpal	H	T	H	T	T	T	T	T	T	H	H	T	H	H	H	H	H	T	T	T	
Hannah	H	T	H	H	H	T	T	H	T	T	T	T	H	H	H	H	H	T	T	H	
Ben	H	H	T	H	H	T	H	T	H	T	T	T	H	T	T	T	H	T	T	H	
Kiran	H	T	T	H	T	H	H	H	T	T	H	H	T	T	H	T	T	T	T	H	
Kate	T	T	T	T	H	H	T	T	T	H	T	T	T	H	H	T	T	T	T	H	
Ani	T	H	H	T	T	H	T	T	H	T	H	T	T	H	H	T	T	H	H	H	
Ellie	H	T	H	H	H	H	T	H	H	H	H	T	T	T	T	T	H	T	H	H	
Megan	T	H	T	T	T	T	T	H	T	T	T	T	H	H	H	H	T	H	T	H	
George	H	T	T	H	H	T	H	T	H	H	T	T	T	H	T	H	T	H	T	T	
Oli	T	H	H	T	T	H	H	T	T	T	H	H	T	T	H	H	T	T	H	H	
Abi	H	T	T	T	H	T	H	H	T	H	H	T	H	T	H	H	H	T	T	H	
Tom	T	T	H	T	H	H	H	H	H	T	T	H	H	H	T	H	T	T	T	T	

50 Rationalizing Denominators

Introduction

Rationalizing the denominator of a fraction does not always seem like a very 'rational' thing to do. Occasionally textbook questions say, for example, 'Rationalize $\frac{4}{\sqrt{6}}$', as though the entire quantity were becoming rational – an impossibility! To rationalize the *denominator* means to convert the fraction so that the *denominator* is a rational number (often an integer). So, for instance, $\frac{4}{\sqrt{6}} = \frac{4\sqrt{6}}{\sqrt{6}\sqrt{6}} = \frac{4\sqrt{6}}{6} = \frac{2\sqrt{6}}{3}$, which now has a rationalized denominator, though the quantity as a whole is, of course, just as irrational as it was at the beginning (there is no 'cure' for irrationality!). This can often feel like an isolated technique – a trick to be performed on demand rather than with any mathematical purpose in mind. Hopefully learners will appreciate its usefulness in simplifying expressions through the work in this lesson.

Aims and Outcomes

- rationalize denominators of the form $a\sqrt{b}$ by multiplying numerator and denominator by $\sqrt{b}$ and simplifying
- rationalize denominators of the form $a\sqrt{b} \pm c\sqrt{d}$ by multiplying numerator and denominator by $\sqrt{b} \pm \sqrt{d}$ and simplifying
- simplify expressions involving surds

Lesson Starter (10 min)

Think of two numbers that multiply to make 1.

And another example. And another example, etc.

Try to make your examples as interesting/surprising/creative/unusual as possible. Aim to shock us!

For example:

$1 \times 1 = 1$

$2 \times \frac{1}{2} = 1$

$\pi \times \left(\frac{1}{\pi}\right) = 1$

$(7 + 3) \times \left(\frac{1}{135 - 125}\right) = 1$, etc.

Learners may realize that $n \times \left(\frac{1}{n}\right) = 1$, in general, where $n \neq 0$, so the problem can be thought of as being about reciprocals that don't look like reciprocals.

Main Lesson (25 min)

Depending on whether learners have been working with surds recently or not, they may or may not think of incorporating them here. The advantage of surds in this task is that the reciprocal of an expression involving surds frequently looks very different when simplified. So examples such as $(\sqrt{15}+\sqrt{14})(\sqrt{15}-\sqrt{14}) = 1$, which exploit 'the difference of two squares' may be useful.

Encourage learners to find some more like this.

Learners may realize that $(\sqrt{n}+\sqrt{n-1})(\sqrt{n}-\sqrt{n-1}) = 1$, in general, and may need encouragement to see that although this is true only when $n \geq 1$ it is not necessary for n to be an integer. For example, $(\sqrt{15\frac{1}{5}}+\sqrt{14\frac{1}{5}})(\sqrt{15\frac{1}{5}}-\sqrt{14\frac{1}{5}})=1.$

Give out the Task Sheet. It may be possible for learners to check their ideas on a modern mathematical calculator which displays and handles surds in exact form.

Plenary (20 min)

See what ideas learners have constructed. All of the expressions given on the sheet make 1 except for $(3 + \sqrt{2})(3 - \sqrt{2})$, which is equal to 7. (It makes 1 if the threes are changed into $\sqrt{3}$'s.)

Homework (5 min)

Try to find five examples each where $a\sqrt{b}=b\sqrt{a}$ *or where* $a\sqrt{b}=\frac{1}{b\sqrt{a}}$.

In the first case, this simplifies to $a^2b - ab^2 = 0$ (where $a, b \geq 0$), so $ab(a - b) = 0$, which means that either $a = 0$, $b = 0$ or $a = b$. So possible solutions would be $3\sqrt{0}=0\sqrt{3}$, $0\sqrt{0}=0\sqrt{0}$ or $7\sqrt{7}=7\sqrt{7}$, etc.

In the second case, simplifying gives $a^2bb^2a = 1$ (where $a, b > 0$), so $a^3b^3 = 1$, which means that $(ab)^3 = 1$ so that $ab = 1$. So one possible solution would be $\frac{2}{5}\sqrt{\frac{5}{2}}=\frac{1}{\frac{5}{2}\sqrt{\frac{2}{5}}}$.

To make it harder

A challenging problem for learners comfortable with this material would be to simplify $\frac{1}{\sqrt{1}+\sqrt{2}}+\frac{1}{\sqrt{2}+\sqrt{3}}+\frac{1}{\sqrt{3}+\sqrt{4}}+...+\frac{1}{\sqrt{1599}+\sqrt{1600}}$.

If you rationalize the denominators, you get $\frac{\sqrt{2}-\sqrt{1}}{2-1}+\frac{\sqrt{3}-\sqrt{2}}{3-2}+\frac{\sqrt{4}-\sqrt{3}}{4-3}+...+\frac{\sqrt{1600}-\sqrt{1599}}{1600-1599}$, and since all the denominators are 1, this is just $(-\sqrt{1}+\sqrt{2})+(-\sqrt{2}+\sqrt{3})+(-\sqrt{3}+\sqrt{4})+...+(-\sqrt{1599}+\sqrt{1600})$, where all the terms cancel out except the first and the last, so the answer is $40 - 1 = 39$. (This is called the 'method of differences'.)

Learners should try to construct other problems like this.

Another problem for keen learners would be to consider what kind of meaning, if any, can be attached to statements like $(\sqrt{-3}+\sqrt{-4})(\sqrt{-3}-\sqrt{-4})= -3 - (-4) = 1$, which involve the square roots of negative numbers.

To make it easier

Learners who find this work very difficult could begin with fractions with the simplest kind of irrational denominator, such as $\frac{4}{\sqrt{6}}$, and try to rationalize those.

They could also look at a 'surdy' expression and try to estimate its approximate value before and after rationalizing the denominator, checking afterwards on a calculator.

For example,

How big do you think $\frac{5}{\sqrt{3}}$ *is? Why?*

$\frac{5}{\sqrt{3}} = \frac{5}{3}\sqrt{3} \approx \frac{5}{3} \times 1.73\ldots \approx 3$ is perhaps easier than $\frac{5}{\sqrt{3}} = 5 \div 1.73\ldots \approx 3$.

Is this always the case?

Probably not, since $\frac{1}{\sqrt{3}}$ may be simpler to take in and estimate than $\frac{\sqrt{3}}{3}$, although different learners might have different views.

One doesn't equal ... 1!

Make up **ten** expressions involving surds so that **nine** of them are equal to 1 and ***one** of them* isn't.

See if another group can find which one **doesn't** equal 1 – without using a calculator!

Make sure that they check all the expressions and don't stop when they think they've found the odd one out!

Here are some expressions that may give you ideas. Do all of these equal 1? Why / why not?

$$\frac{\sqrt{18}}{3\sqrt{2}}$$

$$\frac{\sqrt{3}+\sqrt{12}}{\sqrt{27}}$$

$$(3+\sqrt{2})(3-\sqrt{2})$$

$$(\sqrt{1}+\sqrt{2}+\sqrt{3})\left(\frac{\sqrt{3}-\sqrt{2}-\sqrt{1}}{-2\sqrt{2}}\right)$$

$$(\sqrt{3}+\sqrt{2})(\sqrt{3}-\sqrt{2})$$

$$\frac{\sqrt{32}+\sqrt{2}}{\sqrt{8}+\sqrt{18}}$$

$$\frac{1}{\sqrt{3}}\left(\frac{(\sqrt{3})^2-1}{2\sqrt{3}}+\frac{1}{\sqrt{3}}+\frac{2}{\sqrt{12}}\right)$$

What expressions can you invent that equal 1?

Plan how to convince other people that they really equal 1.

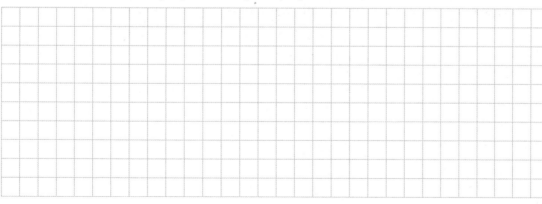

51 Recurring Decimals

Introduction

Learners often do not connect methods for converting terminating decimals (such as 0.13) into simplified fractions with methods for converting *recurring* decimals (such as $0.\dot{1}\dot{3}$) into simplified fractions. There are many 'recurring' misconceptions around this area, such as thinking that 0.3 (not recurring) or 0.33 (not recurring) or 33.3 per cent (without the final 3 recurring) is equal to $\frac{1}{3}$, or giving answers such as $\frac{13}{100}$ to a question asking for $0.\dot{1}\dot{3}$ as a simplified fraction. Several different notations are commonly used to indicate a recurring unit within a decimal. An ellipsis (…) is suitable only in contexts where no ambiguity can result over exactly which digits are repeating, so it would probably be unsuitable in this lesson. More helpful are dots (used here) or a vinculum or brackets indicating the recurring portion; for example, $0.1356356356\ldots = 0.1\dot{3}5\dot{6} = 0.1\overline{356} =$ 0.1(356).

Aims and Outcomes

- convert a recurring decimal into a fraction
- find all possible numbers made by combinations of given digits
- use correct notation for recurring decimals

Lesson Starter (10 min)

What numbers can you make from the digits 1, 2 and 3, using each once only?

How can you show that you have found all the possibilities?

The six possibilities are 123, 132, 213, 231, 312 and 321. Learners might wish to list them in a 'systematic' order to demonstrate that all possibilities have been found or use a tree diagram such as:

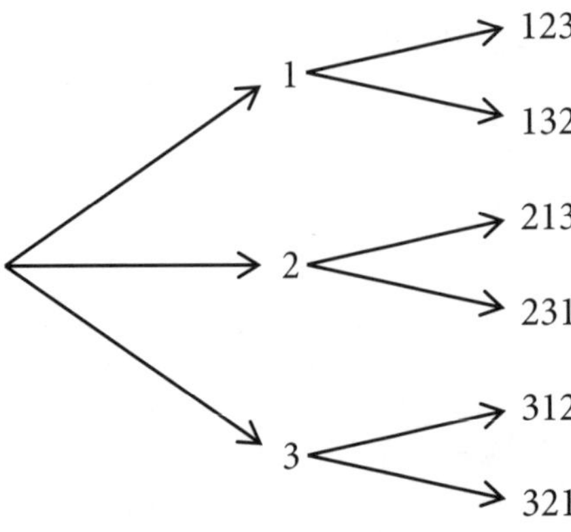

They could also argue that there must be $3 \times 2 \times 1$ possible combinations, so provided that we have six different answers then we must have found them all.

What if you can have 'a dot' as well?

Interpreting the 'dot' as a decimal point should lead to the following six possibilities: 1.23, 1.32, 2.13, 2.31, 3.12, 3.21, with learners perhaps asking whether '.123', for instance, is acceptable without an initial zero.

What if you can have 'another dot' as well, or as many 'dots' as you like?

This may be mystifying, and learners may wonder whether a number can have two decimal points in it. But a dot can go *over* a digit to indicate 'recurring', or 'three dots' (an ellipsis) can be plugged onto the end to indicate that some digits are going to recur.

Another 12 numbers would be possible by placing, for each one, the dot on either the third digit or on both the second and the third digits; for example, from 1.23 you could have $1.2\dot{3}$ or $1.\dot{2}\dot{3}$ – but $1.\dot{2}3$ would not be allowed, since the '3' after the 'recurring 2' would not make sense – when would it appear? Not until *after* 'infinitely many 2s'!

Main Lesson (25 min)

Give out the Task Sheet. Learners could use a mathematical calculator to make the conversions to fractions and look for patterns, or they could take the task as an opportunity to practise a technique such as the following:

Let $x = 8.\dot{0}\dot{1}$.

Then $100x = 801.\dot{0}\dot{1}$, so subtracting gives

$99x = 801 - 8 = 793$

$x = \frac{793}{99} = 8\frac{1}{99}$

Here, multiplying by 100 (or 10^n where n is any even number greater than zero) leads to cancelling out of the recurring decimal in the subtraction step. In general, with an n-unit repeating decimal, multiply by 10^n.

The subtraction step is a subtracting of one infinite series from another, so you may feel that this requires some justification. Learners who believe a statement like $\frac{1}{3} - \frac{1}{6} = \frac{1}{6}$ may be convinced if they look at the 'cancelling out' in the decimal expansions.

Plenary (20 min)

The answers are:

Terminating: $1.8 = \frac{9}{5}$, $1.08 = \frac{27}{25}$, $8.1 = \frac{81}{10}$, $8.01 = \frac{801}{100}$, $0.18 = \frac{9}{50}$, $0.81 = \frac{81}{100}$

Recurring: $1.\dot{8} = \frac{17}{9} = 1\frac{8}{9}$, $1.0\dot{8} = \frac{49}{45} = 1\frac{4}{45}$, $1.\dot{0}\dot{8} = \frac{107}{99} = 1\frac{8}{99}$, $8.\dot{1} = \frac{73}{9} = 8\frac{1}{9}$, $8.0\dot{1} = \frac{721}{90} = 8\frac{1}{90}$, $8.\dot{0}\dot{1} = \frac{793}{99} = 8\frac{1}{99}$, $0.1\dot{8} = \frac{17}{90}$, $0.\dot{1}\dot{8} = \frac{2}{11}$, $0.8\dot{1} = \frac{73}{90}$ and $0.\dot{8}\dot{1} = \frac{9}{11}$

Learners may notice things like $0.8\dot{1} \times 10 = 8.\dot{1}$.

Homework (5 min)

Choose another three numbers and repeat the task. Perhaps let two of the numbers be the same, so as to limit the number of possibilities and make the task more manageable.

To make it harder

Confident learners could try to use the method to show that $0.\dot{9} = 1$, for instance. They could also investigate when a fraction will lead to a recurring, rather than a terminating, decimal. Provided the fraction is in its simplest form, it is dependent solely on the value of the denominator. Any denominator that can be expressed as a product of powers of 2 and 5 only will lead to a terminating decimal expansion; all other fractions will give recurring decimals. Learners might like to find and explain this result and consider what happens in other bases, which might help them to see why twos and fives are special in base 10.

To make it easier

All learners will be able to make numbers from combining digits. Some learners may benefit from the support of a calculator to help with the conversions.

180

Make *all possible* decimal numbers using the three digits 1, 8 and 0 exactly once each.

Check whether any of your numbers are the same as each other.

Remember to include *recurring* decimals as well as terminating ones.

Convert each of your decimals into a simplified fraction.

Which are easy and which are hard? Why?

What patterns can you find? Can you explain them?

52

Reverse Percentages

Introduction

Finding the *original* amount, *before* a specified percentage increase or decrease, is often done incorrectly by learners. For example, when trying to solve the problem: 'After a 20 per cent increase, some shoes sell for £30. How much were they before?', it is tempting to work out 20 per cent of £30 and subtract it, giving £24, but this is wrong, and learners often find it hard to see why. This lesson aims to shed some light on this type of problem.

Aims and Outcomes

- find a percentage increase or decrease of an amount
- find a reverse percentage

Lesson Starter (10 min)

'Multiplying makes things bigger' – when is that correct and when is it wrong? Why?

Learners could discuss this in pairs, trying to come up with examples and explanations.

For example:

$3 \times 1 = 3$ (multiplying by 1 keeps the value the same; multiplying by three makes the value bigger)

$3 \times 0 = 0$ (multiplying by zero makes the value disappear to nothing; multiplying by three leads to no change here)

$3 \times -1 = -3$ (multiplying by a negative number makes a positive number get smaller but a negative number get bigger)

$3 \times 0.1 = 0.3$ (multiplying by a number between zero and 1 makes a positive number get smaller)

Learners sometimes use the words 'decimal' or 'fraction' to refer to numbers between 0 and 1, even though fractions and decimals can lie outside this range, and this may benefit from clarification. This is exacerbated by the common usage of 'just a fraction' to mean 'a very small part'.

Main Lesson (25 min)

Let's stick with positive numbers only for now. When does multiplying make something bigger?

When the 'multiplier' is more than one.

What happens when the multiplier is equal to one or less than one?

Start with an amount of money, say, £30, and multiply by 1.2. What happens?

Try to describe how much bigger the amount of money gets. What if you started with £40 instead?

This should lead to some talk about proportions of the original amount being added on – a 20 per cent increase.

Give learners the Task Sheet. They could use a calculator or not, as you wish. The aim is that they see for themselves, without being told it, that the original ('old') amount is the 'new' amount divided by the 'multiplier' (1.2 in this case). Learners may suggest going back by picking various trial values (trial and improvement) and multiplying each one by 1.2. Division may be suggested if you ask something like: *I think of a number, I times by 1.2 and I get 66. How can you find the number I started with?*

Plenary (20 min)

The answers are:

'Old' amount	Multiplier	'New' amount	Increase
£10	× 1.2	£12	£2
£20	× 1.2	£24	£4
£30	× 1.2	£36	£6
£40	× 1.2	£48	£8
£50	× 1.2	£60	£10

What patterns have you found?

A multiplier of 1.2 increases by 20 per cent.

Why does that happen? Can you extend this pattern?

What multiplier would you need for an n% *increase? An* n% *decrease?*

A multiplier of $1 + \frac{n}{100}$ leads to an n% increase, and a multiplier of $1 - \frac{n}{100}$ leads to an n% decrease. (Learners may not need to express this so generally in order to appreciate the pattern.)

After a 20 per cent increase, some shoes sell for £30. How much were they before?

The answer is $\frac{30}{1.2}$ = £25. (Learners can check it by doing £25 × 1.2 = £30.)

Here's a different way: Twenty per cent of £30 is £6. £30 – £6 = £24, which is wrong by £1. *Why does that happen?* Because we added on 20 per cent of £25 but (mistakenly) took off 20 per cent of £30, which is £1 more! Learners may not appreciate this point fully merely by hearing others explain it, however well – it may be worth asking learners to 'explain it to your neighbour' or write down an explanation in their own words. Can they invent their own examples of this where all the amounts are integer numbers of pounds?

Homework (5 min)

Make up some reverse percentage problems (finding the 'old' amount from the 'new' amount) by starting with the old amount and multiplying. Solve them by division, as if you didn't know the answer. Then swap your questions with someone else and see if you can solve each other's. Make sure you're confident what the answers to your questions are!

To make it harder

Harder percentage changes (such as VAT at 17.5 per cent, say) lead to multiplication and division by multipliers of 1.175 and 0.825, which can be challenging. Other difficult percentage changes are 0.1 per cent or 250 per cent, etc. Confident learners might work on reversing *successive* percentage changes; for example, a 20 per cent decrease, followed by a 3 per cent increase, followed by …, etc.

To make it easier

Some learners may try to cling to methods that involve working out the increase or decrease and adding or subtracting. This may be fine for finding 'new' amounts but will not help them with finding the 'old' amount. A preparatory goal may be to extend their comfort zone to using the multiplier method to find new amounts and to leave tackling reverse percentage problems for another time.

Reverse Percentages

Fill in the gaps in this table.

Check first that you agree with the third line that is given!

'Old' amount	Multiplier	'New' amount	Increase
£10	× 1.2		
£20	× 1.2		
£30	× 1.2	£36	£6
£40	× 1.2		
£50	× 1.2		

Compare the increase amounts with the old amounts.

Can you find a connection?

Imagine that you knew that the new amount was £150.

How could you work out the old amount?

Write down any ideas that you have.

Make up an 'old' amount of money.

Multiply by 1.2.

Tell someone else the answer.

Can they work out the amount you started with without you telling them?

How would it work with different multipliers, instead of 1.2?

What if the multiplier were less than 1 – say 0.8?

How would this make a difference?

53 Rounding

Introduction

It is sometimes ambiguous in mathematics lessons whether a length, say, given as 10 cm, is expected to be taken as precisely 10 cm long or whether it is a measurement with a certain degree of error. Perhaps the length (l) lies in the interval [9.5, 10.5) – i.e., $9.5 \le l < 10.5$ – or perhaps the value is accurate only to 1 significant figure, in which case l is in the wider interval [5, 15), i.e., $5 \le l < 15$. (When the bracket notation is used, square brackets indicate a 'closed' interval [*including* the value at that end] and curved brackets indicate an 'open' interval [*excluding* the value at that end].) Sometimes rounding is an unavoidable consequence of measurement; other times it is carried out for convenience, because we do not need to know the exact value. This lesson aims to provoke thought about rounding by introducing the 'floor' and 'ceiling' functions, which learners may not have met explicitly before. It may not be especially important for them to know these definitions, but working in this context could be helpful for appreciating what is going on when rounding numbers. (For more on rounding, see Lesson 62.)

Aims and Outcomes

- examine the conventions that lie behind how rounding is carried out
- practise using inequalities to express ranges of values
- use the 'floor' and 'ceiling' functions

Lesson Starter (5 min)

'One of the dinosaur skeletons at the National History Museum is 100 million years and two weeks old.'

'How do you know that?'

'When I visited the museum, they said it was 100 million years old, and that was two weeks ago.'

Why is this silly?

Learners should realize that '100 million years' does not mean *exactly* 100 million years!

Between what possible values do you think the age could be, if it's stated as '100 million years'?

There are several possible answers.

Main Lesson (25 min)

Give learners the Task Sheet and encourage them to make sense of the definitions. If learners are uncertain or confused, one way to proceed is to decline to offer explanation but instead to be willing to answer questions such as 'What is floor of 5.6?' or 'Is ceiling of –11.2 equal to –11 or –12?' This can be a more independent way of learners clarifying their understanding.

At any stage, it is helpful to insert numbers in place of x or y to get a sense of what is going on.

Plenary (25 min)

These graphs use the convention that a *filled-in* dot *includes* that value in the marked region, and a *hollow* dot *excludes* it. Making a 'staircase' graph, with vertical line segments at integer values of x, is not really appropriate, since those line segments suggest multiple values of y for integer values of x, which would prevent these relations from being functions. The graphs are single-valued everywhere but *discontinuous* (can't be drawn without taking your pen off the paper, like $y = \frac{1}{x}$ at $x = 0$).

$y = \lfloor x \rfloor$

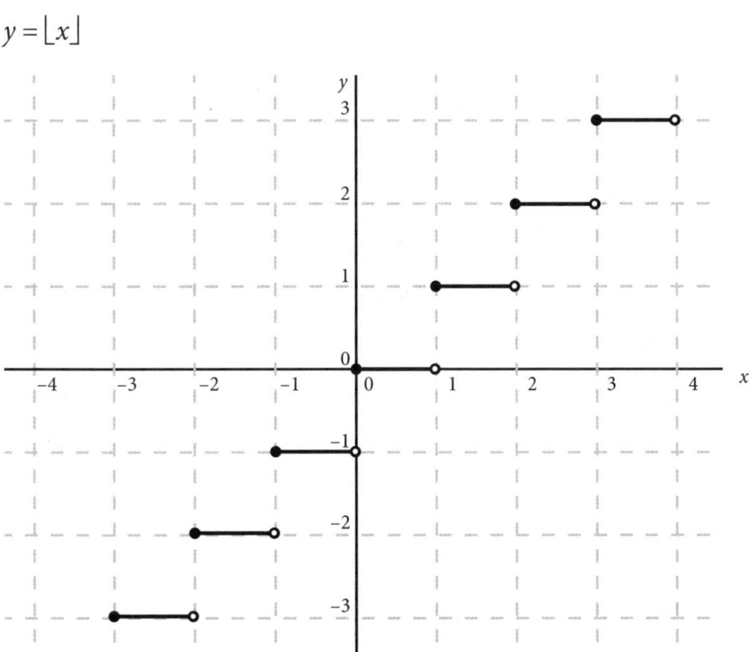

$y = \lceil x \rceil$

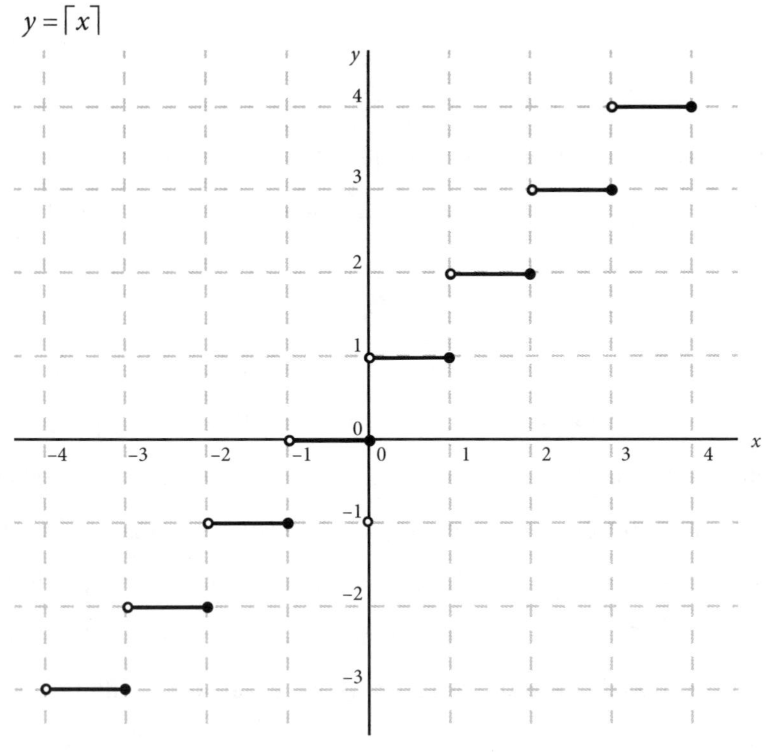

$y = x$ rounded to the nearest interger ($y = \lfloor x + 0.5 \rfloor$)

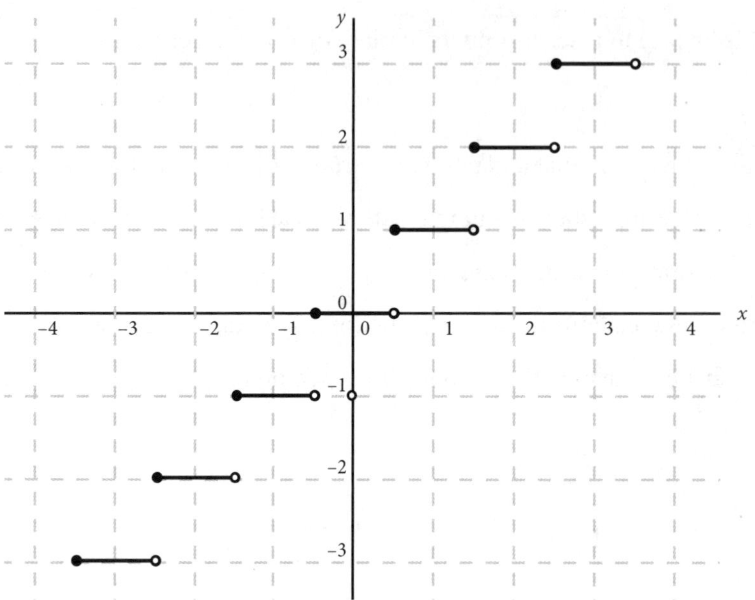

Equations such as $\lfloor x \rfloor = 5$ (solution: $5 \leq x < 6$) and $\lceil x - 3 \rceil = 10$ (so, $9 < x - 3 \leq 10$, giving the solution: $12 < x \leq 13$) may be solved from the above graphs or by intelligent use of number lines or 'logical thinking'. In general, $\lfloor x \rfloor = k$, where k is an integer, is equivalent to $k \leq x < k + 1$, and $\lceil x \rceil = k$ is equivalent to $k - 1 < x \leq k$. Getting learners to formulate this precisely can be challenging and worthwhile.

Other relevant results are:

$\lfloor x \rfloor + \lceil -x \rceil = 0$ for all values of x

$\lceil x \rceil - \lfloor x \rfloor = 0$ if x is an integer; otherwise, it equals 1

$\lceil x \rceil + \lceil y \rceil \geq \lceil x + y \rceil \geq \lceil x \rceil + \lceil y \rceil - 1$

$\lfloor x \rfloor + \lfloor y \rfloor \leq \lfloor x + y \rfloor \leq \lfloor x \rfloor + \lfloor y \rfloor + 1$

Homework (5 min)

Find out about the different rules that are sometimes used for rounding values which are exactly half way between integers. According to some rules, 8.5 would round to 8 and according to others it would round to 9. Why?

It is common to round 'up' the half-way points, so 8.5 would round to 9. However, if you keep on doing this with all the 'half' numbers, this can introduce a bias into statistical data, in which quantities become, on average, overestimated. So in some situations, you might prefer to throw a coin to decide whether to round up or down, or you might round to the nearest *even* number (so in this case 8.5 would go *down* to 8 but 9.5 would go *up* to 10). Even if you stick to the normal 'round up' rule, you have to decide what to do with negative numbers, such as –2.5. Strictly rounding 'up' (i.e., in the positive infinity direction) would make that –2, but often instead the convention is to round 'away from 0', which would instead make it –3. This is always done with physical quantities.

For example, the charge on an electron is $-1.602176487 \times 10^{-19}$ C, but if you were rounding this to five significant figures you would definitely round 'up in magnitude' to -1.6022×10^{-19} C.

To make it harder

Learners who make good progress could try to describe 'ordinary rounding to the nearest integer' using the floor or ceiling functions. When x is rounded to the nearest integer, the answer is $\lfloor x + 0.5 \rfloor$. This may be seen most easily by considering a number line or comparing the graphs of $y = \lfloor x \rfloor$ and $y = \lfloor x + 0.5 \rfloor$.

How could you describe rounding x *'correct to one decimal place'?* This could be $\frac{\lfloor 10x + 0.5 \rfloor}{10}$. In general, rounding x 'correct to n decimal places' could be written as $\frac{\lfloor 10^n x + 0.5 \rfloor}{10^n}$.

Keen learners could also worry about how many solutions there are to some of their inequalities. *What if the solutions have to be* integers? *How many then?*

Suppose that for now all solutions have to be integers. (Diophantine equations are ones where the solutions have to be integers.) For example, with an equation like '$3x - 5 = 120$ (correct to two significant figures)', suppose that the 'correct to two significant figures' in all these problems always relates only to the number immediately before it; 120 in this case, not the 3 or the 5. (But what if the 3 and the 5 are *also* only correct to two significant figures?) So this is equivalent to the double inequality $115 \le 3x - 5 < 125$ or $120 \le 3x < 130$, so $40 \le x < 43\frac{1}{3}$, so since x is an integer it must be 40, 41, 42 or 43 only, so there are exactly four solutions. Learners may not express the problem so formally in this way, using inequalities. They are probably more likely to solve the equations $3x - 5 = 15$ and $3x - 5 = 125$ or begin by solving $3x - 5 = 120$ and use trial and improvement, providing lots of opportunities to practise rounding along the way.

To make it easier

Learners who find this hard may need to experiment with many possible decimal values, particularly the 'point fives' midway between integers.

Floor and Ceiling Functions

If you are already on an integer, you stay there, so $\lfloor 3 \rfloor = 3$ and $\lceil 3 \rceil = 3$

When you are in between two consecutive integers, *floor* ($\lfloor\ \rfloor$) gives the lower one, and *ceiling* ($\lceil\ \rceil$) gives the higher one.

For example, with floor, $\lfloor 3 \rfloor = 3$, $\lfloor 3.2 \rfloor = 3$, $\lfloor 3.5 \rfloor = 3$, $\lfloor 3.9 \rfloor = 3$, and with ceiling, $\lceil 3 \rceil = 3$, $\lceil 3.2 \rceil = 4$, $\lceil 3.5 \rceil = 4$, $\lceil 3.9 \rceil = 4$.

The same thing works with negative numbers, so that $\lfloor -3.2 \rfloor = -4$ and $\lceil -3.2 \rceil = -3$.

Try illustrating these on a vertical number line.

Draw graphs of $y = \lfloor x \rfloor$ and $y = \lceil x \rceil$ on the same axes.

Also draw the graph of $y = x$ (rounded to the nearest integer).

Make up and solve equations like $\lfloor x \rfloor = 5$, $\lceil x - 3 \rceil = 10$, etc.

Work out $\lfloor x \rfloor + \lceil -x \rceil$ for different values of x.

What do you notice? Make a conjecture and try to prove it.

Work out $\lceil x \rceil - \lfloor x \rfloor$ for different values of x.

What do you notice? Make a conjecture and try to prove it.

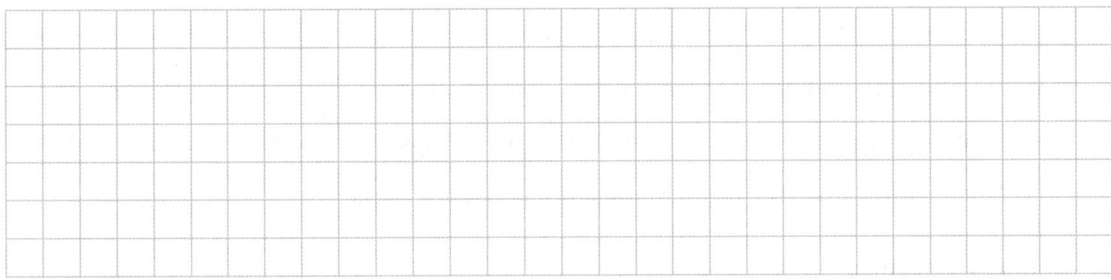

Work out $\lceil x \rceil + \lceil y \rceil$ and $\lceil x + y \rceil$ for different pairs of values of x and y.

Which comes out larger? Make a conjecture and try to prove it.

Work out $\lfloor x \rfloor + \lfloor y \rfloor$ and $\lfloor x + y \rfloor$ for different pairs of values of x and y.

Which comes out larger? Make a conjecture and try to prove it.

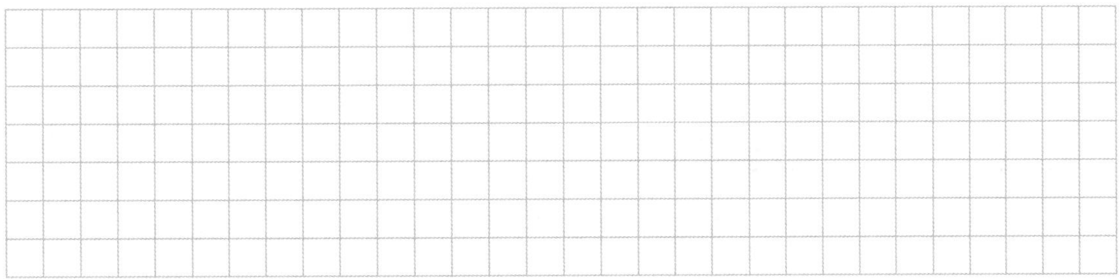

54 Set Theory

Introduction

The idea of this lesson is to avoid giving definitions, as a lecturer might – such material can be almost immediately forgotten! – and instead offer a 'set' of true statements written symbolically and ask learners to use their sense-making powers to work out what it all might mean. Professional mathematicians can be in this position when reading mathematics that is a little outside their field, trying to grasp what is going on and inferring the meanings of the symbols and statements from the context. All learners will have gaps in their mathematical knowledge, so this process would seem to be a genuinely mathematical one and relevant in any situation where some knowledge is lacking. It is perhaps a more independent approach than looking it up in a textbook! Learners are encouraged to work inductively to build 'concept images' relating to sets – these can later be developed into more formal 'concept definitions'. (See Alcock, L. and Simpson, A. (2009), *Ideas from Mathematics Education*. Birmingham: The Higher Education Academy, chapter 1.)

Aims and Outcomes

- consider intersecting sets and their pictorial representation
- make sense of unfamiliar symbols in the context of Venn diagrams

Lesson Starter (15 min)

Choose two non-mutually exclusive and non-exhaustive categories appropriate for your learners; for example, A = {people who do Art}; B = {basketball players}, or whatever is relevant and of interest to the class you teach. Make sure that there will be at least one person in each of the four regions of the Venn diagram, and that the person in the 'outer' region is not going to be made to feel deficient because of it!

Draw the Venn diagram – learners may well be familiar with such pictures.

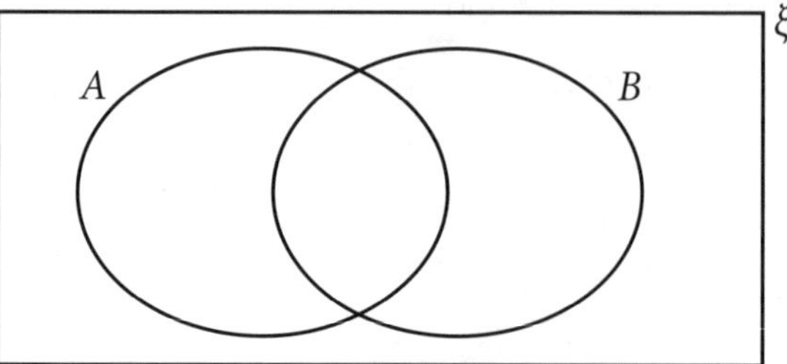

Pick a learner and ask them: *Where do you belong?* If this is insufficient, you could ask *Do you do Art? Do you play basketball?* (even if you know the answers to these questions). Then write their initials in the appropriate region. Then invite other learners (everyone if you have a small class) to come and put their initials in the appropriate region. Arguments are to be expected ('I go to Art club but don't do it for GCSE', 'I did do basketball but I don't any more', etc.) and negotiating around these is all part of the game.

If it hasn't been commented on, draw attention to the universal set symbol (ξ) and ask what learners think it means. It will be either {everyone in our class} or {everyone who put their initials on the board}.

If you wish, you could pick a set of initials on the board and ask, *What would happen if this person moved here?* and drag your finger to another region. Learners can answer in terms of the context: 'It would mean she gave up basketball but carried on doing Art', etc.

Main Lesson (20 min)

Give learners the Task Sheet and avoid telling them what the symbols mean. Invite them to look for patterns and structure. The hardest thing to figure out may be the $n(A)$ notation, but it may come suddenly in a flash of inspiration. Such moments tend to be far more memorable than a quick point made by a teacher.

Learners may wish to draw multiple Venn diagrams, shading in and labelling the relevant regions. This may be the clearest way to summarize their conclusions.

Plenary (20 min)

Each group of learners could describe and explain one symbol or feature. It may be worth bearing in mind that the person who gets the most out of an explanation is frequently the explainer. The main value in learners explaining to one another is likely to be for those doing the explaining. The teacher could perhaps produce a 'better', clearer explanation, but that is not the point!

Homework (5 min)

Make up a sheet like the Task Sheet, with two different starting sets A and B. Learners could be asked to keep the algebra the same and change the lists of elements for each one, to match their chosen sets, or be invited to invent different statements – though this may end up being very time consuming to mark, unless learners mark each other's!

To make it harder

Learners who require additional challenges could be asked to find, and prove visually, identities such as $A \cup B = A + B - A \cap B$. They could also try to find the corresponding statement for *three* circles.

The answer is $A \cup B \cup C = A + B + C - (A \cap B) - (A \cap C) - (B \cap C) + (A \cap B \cap C)$.

Even with just two sets, A and B, using complements (A' and B') can make statements quite challenging; e.g., $A' \cap B' = \xi - (A \cup B)$. Learners could also explore commutativity, associativity and distributivity.

Another interesting task is the following: *What is the maximum number of regions you can get with n overlapping circles?*

Learners sometimes assume that it is 2^n, because with one circle you get two regions (inside and outside), with two circles you get four regions and with three circles you can get eight regions, but with four circles there are only *14* regions (not 16), and in fact *plane division by circles*, as it is called, follows the formula $n^2 - n + 2$. (This is a good example of the dangers of assuming that a simple rule will continue for all values of n.) Learners could experiment with ellipses instead of circles, where 14 regions are possible with just *three* ellipses, the general rule this time being $2(n^2 - n + 1)$. (For comparison, the corresponding formula for *plane division by lines* is $\frac{1}{2}(n^2 + n + 2)$.)

To make it easier

If learners are unfamiliar with working in this kind of way, then it is quite likely that the majority of the class may almost immediately claim to be stuck! Avoid telling learners the answers but try to encourage them to plug away at it and make some sense out of the statements. You might want to reassure learners that it is OK to be confused for a while.

Set Theory

ξ = {integers from 1 to 12 inclusive} = {1, 2, 3, 4, 5, 6, 7, 8, 9, 10, 11, 12}

A = {even numbers}

B = {multiples of 3}

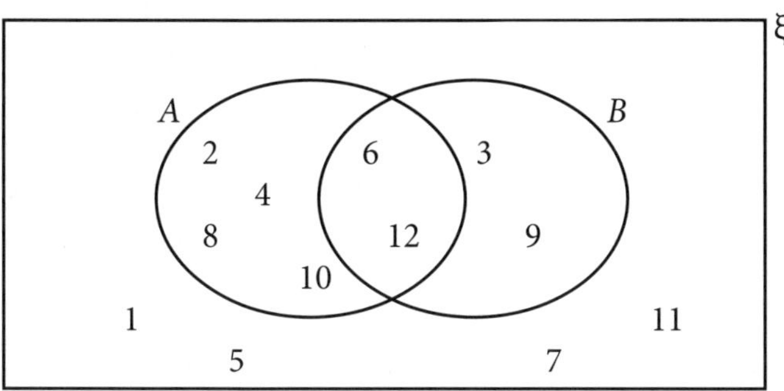

Use the diagram above to make sense of the symbols and statements below.

1	$A \cap B = \{6, 12\}$	$n(A \cap B) = 2$
2	$A \cup B = \{2, 3, 4, 6, 8, 9\ 10, 12\}$	$n(A \cup B) = 8$
3	$(A \cap B)' = \{1, 2, 3, 4, 5, 7, 8, 9\ 10, 11\}$	$n((A \cap B)') = 10$
4	$A \cap B' = \{2, 4, 8, 10\}$	$n(A \cap B') = 4$
5	$(A \cup B)' = \{1, 5, 7, 11\}$	$n((A \cup B)') = 4$
6	$A \cup B' = \{1, 2, 4, 5, 6, 7, 8, 10, 11, 12\}$	$n(A \cup B') = 10$
7	$A' \cap B = \{3, 9\}$	$n(A' \cap B) = 2$
8	$A' \cup B = \{1, 3, 5, 6, 7, 9, 11, 12\}$	$n(A' \cup B) = 8$
9	$A' = \{1, 3, 5, 7, 9, 11\}$	$n(A') = 6$
10	$B' = \{1, 2, 4, 5, 7, 8, 10, 11\}$	$n(B') = 8$
11	$\xi = \{1, 2, 3, 4, 5, 6, 7, 8, 9, 10, 11, 12\}$	$n(\xi) = 12$
12	$9 \in B$	
13	$9 \notin A$	
14	$6 \in A \cap B$	
15	$9 \notin A \cap B$	

Illustrate your conclusions clearly.

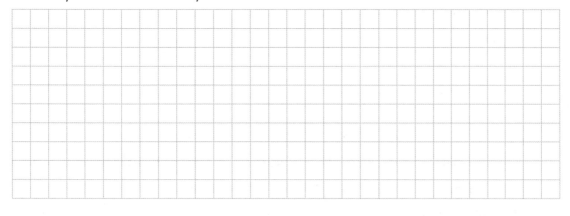

55 Similarity

Introduction

This is an important topic that brings together ideas from ratio, enlargements, scale factors and proportionality. Similarity is one of the big themes in Classical geometry. When a geometry problem can be solved 'merely' by using ratio and similar triangles, many mathematicians would regard this as more elegant than using the heavier machinery of calculating sin, cos and tan, for instance. Learners need to appreciate that 'similar' is an ordinary word that also can have a technical mathematical meaning. You might think that two rectangles look similar, but they are only *mathematically* similar if their sides are in the same ratio as each other. All circles are similar and all squares are similar, but not all rectangles are similar – it might be good to ask learners to explain why.

Aims and Outcomes

- understand the conditions under which two shapes are similar
- understand the properties of similar shapes

Lesson Starter (15 min)

Look at this drawing, made up of two pairs of parallel lines and one diagonal:

(You could consider drawing this in a less traditional orientation to dispel the popular notion that a shape drawn on the board has a special mathematical name only if at least one of its sides is parallel to the floor!)

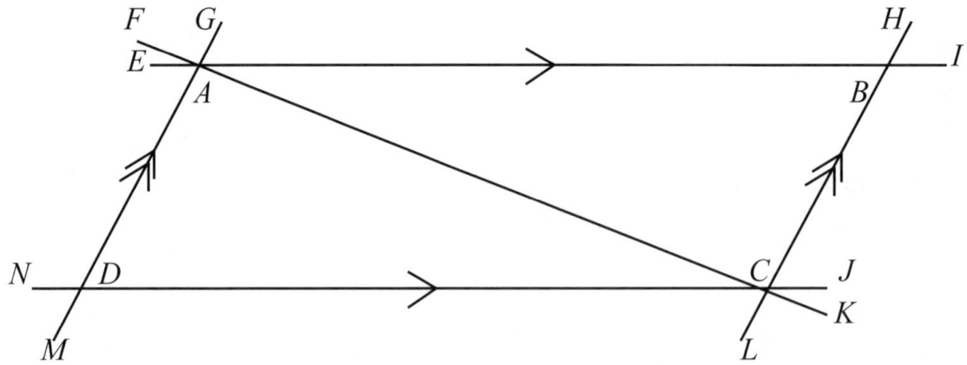

What can you say about this shape? It is a quadrilateral with parallel sides, equal-length opposite sides, equal opposite angles, is called a parallelogram, it contains two congruent triangles, etc. Encourage learners to make lots of observations and comments.

Depending on whether learners are familiar with the *ABC* notation for angles and with ideas such as 'corresponding angles', you could ask them to describe a pair of corresponding angles or a pair of supplementary angles (adding up to 180°). Unless they use the *ABC* notation, they are likely to struggle to say from their seat which angle they mean. There will be lots of pointing and phrases like 'that bit around the thing' and learners will want to come up to the board. So it is a natural opportunity to introduce (or remind learners of) the *ABC* notation.

Then ask for:

- a pair of corresponding angles
- a pair of alternate angles
- a pair of vertically opposite angles
- etc.

Main Lesson (20 min)

Add another (horizontal) line parallel to *AB* and *CD*, but not necessarily bisecting *BC* and *AD*.

What has happened now?

What about the new angles we have created?

What about the new shapes?

Similar shapes are produced, since angles in the same relative positions are equal to each other.

Give out the Task Sheet and ask learners to measure accurately (say, correct to the nearest millimetre) and to work out the ratios correct to one decimal place.

Plenary (20 min)

The answers are, in millimetres: $(a, b, c) = (18, 48, 36)$; $(a', b', c') = (34, 90, 68)$; and, in degrees: $(A, B, C) = (19, 120, 41)$.

The ratios, correct to one decimal place, are:

$\frac{b}{a}=2.7$ $\frac{c}{a}=2.0$

$\frac{a}{b}=0.4$ $\frac{c}{b}=0.8$

$\frac{a}{c}=0.5$ $\frac{b}{c}=1.3$

$\frac{b'}{a'}=2.6$ $\frac{c'}{a'}=2.0$

$\frac{a'}{b'}=0.4$ $\frac{c'}{b'}=0.8$

$\frac{a'}{c'}=0.5$ $\frac{b'}{c'}=1.3$

$\frac{a}{a'}=0.5$ $\frac{b}{b'}=0.5$ $\frac{c}{c'}=0.5$

$\frac{a'}{a}=1.9$ $\frac{b'}{b}=1.9$ $\frac{c'}{c}=1.9$

So the two triangles are similar, with scale factor about 2.

You could then think about combining two similar triangles by joining them in different ways:

1. Fit the smaller one inside the larger one.

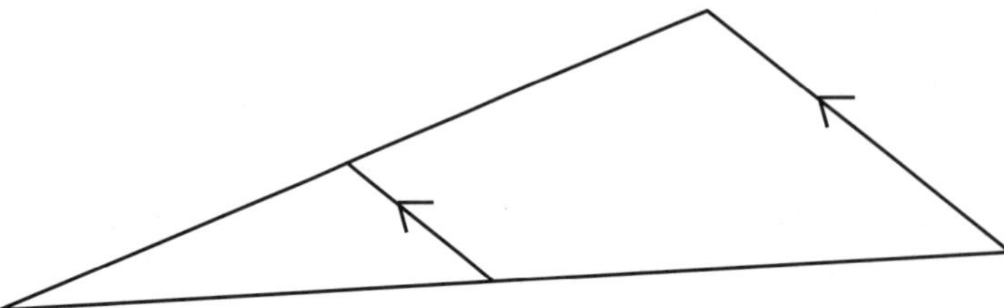

How do you know that the lines marked as parallel really are?

The converse of the idea that *corresponding* angles on parallel lines are equal is that equal angles mean that you have parallel lines.

2. Rotate one of them 180° and let them meet at a pair of corresponding vertices.

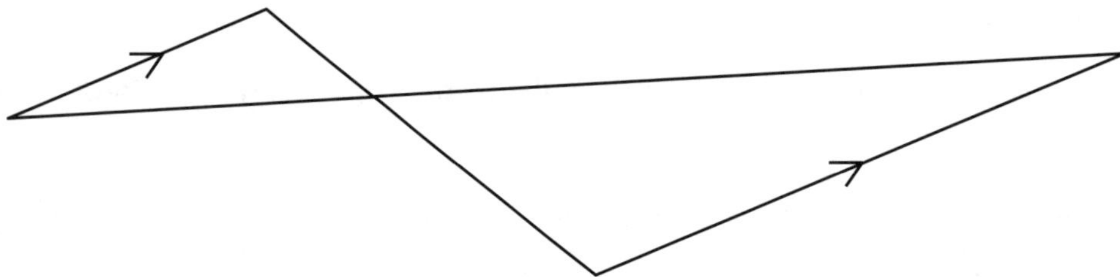

How do you know that the lines marked as parallel really are this time?

Here, the converse of the idea that *alternate* angles on parallel lines are equal is that when you have equal angles it means that you must have parallel lines.

3. Reflect one of them and rotate it to superimpose on the other.

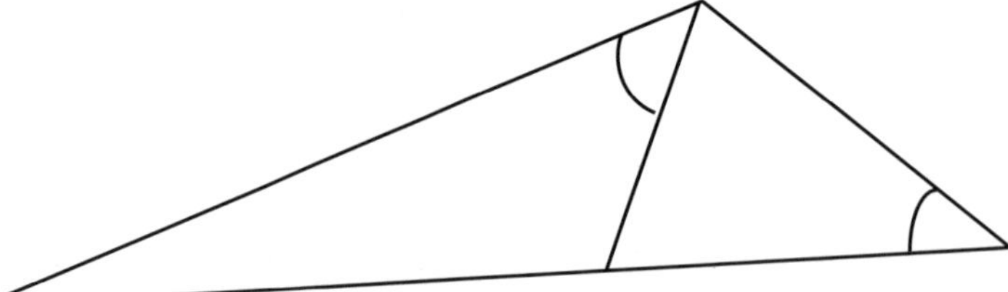

How do you know that the marked angles are equal? This time it is 'by construction', since we started with those angles being equal, since we said that the original shapes were similar.

4. And the special case where the created triangle is also similar to the first two.

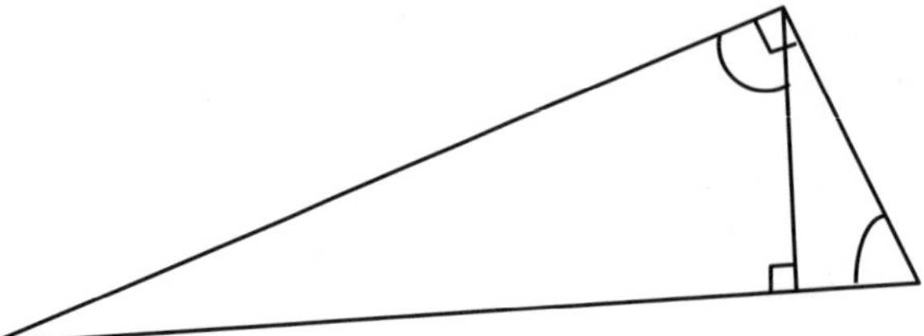

Learners could be invited to construct problems based on some or all of these diagrams by placing known lengths in strategic positions and requiring the calculation of particular unknown lengths.

Homework (5 min)

Confident learners could be asked to use the idea of similar triangles to prove Pythagoras' Theorem from a diagram such as this:

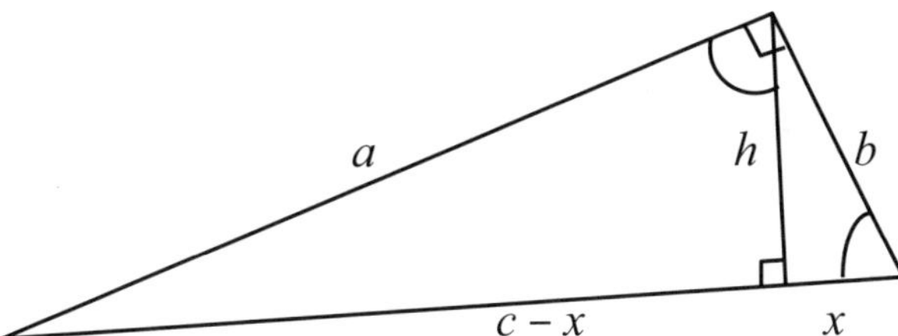

The c-side has been split by the altitude into $c - x$ and x.

Using similar triangles, $\frac{b}{x} = \frac{c}{b}$, so $b^2 = cx$. Also, $\frac{a}{c-x} = \frac{c}{a}$, so $a^2 = c(c - x) = c^2 - cx$, and since $b^2 = cx$ that means that $a^2 = c^2 - b^2$ or $a^2 + b^2 = c^2$.

This is thought to derive from an ancient Hindu source, but was written down by Adrien-Marie Legendre (1752–1833).

A quicker proof based on similar triangles is to say that the area of similar shapes is proportional to the *square* of their corresponding sides (since *area* scale factor is equal to the square of the *linear* scale factor). So viewing the shape as a large triangle split into two smaller triangles (such that all three triangles are similar): area of large triangle = area of medium-sized triangle + area of small triangle.

Taking the hypotenuses of each triangle as the corresponding sides gives $kc^2 = ka^2 + kb^2$, where k is a positive constant, so $a^2 + b^2 = c^2$. (See also Lesson 45.)

To make it harder

Learners who are comfortable with these ideas might like to find out about the *Intercept Theorem* (also sometimes called Thales' theorem) and examine some Euclidean proofs built on the idea of similar triangles. For a 3D example, see Lesson 61.

To make it easier

Learners who are stuck might find that it helps to construct triangles for themselves and cut them out of paper. Then vertices may be superimposed to show equality of angles in similar triangles.

Similarity

The diagrams below *are* drawn accurately.

What is the same and what is different about these shapes?

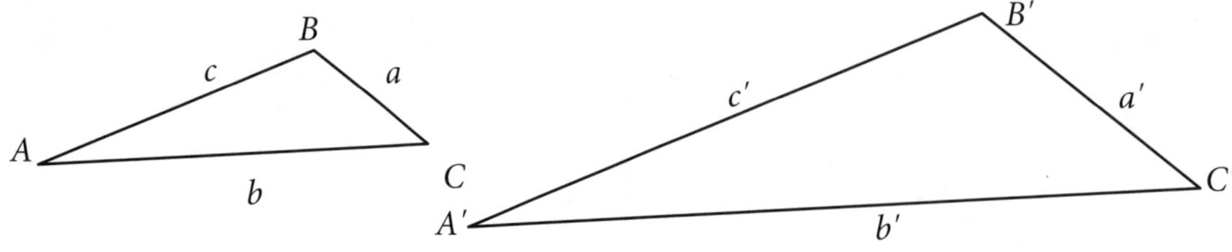

Measure the angles. How do they compare?

Measure the lengths of the sides.

How do they compare on the different shapes?

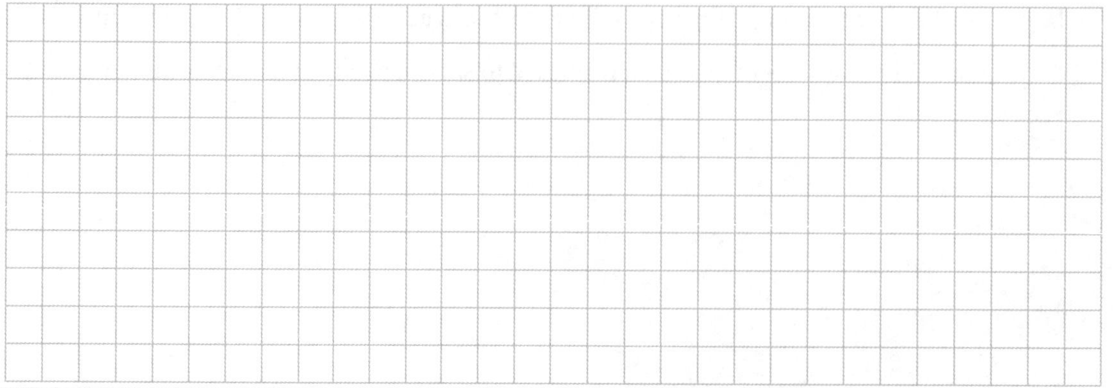

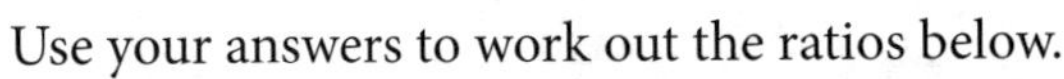

Use your answers to work out the ratios below.

Round your answers to one decimal place if necessary.

Which ratios are the same as each other? Why do you think that is?

$\frac{b}{a}=$ $\frac{c}{a}=$

$\frac{a}{b}=$ $\frac{c}{b}=$

$\frac{a}{c}=$ $\frac{b}{c}=$

$\frac{b'}{a'}=$ $\frac{c'}{a'}=$

$\frac{a'}{b'}=$ $\frac{c'}{b'}=$

$\frac{a'}{c'}=$ $\frac{b'}{c'}=$

$\frac{a}{a'}=$ $\frac{b}{b'}=$ $\frac{c}{c'}=$

$\frac{a'}{a}=$ $\frac{b'}{b}=$ $\frac{c'}{c}=$

Summarize which ratios are equal to each other in similar shapes.

Why do you think that this should be?

56 Simpson's Paradox

Introduction

Proportional thinking can be very hard, with learners often wanting to work additively rather than multiplicatively. For example, learners may think that ratios such as 3:4 and 4:5 are equal, because in each case the second category is 'one more' than the first, even though that extra one represents $\frac{1}{7}$ of the whole in the first case but only $\frac{1}{9}$ of the whole in the second case. Notions of 'multipliers' or 'scale factors' can be a way of moving learners into thinking about how many *times* one number is bigger than another, rather than what needs to be added. In this lesson, a counterintuitive task attempts to draw learners into this sort of thinking.

Aims and Outcomes

- appreciate the importance of multiplicative comparisons in certain situations
- compare numerical proportions in different sets of data
- handle paradoxical data intelligently

Lesson Starter (10 min)

Look at this data:

	Improved	Got worse
Medicine A	5	6
Medicine B	3	4

Which medicine do you think is better? Why?

Learners may raise all sorts of issues, such as it depending on who the patients were, what underlying conditions they may have had, etc. Or, if those who get better are, say, predominantly children rather than adults, then maybe fewer children improving could be better than more adults improving? But ignoring these kind of objections, this data should prompt a discussion relating to ratio. Someone may suggest (or the teacher could) that the two medicines are equally good, since in both cases one more person got worse than got better. Some learners will probably see difficulties with this claim. For comparison purposes you might find it helpful to imagine a third medicine (or more) with numbers such as:

	Improved	Got worse
Medicine C	100	101

Medicine C would clearly be better than either A or B, since medicine C is almost 50:50 in terms of improving or getting worse, whereas medicines A and B have a much bigger relative difference. An argument such as '$\frac{5}{11} > \frac{3}{7}$, so medicine A is more effective' can be developed.

Main Lesson (25 min)

Once learners begin to accept that they need to work with fractions or ratio, give out the Task Sheet and see whether learners can appreciate the paradox.

Changing the numbers and trying to replicate the paradox can lead to valuable practice of comparing proportions. It is quite hard to find numbers such that the paradox occurs: maybe that is a good thing?!

Plenary (20 min)

In Study 1, $\frac{5}{11} > \frac{3}{7}$, so medicine A is more effective.

In Study 2, $\frac{6}{9} > \frac{9}{14}$, so medicine A is more effective, again.

With the combined results, $\frac{11}{20} < \frac{12}{21}$, so this time medicine B is more effective!

So suppose that you are going to take either medicine A or medicine B and you talk to your doctor and she says: 'There have been two studies on which is better. Study 1 showed that medicine A is better, and Study 2 backed that up, because it also showed that medicine A is better. And on the basis of those two studies I would recommend medicine B.' What would you think? This is a statistical paradox called *Simpson's Paradox*. If anyone claims not to care, the medicinal context makes it easy to ask: *But suppose it was you and it mattered – which medicine would you choose to take?* It is hard to resolve this paradox!

Homework (5 min)

Learners could find out about real-life situations in which Simpson's Paradox has appeared or try to think of scenarios in which this could happen.

There are many fairly well-reported real life examples, such as in medicine – a frequently described case being one involving the treatment of kidney stones. Another often-quoted example relates to the batting averages of professional baseball players, and learners could find out more about these or other occurrences of the paradox.

Learners could also be encouraged to find out about *confounding variables* (also called *lurking factors*!) and the idea that in statistics correlation does not necessarily imply causation (i.e., correlation and causation don't perfectly correlate!). They could also find out about Edward Simpson (b. 1922), who Simpson's Paradox is named after.

To make it harder

Learners who are confident with this work could try to model the situation algebraically and look for conditions on the numbers if this paradox is going to arise. *Is it so surprising and counterintuitive simply because it happens so rarely?*

To make it easier

All learners should be able to express an opinion about which medicine is better. Different examples may help learners who cling to additive rather than multiplicative thinking to develop their ideas.

Getting Better or Getting Worse?

Look at these two sets of data from imaginary studies:

Study 1

	Improved	Got worse
Medicine A	5	6
Medicine B	3	4

Which medicine do these results suggest is better? Why?

Study 2

	Improved	Got worse
Medicine A	6	3
Medicine B	9	5

Which medicine do these results suggest is better? Why?

Now the results from the two studies are combined:

Combined Results

	Improved	Got worse
Medicine A	11	9
Medicine B	12	9

The '12' in this table comes from the '3' in the first table and the '9' in the second table.

Make sure you can see where the 11 and the two 9s in this table come from.

Which medicine do the combined results suggest is better? Why?

Make up different numbers for the two studies.

Which medicine appears to be better?

What happens when you work out the combined results? Why?

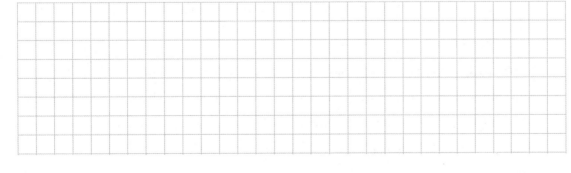

57 Solving Quadratic Equations

Introduction

Quadratic equations can feel completely different from linear equations. With linear equations, learners get used to doing the same operations to both sides, closing in on the unknown letter until the solution is obtained, rather like making the unknown letter the subject. With quadratics, the focus changes to making the equation equal to zero (as though this time zero becomes the subject) and then trying to factorize ('find two numbers with a sum of this and a product of this'), which can feel rather like the trial and improvement method of finding solutions to equations. Then you finish with a completely different-sounding sort of argument where you say 'either this is zero or this is zero' and end up with two solutions rather than just one. And then there are the cases where you can't factorize and have to complete the square or use 'the formula'; or you *can* factorize but it's hard because the coefficient of x^2 is not 1, and so on ... It is no wonder that this can seem like a completely different topic from ordinary 'solving equations'. The intention of this lesson is to bring these ideas together a bit more. If you have anonymous incorrect work handy (you could keep notable examples from previous years' learners), you could use that as a discussion point in a similar way to the items used in this lesson.

Aims and Outcomes

- consider and practise different methods of solving quadratic equations
- constructively critique another learner's work

Lesson Starter (10 min)

What different ways are there of solving a quadratic equation? List as many as you can think of. Make up a different example equation for each method so that your example is a question that you would choose to solve that way: for example, simple factorizing (e.g., monic: $x^2 + 5x - 36 = 0$, $(x + 9)(x - 4) = 0$, *etc.), harder factorizing (e.g., non-monic:* $12x^2 + 13x - 14 = 0$, $(3x - 2)(4x + 7) = 0$, *etc.), completing the square or using 'the formula' (e.g.,* $5x^2 + 3x - 7 = 0$*), etc.*

Main Lesson (25 min)

Give out the Task Sheet and invite learners to ponder the attempted solutions. A constructive and positive atmosphere, rather than an critically negative one, is helpful. Perhaps on another occasion learners might feel brave enough to share some of their own errors for discussion, for everyone's benefit, if the classroom climate seems safe enough?

Plenary (20 min)

The first step (+120) is carried out correctly, but is a 'backwards move'. The equation as given is helpfully set up with zero on the right-hand side. Square-rooting both sides would be valid but would lead to $\sqrt{y^2-2y}$ on the left-hand side. The writer has square-rooted the y^2 but not the *whole* of the left-hand side. The next step, dividing by $2y$, is incorrect on the left-hand side. To remove the $-2y$ there the writer could have added $2y$, but this would not have enabled him or her to collect all the y's into one letter, as they do in the next step. Is this a deliberate 'fudge', perhaps? The last two steps are correct starting from this point, except that when taking the final square root there are two possibilities, so they might have written $y=\pm\sqrt{\frac{\sqrt{120}}{2}}$. If he or she had attempted to substitute back in to the original equation they might have discovered their error. And square roots within square roots (i.e., fourth roots) are not an expected feature of solving quadratic equations!

A more conventional (and correct) solution, of course, would have been along these lines:

$y^2 - 2y - 120 = 0$

$(y - 12)(y + 10) = 0$

so either $y - 12 = 0$ or $y + 10 = 0$

so either $y = 12$ or $y = -10$.

Although this would probably be the easiest way to solve this equation, it is very different from the writer's attempt. He or she may not formally have been trying to 'complete the square' but this seems to be the direction in which their instincts took them. So learners might like to try to modify the writer's method so that it works and offer encouragement in this direction:

$y^2 - 2y - 120 = 0$

$y^2 - 2y = 120$

$(y - 1)^2 - 1 = 120$

$(y - 1)^2 = 121$

$y - 1 = \pm\sqrt{121}$

$y - 1 = \pm 11$

so either $y - 1 = 11$ or $y - 1 = -11$,

so either $y = 12$ or $y = -10$.

In the second case, it would be straightforward to write that $x = 3$ or 4 right away. Instead, the learner expands and simplifies correctly but mis-assigns a, b and c in the formula. (Underneath the correcting fluid on the original you can just see that they had done it correctly initially and then changed it!) He or she evaluates $b^2 - 4ac$ incorrectly and fails to check to see if their answers are correct by substituting back into the original equations.

Both attempts could be seen as 'near misses' from learners who know a thing or two about solving equations. In both cases, a factorizing method would be have been quick and much easier.

Homework (5 min)

Look back through previous work you have done on solving quadratic equations. Find some errors and try to understand them. If you think they might be interesting and instructive, and you are willing to share them, be ready to do so next time. Otherwise, try to make a list of advice for solving equations – 'tips for beginners', perhaps – the sort of thing that might be useful to someone in your Year or the Year below.

To make it harder

Learners who are confident with the different methods might like to write a flow chart that someone could follow to decide which method to use on a quadratic (see facing page). Perhaps assume that the quadratic has been rearranged (if necessary) into the 'standard' form $ax^2 + bx + c = 0$, where $a \neq 0$. Questions in the flow chart could check things like 'Is $a = 1$?' or 'Is $b^2 - 4ac$ a perfect square?', etc. It would be better here to use 'the formula' only as a last resort.

To make it easier

Learners who are not yet confident solving quadratics should find this lesson an excellent opportunity to raise queries and look at alternative methods.

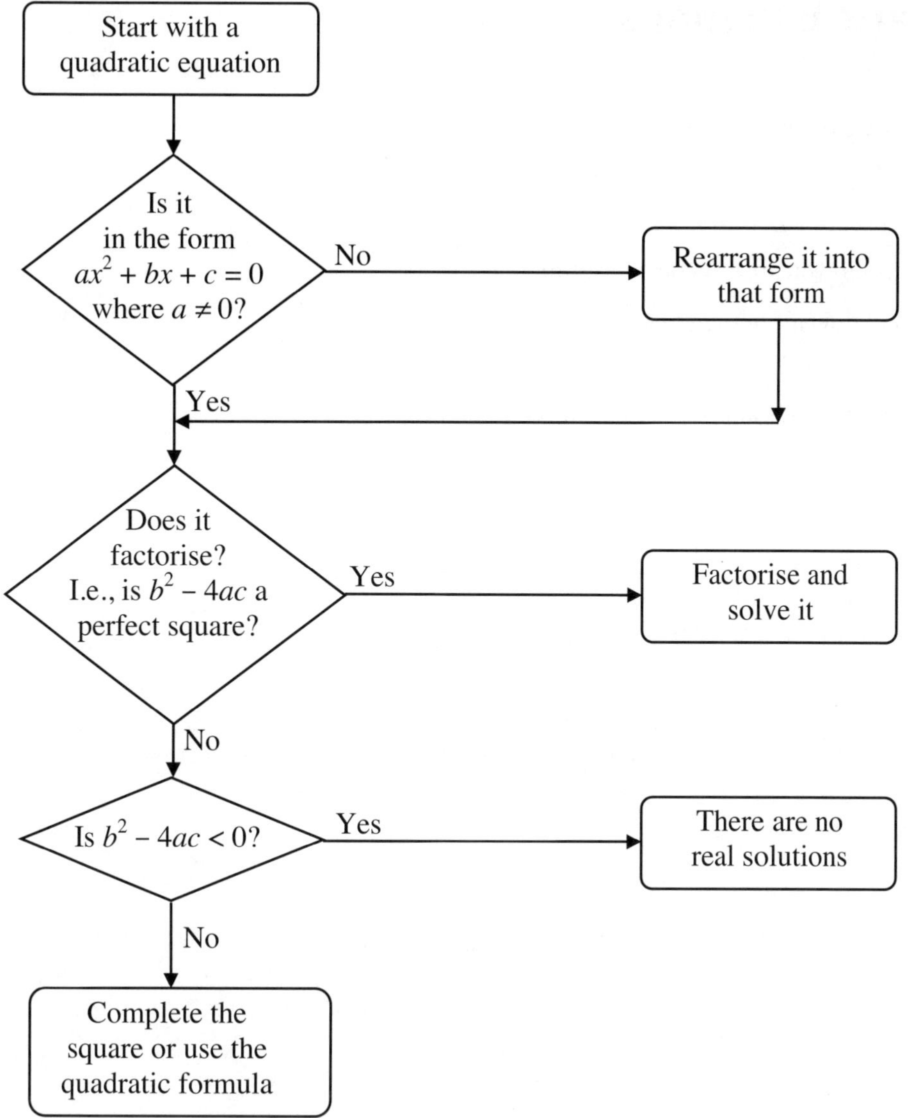
Start with a quadratic equation
Is it in the form $ax^2 + bx + c = 0$ where $a \neq 0$?
No
Rearrange it into that form
Yes
Does it factorise? I.e., is $b^2 - 4ac$ a perfect square?
Yes
Factorise and solve it
No
Is $b^2 - 4ac < 0$?
Yes
There are no real solutions
No
Complete the square or use the quadratic formula

Quadratic Equations

A. Here is a question:

Solve the equation $y^2 - 2y - 120 = 0$.

How would you answer this question?

Do you know more than one way of doing it?

Here is someone's answer – it doesn't come out right:

$$y^2 - 2y - 120 = 0$$
$\downarrow$ $+120$
$$y^2 - 2y = 120$$
$\downarrow$ $\sqrt{\ }$
$$y - 2y = \sqrt{120}$$
$\downarrow$ $\div 2y$
$$y = \frac{\sqrt{120}}{2y}$$
$\downarrow$ $\times y$
$$y^2 = \frac{\sqrt{120}}{2}$$
$\downarrow$ $\sqrt{\ }$
$$y = \sqrt{\frac{\sqrt{120}}{2}}$$

What *positive* feedback would you give to the person who wrote this answer?

How would you criticize what they have written?

Why is the answer wrong?

Find as many things to say as you can.

B. Here is another question:

Solve the equation $(x - 3)(x - 4) = 0$.

How would you answer this question?

Do you know more than one way of doing it?

Here is someone's answer – it doesn't come out right:

$(x - 3)(x - 4) = 0$

$x^2 + 12 - 4x - 3x = 0$

$x^2 + 12 - 7x = 0$

$a = 1 \quad b = 12 \quad c = -7 \quad b^2 = 144$

$$x = \frac{-b \pm \sqrt{b^2 - 4ac}}{2a}$$

$$= \frac{-12 \pm \sqrt{144 - 4 \times 1 \times -7}}{2 \times 1}$$

$$= \frac{-12 \pm \sqrt{133}}{2}$$

$x = -0.23$

or

$x = -11.76$

What *positive* feedback would you give to the person who wrote this answer?

How would you criticize what they have written?

Why is the answer wrong?

Find as many things to say as you can.

58 Straight-Line Graphs

Introduction

A 'line' in mathematics is usually taken to mean 'straight line', so 'straight' is perhaps redundant here but is often added for emphasis. Sometimes learners think that all 'proper mathematical graphs' are straight lines and are surprised when they meet examples such as $y = x^2$. This lesson is very straightforward, simply using graph-drawing software to draw lots of examples of straight-line graphs and looking for similarities and differences. The idea is to put the responsibility onto the learners for describing the behaviour of the graphs in sufficient detail for them to able to reconstruct them in the future, when away from the computer, just by using their notes. Textbooks sometimes overlook the fact that not all straight-line graphs have equations of the form $y = mx + c$; vertical lines (infinite gradient) have the form $x = k$, so this is included as well.

Aims and Outcomes

- know that the graph of $x = k$ is a vertical line passing through $(k, 0)$
- understand the effect on the graph of changing m and c in the equation $y = mx + c$

Lesson Starter (20 min)

Draw the first one of these shapes on the board. Challenge learners: *Can you draw it without taking your pen off the paper/board and without going over any line you've already drawn?* (Some learners may have seen this idea before – that's OK: it's going to get harder!)

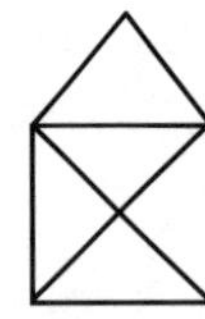
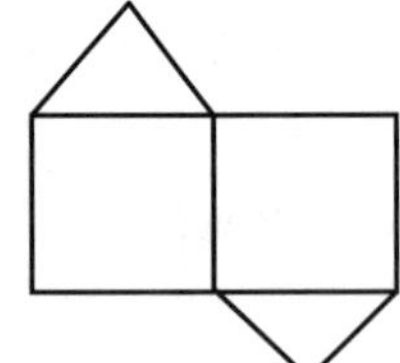
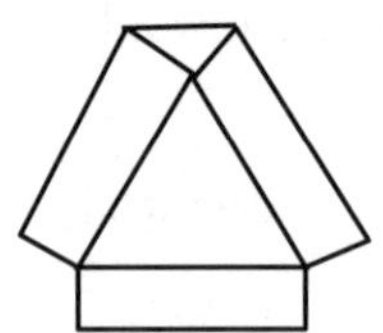

Let learners have a few goes, and when one shape is successfully completed move on to the next. Be careful how you draw the shapes on the board, or have them prepared, otherwise you may give away an answer! If you feel the need to give hints, then suggest where someone should start, but it is more fun just to let learners try.

The first four shapes each contain exactly two 'odd nodes' – i.e., points with an odd number of line segments coming out from them. You must start at one of these odd nodes and finish at the other. (These drawings are called *traversable* graphs.) The fifth shape has no odd nodes, so *should* be easier: one way is to do the hexagon and then go round the shape again putting a triangle on each side.

What makes each one of these hard/easy/possible/impossible?

What changes a possible one into an impossible one or vice versa? Can a single line segment do it? When? Why?

How are you choosing where to start/go next? Does it matter? When? Why?

Mathematically, you could say that these aren't lines. *Do you know why?* These are 'line segments', because a line extends infinitely far in both directions. You can even have a half-line (e.g., $y = x$, $x \geq 0$) which extends infinitely far in one direction but has a definite stopping point at the other end at a certain specific point. For the rest of the lesson we are considering lines.

Main Lesson (20 min)

Give out the Task Sheet. Learners will need access to graph-drawing software or graphical calculators, either individually or in pairs, in order to experiment with drawing numerous straight-line graphs instantly, varying the parameters m and c. It would be possible for the teacher to use one computer with a projector, but this denies learners the hands-on element and the opportunity to pursue their own queries, which may be different from those of the majority of the class.

Plenary (15 min)

The $x = k$ and $y = c$ ($m = 0$) cases should be fairly straightforward and learners should therefore probably spend most of their time on the $y = mx + c$ case. The hardest (but most worthwhile) part will be articulating what happens as m increases/decreases and is positive/negative. It may be easier to set $c = 0$ initially in order to focus fully on changes in m. A really good quantitative sense of this family of graphs will be very valuable to learners in many future topics and you could emphasize this. The m and the c behave independently, so can be studied separately.

Homework (5 min)

Make an octagon using eight straight-line graphs – what are their equations? How symmetrical can you make the octagon? Can you make it a regular *octagon?*

One solution, though not regular, would be $y = 2$, $y = 3 - x$, $x = 2$, $y = x - 2$, $y = -1$, $y = x - 1$, $x = -1$, $y = x + 2$.

Is a regular octagon easier to do than a regular hexagon? (See the differentiation task below.) It is easier to get the equations of graphs at 45° to each other than at 60°. You could think of this as being related to the fact that tan 45° = 1.

Learners might like to try to make a family of 'concentric' similar polygons and look for patterns in their equations.

Learners might find it easier to centre the polygons on the origin and exploit symmetry, or they may find that this makes it harder, because of negative intercepts – and therefore this might make an appropriate extra challenge.

To make it harder

Similar to the homework task, learners who are confident could try to draw a *hexagon* using six straight-line graphs, giving their equations. *How symmetrical can you make the hexagon? Can you make it a* regular *hexagon?* Hexagons with two lines of symmetry are fairly easy (e.g., $y = x + 1$, $y = 1$, $y = 2 - x$, $y = x - 2$, $y = -1$, $y = x - 1$). Getting a *regular* hexagon is challenging, and some trigonometry in right-angled triangles, or Pythagoras' Theorem, will be needed. Learners might want to begin by drawing an equilateral triangle (e.g., $y = \sqrt{3}x$, $y = -\sqrt{3}x + \sqrt{3}$, $y = 0$) and then extend this into a regular hexagon by adding the necessary lines parallel to these (e.g., $y = \sqrt{3}x - 2\sqrt{3}$, $y = -\sqrt{3}x + 3\sqrt{3}$, $y = \sqrt{3}$).

Confident learners might also like to describe the appearance of the line $ax + by = d$, perhaps by drawing several possibilities, or thinking about it, or rearranging $y = mx + c$.

To make it easier

Learners who find this difficult could begin by restricting themselves to horizontal and vertical lines only.

Straight-Line Graphs

Change the numbers in **bold**. Try big values and small values.

Remember to try negative values as well as positive values.

Look at what happens to the graphs as you vary the numbers.

Describe carefully the effect of having different numbers in each case.

$x = \mathbf{5}$

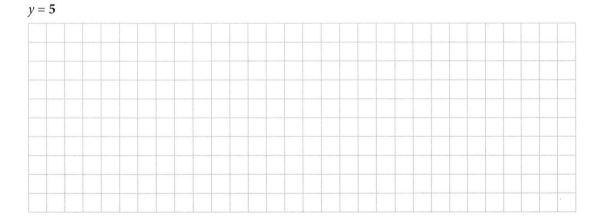

$y = \mathbf{5}$

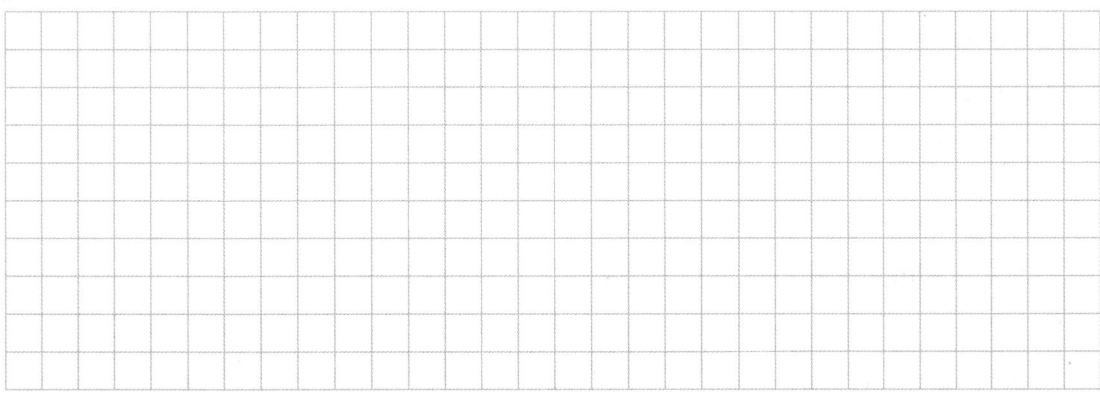

$y = \mathbf{5}x + \mathbf{6}$

59 Surds

Introduction

Surds sometimes appear to learners to be mysterious objects obeying odd rules and existing only in order to have peculiar operations done to them! This lesson seeks to exploit the surprise factor when one surd-infested expression turns out to be equal to another! Learners unfamiliar with surds may take some time to become used to the fact that, for example, $\frac{\sqrt{2}}{2}=\frac{1}{\sqrt{2}}$. Constructing their own examples is a good way to become comfortable in this territory, both simplifying and deliberately 'complicating' expressions involving surds. There is no need to include ± symbols when simplifying, say $\sqrt{8}$, writing $\pm 2\sqrt{2}$, since the square root symbol is taken to mean the *positive* square root. So it is fine to write that $\sqrt{8} = 2\sqrt{2}$, even though the solutions to the equation $x^2 = 8$ are $x = \pm\sqrt{8} = \pm 2\sqrt{2}$.

Aims and Outcomes

- simplify surds using rules such as $\sqrt{a}\sqrt{b}=\sqrt{ab}$ and $\frac{\sqrt{a}}{\sqrt{b}}=\sqrt{\frac{a}{b}}$, $b \neq 0$
- understand surds as irrational roots

Lesson Starter (10 min)

Which of these do you think is the odd one out and why?

$$\sqrt{3}, \sqrt{4}, \sqrt{5}, \sqrt{6}, \sqrt{7}, \sqrt{8}$$

As always with this sort of question, there are different possible answers, but one possibility is that $\sqrt{4}$ is the only one that is not a surd, because it is an integer. If a different answer is given, for a correct reason, you could just accept it and ask if anyone has another answer. For example, $\sqrt{8}$ is the only surd that can be simplified (to $2\sqrt{2}$), $\sqrt{3}$ is the only one less than 2, or the only one which when raised to the power of 4 gives a single-digit answer, $\sqrt{7}$ is the only one which when squared is in the seven-times table, etc.

You might want to say that when you square root an integer you either get an integer (if the original number was a perfect square) or an irrational number (a non-repeating non-terminating decimal that cannot be expressed exactly as an integer divided by another integer). The latter kind are called surds. Other irrational roots, such as $\sqrt[3]{7}$, are also called surds, but there are plenty of irrational numbers, such as π, that are not surds.

Main Lesson (25 min)

What goes in the gap?

$$\sqrt{2}, \sqrt{8}, \sqrt{18}, \_\_\_\_\_, \sqrt{50}$$

This is easier than it looks. The numbers under the square root sign make a quadratic sequence (+ 6, + 10, + 14, + 18), which some learners may spot, but there is probably too little data for them to be absolutely sure about this. However, if you simplify the surds, you realize that this is a linear sequence: the $\sqrt{2}$-times table, in fact.

$$\sqrt{2}, 2\sqrt{2}, 3\sqrt{2}, \_\_\_\_\_\_, 5\sqrt{2}$$

So the answer is $4\sqrt{2}$ or $\sqrt{32}$.

Ask learners to make up another example like this and to try it out on a friend. They could do, say, the $\sqrt{3}$-times table, or be a little more adventurous and try something like $\sqrt{2}$, $\sqrt{12}$, ______, $\sqrt{80}$, $\sqrt{150}$, which is $1\sqrt{2}$, $2\sqrt{3}$, $3\sqrt{4}$, $4\sqrt{5}$, $5\sqrt{6}$, so the answer is $3\sqrt{4}$, which is just 6. Another possibility is to start the other way round with something like $\sqrt{3}$, ______, 3, $2\sqrt{3}$, $\sqrt{15}$, $3\sqrt{2}$, which is $\sqrt{3}$, $\sqrt{6}$, $\sqrt{9}$, $\sqrt{12}$, $\sqrt{15}$, $\sqrt{18}$, so the answer is $\sqrt{6}$. These can be trickier to spot. Choosing which member of the sequence to leave out raises interesting issues.

Then you could ask learners to simplify these: $\sqrt{20}$, $\sqrt{45} - \sqrt{5}$, $\sqrt{80} - \sqrt{20}$, $\frac{10}{\sqrt{5}}$. They should all come out to $2\sqrt{5}$.

Can they think of any more 'surdy' expressions that are equivalent to $2\sqrt{5}$?

This gives an opportunity to (re-)examine rules such as $\sqrt{a}\sqrt{b} = \sqrt{ab}$ and $\frac{\sqrt{a}}{\sqrt{b}} = \sqrt{\frac{a}{b}}$, $b \neq 0$ and how they help with manipulating surds. Learners may find more than one way to explain equivalence; for example, $\frac{10}{\sqrt{5}} = \frac{10\sqrt{5}}{5}$ $2\sqrt{5}$ or, alternatively, $\frac{10}{\sqrt{5}} = \frac{2\sqrt{5}\sqrt{5}}{\sqrt{5}} = 2\sqrt{5}$ or $\frac{10}{\sqrt{5}} = \frac{\sqrt{100}}{\sqrt{5}} = \sqrt{\frac{100}{5}} = \sqrt{20} = \sqrt{4}\sqrt{5}$ $= 2\sqrt{5}$, etc. This is a good way of seeing the interconnectedness of these properties and validating different learners' ways of thinking.

Then give out the Task Sheet and ask learners to work on expressions equal to $3\sqrt{5}$ instead.

Plenary (20 min)

It will be good to share on the board some of the different examples that learners have constructed. If some turn out not to equal $3\sqrt{5}$ the process of establishing that will be just as worthwhile in terms of developing facility with surds.

Homework (5 min)

Pythagoras' Theorem is an obvious context in which to work with surds. You could ask learners to work with a 4 × 4 square grid of dots and try to find all the different possible lengths of line segments that can be drawn from dot to dot. You can have lengths of 1, 2, or 3 (horizontally or vertically) or $\sqrt{2}$, $2\sqrt{2}$ or $3\sqrt{2}$ (lines at 45°) or $\sqrt{5}$, $\sqrt{10}$ or $\sqrt{13}$; i.e., 9 possibilities altogether. These are all shown below:

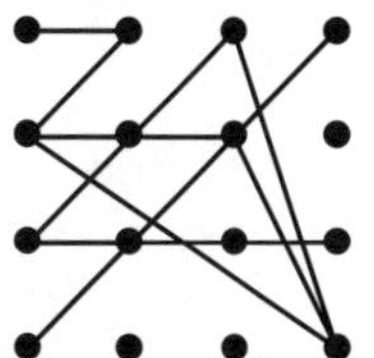

With an $n \times n$ grid there are $\frac{1}{2}n(n+1) - 1$ (i.e., one less than the nth triangle number) ways initially, but whenever you obtain Pythagorean Triples (such as $3^2 + 4^2 = 5^2$) you end up with an integer length that you have already counted, rather than a new surd, and that reduces the total by one. In other situations where $a^2 + b^2 = c^2 + d^2$ (where none of a, b, c or d is 0), the total will be reduced again because you obtain a surd identical to one found previously. This can be a fruitful area for learners to work on, perhaps gathering data for homework and then discussing in class whether anyone found any breaks in their patterns caused by this. Sometimes learners will assume that a pattern continues and that they 'must have missed one' rather than notice that something has changed. Honesty is the best policy!

To make it harder

Keen learners could try the homework task on a 3D $n \times n \times n$ lattice. Alternatively they could find out about *tetration* (also known as 'superexponentiation', or 'power towers'), such as $2^{2^{2^2}}$, sometimes written as ${}^4 2$, where ${}^4 2 = 2^{2^{2^2}} = 2^{2^4} = 2^{16} = 65536$. Here, 2 is the 'base number' and 4 is the 'height number', the number of times 'to the power of' appears. There are links here with *Graham's number* and *Skewes' number*, which learners might like to find out about.

Learners might also like to attempt to *prove* that $\sqrt{a}\sqrt{b} = \sqrt{ab}$ and $\frac{\sqrt{a}}{\sqrt{b}} = \sqrt{\frac{a}{b}}$, $b \neq 0$. One possibility is to write $\left(\sqrt{a}\sqrt{b}\right)\left(\sqrt{a}\sqrt{b}\right) = \left(\sqrt{a}\sqrt{a}\right)\left(\sqrt{b}\sqrt{b}\right) = ab$, but $\left(\sqrt{ab}\right)\left(\sqrt{ab}\right)$ is also equal to ab, so $\sqrt{a}\sqrt{b} = \sqrt{ab}$. A similar approach will work with $\frac{\sqrt{a}}{\sqrt{b}} = \sqrt{\frac{a}{b}}$, but not with $\sqrt{a} \pm \sqrt{b}$, which is not equal to $\sqrt{a \pm b}$, and it may be helpful to try it and see why not.

To make it easier

Learners who find this hard could begin by trying to find any equivalent surd statements, such as $\sqrt{40} = 2\sqrt{10}$.

Everything has to equal ... $3\sqrt{5}$!

Choose numbers for the *s below to make the expressions equal to $3\sqrt{5}$.

The *s can be different each time.

$\sqrt{*} = 3\sqrt{5}$

$\sqrt{*} + \sqrt{*} = 3\sqrt{5}$

$\sqrt{*} - \sqrt{*} = 3\sqrt{5}$

$2\sqrt{*} - \sqrt{*} = 3\sqrt{5}$

$\frac{\sqrt{*}}{\sqrt{*}} = 3\sqrt{5}$

$\frac{2\sqrt{*}}{\sqrt{*}} = 3\sqrt{5}$

$\frac{\sqrt{*}}{2\sqrt{*}} = 3\sqrt{5}$

$\frac{1}{\sqrt{*}} = 3\sqrt{5}$

$\frac{*}{\sqrt{*}} = 3\sqrt{5}$

$\frac{\sqrt{*}}{*} = 3\sqrt{5}$

$(\sqrt{*} + \sqrt{*})(\sqrt{*} - \sqrt{*}) = 3\sqrt{5}$

What other kinds of expressions can you find that are equal to $3\sqrt{5}$?

Try to be as creative and inventive as you can.

Try to make expressions that look nothing like $3\sqrt{5}$ but are equal to it.

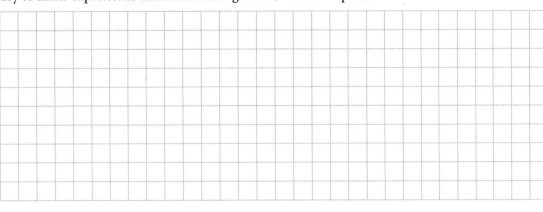

60 Surface Area and Volume of a Cuboid

Introduction

This is a similar maximization problem to 'max-box', the well-known investigation in which learners try to make the maximum volume box out of a certain sized piece of paper (see, for example, Foster, C. [2003], *Instant Maths Ideas for Key Stage 3 Teachers: Shape and Space*. Cheltenham: Nelson Thornes, p. 91). Here, though, the dimensions of the box are restricted to multiples of 2 cm, which adds a constraint requiring considerable thought to accommodate. Learners (and teachers!) may be surprised by the vastly different number of cubes that it is possible to wrap in what seem like only slightly different arrangements.

Aims and Outcomes

- solve a challenging problem using surface area and volume of cuboids

Lesson Starter (10 min)

Do you use wrapping paper to wrap up presents? Do you recycle the paper when you receive a present?

Apparently the UK uses about 80 km² of wrapping paper every Christmas. *Do you think that is a lot? Why / why not?* (See https://www2.le.ac.uk/ebulletin/news/press-releases/2000-2009/2007/12/nparticle.2007-12-04.6745557516 for some mathematical formulae and rules about how to wrap presents more efficiently and reduce your 'present footprint'!) Learners might like to try to visualize the size of this area, perhaps by relating it to a 9 km × 9 km area in the locality.

Estimate the mass *of 80 km² of wrapping paper.*

Ordinary A4 paper is around 80 gsm (gram/m²). Wrapping paper is much thinner, so maybe you could assume that it has about a quarter the surface density of this? That gives 1600 tonnes of wrapping paper! (See www.wasteonline.org.uk/resources/InformationSheets/ChristmasRecycling.htm for more details.)

Main Lesson (25 min)

Suppose that you have a single sheet of A4 paper and that you can cut it however you wish, but any part that you cut off (i.e., becomes separate from the larger main part of the sheet) cannot be used. What is the maximum number of plastic cubes you can wrap up? You can use sticky tape to hold the paper, but no part of any of the cubes should be visible at the end. Estimate roughly how many cubes you think you might be able to do.

Then give out the Task Sheet and encourage learners to work on 48 cubes and then as many as they think might be possible. You may or may not wish to provide cubes, scissors, etc. One option is to give each group *one* cube only. Then they have to think and calculate what *would* happen rather than actually do it.

Plenary (20 min)

Forty-eight cubes can be $1 \times 1 \times 48$, $1 \times 2 \times 24$, $1 \times 3 \times 16$, $1 \times 4 \times 12$, $1 \times 6 \times 8$, $2 \times 2 \times 12$, $2 \times 3 \times 8$, $2 \times 4 \times 6$ or $3 \times 4 \times 4$ (nine ways). The $3 \times 4 \times 4$ cuboid is closest to a cube shape and will have the smallest surface area, but you also have to allow for the $1{:}\sqrt{2}$ ratio of A4 paper, the chosen net, and the fact that you need to be able to fold appropriately at the corners. $3 \times 4 \times 4$ works as shown:

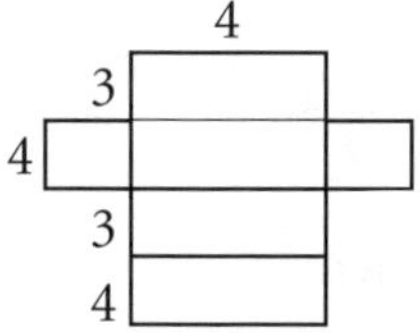

(Each of these is contained within a 20 cm × 28 cm rectangle.)

It is also possible to do 48 cubes as $2 \times 3 \times 8$:

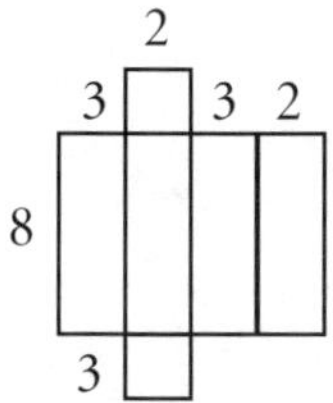

Given that 48 cubes fit with little paper left over, learners may be surprised that it is possible to do 60 cubes ($2 \times 3 \times 10$) by slightly modifying this arrangement:

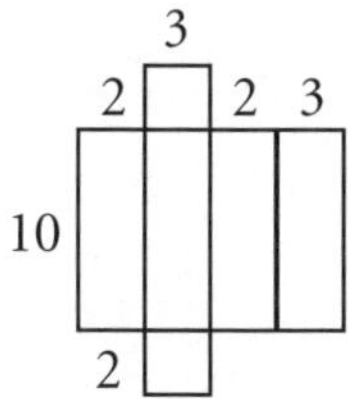

When learners eventually discover that they can do $3 \times 3 \times 8 = 72$, it is frequently thought that this is the best solution, but in fact $3 \times 4 \times 7 = 84$ is also possible. (Other more fiddly solutions, such as $2 \times 3 \times 12 = 72$, can also be done.)

Homework (5 min)

What if you had a sheet of A3 *paper instead of* A4 *paper. How many cubes could you wrap?* A3 paper has twice the area of A4 paper, but doubling the answer for A4 paper will not be correct! In fact, twice the surface area ought to mean $\left(\sqrt{2}\right)^3 = 2\sqrt{2}$ times the volume, so if 84 cubes were possible with A4 then you might expect about 237 cubes to be possible now, but that doesn't take account of the fact that the number of cubes in each direction must be an integer. $4 \times 5 \times 9 = 180$ would certainly fit (by multiplying 3, 4 and 7 by $\sqrt{2}$ and rounding down), but learners can certainly do much better by jiggling the cubes around.

To make it harder

An extra challenge for any group finishing early would be to ask: *What if cutting of the paper (and using the cut off pieces) were allowed? What would be the most cubes that could be wrapped in that case?* The answer is that you could (just!) manage 125 by doing a $5 \times 5 \times 5$ cube, since you can almost get six 10 cm × 10 cm squares from an A4 sheet. Two of the 'squares' will be only 9.7 cm in one direction, but you can easily cut out the two necessary 0.3 cm × 10 cm pieces from the unused 1 cm × 29.7 cm strip down the side of the paper.

To make it easier

If learners are really struggling with this task, then you could give them some cubes to use.

Wrapping Cubes

Each cube is 2 cm along each edge.

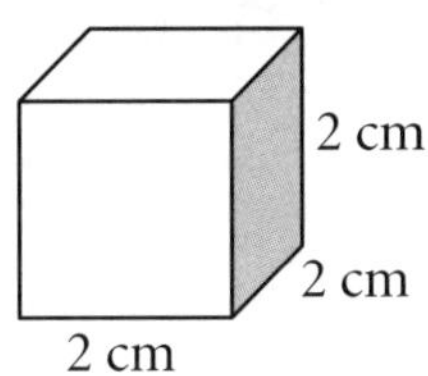

A4 paper is 21 cm × 29.7 cm.

Start with 48 cubes.

Arrange them into a cuboid.

In how many ways is it possible to do this? Why?

How do you know that you have found all the possibilities?

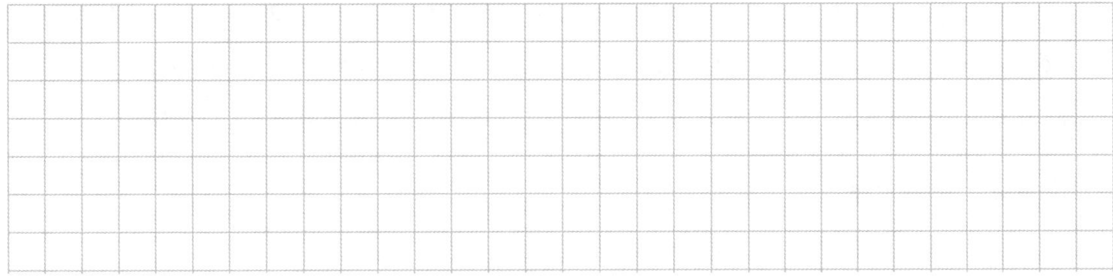

Which arrangement do you think will use the least paper to wrap up? Why?

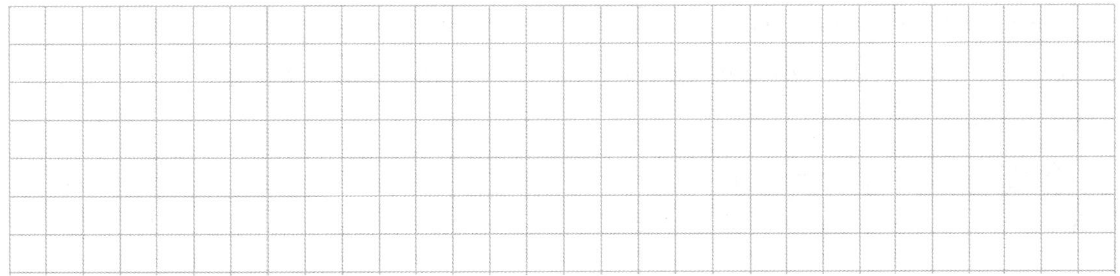

Try to find ways of wrapping more than 48 cubes.

Remember that any pieces that are cut off from the main sheet are not allowed to be used.

61 Surface Area and Volume of a Sphere

Introduction

It sometimes seems as though formulae such as $S = 4\pi r^2$ and $V = \frac{4}{3}\pi r^3$ come down from space and 'just are'. The most common proofs involve calculus, but there is a lot of useful mathematical thinking involved in trying to make sense of non-calculus proofs of these formulae. This lesson can work well whether or not learners are already familiar with these results. If you know nothing about the origin of a formula, using it can sometimes lead to a view that mathematicians are 'other people, out there somewhere' who produce these clever things, and that we ordinary folks just use their results. This can limit what learners think they are capable of achieving, so it is nice to try to take away the mystery and give access to the thinking behind formulae such as these.

Aims and Outcomes

- analyse a proof of the formulae for surface area and volume of a sphere
- understand dissection proofs based on imagining a solid cut up into infinitely many tiny pieces

Lesson Starter (5 min)

Which would take more paint to cover, a cube or a sphere? Suppose that they have the same 'dimensions'; i.e., that the diameter of the sphere is equal to the side length of the cube.

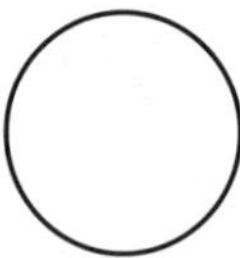

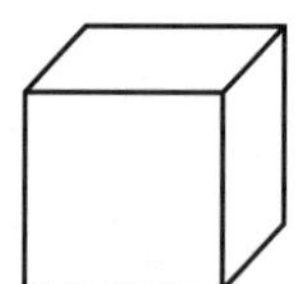

Learners should be able to think this through visually, whether or not they know any formulae. Suppose that the radius of the sphere is r. Then the side lengths of the cube are $2r$. So the surface area of the cube $= 6(2r)^2 = 24r^2$, which is nearly twice as much as $4\pi r^2$, the surface area of the sphere. Similarly, the volume of the cube $= (2r)^3 = 8r^3$, which is almost twice the volume of the sphere, $\frac{4}{3}\pi r^3$. When you consider that the sphere fits snugly inside the cube, the factor of almost two is perhaps quite surprising.

Main Lesson (25 min)

Invite learners to work through the Task Sheet, perhaps discussing in pairs before writing down their (agreed) answers. Making sense of the diagrams, and the argument, can be quite difficult. Learners may not be used to following through a mathematical proof on paper like this.

Plenary (25 min)

The surface area of the cylinder is $2\pi r \times$ length $= 2\pi r \times 2r = 4\pi r^2$.

The hardest part is probably seeing that the triangles are similar, giving $\frac{y}{l} = \frac{x}{r}$, and both, incidentally, equal to sin θ. Angle-chasing should convince learners that the two angles marked θ are the same. This depends on the idea that the surface of the sphere will be perpendicular to the radius (in the same way that a tangent to a circle is perpendicular to the radius). Algebra converts this into $2\pi ry = 2\pi xl$, which is hopefully recognized as the area of that slice of the cylinder (on the left-hand side) and the area of that slice of sphere (on the right-hand side). So each bit of sphere has the same area as the bit of cylinder in the same slice. So going through the whole sphere, slice by slice, the surface area of the whole sphere is equal to that of the whole cylinder: $4\pi r^2$. The volume formula is exact, because we can make the little pieces as small and as numerous as we like. But if learners are suspicious of these cut-it-into-tiny-bits-and-say-the-sides-are-straight kinds of arguments, then that is not unreasonable. Sometimes 'proofs' like this do lead you astray, so they are wise to be cautious.

Homework (5 min)

Find out about square fruit such as 'square' (actually cubic) watermelons, invented in Japan. They are fashionable and easier to pack, store and slice. They are easy to grow, using polycarbonate boxes. Google it for some striking pictures: see http://news.bbc.co.uk/1/hi/world/asia-pacific/1390088.stm.

To make it harder

Keen learners could find out what a 'spherical triangle' is and what its angles add up to (and why). They could also find out about the *Banach–Tarski Paradox*, which says that you can cut up a solid ball and put the pieces back together to make *two* solid balls, identical in size to the original one! Alternatively they could find out about other proofs that depend on cutting up a shape into infinitely many infinitesimally small pieces and adding them up – ultimately this is the idea behind integral calculus.

To make it easier

Learners are likely to find the argument on the Task Sheet difficult to follow. Some learners might find that accurate drawings (or building models, even) help them to appreciate what is going on.

Surface Area and Volume of a Sphere

Take a sphere of radius r and slip it inside a hollow cylinder of radius r and length $2r$ so it fits exactly in both directions.

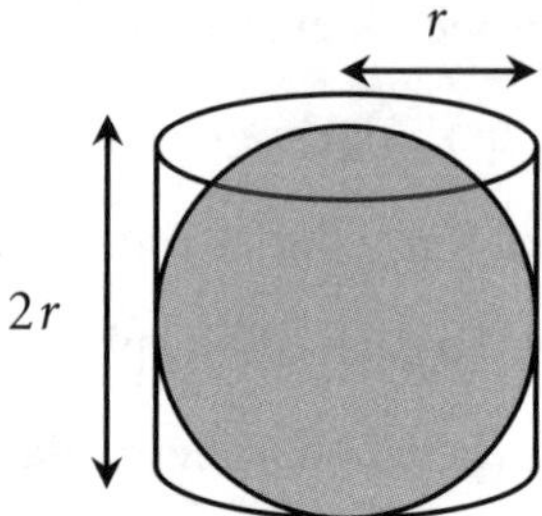

Surface Area

Work out the outside surface area of the cylinder. (It has no ends.)

This is the same as the surface area of the sphere. To see why, imagine a narrow horizontal slice through the sphere (shown in grey) and cylinder. The side of the sphere will be *almost* straight if it is a *very thin* slice.

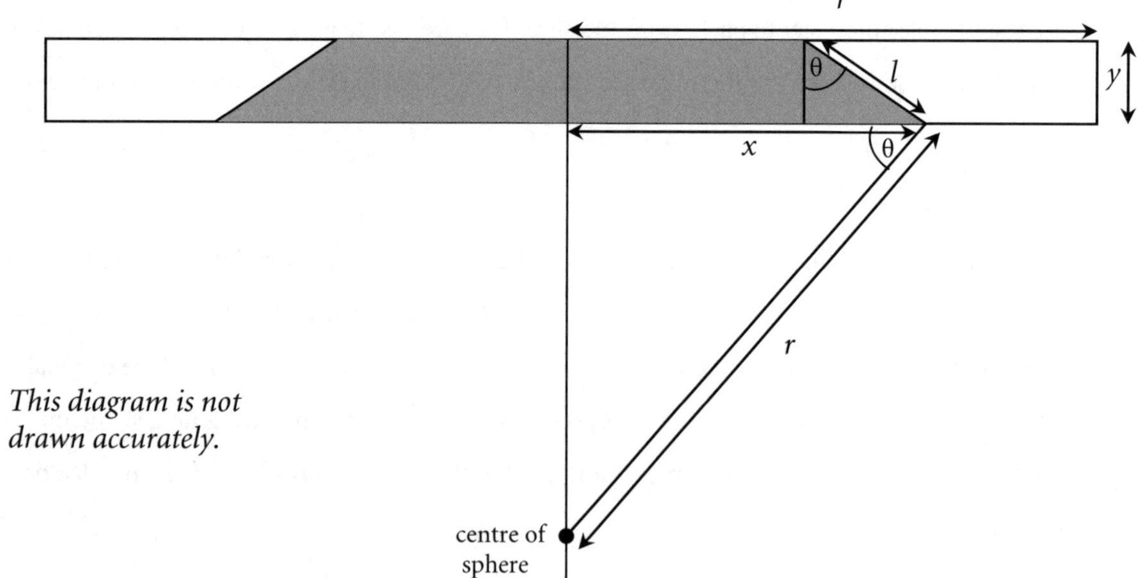

This diagram is not drawn accurately.

Two angles have been labelled as θ because they are the same size. Explain why they are the same size.

Explain from the diagram why $\frac{y}{l} = \frac{x}{r}$

Use this to show that $2\pi ry = 2\pi xl$. Which areas are these?

Why does this mean that the surface area of a sphere must be $4\pi r^2$?

Volume

Imagine a very large number of tiny pyramids with their apexes all meeting at the centre of a sphere and their bases making up the sphere's entire surface.

Their total volume will be the total volume of the sphere.

The volume of each one will be $\frac{1}{3} \times$ base area $\times$ height.

The height of each pyramid is the radius of the sphere.

And the total base area of all the pyramids is $4\pi r^2$.

So the total volume must be:

$$\text{volume} = \frac{1}{3} \times \text{total base area} \times \text{height}$$

$$= \frac{1}{3} \times 4\pi r^2 \times r$$

$$= \frac{4}{3}\pi r^3$$

Do you think this answer is approximate or exact? Why?

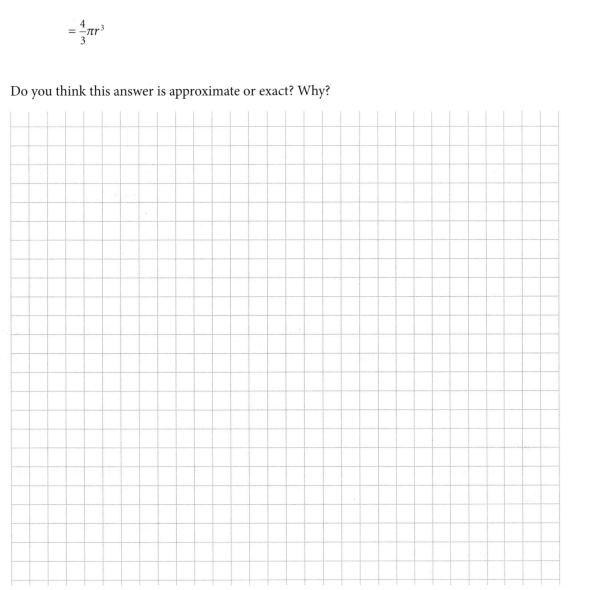

62

Tetraphobia

Introduction

This lesson brings together some simple work on multiplying, ordering and rounding decimals. The novelty is the emergence of sequences in which certain numbers are 'missing'. There is plenty of scope for learners to practise working with decimals and rounding while constructing interesting sequences and looking for what it is that determines which number will be missing. Learners may be quite surprised that sequences like this can be made quite so easily. For more on rounding, see Lesson 53.

Aims and Outcomes

- practise rounding decimals correct to the nearest integer
- work on surprising omissions in apparently linear sequences

Lesson Starter (15 min)

What comes next?

1, 2, 3, 4, …

Can you think of any reason why it wouldn't *be 5? Come up with an alternative answer* and reason.

Do you know your 1.1-times table? You could do some class chanting: 1.1, 2.2, 3.3, 4.4, 5.5, 6.6, 7.7, 8.8, 9.9, (learners may chant '10.10', or pause, here!) 11, 12.1, …

Let's round all these numbers to the nearest integer:

1, 2, 3, <u>4, 6,</u> 7, 8, 9, 10, 11, 12, …

Will any other integers be missing apart from 5? Why?

Learners may think that '5s are bad' in some sense and expect 15 to be missing, but 15, and 50, are present. Sixteen is the next missing number, then 27, etc. In general, the missing numbers are $11n - 6$, where n is an integer.

Rehearse how to round to the nearest integer, including rounding 'up' the 0.5s.

Main Lesson (20 min)

Ask learners to try some different decimal times tables rounded to the nearest integer and give out the Task Sheet.

'Tetraphobia' is a fear of the number four. See if learners can make a sequence suitable for someone 'allergic to four'!

Can you make any number you wish to be missing? How?

Learners could use spreadsheets to help them focus on the ideas behind which number may be omitted. Alternatively, you might wish them to practise their sequences and rounding (with or without the aid of a calculator).

Plenary (20 min)

Rounding the 1.13-times table, for instance, gives 1, 2, 3, 5, 6, 7, … (4 missing).

To make the number 10, say, missing, one way is to try to hit something around 9.4, say, on the ninth term, so work out $\frac{9.4}{9} = 1.0\dot{4}$. Perhaps then try the 1.05-times table (which works) – the 1.04-times table leaves out 13. Learners may come up with other approaches and ideas. The patterns are complicated, since the 1.06-times table leaves out 9.

In which cases are no *numbers missing? Why?*

Homework (5 min)

Find out what Wittgenstein's finite rule paradox *is.*

It says that there are always infinitely many possible ways of continuing a sequence when you are given any finite number of terms: there are always an infinite number of possible rules that could be being followed.

Find examples of sequences that 'go wrong' at some point.

For example, there is a formula for π that works for the first 42 billion digits and then goes wrong!

$$\left(\frac{1}{10^5}\sum_{n=-\infty}^{\infty} e^{-\frac{n^2}{10^{10}}}\right)^2 \approx \pi$$ (See www.rowan.edu/open/depts/math/osler/Billions_pi_digits.pdf.)

Learners could also find out more about tetraphobia – there is a real aversion to the number four in some parts of East Asia (similar to triskaidekaphobia [fear of the number 13] in the West) due to a similarity between the sound of the word for 'four' and the word for death. The phone manufacturer *Nokia*, for instance, apparently avoids using four in the model numbers of their phones.

To make it harder

Learners who want a greater challenge could work on the following questions:

What happens if you use negative *numbers?*

What happens if instead of 'normal' rounding you use floor *or* ceiling *functions?*

Can you generate 'missing term sequences' in these situations?

They could also try to make tables squares arising from having the numbers around the edge as the 1.1-times-table, say, rather than the 1-times table; i.e.,

	1.1	**2.2**	**3.3**	**4.4**	**5.5**	**6.6**	**7.7**	**8.8**	**9.9**	**11**
1.1	1.21	2.42	3.63	4.84	6.05	7.26	8.47	9.68	10.89	12.1
2.2	2.42	4.84	7.26	9.68	12.1	14.52	16.94	19.36	21.78	24.2
3.3	3.63	7.26	10.89	14.52	18.15	21.78	25.41	29.04	32.67	36.3
4.4	4.84	9.68	14.52	19.36	24.2	29.04	33.88	38.72	43.56	48.4
5.5	6.05	12.1	18.15	24.2	30.25	36.3	42.35	48.4	54.45	60.5
6.6	7.26	14.52	21.78	29.04	36.3	43.56	50.82	58.08	65.34	72.6
7.7	8.47	16.94	25.41	33.88	42.35	50.82	59.29	67.76	76.23	84.7
8.8	9.68	19.36	29.04	38.72	48.4	58.08	67.76	77.44	87.12	96.8
9.9	10.89	21.78	32.67	43.56	54.45	65.34	76.23	87.12	98.01	108.9
11	12.1	24.2	36.3	48.4	60.5	72.6	84.7	96.8	108.9	121

Rounding the answers in the table to the nearest integer produces the following:

	1.1	**2.2**	**3.3**	**4.4**	**5.5**	**6.6**	**7.7**	**8.8**	**9.9**	**11**
1.1	1	2	4	5	6	7	8	10	11	12
2.2	2	5	7	10	12	15	17	19	22	24
3.3	4	7	11	15	18	22	25	29	33	36
4.4	5	10	15	19	24	29	34	39	44	48
5.5	6	12	18	24	30	36	42	48	54	61
6.6	7	15	22	29	36	44	51	58	65	73
7.7	8	17	25	34	42	51	59	68	76	85
8.8	10	19	29	39	48	58	68	77	87	97
9.9	11	22	33	44	54	65	76	87	98	109
11	12	24	36	48	61	73	85	97	109	121

Learners could investigate which numbers are present in the table and why.

To make it easier

All learners should be able to engage with notions of sequences of small positive integers.

Tetraphobia

Make up rules for sequences which appear to leave out particular terms.

For example, can you invent a rule for a sequence which goes:

1, 2, 3, 5, 6, 7, ...

(The number 4 is missing from this sequence!)

Experiment with other rules to see which numbers are omitted.

Try to find a way of making sequences which leave out particular terms.

Write about what you have discovered.

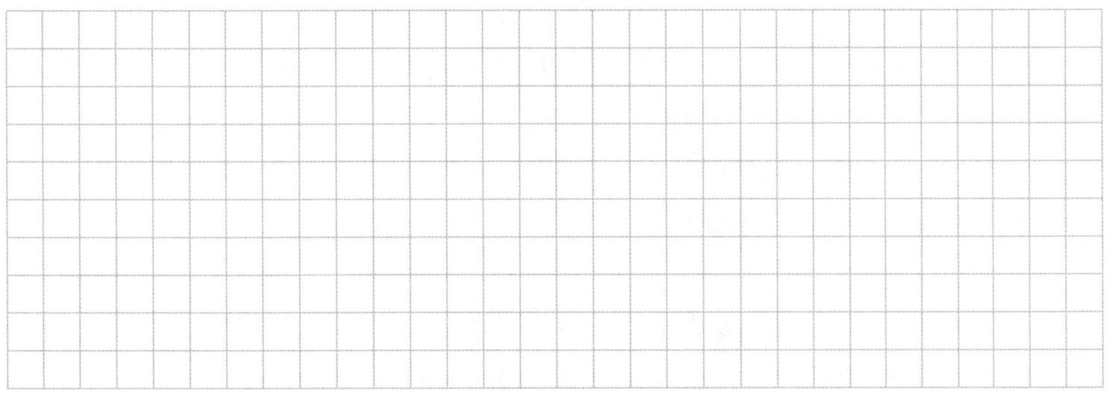

63 The Cosine Rule

Introduction

It is nice to think of the cosine rule as a modification to Pythagoras' Theorem to take account of *non*-right-angled triangles. Learners will be used to $a^2 + b^2 = c^2$, and they may realize that if $C > 90°$ then $a^2 + b^2 < c^2$ (obtuse-angled triangles), just as $a^2 + b^2 > c^2$ when $C < 90°$ (acute-angled triangles). The 'c-side' (the longest side, or the hypotenuse when the triangle is right-angled) gets longer when the angle C gets bigger (the *hinge theorem*). Pythagoras' Theorem can be thought of as the 'special case' of equality in between these extremes. Adapting the formula to account for this gives the cosine rule: $a^2 + b^2 = c^2 + 2ab\cos C$. When $C > 90°$, $\cos C$ is negative, so $a^2 + b^2 < c^2$; when $C < 90°$, $\cos C$ is positive, so $a^2 + b^2 > c^2$. Although it is nice to see the $2ab\cos C$ as the 'extra' bit, it is of course an *area* rather than a *length*, so it is difficult to relate to diagrams where the a and b sides rotate apart as angle C increases or decreases and the c-side gets consequently longer or shorter. The area connection comes out of this lesson.

Aims and Outcomes

- appreciate the cosine rule qualitatively as a modification to Pythagoras' Theorem for non-right-angled triangles
- work through and understand a proof of the cosine rule

Lesson Starter (10 min)

I want you to close your eyes (if you wish) and imagine the seaside. No, I mean the 'c-side' of a right-angled triangle, where a *and* b *are the 'legs' and the* c*-side is the hypotenuse.* (Learners may find it helpful to remember the word 'hypotenuse' by visualizing a hippopotamus at the seaside. On the other hand, they may not!) It could be beneficial to try to do this without drawing anything on the board or allowing learners to sketch on paper.

Label the angles with the same letter as the opposite *sides. Which angle is the right angle?* C is the right angle, opposite the hypotenuse.

Imagine sides a *and* b *staying the same length but angle* C *getting* smaller *than 90°. Describe what happens to the* c*-side.* It gets smaller.

What does the triangle *become like?* It becomes acute-angled.

Imagine sides a *and* b *staying the same length but angle* C *getting* larger *than 90°. What happens to the* c*-side?* This time it gets larger and the triangle becomes obtuse-angled.

Do you think that Pythagoras' Theorem $a^2 + b^2 = c^2$ *still works for acute-angled or obtuse-angled triangles? Why / why not?* Learners may be able to see that for acute-angled triangles $c^2 < a^2 + b^2$

whereas for obtuse-angled triangles $c^2 > a^2 + b^2$. Pythagoras' Theorem is for the special in-between case of right-angled triangles.

Main Lesson (25 min)

Give out the Task Sheet and ask learners what they see in the diagrams. Since the diagrams are accurately drawn, learners could use rulers and protractors to establish what shapes are intended. You might simply prefer to say that things which look like squares *are* squares.

How many different lengths are there? There are only three, so they can be labelled a, b and c.

How many different angles are there? This depends on what you count as an angle, but all angles can be seen as consisting of 90° and/or any of the three acute angles A, B and C. The triangles are scalene and angles A, B and C lie opposite to sides a, b and c respectively.

Invite learners to complete the sheet.

Plenary (20 min)

To be successful, the labelling needs to be done consistently. If learners have not followed the instruction that $a > c > b$ but have been consistent about it, then they should still obtain a version of the cosine rule, just with letters interchanged, so this does not really matter and might be a useful discussion point.

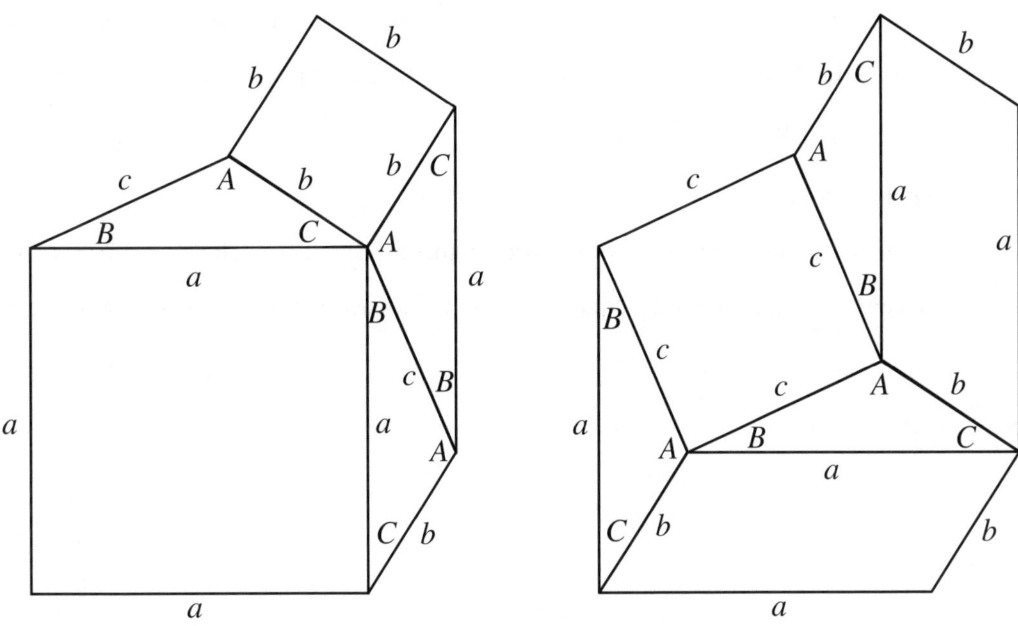

Triangle T is always the same way round, just rotated. (Incidentally, $T = \frac{1}{2}ab \sin C$ or $\frac{1}{2}ac \sin B$ or $\frac{1}{2}bc \sin A$ – see Lesson 4.) Learners may be satisfied that the two diagrams have the same total area by imagining journeying round the edge (as with a turtle in *Logo*-style geometry software) and considering the distance travelled and angle turned through at each vertex. Since these match then the two diagrams must have the same total area.

It is worth establishing that the squares in each diagram are definitely not just rhombuses but have 90° corners. The parallelograms must be parallelograms because they have two pairs of opposite sides equal.

The height of the parallelogram is $b \cos C$, so the area is $ab \cos C$, since the area of a parallelogram is equal to the base multiplied by the perpendicular height. (It can be sheared into a rectangle with the same base and height without changing the area.)

You might wish to consider how the cosine rule plugs the gap in triangle problems that cannot be solved with the sine rule. The two cases that are not easily dealt with using just the sine rule are SSS (all the sides given) and SAS (two sides with the included angle). Since the cosine rule is more cumbersome than the sine rule, it is probably more efficient to use it only in these situations, and, in each case, after one application, there is enough information available then to use the sine rule to find any other required quantities.

Homework (5 min)

Learners could devise three non-right-angled triangle problems which can be solved by using the sine rule and three that can be solved by using the cosine rule. *Can any of the problems be solved using the other rule? Why / why not?*

To make it harder

Learners who are confident with this work might like to consider the case where $C > 90°$ and a different diagram is needed. Can they construct it? This is pretty difficult – a search on the internet will reveal the diagram if necessary!

To make it easier

Learners may need to use rulers and protractors to identify which line segments and angles in the diagrams are supposed to be equal. Some initial measurement may support later generalization.

The Cosine Rule

Look at these two diagrams, which are drawn accurately.

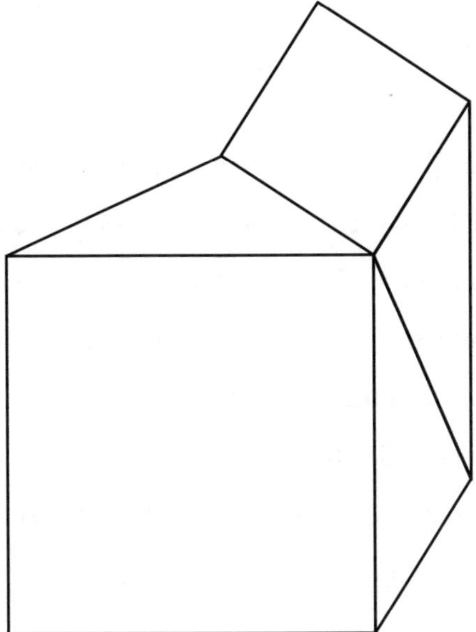

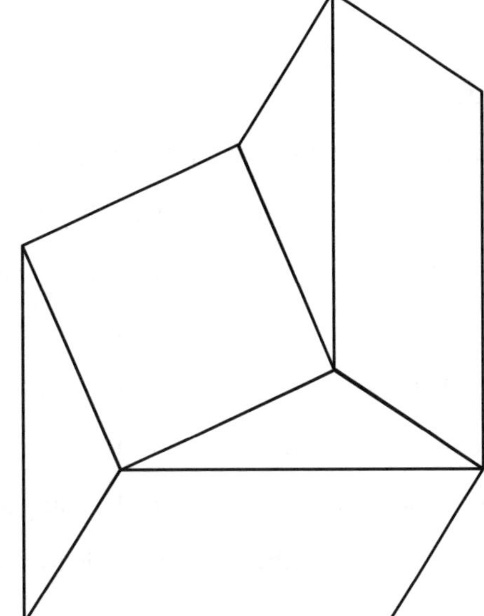

The left diagram contains two squares and three congruent triangles.

The right diagram contains one square, two parallelograms and three more of the same congruent triangles.

Label each of the triangles with a, b, c, A, B and C so that $a > c > b$.

Label the *areas* of the squares: a^2 and b^2 are in the left diagram and c^2 is in the right.

Label the areas of the triangles as T.

How can you be sure that the total areas of both diagrams are the same?

In the right diagram, the (horizontal) 'base' of the bottom parallelogram is a.

Use trigonometry to find an expression for the *perpendicular height* (vertical) in terms of b and C.

So what is the area of the parallelogram?

Explain how together the diagrams illustrate the following equation:

$$a^2 + b^2 + 3T = c^2 + 2ab \cos C + 3T$$

Therefore, $\mathbf{a^2 + b^2 = c^2 + 2ab \cos C}$, which is called the **cosine rule**.

64 The Sine Rule

Introduction

The sine rule is a useful general statement about triangles and may be the first occasion when learners use trigonometry in non-right-angled triangles. Sometimes learners who have encountered the sine rule like it so much that they begin to use it even in right-angled triangles as well, instead of reverting to the sin, cos or tan ratios themselves. They may even think that 'use the sine rule' means 'use sin'. Although it is nice to see that substituting 90° as one of the angles leads to sin 90° being 1 and the original trigonometrical ratio, it is good if learners realize that always using the sine rule in right-angled triangles would be like using a sledgehammer to crack a nut – a little inefficient. It would be a little like using the quadratic formula to solve $x^2 = 36$.

Aims and Outcomes

- consider when the sine rule is useful for solving triangles
- prove the sine rule

Lesson Starter (10 min)

Close your eyes (if you wish). Imagine a triangle with sides 10 cm, 8 cm and 3 cm. Describe what it is like. It is obtuse-angled scalene. You could push for comments on the angles: *Where is the biggest angle (the obtuse one)? How do you know? Which of the other two angles is bigger? Why?*

It might be helpful to label *a*, *A*, *b*, *B*, *c*, *C* (sides lower case; angles/vertices upper case).

Are we all thinking of the same triangle or could we have different pictures in our heads? Why? They could be mirror images of each other and could, of course, have different orientations.

The so-called hinge theorem makes the (perhaps obvious?) point that the largest side in a triangle is always opposite the largest angle, the medium-length side is always opposite the medium-sized angle and the smallest side is always opposite the smallest angle. The side lengths are not *proportional* to the angle sizes, however, but to the *sine* of the angles. This is one way of looking at what the sine rule says: ; i.e., $\frac{a}{\sin A} = \frac{b}{\sin B} = \frac{c}{\sin C}$; i.e., $p \propto \sin P$, where the side of length p is opposite the angle P. This is complicated, though, by the fact that when $90° < P < 180°$ sin *decreases*.

Main Lesson (25 min)

Give out the Task Sheet and ask learners to complete the first three sections. Then draw the class together and establish that the equation $b\sin A = a\sin B$ can be rearranged to give $\frac{a}{\sin A} = \frac{b}{\sin B}$, and that this can be extended to $\frac{a}{\sin A} = \frac{b}{\sin B} = \frac{c}{\sin C}$. Learners may need some persuading that it is equally acceptable to write these equations 'upside down' as $\frac{\sin A}{a} = \frac{\sin B}{b} = \frac{\sin C}{c}$, either by rearranging the original $b\sin A = a\sin B$ differently or by 'inverting' both sides of $\frac{a}{\sin A} = \frac{b}{\sin B}$, etc. The versions with the sin's on the top are more convenient when finding *angles*.

Ask learners to look at the table in section 4 and decide which combinations of information enable them to use the sine rule to 'solve the triangle' (i.e., find all the remaining sides and angles).

Plenary (20 min)

This final plenary is an opportunity to discuss the work resulting from section 4 of the Task Sheet. The sine rule is ideal when one value is missing from two pairs of side-opposite-angle pieces of information; for example, a, b and A are known and B is to be found, or A, B and a are known and b is to be found. But it can also be used when the 'wrong' pair of angles is known, because the third one can be found by using the fact that the sum of the interior angles of a triangle is always 180°. So, for example, if A, C and a are known, then either b or c can be found, since if b is required then B can first be calculated, using $B = 180 - A - C$, and both A and C are known. Finding angles can be more problematic, because of the possibility of the 'ambiguous case', but a similar process enables, say, B to be found when a, b and A are known, and then you can go on to calculate C, if you wish, using $C = 180 - A - B$.

Homework (5 min)

Make up and answer six questions involving finding sides or angles in non-right-angled triangles. In one of the questions, make it impossible to do using the sine rule, but don't indicate which one!

To make it harder

Learners who complete these tasks early could find out about the 'ambiguous case', which happens when finding an angle, B, say, given an *acute* angle A and sides a and b such that $b \sin A < a < b$. Drawing a diagram and imagining making the construction with compasses will show that two triangles are possible, and therefore that angle B may be or $\sin^{-1}\left(\frac{b\sin A}{a}\right)$ or $180° - \sin^{-1}\left(\frac{b\sin A}{a}\right)$.

To make it easier

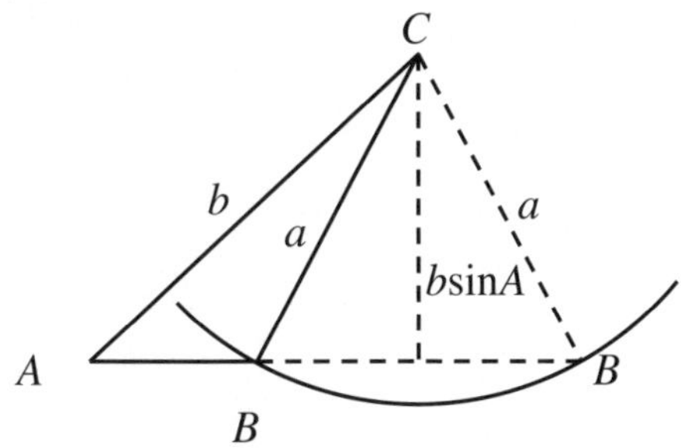

Some accurate drawing of triangles, using compasses and/or protractors, may help some learners to visualize what is going on.

The Sine Rule

Look at the diagram below.

Uppercase letters indicate angles.

Lowercase letters indicate side lengths.

Side a is opposite angle A, etc.

The *altitude* (marked h) divides the triangle ABC into two right-angled triangles, one on the left and one on the right.

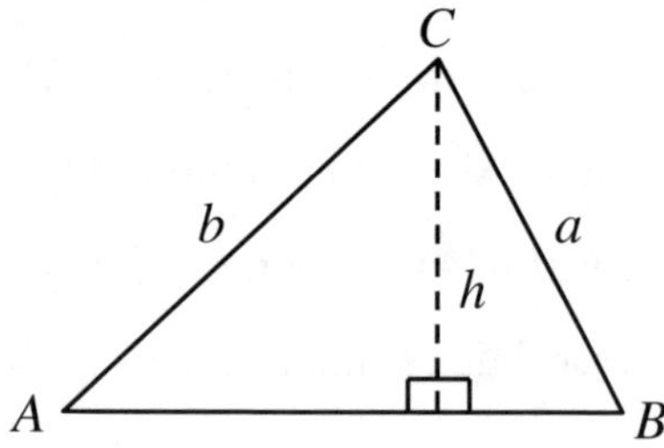

1. Use trigonometry in the left triangle (drawn again below) to find an expression for h in terms of **angle A and side b**.

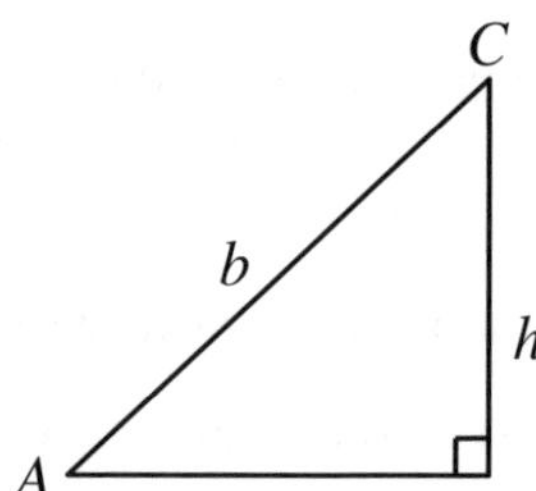

2. Use trigonometry in the right triangle (drawn again below) to find an expression for h in terms of **angle B and side a**.

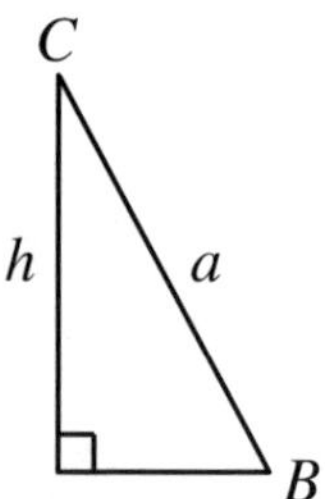

3. Put your answers together and write about what this tells you.

   Can you involve angle C and side c in this?

4. Suppose you are given *any three* pieces of information (indicated by ticks below). Which of the remaining three pieces of information could you work out by using the sine rule? Why?

Try to cover all possibilities.

	a	*b*	*c*	*A*	*B*	*C*	**Conclusions**
	✓			✓	✓		

65 Throwing a Coin

Introduction

Learners sometimes have the misconception that if an experiment has two possible outcomes then they must be equally likely, so that each has a probability of $\frac{1}{2}$. In real life, of course, they know that 'winning the lottery' and 'not winning the lottery' are not equally likely, but it is common for learners to think that 'mathematically' (whatever this means) the chance is $\frac{1}{2}$, even though it isn't really. This sense that mathematics can sometimes say nonsense is worth addressing. In this lesson, learners find the probability of a coin falling across a line by actually doing it. They should see that the probability depends on things like the length of the stick and the positions of the lines rather than always being 50:50.

Aims and Outcomes

- consider practical factors that will minimize bias in an experiment
- use an experimental relative frequency approach to estimate a probability

Lesson Starter (5 min)

Have you ever tried to walk along the pavement without stepping on the cracks? Some people are superstitious about it.

If you throw an ordinary circular coin at random onto some paving slabs, what is the probability that the coin will land across a crack? What will the probability depend on?

Some learners may think that the coin will either land across a crack or won't land across a crack, so it is 50:50, but these two events are not necessarily equally likely. It will depend on how the coin is thrown, the size of the coin and the size and shape of the paving slabs. For example, if square paving slabs have an area smaller than the area of the circular coin, then the coin is bound to land across a crack. (Even if the area of the square is greater than the area of the circle, the probability may still be 1, and this might be something for learners to investigate.)

What things will it be sensible to disregard? We will need to assume that the ground is flat, the coin doesn't land on its side or roll out of the paved area, there are no earthquakes or significant fluctuations in the earth's gravitational field, etc!

Main Lesson (30 min)

Give learners the Task Sheet and a coin (e.g., a UK ten-pence coin), unless they are going to provide their own. Different groups could use different-sized coins to see what the effect of the coin size is. The Task Sheet has lines and squares with lengths of 4.9 cm. (This is twice the diameter of a UK ten-pence coin.)

Learners could also try using other size grids – they may need to construct their own lines, grids and dots.

If they drop a coin onto a sheet of squared dotty paper, what is the probability that the coin will cover a spot? What if they use isometric dotty paper instead? Does it matter?

Learners could try to calculate the theoretical probabilities, and then see whether experiment verifies their predictions. Thinking about where the centre of the coin can be, and drawing diagrams such as the one below, can be helpful. It may be important how the coin is thrown. One possibility is to throw the coin *upwards*, or to insist on some spin, so that it falls more randomly onto the grid than may be the case if it is simply dropped.

Learners may think that to make the experiment fair they need to drop the coin from the same height each time. Alternatively, they may think exactly the opposite if we are trying to be random!

Plenary (20 min)

Learners may be surprised that the locus of the centre of the coin, where the coin *just touches* a crack, is a *square* and not a 'rounded rectangle'.

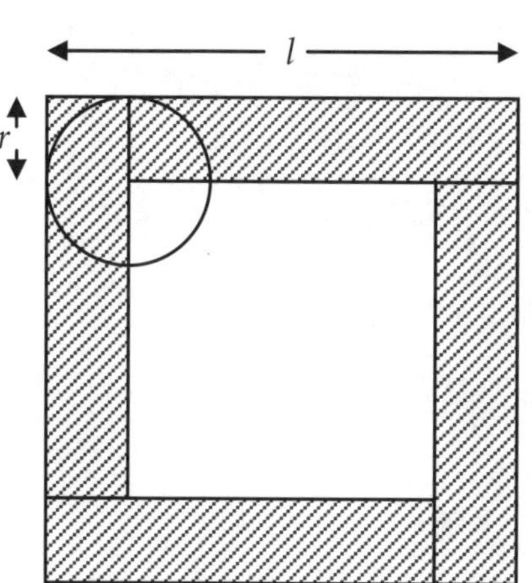

$$p(\text{coin falls across a crack}) = \frac{4(l-r)}{l^2}$$

On lines (with spacing l), the probability of the coin (radius r) falling across a crack is $\frac{2r}{l}$, provided that $2r < l$, otherwise the probability is 1.

On squares (with side length l), the probability of the coin (radius r) falling across a crack is $\frac{4(l-r)}{l^2}$, provided that $2r < l$, otherwise the probability is 1.

On squared dotty paper (with side length l), the probability of the coin (radius r) falling over a dot is $\frac{\pi r^2}{l^2}$, provided that $2r < l$, otherwise it gets very complicated! (This assumes that the area of a dot is negligible.)

Note that these equations are dimensionally correct, since probability is a dimensionless number.

Learners may be surprised that they do not need the formula for the area of a circle in the lines and the squares cases, only for situations involving the dotty grid.

In particular, if $l = 4r$, the probability is $\frac{1}{2}$ for the lines and $\frac{3}{4}$ for the squares. If $l = 3r$, the probability is $\frac{2}{3}$ for the lines and $\frac{1}{2}$ for the squares.

Homework (5 min)

Learners could design a coin and paving slab situation so that the probability of the coin landing across a crack is $\frac{1}{2}$.

To make it harder

Learners who want an extra challenge could use a stick (e.g., a headless matchstick) instead of a coin. So long as the lines are further apart than the length of the stick, the probability of it falling across a crack is $\frac{2l}{\pi s}$, where s is the spacing between the lines and l is the length of the matchstick. Learners can use this result to design an experiment to get a value of π. (This is known as *Buffon's Needle* after Comte de Buffon [1707–1788].)

To make it easier

Some learners may need support in keeping count of the number of throws and the number of 'successes'.

Throwing a Coin

Squares

Lines

66

Trial and Improvement

Introduction

Trial and improvement is a powerful method for finding solutions to equations. The sorts of equations that learners commonly meet in school (such as linear equations and quadratic equations) are deliberately constructed to be solvable by algebraic methods. But it is probably the case that most equations that arise in real-life or scientific contexts cannot be solved by 'doing the same things to both sides' and numerical/graphical methods have to be used, often on computer. There is a subtle but important distinction between 'solving' an equation algebraically, in which by logical steps you show what all the solutions must be, and 'finding a solution' by numerical methods, such as trial and improvement – you are generally not locating the solution precisely, and nor are you establishing that the solution(s) you find is/are the only one(s). However, you are checking that the solutions that you find are (approximately) correct because they satisfy the equation.

Textbook equations for trial and improvement are often readily solvable by other means generally encountered by this stage. Presumably this is to make it easier for the author to supply the answers, but this can be de-motivating for learners. Exponential equations are likely to be less familiar territory, as logarithms are unlikely to be well known (if at all) – and indeed this lesson could be an opportunity to encourage competent learners to explore them a little. Also, the monotonically increasing nature of exponential curves makes them a natural choice for finding in-between values in a commonsense way, as does the fact that each equation has exactly one solution.

Aims and Outcomes

- explore exponential growth
- solve equations by trial and improvement

Lesson Starter (10 min)

Suppose that the number of bacteria in a colony doubles every six hours. If you start off with 10 000 bacteria how many will there be after a week? There will be about 10^{12}!

Estimates say that there are about 10^{12} bacteria on the surface of the adult human body. (Data for *teenagers* is not available, but is obviously likely to be many times higher!) *Inside* the human body there are estimated to be around 10^{15} bacteria (this means that there are about ten times as many bacteria as there are cells!), consisting of somewhere between 500 and 100 000 different species. For comparison, the brain contains about 10^{11} neurons, so bacteria well outnumber brain cells!

What would the graph of 'number of bacteria' against 'time' look like? Learners could sketch their ideas, maybe on mini-whiteboards. *What sort of formula might fit this?* The shape will be an exponential increase, with a formula something like $y = 10000 \times 2^x$, where y is the number of bacteria and x is the time. Here x is measured in units of six hours, and tells us how many times to double the initial 10 000. If you want the time (t) in days then the formula will become $y = 10000 \times 2^{4t} = 10000 \times 16^t$.

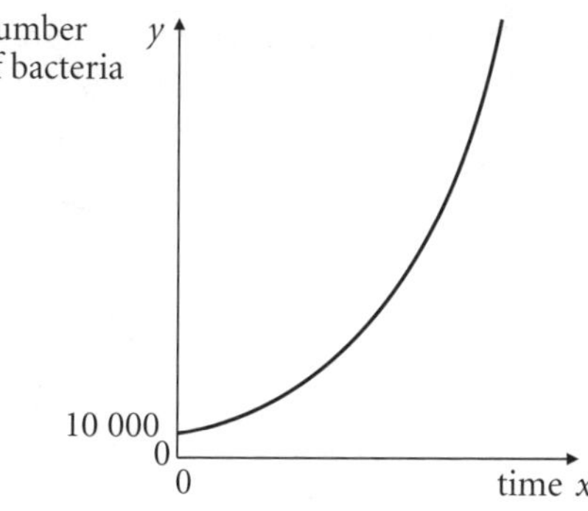

Main Lesson (25 min)

Suppose we count bacteria in thousands and suppose the number of bacteria starts at one (i.e., one thousand) and doubles every day.

After how many days will there be sixteen (thousand)?

Working it through, 1, 2, 4, 8, 16, so the answer is, after four days.

At what point will there be ten (thousand) bacteria? Presumably some time between three days and four days.

What equation represents this? $2^x = 10$. Learners may initially confuse this equation with $2x = 10$ and therefore think that the answer is 5. Working out 2^5 should convince them that this is wrong. If there are 16 000 after four days then there cannot be 10 000 after five days. This sort of error gets (much) worse with bigger numbers (the lines $y = 2x$ and $y = 2^x$ diverge very quickly) – with an equation such as $2^x = 100$, 2^{50} will turn out to be *far* too big! Learners may need encouragement to be careful in their handwriting so that 2^x doesn't look like $2x$. Some may also confuse an equation like $2^x = 100$ with the equation $x^2 = 100$, and therefore may think that $x = 10$ (and possibly -10) is the solution. Substituting 10 back into the equation should persuade them that 10 is much too large to be a solution.

Give out the Task Sheet and let learners work on finding solutions to the given equations, along with others of their choice.

Plenary (20 min)

Estimating where to start the trial and improvement process is good for becoming familiar with the powers of 2.

The solution to the equation $2^x = 30$, say, is $x = \log_2 30 = \frac{\log 30}{\log 2} = 4.9069$ (correct to 5 significant figures). Because of the context of the questions, learners may wish to convert numbers such as this (in days) into days, hours, minutes and seconds – see below (correct to the nearest second). These answers should match those obtained by trial and improvement, albeit probably with greater accuracy.

y (thousands)	x (days) (correct to 5 significant figures)	Days	Hours	Minutes	Seconds
10	3.3219	3	7	43	34
20	4.3219	4	7	43	34
30	4.9068	4	21	45	55
40	5.3219	5	7	43	34
50	5.6438	5	15	27	9
60	5.9068	5	21	45	55
70	6.1292	6	3	6	10
80	6.3219	6	7	43	34
90	6.4918	6	11	48	16
100	6.6438	6	15	27	9

It is worth being careful about terminology during this lesson. In the expression 2^5, the '5' may be called the index or the exponent (or even the logarithm of 32 to base 2), but care is needed over the word 'power'. 2^5 can be described as the 'fifth power of 2', but to say that we have a 'power of 5' can be misleading: 5^2 is the (second) 'power of 5'.

Homework (5 min)

Find out what logarithms are. Explore the log button on the calculator by trying log 10, log 100, log 1 000 000, log 0.001, etc. Make a conjecture about what the log function does. Try to solve equations like $\log x = 0.1$ *or* $\log x = 0$ *or* $\log x = \frac{1}{2}$. The solutions are -1, 1 and $\sqrt{10}$. *Try sketching the graph of* $y = \log x$. *Why does 'second-function-log' (or 'shift-log' or 'inverse-log') on the calculator correspond to* 10^x*?*

To make it harder

Learners who know about logs might be able to follow a *proof by contradiction* that log 2 is irrational:

Suppose that log 2 is *rational*, in which case we can write $\log 2 = \frac{a}{b}$, where a and b are positive integers. Rearranging this gives $10^{\frac{a}{b}} = 2$ or $10^a = 2^b$, which is impossible, since 5 is definitely a factor of the left-hand side but 5 is definitely *not* a factor of the right-hand side. So our initial statement that '$\log 2 = \frac{a}{b}$ where a and b are positive integers' must be false, so log 2 is irrational. This is always going to happen unless we log a power of 10 instead of 2. (In some ways this is an easier proof of irrationality than the more common proof that $\sqrt{2}$ is irrational.)

To make it easier

Some learners may benefit from help constructing a table to record their 'trials' and in deciding whether to go for a higher or lower number next time – a number line may help with this.

Exponential Equations

Use trial and improvement to find the solutions to these equations.

Decide how many decimal places you think is sensible.

$2^x = 10$ $2^x = 20$ $2^x = 30$ $2^x = 40,$ …

Do you see any patterns in your answers?

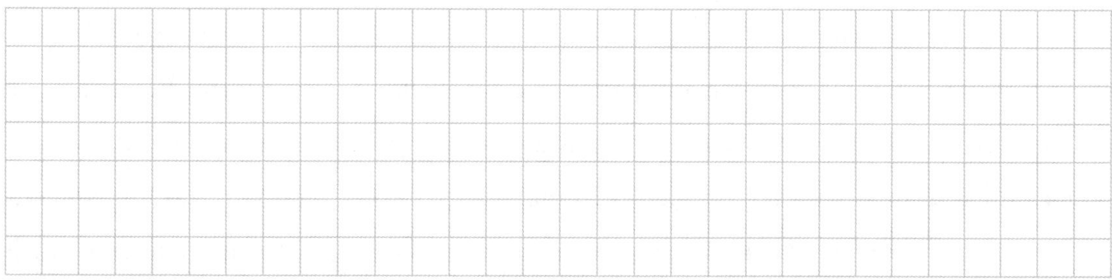

Draw a graph of $y = 2^x$, with the y-axis going from 0 up to about 100 and the x-axis going from 0 to 6.

Use the graph to find solutions to the equations above.

Is this easier than using trial and improvement?

Which method do you think is more accurate?

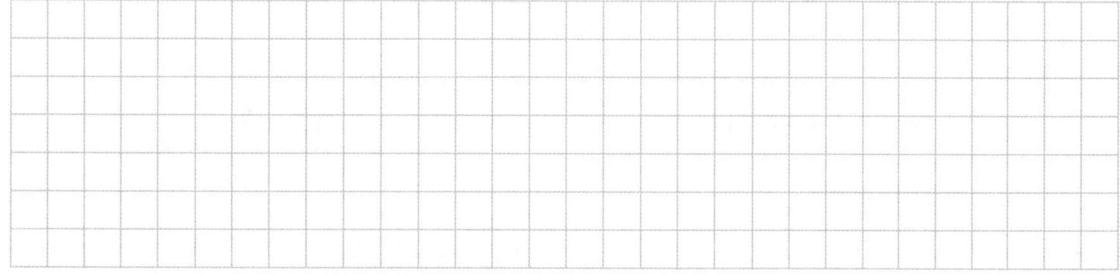

Make up and solve some exponential equations with bases other than 2.

For example, $10^x = 500$ or $3.5^x = 10$.

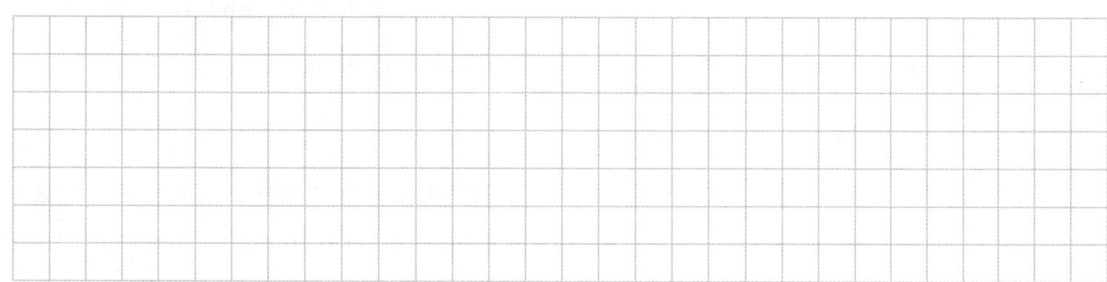

67 Trigonometry

Introduction

Teachers have differing opinions regarding measurement in pure mathematics. On the one hand, measuring the sides of right-angled triangles can help learners develop a sense of constant ratio amid changing sizes of triangles, and allow them to check that the sizes of their answers are approximately correct. But on the other hand, mathematics is not science, pure mathematics results contain no experimental errors, mathematical graphs do not have error bars, and if we rely too much on measurement we risk learners thinking that things are true because empirically they seem to be, which could be said to undermine an appreciation of mathematical structure and proof. Perhaps a discussion along these lines at some stage (not necessarily as part of this lesson) can mitigate the problems and widen learners' perceptions of different approaches to learning mathematics. Trigonometry is often learned in a very instrumental way, without much sense that the sizes of the answers are important or plausible, so a certain amount of measuring on accurately constructed triangles could help with this.

Aims and Outcomes

- understand and use trigonometric ratios in similar right-angled triangles

Lesson Starter (5 min)

Cut out the triangles from the sheet. (Photocopied onto card may be best.) *While you are cutting, think about what is the same and what is different about the triangles. Try to find as many things as possible.*

Learners might comment on some triangles being 'the other way round' (i.e., reflections) of others if they are unsure whether triangles may be turned over or not.

Main Lesson (30 min)

After some time, those who have not yet made measurements with ruler or protractor might be invited to do so. One advantage of cutting out the shapes, rather than merely observing them on the page, is that angles and lengths can be compared without measuring them, simply by placing shapes on top of or next to each other. Measurements might be recorded on the individual triangles or collated into some kind of table or chart. Sometimes learners arrange the pieces 'concentrically' or aligned at a common vertex, and these might lend themselves to being presented on posters with annotations.

Plenary (20 min)

Discuss learners' observations. Learners may have a strong feeling that the triangles are in some sense 'all the same', and pushing for more precise articulation may be helpful. Although the angles in any triangle add up to 180° and each triangle is right-angled, there is more to be said about the angles in these triangles. Although the triangles are of varied sizes, the angles are always 35°-55°-90°. So all the triangles are mathematically 'similar', scaled-up or -down versions of each other (enlargements). The intention is for learners to explore the implications of this for the *lengths of the sides.*

You might suggest, for convenience, the common convention of labelling the sides 'hypotenuse' (hyp) for the side facing the right angle, 'opposite' (opp) for the side opposite the 35° angle, say, and 'adjacent' (adj) for the side next to the 35° angle.

The measurements (in centimetres) are:

Adj	Opp	Hyp
2.0	1.4	2.4
3.0	2.1	3.7
5.0	3.5	6.1
6.0	4.2	7.3
7.0	4.9	8.5
8.0	5.6	9.8
9.0	6.3	11.0
10.0	7.0	12.2
12.0	8.4	14.6
15.0	10.5	18.3

Asking learners to make observations from this table may lead to different conjectures. *What happens when 'adj' doubles?*, etc. Multiplicative thinking (as opposed to additive thinking) is going to be critical here.

What is the same on every line?

Learners may suggest dividing or ratio, and you might wish to intervene to achieve this the 'right' way round for the major trigonometric ratios (e.g., opp/adj rather than adj/opp, since that corresponds to tan rather than cot). Having established, for example, that opp/adj is equal to (approximately) 0.7 for each line, if it seems appropriate, you could invite learners to ensure that their calculators are in degrees mode and then enter 'tan 35'. This can be a helpful way of learners making the connection without being explicitly told that 'tan is opp divided by adj'.

Would tan 40 be more or less than tan 35, do you think? Why? More, because if the 35° angle increases it looks as though opp is going to get bigger, even if adj were to stay the same.

Can you say what tan 45 would be without using the calculator? Why? It must be 1, because the triangle becomes isosceles at this stage, and opp = adj.

Can you experiment and find an angle with a tan of as close to 2 as possible? An accurate answer can be found by doing $\tan^{-1} 2 = 63.4°$ (correct to 1 decimal place).

Homework (5 min)

Write about what you have found out about right-angled triangles. What is tan all about? Give some examples, with angles and lengths.

Even if learners' explanations contain inaccuracies and highlight misconceptions, writing about an emerging understanding can be a very helpful process, and give useful feedback to the teacher; any difficulties can be worked on in subsequent lessons.

Another possible task would be to use a calculator to evaluate $\tan x$ for $x = 0°, 5°, 10°, 15°, \ldots$ and draw the graph. Learners can decide when it is sensible to stop. You might or might not wish to warn them that they may get an error for some of the values (i.e., 90°, 270°, etc.) and that that doesn't mean that they have done anything wrong. Again, they can decide what to do about it.

To make it harder

Learners who are confident about the connections between the side lengths of these triangles might be invited to make predictions about as-yet undrawn triangles – for example, if you had a triangle similar to these with an adj of 18 cm, its opp would be 12.6 cm – and then draw the triangle in question to verify the conjecture. Alternatively, they might produce a selection of triangles with a different set of angles (say 30°-60°-90°, for instance) and predict in advance what different results they would expect to obtain. An even more advanced extension would be to look at a set of similar *non*-right-angled triangles to see whether alternative trigonometrical ratios could be defined on triangles all containing a 100° angle, for instance.

To make it easier

All learners should be able to make some statements about the triangles that they have cut out. Some learners may benefit from being given the triangles already cut out.

Triangles

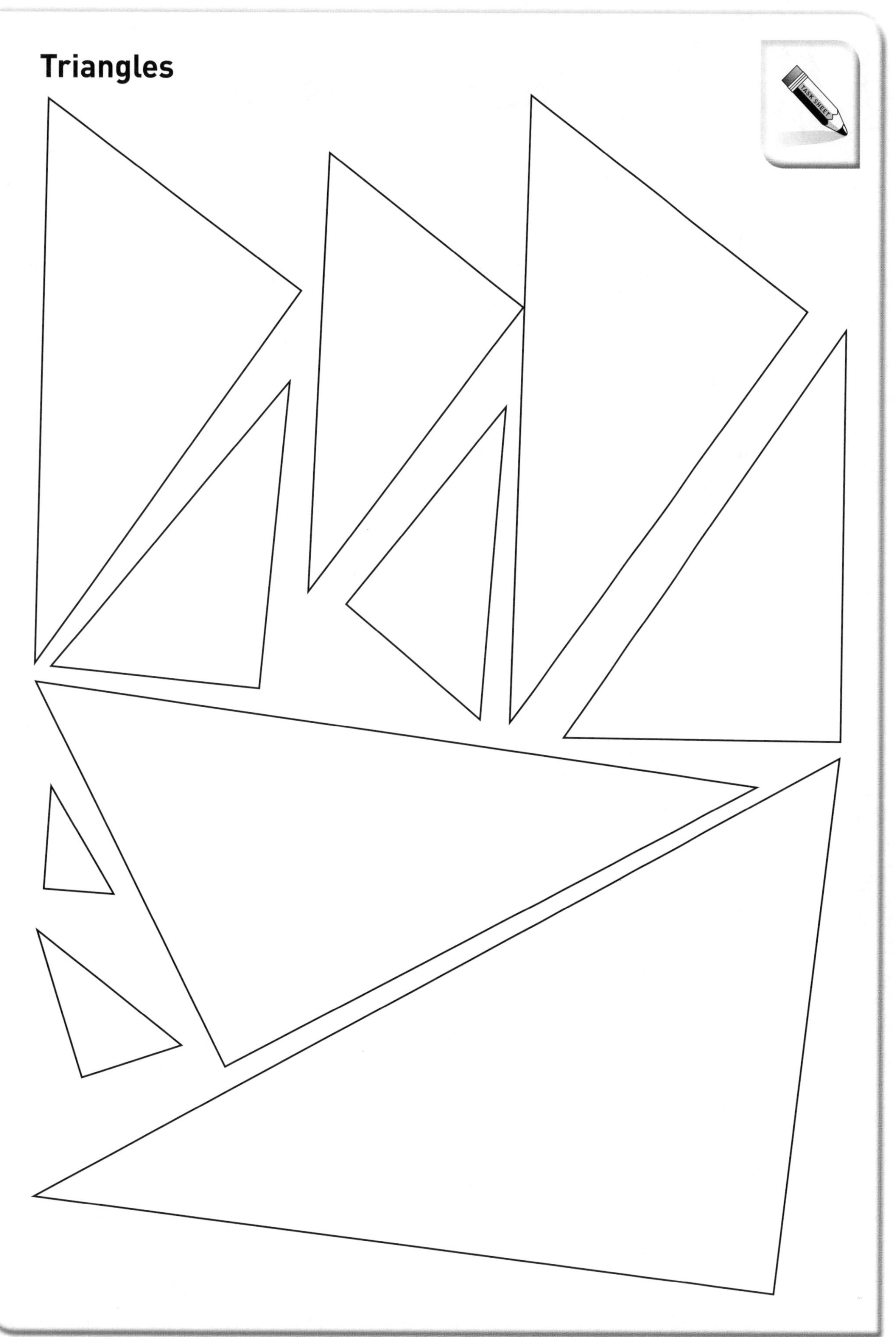

68 Twenty Questions

Introduction

This lesson seeks to involve learners in logical reasoning, ordering of integers and rounding. The scenario is the classic 'I'm thinking of a number …' situation and an attempt to find efficient strategies for working out what the number must be. Learners often approach this sort of problem completely reliant on luck and may be surprised to be asked to think about logical methods. Deliberately considering worst-case scenarios enables an upper limit to be put on the number of questions needed. The approach is similar to the interval bisection method for finding a root of an equation.

Aims and Outcomes

- develop a strategy for a game, considering awkward 'boundary' cases
- use logical reasoning to home in on a number on a number line

Lesson Starter (10 min)

Have you played the game 20 Questions? I think of something and you have to guess what it is. You can ask me up to 20 questions, but I am allowed to answer only 'yes' or 'no' to each one.

You can even get computer versions, which sometimes seem almost psychic! For example, see www.20q.net.

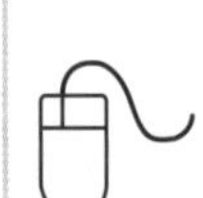

Play the game, thinking of 'something mathematical' (e.g., a triangle, a line, 42, etc.)

Do you think that 20 questions will be enough? Why / why not?

Main Lesson (25 min)

This time, I am going to think of a positive integer between 1 and 1000 (inclusive). How many questions would be the absolute most that you might need, if you were sensible? Do you think that 20 questions would be enough? Why / why not? What strategy would you use to play this?

Ask learners to think about this in groups for a few minutes and have a mini-plenary to share thoughts. They may know the comedy game Numberwang (*That Mitchell and Webb Look* [BBC TV]), where contestants shout out random numbers, one at a time until they win for no apparent reason! Some learners may begin by adopting this sort of approach – 'Is it 42?' – and this is, at least, one possible way of operating, but you could need up to 1000 goes if you did it this way, and were very unlucky – more if you forget what numbers you have tried before! Most learners will see that there are much quicker ways, such as 'Is it a prime number?', but then it may be hard to know what to ask next. The most efficient approach is probably to use 'greater than' and 'less than' statements, although learners sometimes try 'Is it a multiple of two?', 'Is it a multiple of three?', etc., bearing in mind that if the number is not a multiple of two (say) then there is no point asking whether it is a multiple of any multiple of two (like four or six, for example).

Give learners the Task Sheet and encourage them to think through an efficient strategy.

Plenary (20 min)

Since $2^{10} = 1024$, which is more than 1000, 10 questions should be sufficient. This may be surprising to learners, who may initially think that they will need a lot more than 20 questions. The reason is that with each question you eliminate about half of the remaining numbers, so 10 steps should get you down to only one number. After dividing into >500 or ≤500, the next question will ask about 750 or 250, and then 875, 625, 375 or 125, and then 937, 813, 687, 563, 437, 313, 187 or 63, and so on. Each time, half the previous difference is added or subtracted, with rounding as necessary so as to obtain integers. It is important to worry about the 'boundary' numbers (such as 500) and to check that the scheme works for them too. For simplicity, all questions could ask about 'more than'. A number line-diagram may help learners to appreciate what is going on. It will not be possible to continue the flow diagram to the end, because there would be far too many branches to fit onto a piece of paper!

Suppose you have two variables, *max* and *min*, and initially *max* is set to 1000 and *min* is set to 1. At any stage in the game,

max = the last number to which the answer was 'no' and

min = the last number to which the answer was 'yes'.

The current question is: 'Is it more than $\left\lfloor \frac{max + min}{2} \right\rfloor$?', where the brackets indicate the 'floor' function (rounding down). The game ends when $max = min$, and that's the mystery number. Learners may be able to find a simpler way of explaining this!

Since $2^{20} = 1\,048\,576$, which is the first power of 2 greater than 1 000 000, it follows that 20 questions should be enough to guess any number from 1 to 1 000 000. Learners may be surprised how big a range of numbers may be dealt with in relatively few questions, if the questions are carefully chosen. It might be fun to play this game and see it working.

Homework (5 min)

Construct a flow diagram for dealing with polygons (with, say, up to ten sides), where the name the person is thinking of is the most specific mathematical name possible (e.g., although all squares are also rectangles, and many other things, if you were thinking of a square then the answer would be 'square', not 'rectangle' or 'rhombus' or 'parallelogram' or 'kite' or 'quadrilateral', etc.).

To make it harder

Confident learners could consider the effect of including negative numbers or halves as well as positive integers. *Is it easy to modify the process to accommodate these? Why / why not?*

Learners who know a computer programming language, such as BASIC, could try writing a computer program to locate the number by asking appropriate questions.

To make it easier

If 1000 is too daunting to begin with, choosing from the numbers 1 to 20, say, might be more accessible at the start. Here you could certainly do it in 20 questions (!) but learners could work on the smallest number of questions that would *always* be sufficient.

Twenty Questions ... or Fewer

Here is the beginning of a flow chart.

How would you continue it?

Can you eliminate about half of the remaining possible numbers each time?

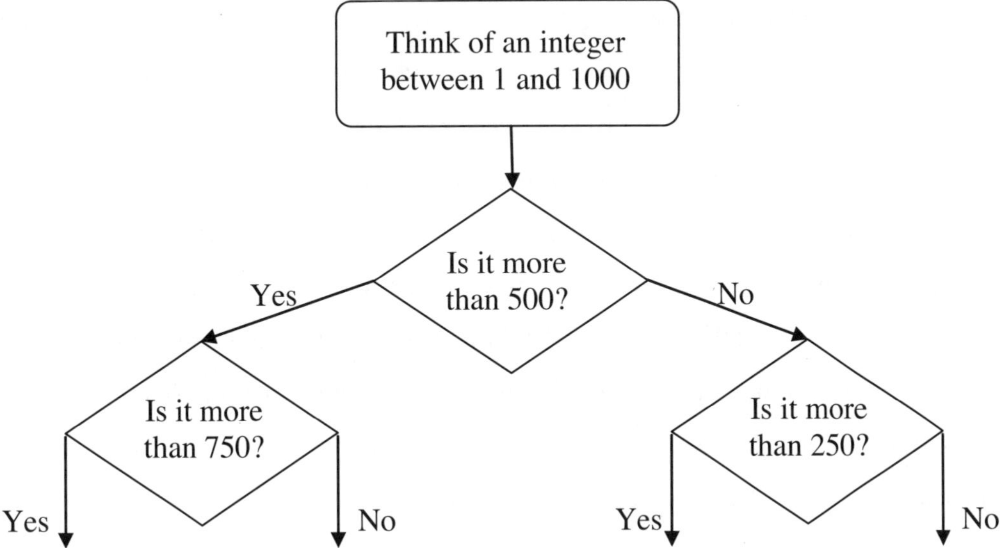

Which are the most 'awkward' numbers to cater for in your flow diagram? Why?

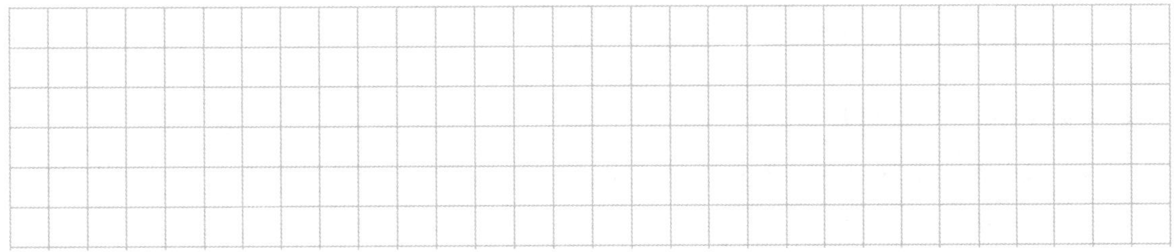

Are you sure that your questions will work for every number? Why?

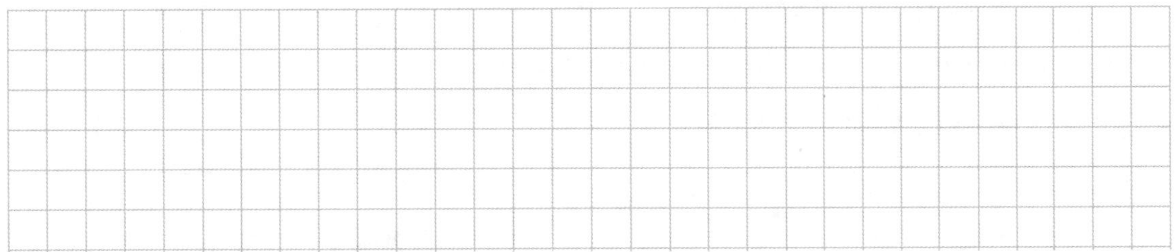

What other different possible question structures could you use to find the number?

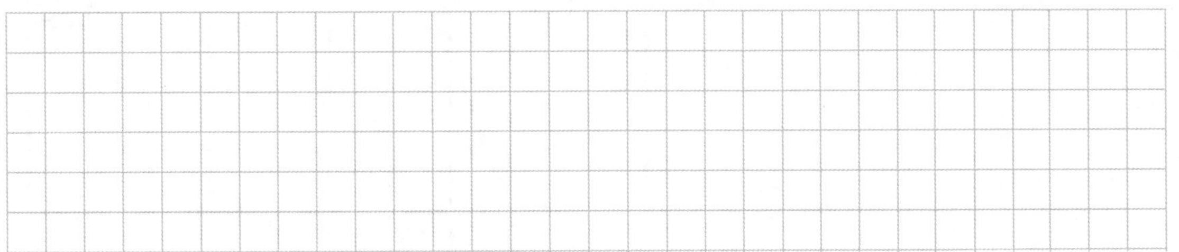

69

Vectors

Introduction

Vectors is typically seen as a hard topic, yet the idea of moving a certain amount in a certain direction is an everyday one. Frequently learners are confused over the difference between a pair of coordinates such as (3, 4) and a vector $\begin{pmatrix}3\\4\end{pmatrix}$. The vector $\begin{pmatrix}3\\4\end{pmatrix}$ represents the displacement from the origin (0, 0) to the point (3, 4) or from any point to another point three units to the right and four units up from there. Coordinates represent one specific point whereas a vector can be thought of as representing a journey *between* two points, or a relationship of translation from one point to another. It is unfortunate that the words 'translation' and 'transformation' are so similar, since of all the transformations the only ones that can be represented by vectors are translations. Matrices (an extension of vectors) can be used for other transformations. At this level, vectors are more likely to be 2D than 3D, despite the fact that we live in a 3D world.

Aims and Outcomes

- understand addition and subtraction of vectors, and multiplication of a vector by a scalar
- use vectors to represent translations in the plane

Lesson Starter (10 min)

If you have a data projector, first show the polygon below *without* the grid. Then add the grid background over the top.

Look at this shape. Say what you see.

Try to be accepting rather than overly critical of what learners say, so as to encourage people to contribute whatever draws their attention, rather than feeling that there is some correct/desired answer which they must try to guess.

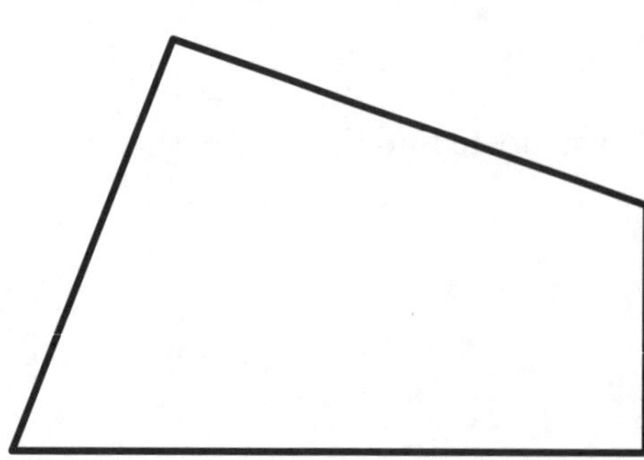

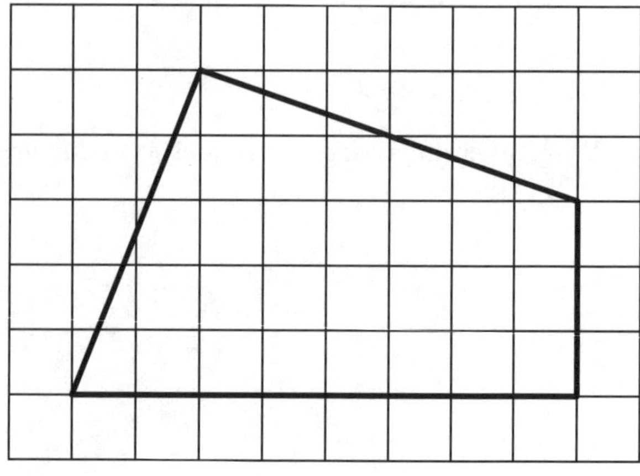

Could you describe this shape, without drawing *anything, in enough detail for someone else to make an* exact *copy? How?*

Do you think the grid makes it easier? Why / why not?

It is likely that learners will envisage tracing around the edge with instructions like 'go two to the right and five up', etc. Eventually it gets tedious keep having to describe right/left/up/down so you can introduce vectors like $\begin{pmatrix} 2 \\ 5 \end{pmatrix}$ as a natural convenience for representing $\begin{pmatrix} \textit{right} \\ \textit{up} \end{pmatrix}$, if learners have not met these before when describing translations. Negative numbers indicate 'left' and 'down'. Discussion may focus on whether the shape contains one or two right angles. (It has only one right angle, the one at the bottom right – the angle at the top is slightly obtuse.)

Main Lesson (25 min)

Give learners the Task Sheet and ask them to answer the questions.

If you wish, further prompts for use with the diagram are:

Say some vectors, like $\overrightarrow{AB}$, that are equal to, for example, $\begin{pmatrix} 3 \\ 3 \end{pmatrix}$.

Say two vectors that are parallel to each other.

Say a vector that is horizontal/vertical.

Say some vectors that add up to the zero vector $\begin{pmatrix} 0 \\ 0 \end{pmatrix}$.

Say two vectors that add up to a horizontal vector.

Say two non-horizontal *vectors that add up to a horizontal vector.*

Make up some questions like these.

Plenary (20 min)

The answers are: $\overrightarrow{BA} = \begin{pmatrix} -3 \\ -3 \end{pmatrix}$, $\overrightarrow{BC} = \begin{pmatrix} 3 \\ 3 \end{pmatrix}$, $\overrightarrow{CD} = \begin{pmatrix} 3 \\ -3 \end{pmatrix}$, $\overrightarrow{BD} = \begin{pmatrix} 6 \\ 0 \end{pmatrix}$, $\overrightarrow{JM} = \begin{pmatrix} 0 \\ -3 \end{pmatrix}$, $\overrightarrow{FH} = \begin{pmatrix} -6 \\ 0 \end{pmatrix}$ and $\overrightarrow{GH} = \begin{pmatrix} -3 \\ 3 \end{pmatrix}$.

Vectors are equal if they are of equal magnitude and are going in the same direction. Learners may comment on the directions associated with negative signs. Vectors such as $\overrightarrow{BA}$ and $\overrightarrow{BC}$ are sometimes described as 'equal and opposite'.

$\overrightarrow{HI} + \overrightarrow{IM} = \overrightarrow{HM}$, even though there is no line drawn in from H to M on the diagram.

$\overrightarrow{HI} + \overrightarrow{LM} = 2\overrightarrow{HI} = 2\overrightarrow{LM} = 2\overrightarrow{HB}$, etc. Vectors don't have to be end to end on the diagram, since parallel vectors of the same length, and going in the same sense, are equal.

$\overrightarrow{AC} + \overrightarrow{CE} + \overrightarrow{EG} + \overrightarrow{GA} = \begin{pmatrix} 0 \\ 0 \end{pmatrix}$. Note that this is the 'zero *vector*' and not the *number* zero. Adding vectors always produces a vector, not a scalar – we are making a vector equation – so the zero vector is the vector that has zero magnitude and 'doesn't go anywhere' (the direction is undefined).

$\overrightarrow{AM} = \overrightarrow{MG}$ is false, because although the vectors have equal magnitude their directions are at right angles.

$\overrightarrow{CK} = \begin{pmatrix} 3 \\ -6 \end{pmatrix} = \overrightarrow{AK} - \overrightarrow{AC}$

$\overrightarrow{AD} + \overrightarrow{DL} = \overrightarrow{AL}$

Homework (5 min)

Make a new diagram on coordinate axes, containing at least eight points. Label them A *to* H. *Write down at least ten vectors, such as* $\overrightarrow{AB}$ = ... *for your diagram, giving them in component form as column vectors.*

To make it harder

A learner who makes quick progress could try the following problem:

Do you know how a knight moves on a chessboard? A knight can move two squares horizontally and one square vertically or two squares vertically and one square horizontally. It can go left/right and up/down.

If it starts here (e.g., bold '8' square below), which squares can it go to? It can get to any of the eight shaded squares.

How many different *squares can it get to from this square? From this square?*, etc.

Write in each square on the board the number *of different squares the knight can get to (in one move), starting from that square.*

2	3	4	4	4	4	3	2
3	4	6	6	6	6	4	3
4	6	8	8	8	8	6	4
4	6	8	**8**	8	8	6	4
4	6	8	8	8	8	6	4
4	6	8	8	8	8	6	4
3	4	6	6	6	6	4	3
2	3	4	4	4	4	3	2

Chess pieces are generally more powerful if they are placed near the centre of the board, and you can see that this is particularly true for the knights.

To make it easier

Learners who find this difficult could create more examples of different vectors on 1 cm × 1 cm squared paper, drawing and labelling each one, before trying to find relationships between their various vectors.

Vectors

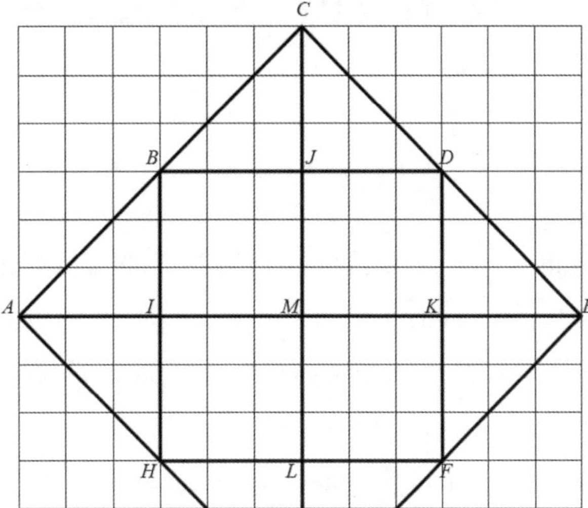

$\overrightarrow{AB} = \begin{pmatrix} 3 \\ 3 \end{pmatrix}$, $\overrightarrow{BI} = \begin{pmatrix} 0 \\ -3 \end{pmatrix}$, etc.

Write down vectors for $\overrightarrow{BA}$, $\overrightarrow{BC}$, $\overrightarrow{CD}$, $\overrightarrow{BD}$, $\overrightarrow{JM}$, $\overrightarrow{FH}$, and $\overrightarrow{GH}$.

Compare your answers.

What do you notice?

What else do you notice?

Can you explain your observations?

Does it make sense to write $\overrightarrow{HI} + \overrightarrow{IM}$? Why / why not?

What would the answer be? Why?

Does it make sense to write $\overrightarrow{HI} + \overrightarrow{LM}$? Why / why not?

What would the answer be? Why?

Work out $\overrightarrow{AC} + \overrightarrow{CE} + \overrightarrow{EG} + \overrightarrow{GA}$? Explain your answer.

Write down four more vector sums with the same answer as this.

How did you choose them?

Why is it wrong to write $\overrightarrow{AM} = \overrightarrow{MG}$?

Work out $\overrightarrow{CK}$. Could you do it if all you knew was $\overrightarrow{AC}$ and $\overrightarrow{AK}$? How? Find a connection.

Find a connection between $\overrightarrow{AD}$, $\overrightarrow{DL}$ and $\overrightarrow{AL}$.

70 Winner Takes All!

Introduction

Handling uncertainty is a vital skill in life – weaknesses in assessing risk lead people into unwise decisions or missed opportunities that they may later regret. Some teachers/learners/parents may be uneasy about a context that relates to gambling, so the monetary aspect of this lesson could be omitted or modified if you wish. Alternatively, it may be argued that a mathematical perspective on gambling is likely to *discourage* rather than encourage involvement in the gaming industry! Ability to weigh up alternative outcomes helps people to avoid being taken in by 'too good to be true' setups.

Aims and Outcomes

- calculate conditional probabilities in 'without replacement' situations
- understand when a game is fair or unfair

Lesson Starter (10 min)

Suppose that you have a spinner that is equally likely to stop at any point on the edge and looks like this:

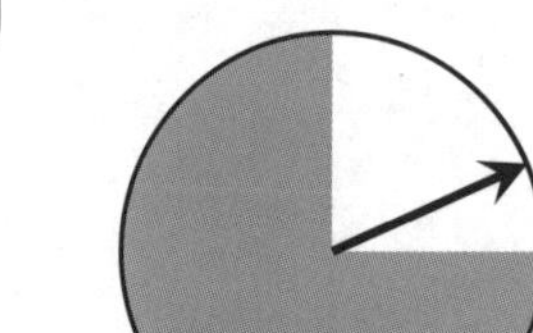

Is this a 'fair' spinner?

Some learners might call it fair because it is equally likely to stop at any angle, but others might say it is unfair because it is three times more likely to stop in the grey than in the white. It is exactly what it appears to be – it doesn't conceal the bias towards grey, so in that sense learners might think it is 'honest'. It doesn't matter so long as learners are satisfied that $p(\text{grey}) = \frac{3}{4}$ and $p(\text{white}) = \frac{1}{4}$.

What if the same amount of white area were split into several smaller sectors arranged at various positions around the spinner? Would that make a difference? Why / why not?

It would not make any difference, provided that the total area stays the same. (Learners sometimes confuse this with situations in darts, say, where hitting either of two small regions is generally harder than hitting one large region with the same total area. Similarly, hitting a 4 cm × 4 cm square, say, is much easier than hitting a 0.16 cm × 100 cm rectangle, although they have the same area, but this is because of human skill and aim rather than probability, so is not relevant here.)

You are going to predict whether the spinner will stop on white or grey. You get a point (or £1) for every correct prediction. The spinner will be spun 100 times. How many times would you predict 'white' or 'grey'? In what order?

It may be a surprise to learners that if the spinner is truly random (and they are un-psychic!) then they cannot do better than predict grey every time. Commonly, learners think that it is best to predict grey 75 times and white 25 times in some convenient or 'random' ordering. But a two-stage tree diagram will show that the probability of being right then becomes p(predict grey and it is grey) + p(predict white and it is white) $= \frac{3}{4} \times \frac{3}{4} + \frac{1}{4} \times \frac{1}{4} = \frac{5}{8} = 62.5\%$, which is considerably less than the 75 per cent that you might expect to get right (on average) by predicting grey every time. And any other strategy will be worse than 'always grey', no matter how many greys or whites you have already had.

Main Lesson (25 min)

Give out the Task Sheet and ask learners to think about the game, perhaps trying it out a few times (not with real money, of course!). There are many 'dimensions of possible variation' which learners can explore: the number of bags, players, colours, counters per bag, the rules, etc. Tree diagrams will probably be helpful in order to handle the 'without replacement' aspect of the game.

Plenary (20 min)

For the numbers as stated, if Player 2 chooses Bag A,

$$p(win|A) = p(RR) + p(GG) + p(BB)$$

$$= \frac{4}{15} \times \frac{3}{14} + \frac{5}{15} \times \frac{4}{14} + \frac{6}{15} \times \frac{5}{14}$$

$$= \frac{31}{105} = 0.2952\ldots$$

whereas if she chooses Bag B,

$$p(win|B) = p(RR) + p(GG) + p(BB)$$

$$= \frac{3}{12} \times \frac{2}{11} + \frac{4}{12} \times \frac{3}{11} + \frac{5}{12} \times \frac{4}{11}$$

$$= \frac{19}{66} = 0.2878\ldots$$

so these are pretty close, but Bag A is the better bet.

Keeping the number of red, green and blue counters as consecutive integers in the order $R < G < B$, other results (truncated to 3 decimal places) are:

Bag	Red	Green	Blue	Probability of win
A	4	5	6	0.295 ...
B	3	4	5	0.287 ...
C	2	3	4	0.277 ...
D	1	2	3	0.266 ...
E	6	7	8	0.300 ...

As the number of counters becomes larger, the probability tends to $\frac{1}{3}$, since with a lot of counters the three colours become almost equally likely to come out, even when one counter has already been removed.

Homework (5 min)

Learners could invent and analyse another game involving two bags and a certain number of counters in each. Can they make a game which is as fair as possible, or one which looks fair but isn't?

To make it harder

Confident learners could extend the problem to three bags, which would make it a good deal more complicated!

To make it easier

Learners who find this hard could begin with fewer counters in the bags and some practical equipment to support their thinking.

Winner Takes All!

Bags A and B contain red, green and blue counters.

Rules of the Game

1. Player 1 chooses either Bag A or Bag B.
2. Player 2 randomly picks a counter out of whichever bag Player 1 chooses.
3. Player 1 randomly picks a counter out of the same bag.
4. If the counters are of the same colour, Player 1 wins. If not, Player 2 wins.

How many red, green and blue counters should there be in each bag at the beginning to make this a good game? What do you think makes 'a good game'?

Do you think the players should know the contents of the bag before they start? Why / why not?

Suppose it begins as follows:

Bag	Red	Green	Blue
A	4	5	6
B	3	4	5

How likely do you think Player 2 is to win?

Player 2 suggests that they both contribute £5 and whoever wins should receive the £10 at the end. Why is this unfair?

How much do you think each Player should contribute at the beginning to make a £10 prize for the winner fair? Why?

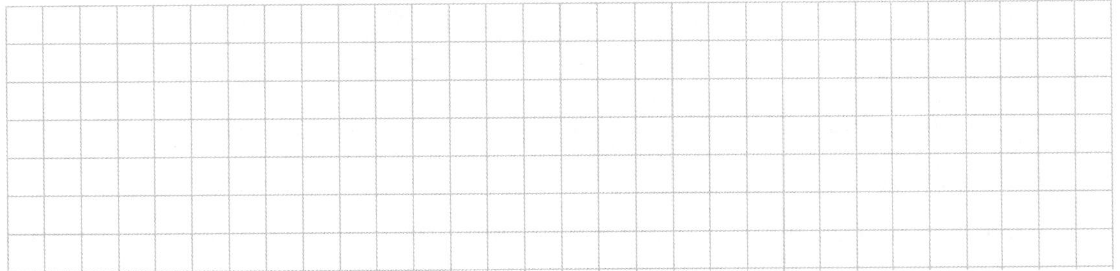

Other Resources

Association of Teachers of Mathematics (1989), *Points of Departure 1–4*. Derby: Association of Teachers of Mathematics.

Bills, C., Bills, L., Watson, A. and Mason, J. (2004), *Thinkers*. Derby: Association of Teachers of Mathematics.

Mason, J. (1999), *Learning and Doing Mathematics*. York: QED.

Mason, J. and Johnston-Wilder, S. (2004), *Designing and Using Mathematical Tasks*. Milton Keynes: Open University.

Ollerton, M. (2009), *The Mathematics Teacher's Handbook*. London: Continuum.

Ollerton, M. (2005), *100 Ideas for Teaching Mathematics*. London: Continuum.

Ollerton, M. (2002), *Learning and Teaching Mathematics Without a Textbook*. Derby: Association of Teachers of Mathematics.

Ollerton, M. and Watson, A. (2001), *Inclusive Mathematics 11–18*. London: Continuum.

Watson, A. (2006), *Raising Achievement in Secondary Mathematics*. Maidenhead: Open University.

Watson, A. and Mason, J. (2005), *Mathematics as a Constructive Activity. New Jersey:* Lawrence Erlbaum.

An excellent website for stimulating learners' mathematical thinking is http://nrich.maths.org/. Many other excellent books and resources are available at www.atm.org.uk.

Other books by Colin Foster

Foster, C. (2009), *Mathematics for Every Occasion*. Derby: Association of Teachers of Mathematics.

Foster, C. (2008), *50 Mathematics Lessons: Rich and Engaging Ideas for Secondary Mathematics*, London: Continuum.

Foster, C. (2008), *Variety in Mathematics Lessons*. Derby: Association of Teachers of Mathematics.

Foster, C. (2003), *Instant Maths Ideas for Key Stage 3 Teachers: Data, Numeracy and ICT*. Cheltenham: Nelson Thornes.

Foster, C. (2003), *Instant Maths Ideas for Key Stage 3 Teachers: Number and Algebra*. Cheltenham: Nelson Thornes.

Foster, C. (2003), *Instant Maths Ideas for Key Stage 3 Teachers: Shape and Space*. Cheltenham: Nelson Thornes.

Index

Numbers refer to *Lesson* numbers, not page numbers.